Information Efficiency and Anomalies in Asian Equity Markets

The efficient market hypothesis (EMH) maintains that all relevant information is fully and immediately reflected in a stock price and that an investor will obtain an equilibrium rate of return. This has far-reaching implications in terms of capital allocation and stock price predictability, as well as the possibility of any profitable trading strategies that can be used to 'beat the market'. Equity market anomalies reflect that the market is inefficient and, hence, contradicts the EMH.

This book gathers both theoretical and practical perspectives by including research issues, methodological approaches, practical case studies, uses of new policy, and other points of view related to stock market efficiency to help address the future challenges facing global stock markets and economies. *Information Efficiency and Anomalies in Asian Equity Markets* is an insightful resource that will be useful for students, academics and professionals alike.

Qaiser Munir is an associate professor in the Faculty of Business, Economics and Accountancy at Universiti Malaysia Sabah, Malaysia. He has been an academic in the applied economics discipline for over eight years. Since 2008, he has worked on various projects and consultancies, including projects funded by the Ministry of Higher Education, Malaysia. His research interests include applied economics, financial economics, development economics, and applied econometrics. Dr. Munir is presently serving as chief editor of the *Malaysian Journal of Business and Economics* and has reviewed a number of articles for the *Economic Bulletin*, the *Journal of Economic Studies* and other academic journals. He has won numerous excellence awards for teaching during his career.

Sook Ching Kok is a senior lecturer and PhD candidate at the Faculty of Business, Economics and Accountancy at Universiti Malaysia Sabah, Malaysia. Her main research interest is in financial economics. She has worked on various projects, including those funded by the Ministry of Higher Education, Malaysia.

Routledge Studies in the Modern World Economy

For a full list of titles in this series, please visit www.routledge.com/series/SE0432

Information Efficiency and Anomalies in Asian Equity Markets

Theories and evidence

**Edited by Qaiser Munir
and Sook Ching Kok**

LONDON AND NEW YORK

First published 2017
by Routledge

2 Park Square, Milton Park, Abingdon, Oxfordshire OX14 4RN
52 Vanderbilt Avenue, New York, NY 10017

Routledge is an imprint of the Taylor & Francis Group, an informa business

First issued in paperback 2020

British Library Cataloguing in Publication Data
A catalogue record for this book is available from the British Library

Library of Congress Cataloging in Publication Data
Names: Munir, Qaiser, 1968– editor. | Kok, Sook Ching, editor.
Title: Information efficiency and anomalies in Asian equity markets :
    theories and evidence / edited by Qaiser Munir and Sook Ching Kok.
Description: Abingdon, Oxon ; New York, NY : Routledge, 2017. |
    Series: Routledge studies in the modern world economy ; 162 |
    Includes bibliographical references and index.
Identifiers: LCCN 2016025427 | ISBN 9781138195387 (hardback) |
    ISBN 9781315638195 (ebook)
Subjects: LCSH: Capital market—Asia. | Stock exchanges—Asia. |
    Information theory in finance—Asia. | Finance—Asia.
Classification: LCC HG5702 .I54 2017 | DDC 332.64/25—dc23
LC record available at https://lccn.loc.gov/2016025427

ISBN: 978-1-138-19538-7 (hbk)
ISBN: 978-0-367-59592-0 (pbk)

Typeset in Galliard
by Apex CoVantage, LLC

Contents

Figures

Tables

Contributors

Andrei Anghel is a chartered financial analyst (CFA) and a member of the CFA Society of Romania. He is an experienced capital market practitioner, having worked as a financial analyst (2004–2007), authorized investment consultant (2008–2015), and portfolio manager (2007–present).

Sok-Gee Chan is a senior lecturer at the Faculty of Business and Accountancy, University of Malaya. Her research areas include corporate governance and bank efficiency, economic efficiency analysis and value-added tax.

Ricky Chee-Jiun Chia teaches at the Labuan School of International Business and Finance, Universiti Malaysia Sabah. His research interests include applied econometrics, technical analysis in studying issues related to international economics, financial economics, macroeconomics, international finance and banking.

Muhammad A. Cheema is a senior lecturer in finance at Curtin University, Sarawak, Malaysia. His research and teaching interests are in behavioural finance, capital markets, stock market anomalies, financial literacy and derivative securities.

Sook Ching Kok is a senior lecturer and PhD candidate at the Faculty of Business, Economics and Accountancy at Universiti Malaysia Sabah, Malaysia. Her main research interest is in financial economics. She has worked on various projects, including projects funded by the Ministry of Higher Education, Malaysia.

Hooi Hooi Lean is a professor of economics at the School of Social Sciences, Universiti Sains Malaysia. She has published more than 100 journal articles in many renowned international journals. Her H-index is 26, and there are more than 2000 citations to her works. She has been awarded the ASEAN-ROK Academic Exchange Fellowship in 2007, the Democratic Pacific Union Visiting Fellowship in 2008, the International HERMES Fellowship in 2009 and the Faculty Exchange Fellowship from Georg-Simon-Ohm University in 2012.

Shiok Ye Lim received her master's degree in the field of international finance economics from Universiti Malaysia Sabah in 2011.

Evgeniya Mikova is a doctor of philosophy and a lecturer at the Department of Finance at the National Research University Higher School of Economics. She is also an analyst of the Research & Training Laboratory of Financial Markets Analysis.

Vinod Mishra is a senior lecturer in the Department of Economics in the Monash Business School, Monash University, Australia. His research interests include applied industrial organization, financial economics, high-frequency financial data analysis, labour economics, development economics and energy economics.

Qaiser Munir is an associate professor in the Faculty of Business, Economics and Accountancy at Universiti Malaysia Sabah, Malaysia. He has been an academic in the applied economics discipline for over eight years. Since 2008, he has worked on various projects and consultancies, including projects funded by the Ministry of Higher Education, Malaysia. His research interests include applied economics, financial economics, development economics and applied econometrics. Dr. Munir is presently serving as the chief editor of the *Malaysian Journal of Business and Economics* and has reviewed a number of articles for the *Economic Bulletin*, the *Journal of Economic Studies* and other academic journals. He has won numerous teaching excellence awards during his career.

Gilbert V. Nartea is an associate professor and a chairperson in the Department of Finance at the University of Waikato, New Zealand. His research interests are in empirical asset pricing, behavioural finance, decision analysis, risk management and investments.

Massimiliano Serati is an associate professor of economic policy at Carlo Cattaneo University – LIUC and the head of LIUC-Centro di Ricerca per lo Sviluppo del Territorio. His main research interests are time series econometrics, macroeconomic forecasting, business cycle analysis, monetary policies and labour market economics.

Russell Smyth is a professor of economics in the Department of Economics in the Monash Business School, Australia. His research interests include development economics, energy economics, financial economics, labour economics and empirical legal studies. He is an associate editor of *Energy Economics and Economic Modelling* and sits on the international advisory board of the *Journal of Empirical Legal Studies*.

Tamara Teplova is a doctor of sciences and a professor of the Academic Department of Finance, National Research University Higher School of Economics and the head of the Research & Training Laboratory of Financial Markets Analysis.

Piyapas Tharavanij is the director of the financial academic department at the College of Management, Mahidol University (CMMU), Bangkok, Thailand. Prior to joining academia, he worked as an analyst at Siam Commercial Bank. Later, he worked as a regulator with the Thailand Securities Exchange Commission (SEC).

Cristiana Tudor is a professor at the Department of International Business and Economics and member of the International Research Center in applied mathematics at the Bucharest University of Economics. She is co-founder of the Romanian Quantitative Finance Association (QUANTFIN), which is designed to provide research for capital market professionals and policy makers and to support the overall development of the Romanian capital market. She has received the Excellency Diploma for Academic Research from the Bucharest University of Economics (in 2007, 2012 and 2013).

Geok Peng Yeap is a PhD candidate at the School of Social Sciences, Universiti Sains Malaysia and a lecturer at Sentral College Penang, Malaysia. Her research interests include financial economics, housing economics, the stock market and macroeconomics.

Arianna Ziliotto is a lecturer and researcher at Carlo Cattaneo University – LIUC. She teaches a course on international financial and foreign exchange markets, and her main research interests cover quantitative finance, financial market efficiency and time series econometrics. She is also a risk and supervisory reporting manager for an Financial Conduct Authority-regulated investment firm and previously worked as a fixed income and derivatives trader on major Italian- and German-regulated markets.

Preface

When I began this book project, my intent was to address the issues regarding informational efficiency and anomalies in the context of Asian equity markets. The dynamic connectedness of Asian equity markets vis-à-vis other major global markets has made the Asian markets more influential in affecting the world economy. It may also have impacted the transmission of external shocks via equity prices and volatilities during financial crises. In a recently published International Monetary Fund working paper, Guimarães-Filho and Hong (2016) have highlighted the relevance of Asian emerging market development to the global economy and financial stability. Clearly, these emerging markets are receiving growing attention in research due to their increasing economic importance. This edited book presents a selection of chapters offering insights on Asian equity markets. In certain chapters, a comparison between emerging markets and developed markets within or beyond the Asian context is provided. Understanding the contents of this book will definitely help to identify investment opportunities, and it is deemed important for policy implications.

The other main goals of this edited book are fourfold. First, we seek high quality, scientific research chapters providing a wide array of efficiency measurement- and stock price forecasting-related subjects that contribute to the advancement of knowledge in the use of novel computational methods, for the analysis of informational efficiency and anomalies in equity markets. The primary implication of equity market efficiency is central to capital allocation effectiveness, stock price forecasting, and the practicality of specific trading rules consistently resulting in an abnormal return. Second, this book aims to shed light on the intellectual history of efficient markets to track the origin and development of the efficient market hypothesis (EMH), the competing theories of equity market anomalies from rational and behavioural perspectives and the main classifications of anomalies. Third, this book aims to assemble current empirical works to provide insight into effective efficiency measures, equity market anomalies and potential profitable trading strategies. Fourth, we encourage the exchange of ideas among authors/ researchers/policy makers with respect to equity market efficiency and the related issues of globalization, financial crisis, and economic turbulence. This helps to address the future challenges facing global equity markets and economies. In brief, this book gathers both theoretical and practical perspectives by including research issues, methodological approaches, practical case studies, and the uses of new policy and other points of view related to equity market efficiency.

The target audience

The target audience for this publication is academics, researchers, postgraduate students, undergraduate students (majoring in finance and financial economics), financial analysts, portfolio managers, investors, policy makers, and financial system regulators engaged in various disciplines, including economics, business, finance, accounting, international capital flow liberalization, and regulation.

Contents and organization

There are 13 chapters in this book. A brief description of each chapter is as follows:

Chapter 1 is the introduction to equity market informational efficiency. This chapter has two objectives: first, to give an overview of the underlying theories and core concepts in this field; and, second, to provide a broad picture of this research area.

Chapter 2 elucidates the concepts, standard classifications, theories and empirical evidence of equity market anomalies. This chapter sheds light on the main categories of anomalies and discusses a number of competing theories related to anomalies.

Chapter 3 examines the random walk hypothesis using index-level monthly data for the small and medium segment of the National Stock Exchange of India. The authors highlight the importance of addressing heteroscedasticity when testing for a random walk with high-frequency financial data.

Chapter 4 investigates the co-movement between the Malaysia Stock Market Index FTSE KLCI with crude oil prices, gold prices and exchange rates. The methodology used is based on the autoregressive distributive lag model (ARDL) approach to cointegration of Pesaran *et al.* (2001).

Chapter 5 attempts to identify the behaviour of major Asian equity markets during the Asian financial crisis, by examining the existence of the day-of-the-week effect in the markets. The EGARCH–mean model is adopted to examine the equity market anomalies.

Chapter 6 presents the theoretical background of the reversal effect and presents the evidence for when the contrarian strategy works most effectively. This chapter also highlights the practical implication of the contrarian strategy across the selected Asian markets.

Chapter 7 covers the theoretical framework of the momentum effect and presents the international evidence of the existence of this pattern in the equity market. This chapter also offers a comprehensive approach to the decision-making process of investors when they are constructing momentum strategy and choosing the most profitable design.

Chapter 8 investigates the profitability of the momentum trading strategy in the stock exchanges of Shanghai, Shenzhen and Hong Kong. The analysis takes into account the effectiveness of the momentum trading strategy during a financial or stock market crisis.

Chapter 9 re-examines one of the simplest and most famous technical trading rules, the moving average, for representative indices of Asian equity markets (NIKKEI for Japan, HANGSENG for Hong Kong, SSE composite for China, and BSE SENSEX for India).

Chapter 10 explores the issues of technical trading rules in Asian equity markets. These include an overview of technical trading and market efficiency, the EMH and the theories that challenge the EMH paradigm, empirical evidence, trading rules and data-snooping biases.

Chapter 11 presents an innovative framework of testing for semi-strong market efficiency in a comparative way, with a special focus on Asian, European and US equity price reactions to macroeconomic impulses under stressed market conditions.

Chapter 12 examines the long-run causality between the return of banking stocks and the efficiency level in ASEAN-5. The panel vector error correction model (VECM) method is used to estimate the short-run and long-run causalities between bank efficiency level and stock price return.

Chapter 13 examines the asymmetric effect of negative and positive shocks on FTSE KLCI during certain periods of elections in Malaysia. The threshold generalized autoregressive conditional heteroscedasticity (TGARCH) and exponential generalized autoregressive conditional heteroscedasticity (EGARCH) models are adopted for analysis.

Acknowledgements

The editor(s) would like to acknowledge the help of all the people involved in this project: more specifically, Ms. Winnie binti Abdul Nasir, who provided overall support during this project, and the authors and reviewers that took part in the review process. Without their support, this book would not have become a reality.

First, the editors would like to thank each one of the authors for their contributions. Our sincere gratitude goes to the chapter authors who contributed their time and expertise to this book.

Second, the editors wish to acknowledge the valuable contributions of the reviewers towards the improvement of quality, coherence and content presentation of the chapters. Most of the authors also served as referees; we highly appreciate their taking on this double task.

Qaiser Munir
Universiti Malaysia Sabah, Malaysia

1 Equity market informational efficiency

History and development

Qaiser Munir and Sook Ching Kok

1.0 Introduction

In economics and finance, the term 'efficiency' has several distinct connotations. This term can be used to refer to allocation efficiency, informational efficiency, operational efficiency or technical efficiency.[1] At the outset, it is necessary to clarify that in this chapter 'efficiency' only refers to informational efficiency, such that prices are based on the best available information (Howell and Bain, 2005: 540). According to Latham (1986), the most common implicit definition for informational efficiency is that prices will not change if all private information is publicized. Zou (2011) interprets this type of efficiency as the effectiveness of market information.

As such, an efficient market, as it is generally understood and practiced, is a market in which investors are unable to earn consistent excess profits from trading stocks. Fama (1970) precisely defines an efficient market as one in which security prices fully reflect available information. Earlier, Fama (1965) stated that an efficient market should contain a sufficiently large number of participants who are rational profit-maximizers and have almost free access to all relevant information. Their competition causes stock prices to incorporate information promptly. Beechey, Gruen and Vickery (2000) believe that efficient markets adjust instantaneously to new information. According to Malkiel (2003), efficient markets are devices that reflect new information quickly and for the most part accurately. In such markets, therefore, investors are not likely to anticipate the future direction of security prices. Even good analysts cannot outwit the market. Thus, it is possible for investors to obtain an above average return without taking an above average risk.

It is well acknowledged that the fundamental principle of all gambling is simply equal conditions. This idea was addressed by the Italian mathematician Girolamo Cardano in *Liber Aleae*, or *The Book of Games of Chance*, published in 1564. Another landmark event in the history of EMH was the discovery of Brownian motion in 1828 by the Scottish botanist Robert Brown. He noticed that grains of pollen suspended in water display quick oscillatory motion. As articulated in 1863 by the French stockbroker Jules Regnault, security price deviation is directly proportional to the square root of time. According to Regnault, as in a game of heads or tails, stock price movements are independent (Jovanovic and Gall, 2001). In 1888, the British logician and philosopher John Venn explained the concepts of random walk and Brownian motion. The term 'efficient markets' was probably first mentioned clearly in a book entitled *The Stock Markets of London, Paris and New York*, which was published in 1889 and written by George Gibson. A breakthrough in the history of EMH was made by Louis Bachelier, a French mathematician. In his PhD thesis published in 1900, he developed the mathematics and statistics of Brownian motion (Bachelier, 2006). At that time, his work did not gain much attention (Sewell, 2011). In 1905, the Einstein's theory was introduced and provided a better understanding of the formulation of diffusion equation for Brownian particles and diffusion coefficient to measurable physical quantities (Berkyürek, 2012). In the same year, a professor and fellow of the Royal Society, Karl Pearson (1905), in *Nature* described a random walk as the drunkard's walk. Samuelson (1965) explained the coherence of randomness in stock price movements and efficient markets under the martingale property. In 1965, the two landmark studies of Eugene Fama were published. Fama (1965b) explained how the theory of random walks could pose a great challenge to both technical, or chartist, analysis and fundamental analysis. Meanwhile, Fama (1965a) discussed random walk theory and empirically validated the random walk model. Following the definitive paper of Fama (1970) on the theory of efficient capital markets, the EMH raised a fast-growing interest among researchers, market practitioners, and analysts. In 1991, Fama acknowledged new dimensions of return predictability as part of the weak-form tests, in addition to the more established tests for the predictive power of historical stock prices. Timmermann and Granger (2004) discussed the EMH from the perspective of the modern forecast approach. He postulated the self-destruction of predictability; that is, stable predictable patterns will disappear when they are known to the public and have been extensively exploited.

On the other hand, the validity of market efficiency was criticized in a number of prominent studies. In their findings, Kemp and Reid (1971) showed that stock price movements were conspicuously nonrandom in short time horizons. Hence, it was argued that those findings of randomness in stock price movements could be changed by the method of analysis. Grossman and Stiglitz (1980) assert that perfect informational efficiency is unlikely to hold true, as information costs will limit arbitrage activities. Moreover, Andersen (1983–84) views equity markets as highly imperfect but liable to speculative manias. Furthermore, stock prices are perceived to be too volatile to accord with efficient markets (LeRoy and Porter, 1981; Shiller, 1981). Bondt and Thaler (1985, 1987) discovered market inefficiencies that correspond to the overreaction hypothesis. The finding suggests that overreaction to unexpected news or events is a key feature of equity markets. Jegadeesh and Titman (1993) demonstrated the profitability of momentum-based investing strategies. The finding is clearly different from the outcome of an efficient market, since the momentum effect is the idea that investors usually underreact to firms' earnings information, causing price continuation (Barberis, Shleifer and Vishny, 1997). According to Wilson and Marashdeh (2007), the observed short-run arbitrage opportunities attributed to cointegrated stock prices are evidence against the EMH. However, it is clarified by Fama (1998) that anomalies are chance results that tend to disappear with changes in technique. In the opinion of Malkiel (2003), equity markets are actually more efficient and less predictable than they are thought to be in certain studies. More recently, the financial crisis of 2008–2009 seems to cast some doubt on the validity of market efficiency. In response to this particular issue, Ball (2009) stresses that it is important to understand the basic premise, applicability, and limitations of the EMH; he defends the hypothesis.[2]

Notwithstanding, the EMH is extensively applied in many current studies. This hypothesis has remained vital in dictating the behaviour of stock prices. Today, it is still intact and continues to attract much research interest. Against this background, we aim to give an overview of the underlying theories and core concepts in the field of equity market informational efficiency and to provide a broad picture of this research area. We focus on the intellectual history of EMH to trace the origins and development of theories and empirical works. The remainder of this chapter is organized as follows: Section 2.0 presents efficient market theories; Section 3.0 discusses the EMH and its implications; Section 4.0 explains technical analysis; Section 5.0 illuminates fundamental analysis; Section 6.0 reviews developing trends in the EMH literature. The last section presents our conclusions.

2.0 Efficient market theories

2.1 Theory of efficient capital markets

The underlying idea of equity market efficiency is based on the theory of efficient capital markets and the EMH defined in Fama (1970). The theory has three important assumptions: first, security trading has zero transaction cost; second, information is at no cost to all market participants; third, all participants agree on the implications of current information for current prices and the distributions of future prices for every security. Once the above conditions are fulfilled, it is impossible for the market to be efficient. In fact, this theory is built on the foundation of rational expectations. Muth (1961) describes rational expectations as the optimal forecast using all available information (Muth, 1961). The idea of this theory is expressed in three related models, including the fair game expected returns model, the sub-martingale model, and the random walk model. Equation 1 below shows the fair game model:

$$E\left(\tilde{P}_{j,t+1}|\Phi_t\right)=\left[1+E\left(\tilde{r}_{j,t+1}|\Phi_t\right)P_{jt}\right],\tag{1.1}$$

where E is the expected value operator, P_{jt} is the price of security j at time t, $P_{j,t+1}$ is the price of security j at time $t + 1$, $r_{j,t+1}$ is the one-period percentage return on security j, $\frac{P_{j,t+1}-P_{jt}}{P_{jt}}$, and Φ_t denotes any information set which is fully reflected in the price of security j at time t, P_{jt}. In this model, market equilibrium is expressed in terms of expected return as a function of risk conditioned on the relevant information set. In more detail, security price at time $t + 1$, $P_{j,t+1}$, and the one-period percentage return on security, r_j, t_{+1}, are two random variables that are subject to being changed by the information reflected in security price at time t, P_{jt}. As such, the current price of security fully reflects all available information. This model implies that it is impossible to have any trading systems that relies only on the information set Φt to outperform the market.

An integral part of the efficient capital markets theory is expressed using the sub-martingale model. Equation 2, which follows, shows the model:

$$E\left(\tilde{P}_{j,t+1}|\Phi_t\right) \geq P_{jt}; E\left(\tilde{r}_{j,t+1}|\Phi_t\right) \geq 0. \tag{1.2}$$

This model indicates that the expected return of security conditioned on the information set Φ_t is nonnegative. If the expected price of security for the next period exceeds its current price, the price sequence P_{jt} is said to follow a sub-martingale, whereas if the expected price of security for the next period is equal to its current price, then the price sequence of security follows a martingale. As implied from this model, those trading systems that are based only on the information set Φ_t are unable to provide returns on security greater than the equilibrium return.

It is usual for the word 'martingale' to refer to the strap of a horse's harness that connects the girth to the noseband. It prevents the horse from throwing back its head. Bachelier (2006), therefore, interprets 'martingale' as the gambling strategy that allows free movement in one direction and obstructs movement in the other. This can be applied to the random walk or stochastic process of stock prices, in the sense that the future direction of stock prices is unpredictable based on historical stock prices. Since the expected value of the process is the same as today's value, it is not wise to speculate on stock price changes. Investors will be better-off with the simple buy-and-hold strategy over longer time horizons.

In Fama (1970), the random walk model is a part of the efficient capital markets theory. It is used to describe the stochastic system of security returns generating process that is not expressed clearly in the fair game expected returns model. Equation 3 below is the expression of this model:

$$f\left(r_{j,t+1}|\Phi_t\right) = f\left(r_{j,t+1}\right). \tag{1.3}$$

This model stipulates that security price changes are independent and usually identically distributed. The mean of the distribution for a one-period percentage return on security, $r_{j,t+1}$, is independent of the information available at time t, Φ_t. Thus, the whole distribution is independent of the information set Φ_t. This implies that the order of historical prices cannot be used to anticipate the distributions of future prices.

2.2   Theory of random walks

One of the earliest definitions given for the concept of an efficient market was documented in Fama (1965b: 56) as follows:

> An efficient market is defined as a market where there are large numbers of rational, profit-maximizers actively competing, with each trying to predict future market values of individual securities, and where important current information is almost freely available to all participants.

The foregoing notion that participants are mostly rational profit-maximizers that are highly competitive and have free access to information in an efficient market plausibly explains the logic behind instantaneous stock price adjustments to new information. In other words, stock prices follow a random walk or stochastic process because the market is efficient (Samuelson, 1965; Fama, 1965b). According to Malkiel (2003), randomness in stock price changes occurs simply because prices adjust to news which should be random in nature if it is not being impeded.

The theory of random walk posits that stock price changes have no memory, thus historical stock prices cannot predict future stock price movements in any meaningful way (1965b). As documented in Fama (1965a), this theory has two hypotheses: first, successive price changes are independent; second, price changes conform to some probability distribution. The latter seems to suggest that there is no need to specify the shape of distribution. Specifically, the former is examined by testing the independence assumption or independence proceeds. To test the independence assumption, one has to assess the stochastic properties of stock prices; however, testing independence proceeds may show possible abnormal returns due to the presence of stable predictable price patterns (i.e. return autocorrelation, calendar or seasonal effects, momentum effect, return reversal).

As discussed earlier, the random walk model in Fama (1970) describes the stochastic data-generating process of security prices in which price changes are independent and usually identically distributed. Following that, Fama and French (1988) introduced a random walk with drift model. It demonstrates how stock prices are basically nonstationary processes that contain slowly decaying stationary components. The stationary components are likely to cause weak negative autocorrelation over a short time horizon and stronger negative autocorrelation over a longer time horizon. This suggests that stock prices tend to depart from the intrinsic value temporarily, but they follow a random walk for the most part in a series (refer to Equations 4–6 below).

$$p(t) = q(t) + z(t) \tag{1.4}$$

$$q(t) = q(t-1) + \mu + \eta(t) \tag{1.5}$$

$$z(t) = \phi z(t-1) + \varepsilon(t), \tag{1.6}$$

where $p(t)$ is the logarithm of stock price at time t, $q(t)$ is the random walk component, $z(t)$ is the stationary component, μ is the expected drift, and $\eta(t)$ is a white noise series. Equation (6) shows first-order autocorrelation AR (1), in which $\varepsilon(t)$ denotes white noise, and Φ is less than one but close to one. $p(t)$ is modelled by the sum of $q(t)$ and $z(t)$. If the gain from each month's price shock is less than 1, then $p(t)$ is a nonstationary process. Another expression for a simple random walk model (Tsay, 2010) is as follows:

$$P_t = P_{t-1} + a_t,$$

where P_t is the logarithm of stock price at time t, P_{t-1} is the logarithm of the one-period lag series of P_t, and a_t is a white noise series. A sequence is a white noise process if each value in the sequence has a zero mean and a constant variance and is uncorrelated with all other realizations (Enders, 2015: 49). P_t is determined by P_{t-1} and the disturbance term a_t, which has zero mean and a constant variance and captures all random influences. This model predicts that P_t has equal chances of an increase or a decrease. Next, a random walk with the drift model (Tsay, 2010) is expressed as follows:

$$p_t = \mu + p_{t-1} + a_t,$$

where p_t is the logarithm of stock price at time t, p_{t-1} is the logarithm of a one-period lag of p_t, μ is the constant term where $\mu = (p_t - p_{t-1})$, and a_t is a white noise series. In the model, the drift μ denotes the time trend of p_t.

3.0   The EMH and its implications

The normative appeal of EMH is clear: that security prices fully reflect available information (Fama, 1970, 1991). The EMH is divided into three levels. Weak-form EMH is the assertion that stock prices already fully reflect the information contained in the history of past trading. Semi–strong-form EMH claims that stock prices already reflect all publicly available information. Strong-form EMH affirms that stock prices reflect all relevant information, including the information of insiders. Economists such as Jensen (1978) and Beechey *et al.* (2000) presume that strong-form efficiency may not be literally true unless transaction costs do not exist. Grossman and Stiglitz (1980) point out that perfect market efficiency is constraint by information costs. The weaker versions of efficiency is more realistic based on the conjecture that stock prices will reflect information up to a level where the marginal benefit of acting on information does not exceed the marginal cost of collecting information. Intuitively, a stock market should be at least weak-form efficient to reduce technical trading and alleviate excessive short-horizon investments. Long-term investments contribute to the steady growth of listed firms. This, in turn, fosters more rapid economic growth.

EMH has far-reaching implications. One salient implication of the hypothesis is in terms of capital allocation. From the standpoint of policy makers, market efficiency is crucial for an effective allocation of capital for all sectors in an economy. In an efficient market, stock prices give accurate signals for buy and sell decisions.

This allows investors to trade stocks at fair value. Kok and Munir (2015) emphasize the importance of efficiency in the market for finance stocks, as it can affect the effectiveness of capital allocation across various listed financial firms, including financial holding companies, commercial banks, investment banks, insurance companies, capital market intermediaries and financial companies. In contrast, inefficiency leads to relatively higher information costs and excessive stock price fluctuations. These disincentives will reduce the attraction of equity markets. Lim (2008) mentions that market inefficiency will limit the ability of equity markets to distribute funds among the most productive sectors in an economy. Indeed, market efficiency is deemed important for stimulating economic growth in the majority of countries around the world.

Next, EMH has implications for the predictability of stock prices based on different information subsets. When weak-form efficiency holds, investors are unable to anticipate the future directions of stock prices by using the information of past trading, especially historical stock prices. If equity markets are efficient in the semi-strong-form sense, future stock price movements cannot be predicted based on publicly available information, such as, firm's earnings, dividends, and stock splits. Under the strong-form EMH, stock price prediction is completely impossible. This level of market efficiency implies that it is unlikely for any individuals or groups that have access to and could successfully exploit insider information to yield higher returns than other investors. Laffont and Maskin (1990) argue that a large trader who has insider information usually will find it desirable to make sure the market price of stocks does not uncover his information, if the variability in returns is not considered too large. This leads to a market situation of 'pooling equilibrium' instead of 'separating equilibria'. Thus, insider information may sometimes not be exploited unless, as in the findings of Chau and Vayanos (2008), a monopolistic insider chooses to reveal his private information very quickly to make sure the market will approach continuous trading and he will still obtain the so-called insider's excess profits. In that sense, the market could be strong-form efficient even though there is a monopolistic insider.

The EMH can suggest whether particular investing strategies are effective. If the market is efficient, a buy-and-hold strategy is preferable. Investors may expect to earn abnormal returns through specific trading rules if the market is inefficient. If the market is inefficient in the weak-form sense, technical analysis can be applied to exploit observable patterns in stock prices for anticipating the future directions of prices. Analysts' recommendations for value stock selection are useful when semi-strong-form efficiency does not hold.

Lastly, EMH has implications for the predictability of stock prices in the long run. If stock prices follow a stochastic data-generating process, the impact of shocks on prices is permanent, as a new equilibrium is reached following a shock. This implies that any forecast techniques are futile in the long run. Conversely, if stock prices are stationary, the impact of shocks on prices is transitory. Stock prices have a tendency to revert back to the long-run mean, which allows the prediction of prices using historical data (Narayan and Narayan, 2007; Munir, Kok and Furouka, 2012; Lean, Mishra and Smyth, 2015).

4.0   Technical analysis

During 1899–1902, Charles Henry Dow produced a series of editorials in the *Wall Street Journal* which introduced the basic uptrend, downtrend, and also a line called 'trading sideways' for showing prices fluctuating around the same value. The knowledge was then extended and developed to establish the Dow Theory. Other main contributors to this theory were William P. Hamilton, Robert Rhea, E. George Schaefer, and Richard Russell. The Dow Theory reflects emotions in the marketplace. It is believed that the closing price will capture the psychology or combined judgements of the whole equity market. In addition, this theory predicts that equity markets will enrol trends and exhibit trend reversals. The primary or long-term trend can be either a bull or a bear market. The secondary trend will show temporary reversal(s) in the primary trend.[3] Dow Theory is an example of a technical theory. In general, the tenet of technical theories is that history will repeat itself and thus the patterns displayed in stock prices will recur in the future (Fama, 1965b). It means that historical price data have an impact on prediction and are exploitable for anticipating the future direction of stock prices.

Technical analysis is a technique used for predicting future stock price movements through studying the behaviour of historical stock prices. This technique is also called the 'chartist technique'. There are three main principles of technical analysis: first, market actions update everything; second, there are existing configurations based on historical price data; and, third, history has a tendency to repeat itself. The important elements of this technique are security prices, the repeatability of price trends, and the tendency of prices to enrol trends (Dana and Cristina, 2013). The most common method used is based on basic graphical analysis (i.e. trend line, trend reversal, support and resistance lines). Moving average and trading range break are two simple and popular technical trading rules that have been proven effective in forecasting stock prices. Further, Suzuki and Ohkura (2016) introduce a technical indicator based on chaotic bagging predictors, combining a nonlinear model to capture the complex behaviour of stocks, the bagging algorithm to allow for quantifying and comparing the confidence in predictions, and a two-step method to identify more profitable stocks.

Some studies find that the moving average and trading range break are able to yield positive above average returns, such as Brock, Lakonishok and LeBaron (1991) and Yu, Nartea, Gan and Yao (2013), but other studies, such as Fang, Jacobsen and Qin (2014), disagree. The latter may hint that the market is efficient at least in the weak-form sense or is simply a result of bias. We also notice that in the study of Tian, Wan and Guo (2002), technical forecast power is not empirically supported in the case of the US equity index after 1975, but it is supported in the case of present Chinese stock markets. This shows the different market efficiencies in the two countries. So far, it is generally accepted that under the weak-form EMH, technical analysis is ineffective in forecasting stock prices.

5.0   Fundamental analysis

We note that the effectiveness of technical analysis depends on whether there exist predictable patterns displayed in stock prices. Conversely, the analysts who practice fundamental analysis do not rely on the observed stable price patterns. They analyze various historical data to forecast the future direction of stock prices. Historical data are employed to evaluate the fair or intrinsic value of stocks. Wafi, Hassan and Mabrouk (2015) explain that stock's fair value reflects firms' ability to generate future cash flows and the uncertainty of the future cash flows. Equity valuation is accomplished through the established valuation models, such as, the dividend discount model (DDM), the earning multiplier models (i.e. the price-to-book value ratio, or P/BV ratio, the price-to-cash flow ratio, or P/CF ratio, the price-to-sales ratio, or P/S ratio), the discounted cash flow model (DCFM) and the residual income valuation model (RI). The computed fair value is compared with the market value. Then, analysts select stocks that are undervalued for buy decisions and stocks that are overvalued for sell decisions. This justifies the value of analysts' recommendations, particularly for value stock selection.

To promote the role played by analysts, the improvement and new invention of methods for more accuracy in fundamental analysis is deemed important. It is known that using financial ratios in equity valuation models has proven useful but complicated. Shen and Tzeng (2015) propose using a combined soft computing model that includes the dominance-based rough set approach, formal concept analysis, the decision-making trial and the evaluation laboratory technique. This new invention is specifically for tackling the problem in value stock selection.

In Fama's sense, the semi-strong-form efficiency means stock prices reflect all publicly available information, hence fundamental analysis is ineffective for forecasting stock prices. If the market is efficient in the semi-strong-form sense, even analysts who are expert and highly skilful cannot outwit the market. This outcome of an efficient market is not always preferred, as there will be no scope for entrepreneur activities in equity markets. The role played by good analysts will be reduced because the information contained in analysts' reports is no longer reliably exploitable for abnormal returns. In view of this, Shostak (1997) points out that asset markets cannot be in equilibrium since there are a number of real causes that tend to have prolonged effects on asset prices. This, in turn, allows analysts to do their jobs on data analysis and equity valuation. Today, entrepreneur activities related to fundamental analysis are integrated into the smoothly operating equity market. As there is no clear universal consensus on semi-strong-form efficiency, fundamental analysis remains very important.

6.0   Developing trends in the EMH literature

For at least 45 years since Fama (1970), economists have amassed strong evidence that efficiency varies across different equity markets. A large body of literature has been devoted to this area of research. Most often, the EMH literature is classified into three camps, the studies on weak-form tests, semi-strong-form tests, and strong-form tests. Weak-form tests assess how well historical stock prices can predict future stock price movements. Semi-strong-form tests examine whether the information from public announcements has affected stock prices. Strong-form tests can verify whether insider information is exploitable for earning a higher return than other investors. A brief review of the literature follows.

6.1   *The studies on weak-form tests*

The literature has documented various types of weak-form tests. The most common weak-form tests include 1) testing for the predictive power of a stock's past prices, and 2) testing for different aspects of return predictability. Weak-form efficiency can be assessed by testing the time-varying expected returns of stocks. Fama (1970) has provided the initial definition of weak-form tests. Fama (1991) refines the understanding of weak-form tests by illuminating several important aspects under the rubric of return predictability. Weak-form tests should include past returns (i.e. short-horizon returns, long-horizon returns, the contrarians), other forecasting variables, volatility tests, return seasonality, and cross-sectional return predictability. Next, we provide a brief discussion on the predictive power of a stock's past prices.

The validity of a random walk model can be empirically assessed by detecting stock return autocorrelation, for instance, Fama (1965a), Fama and French (1988), Lo and MacKinlay (1988), Chang, McQueen and Pinegar (1999), and Baur, Dimpfl and Jung (2012). A number of past studies have used unit root tests to examine the stochastic properties of stock prices. Several issues are found to be important in the recent empirical works, including nonlinearity, heterogeneity, structural breaks, cross-sectional dependence, and high-frequency data estimation. If stock prices contain a unit root (nonstationary) or can be characterized as a random walk process, shocks to prices are permanent. This means prices will reach a new equilibrium following a shock. Thus, future prices are unpredictable based on the past movements of prices. Conversely, if stock prices are stationary, the impact of shocks is temporary, as prices will revert back to the long-run mean. Hence, it is possible to predict future stock price movements based on historical price data.

Narayan and Smyth (2006) apply unit root tests with structural breaks and show strong evidence of market efficiency in 14 European markets, including Belgium, Denmark, Finland, France, Germany, Greece, Ireland, Netherlands, Portugal, Norway, Sweden, Switzerland, Turkey and United Kingdom. Meanwhile, the results from the unit root test with structural breaks shown in Chaudhuri and Wu (2003) indicate mean reversion of market index prices in 11 emerging markets over the period January 1985 through February 1997 (Argentina, Brazil, Greece, India, Malaysia, Mexico, Nigeria, Philippines, Taiwan, Venezuela, and Zimbabwe). This finding suggests market inefficiency. Munir *et al.* (2012) adopt a nonlinear threshold autoregressive approach to test for nonlinear unit root in Association of Southeast Asian Nations (ASEAN)-5 market index prices. The study concludes that for the period

January 1990 through January 2009, the EMH is only valid in Malaysia and Thailand but not in Indonesia, Philippines, and Singapore. The EMH for ASEAN-5 markets is re-examined by Lean *et al.* (2015) for the period January 2011 through March 2014 by employing hourly high-frequency data on the market index prices. The findings support efficiency only in the case of Indonesia. Kok and Munir (2015) found that the price series of 28 finance stocks in Malaysia are characterized as random walk processes by testing the series with unit root tests that accommodate nonlinearity, structural breaks and cross-sectional dependence.

6.2   *The studies on semi–strong-form tests*

Testing for the speed of stock price adjustment to public announcement is the core of semi-strong-form tests. Public announcements are relevant to stock price forming, for instance, firm's earnings, dividends, stock splits, and mergers and acquisitions. Foerster and Sapp (2011) find that the simple Gordon growth model is superior to more modern equity valuation models in evaluating the monthly value of the S&P Composite Index. The stocks comprising the index were undervalued during 1871–1913, overvalued during 1914–1981, and priced at fair value after 1981 until 2010. Ziliotto and Serati (2015) propose a framework for examining the semi-strong-form EMH with focus on price reactions to macroeconomic news releases. They give some interesting examples of such macroeconomic impulses: 'Stocks and oil prices sink on US job data' (*Wall Street Journal*, 6 July 2012); 'US stocks rise as job data offset FED stimulus concern' (*Bloomberg*, 8 November 2013); 'US bonds rise on disappointing jobs data' (*Wall Street Journal*, 10 January 2014). It may be that stock prices will depart from intrinsic value under volatility conditions.

Currently, some researchers have been focusing on analyzing the connection between firms' efficiency and stock performance. It is believed that firm profitability is affected by technical or scale efficiencies. However, it is unknown whether such efficiencies are fully reflected in stock returns in certain firms; otherwise, this specific information is exploitable for forecasting stock returns. This topic is especially important when considering financial institutions due to the increased concern of vulnerable banks and other financial conglomerates in the recent financial crises (e.g. the twin crises of Nov 2000 through Feb 2001 in Turkey; the US subprime mortgage crisis in 2006–2007; the 2008–2009 global financial crisis; the 2014 Russian financial crisis). Thus, the research on this topic is of primary interest to the stakeholders of financial institutions as well as policy makers. Kirkwood and Nahm (2005) analyze the case of 10 retail banks listed on the Australian Stock Exchange for the period 1995–2002 and provide evidence that a bank's operation efficiency could predict its stock returns. Gaganis, Hasan and Pasiouras (2013) explore the relation between a firm's efficiency and stock performance for the period 2002–2008 using a sample of 399 insurance companies from 52 countries. The study found a significant positive relationship between profit efficiency and stock returns.

6.3   The studies on strong-form tests

The third camp of EMH literature is based on the strong-form tests. We notice that there are fewer studies of strong-form efficiency than of weak form and semi-strong form. The existing studies, however, show that the strong-form tests are important in assessing the profitability of insider information. It is quite usual to conclude that the market is inefficient in the presence of insider profits. For instance, over the period January 1992 through December 1996, Brio, Miguel and Perote (2002) show that in the Spanish stock market insiders earn higher returns when investing with corporate private information but outsiders are unable to obtain such excess profits. Khan and Ikram (2011) found evidence that mutual funds outperformed the market in India over the period 1 April 2000 through 30 April 2010. Thus, it is concluded that the Indian capital market is strong-form inefficient. Differing from the preceding studies, Chau and Vayanos (2008) infer strong-form market efficiency in the presence of monopolistic insiders. They studied a sample from the US stock market which consists of a large-cap stock (Coca-Cola) and a small cap stock (Bairnco). In their findings, as the monopolistic insiders reveal their information quickly, the market approaches continuous trading while insiders' profits do not converge to zero.

7.0   Conclusions

This chapter has discussed the background of equity market informational efficiency, efficient market theories (the theory of efficient capital markets, the theory of random walks), the EMH and its implications, technical analysis, fundamental analysis, and the developing trends in the EMH literature. Our discussion has focused on the intellectual history of the EMH, which enables us to provide a clear picture of the underlying theories and core concepts as well as the research in this field.

The EMH has a strong foundation, and to date it has remained very important to dictate the behaviour of stock prices. A perfectly efficient market may seem to be unrealistic, as arbitrage activities are constrained by information and transaction costs. In addition, it is possible that insiders' profits are available in equity markets. This suggests that strong-form efficiency is unlikely to happen. However, recent studies, such as Chau and Vayanos (2008), prove that markets may be close to strong-form efficiency. Such evidence offers new insight into the validity of EMH. Meanwhile, extensive evidence of weak-form and semi-strong-form efficiencies are documented in the literature, which shows that efficiency varies across different equity markets. Not surprisingly, some markets are found to be inefficient either in the weak-form or semi-strong-form sense. Thus, the roles played by technical analysis and fundamental analysis are important. In the presence of market inefficiency, the precision of stock price forecasting will be great, depending on the methods used. Analysts need more advanced methods as markets become more efficient. We notice that there are some new inventions, such as the Suzuki and Ohkura (2016) technical indicator and the Shen and Tzeng (2015) combined soft computing model.

In this chapter, we have only sorted the existing studies of EMH based on the well-established weak-form, semi-strong-form, and strong-form tests. Nonetheless, we believe that the current research is moving in other new directions. For example, Lim and Kim (2011) shift their attention towards the link between trade openness and stock market efficiency, and Li, Nishimura and Men (2016) analyze the effect of transaction costs on the profits from predictable long-term memory. Meanwhile, following the general dimensions under the rubric of return predictability in Fama (1991), we further divide the weak-form tests into stock return autocorrelations, the random walk model, calendar effects, long-run return reversal, the short-run momentum effect, and other forecasting variables. The main focus of semi-strong-form tests is on the speed of stock price adjustment in response to public announcement. A new area of interest is in the connection between a firm's efficiency and its stock performance. There are fewer studies of strong-form tests than of weak-form and semi-strong-form tests. Therefore, extension of research in this area is required.

Notes

1 Allocation efficiency means the resources being allocated are going to their most productive use. Operation efficiency indicates that trading is carried out quickly, reliably, and at minimum cost (Howells and Bain, 2005: 540). Technical efficiency reflects a firm's success in producing maximum output from a given set of inputs (Farrell, 1957).
2 We selectively review a number of past studies, which include a chronological review on the history of EMH by Sewell (2011).
3 More details of the Dow Theory are available in Ray (2012).

References

Andersen, T. M. (1983–1984). Some implications of the efficient market hypothesis. *Journal of Post Keynesian Economics, 6*(2), 281–294.

Bachelier, L. (2006). *Louis Bachelier's Theory of Speculation*. Princeton, NJ: Princeton University Press.

Ball, R. (2009). The global financial crisis and the efficient market hypothesis: What have we learned? (Digest Summary). *Journal of Applied Corporate Finance, 21*(4), 8–16.

Barberis, N., Shleifer, A., and Vishny, R. W. (1997). A model of investor sentiment. Working Paper No. 5926. National Bureau of Economic Research (NBER).

Baur, D. G., Dimpfl, T., and Jung, R. C. (2012). Stock return autocorrelations revisited: A quantile regression approach. *Journal of Empirical Finance, 19,* 254–265.

Beechey, M., Gruen, D., and Vickery, J. (2000). The efficient market hypothesis: A survey. Research Discussion Paper No. 2000–01, Economic Research Department, Reserve Bank of Australia.

Berkyürek, D. (2012). *Random Walk. EP499 Graduation Project*. Gaziantep, Turkey: University of Gaziantep Engineering of Physics.

Brio, E. B. D., Miguel, A., and Perote, J. (2002). An investigation of insider trading profits in the Spanish stock market. *The Quarterly Review of Economics and Finance, 42,* 73–94.

Brock, W. A., Lakonishok, J., and LeBaron, B. (1991). Simple technical trading rules and the stochastic properties of stock returns. SFI Working Paper No. 1991-01-006. Santa Fe Institute.

Brown, R. (1828). A brief account of microscopical observations made on the particles contained in the pollen of plants. *Philosophical Magazine, 4*, 161–173.

Cardano, G. (1564). Liber de Ludo Aleae. First published (in Latin) in Vol. 1, *Opera Omnia* edited by Charles Spon, Lyons, 1663. Translated into English by Sydney Henry Could in *Cardano: The Gambling Scholar by Oystein Ore*, Princeton University Press, New Jersey, NJ, 1853. Reprinted in *The Book on Games of Chance*, Holt, Rinehart and Winston, New York, 1961.

Chang, E. C., McQueen, G. R., and Pinegar, J. M. (1999). Cross-autocorrelation in Asian stock markets. *Pacific-Basin Finance Journal, 7*, 471–493.

Chau, M., and Vayanos, D. (2008). Strong-form efficiency with monopolistic insiders. *The Review of Financial Studies, 21*(5), 2275–2306.

Chaudhuri, K., and Wu, Y. (2003). Random walk versus breaking trend in stock prices: Evidence from emerging markets. *Journal of Bank and Finance, 27*, 575–592.

Dana, B. E., and Cristina, S. L. (2013). Technical and fundamental anomalies, paradoxes of modern stock exchange markets. *Economic Science Series, 22*(1), 37–43.

De Bondt, W. F. M., and Thaler, R. H. (1985). Does the stock market overreact? *Journal of Finance, 40*, 793–805.

De Bondt, W. F. M., and Thaler, R. H. (1987). Further evidence on investor overreaction and stock market seasonality. *Journal of Finance, 42*, 557–581.

Einstein, A. (1905). Über die von der molekularkinetischen Theorie der Wärme geforderte Bewegung von in ruhen-den Flüssigkeiten suspendierten Teilchen. *Annalen der Physik, 322*(8), 549–560.

Enders, W. (2015). *Applied Econometric Time Series.* Hoboken, NJ: John Wiley & Sons.

Fama, E. F. (1965a). The behaviour of stock-market prices. *The Journal of Business, 38*(1), 34–105.

Fama, E. F. (1965b). Random walks in stock market prices. *Financial Analysts Journal, 21*(5), 55–59.

Fama, E. F. (1970). Efficient capital markets: A review of theory and empirical work. *The Journal of Finance, 25*(2), 383–417.

Fama, E. F. (1991). Efficient capital markets: II. *The Journal of Finance, 46*(5), 1575–1617.

Fama, E. F. (1998). Market efficiency, long-term returns, and behavioral finance. *Journal of Financial Economics, 49*, 283–306.

Fama, E. F., and French, K. R. (1988). Permanent and temporary components of stock prices. *The Journal of Political Economy, 96*(2), 246–273.

Fang, J., Jacobsen, B., and Qin, Y. (2014). Predictability of the simple technical trading riles: An out-of-sample test. *Review of Financial Economics, 23*(1), 30–45.

Farrell, M. J. (1957). The measurement of productive efficiency. *Journal of the Royal Statistical Society, Series A (General), 120*(3), 253–290.

Foerster, S. R., and Sapp, S. G. (2011). Back to fundamentals: The role of expected cash flows in equity valuation. *North American Journal of Economics and Finance, 22*, 320–343.

Gaganis, C., Hasan, I., and Pasiouras, F. (2013). Efficiency and stock returns: Evidence from the insurance industry. Bank of Finland Research Discussion Paper No.14/2013.

Gibson, G. (1889). *The Stock Markets of London, Paris and New York.* New York, NY: G. P. Putnam's Sons.

Grossman, S. J., and Stiglitz, J. E. (1980). On the impossibility of informationally efficient markets. *The American Economic Review, 70*(3), 393–408.

Howells, P., and Bain, K. (2005). *The Economics of Money, Banking and Finance.* 1st edition. Harlow, UK: Financial Times/Prentice Hall.

Jegadeesh, N., and Titman, S. (1993). Returns to buying winners and selling losers: Implications for stock market efficiency. *The Journal of Finance, 48*(1), 65–91.

Jensen, M. C. (1978). Some anomalous evidence regarding market efficiency. *Journal of Financial Economics, 6*(2/3), 95–101.

Jovanovic, F., and Gall, P. L. (2001). Does God practise a random walk? The 'financial physics' of a nineteenth-century forerunner, Jules Regnault. *The European Journal of the History of Economic Thought, 8*(3), 332–362.

Kemp, A. G., and Reid, G. C. (1971). The random walk hypothesis and the recent behaviour of equity prices in Britain. *Economica,* New Series, *38*(149), 28–51.

Khan, A. Q., and Ikram, S. (2011). Testing strong form market efficiency of Indian capital market: Performance appraisal of mutual funds. *International Journal of Business and Information Technology, 1*(1), 151–161.

Kirkwood, J., and Nahm, D. (2005). Australian banking efficiency and its relation to stock returns. Available at: http://www.econ.mq.edu.au/research/2005/Nahm_kwood_ABE_2.pdf

Kok, S. C., and Munir, Q. (2015). Malaysian finance sector weak-form efficiency: Heterogeneity, structural breaks, and cross-sectional dependence. *Journal of Economics, Finance and Administrative Science, 20*(39), 105–117.

Laffont, J.-J., and Maskin, E. S. (1990). The efficient market hypothesis and insider trading on stock market. *The Journal of Political Economy, 98*(1), 70–93.

Latham, M. (1986). Informational efficiency and information subsets. *The Journal of Finance, 41*(1), 39–52.

Lean, H. H., Mishra, V., and Smyth, R. (2015). The relevance of heteroskedasticity and structural breaks when testing for a random walk with high-frequency financial data: Evidence from ASEAN stock markets. In: *The Handbook of High Frequency Trading.* Boston, MA: Elsevier Inc. Available at: http://dx.doi.org/10.1016/B978-0-12-802205-4.00004-X

LeRoy, S. F., and Porter, R. D. (1981). The present-value relation: Tests based on implied variance bounds. *Econometrica, 49*(3), 555–574.

Li, D., Nishimura, Y., and Men, M. (2016). The long memory and the transaction cost in financial markets. *Physica A, 442,* 312–320.

Lim, K. P. (2008). Sectoral efficiency of the Malaysian stock market and the impact of the Asian financial crisis. *Studies in Economics and Finance, 25*(3), 196–208.

Lim, K. P., and Kim, J. H. (2011). Trade openness and the informational efficiency of emerging stock markets. *Economic Modelling, 28,* 2228–2238.

Lo, A. W., and MacKinlay, A. C. (1988). Stock market prices do not follow random walks: Evidence from a simple specification test. *Review of Financial Studies, 1,* 41–66.

Malkiel, B. G. (2003). The EMH and its critics. *Journal of Economic Perspectives, 17*(1), 59–82.

Munir, Q., Kok, S. C., Furouka, F., and Mansur, K. (2012). The EMH revisited: Evidence from the five small open ASEAN stock markets. *The Singapore Economic Review, 57*(3), 1250021-1–1250021-12.

Muth, J. (1961). Rational expectations and the theory of price movements. *Econometrica*, 29(3), 315–335.

Narayan, P. K., and Narayan, S. (2007). Mean reversion in stock prices: New evidence from panel unit root tests. *Studies in Economics and Finance*, 24(3), 233–244.

Narayan, P. K., and Smyth, R. (2006). Random walk versus multiple trend breaks in stock prices: Evidence from 15 European Markets. *Applied Financial Economics Letters*, 2, 1–7.

Pearson, K. (1905). The problem of the random walk. *Nature*, 72, 294.

Ray, S. (2012). Revisiting the strength of Dow Theory in assessing stock price movement. *Advances in Applied Economics and Finance*, 3(3), 591–598.

Regnault, J. (1863). *Calcul des Chances et Philosophie de la Bourse*. Paris: Mallet-Bachelier et Castel.

Samuelson, P. A. (1965). Proof that properly anticipated prices fluctuate randomly. *Industrial Management Review*, 6(2), 41–49.

Sewell, M. (2011). History of the efficient market hypothesis. Research Note RN/11/04. UCL Department of Computer Science.

Shen, K.-Y., and Tzeng, G.-H. (2015). Combined soft computing model for value stock selection based on fundamental analysis. *Applied Soft Computing*, 37, 142–155.

Shiller, R. J. (1981). Do stock prices move too much to be justified by subsequent changes in dividends?. *The American Economic Review*, 71(3), 421–436.

Shostak, F. (1997). In defense of fundamental analysis: A critique of the efficient market hypothesis. *Review of Austrian Economics*, 10(2), 27–45.

Suzuki, T., and Ohkura, Y. (2016). Financial technical indicator based on chaotic bagging predictors for adaptive stock section in Japanese and American markets. *Physica A*, 442, 50–66.

Tian, G. G., Wan, G. H., and Guo, M. (2002). Market efficiency and the returns to simple technical trading rules: New evidence from U.S. equity market and Chinese equity markets. *Asia-Pacific Financial Markets*, 9(3–4), 241–258.

Tsay, R. S. (2010). *Analysis of Financial Time Series*. 3rd edition. Hoboken, NJ: John Wiley & Sons.

Venn, J. (1888). *The Logic of Chance, and Essay on the Foundations and Province of the Theory of Probability with Special References to Its Logical Bearings and Its Application to Moral and Social Sciences, and to Statistics*. 3rd edition. London: MacMillan.

Wafi, A. S., Hassan, H., and Mabrouk, A. (2015). Fundamental analysis models in financial markets-review study. *Procedia Economics and Finance*, 30, 939–947.

Yu, H., Nartea, G. V., Gan, C., and Yao, L. J. (2013). Predictive ability and profitability of simple technical trading rules: Recent evidence from Southeast Asian stock markets. *International Review of Economics and Finance*, 25, 356–371.

Ziliotto, A., and Serati, M. (2015). The semi-strong efficiency debate: In search of a new testing framework. *Research in International Business and Finance*, 34, 412–438.

Zou, H. (2011). Information efficiency of stock markets. *International Journal of Innovative Management, Information & Production*, 2(3), 40–48.

2 Equity market anomalies

Concepts, classifications, theories and evidence

Qaiser Munir and Sook Ching Kok

1.0 Introduction

At the outset, it is important to understand the meaning of 'anomalies'. In general, anomalies are known as irregularities or deviations from the natural order (George and Elton, 2001). Anomalies that arise from the trading of financial instruments are referred to as the moments when security prices depart from their normal behaviour (Dana and Cristina, 2013). In relation to stock trading specifically, Hubbard (2008) defines anomalies as the trading opportunities derived from the investment strategies that allow for earning above-normal returns.

The existence of anomalies reflects market inefficiency such that stock prices depart from their intrinsic value and the rationality of investors is questionable. In favour of behaviourism, it is argued that the rational theory of choice expressed in the model of decision making under risk can only describe idealist decision makers. Such a model is perceived as explaining the logic of choice as games of chance rather than the psychology of risk and value (Schumpeter, 1954; Tversky and Kahneman, 1986). Stock markets can be occupied by many irrational investors, who may frequently underreact as well as overreact to the information of price forming. As a result, stock prices tend to temporarily deviate from their fundamental value. The influence of psychology on individual decision making has been clearly addressed in previous studies. For instance, the overreaction hypothesis, which concerns return reversal, is formalized in De Bondt and Thaler (1985). As arbitrage is limited, investor sentiment may have a significant impact on prices (Shleifer and Summers, 1990). Barberis, Shleifer and Vishny (BSV, 1997) developed the model of investor sentiment, which describes momentum in stock returns. Noise traders are overconfident (Daniel, Hirshleifer and Subrahmanyam, DHS, 1998). Further, the literature has documented the intuition of investor optimism prior to a holiday, which explains the logic of the holiday effect anomaly (Karadžić and Vulić, 2011).

Despite the theoretical grounds of anomalies, there are several important considerations regarding anomalies that should be taken into account when assessing market efficiency. First, efficiency tests usually incorporate testing for the hypothesis of equilibrium expected asset returns. Thus, the evidence of anomalies can either show market inefficiency or simply the shortcomings of the models used (Schwert, 2003). This is very dependent on whether investors are able to make an excess profit by trading on the observed profit opportunities, for instance, the consideration of transaction costs is unavoidable. Third, the persistence of anomalies is arguable. Borges (2009) finds that the day-of-the-week effect and month-of-the-year effect in 17 Western and Central European stock markets are nonpersistent but attributed to data mining. His finding is consistent with a statement made by Fama (1998: 283): 'Most important, consistent with the market efficiency prediction that apparent anomalies can be due to methodology, and most long-term return anomalies tend to disappear with reasonable changes in technique.' Fourth, some economic advocates believe in the nonpersistence of anomalies in the long run, as anomalies are likely to attenuate, disappear or reverse after being learned and exploited by a large number of investors (Fama, 1970; Schwert, 2003; Timmerman and Granger, 2004). Timmermann and Granger (2004) call this phenomenon 'the self-destruction of anomalies in the long run'. Empirically, it refers to the observation of nonstationarity in security prices. The weakening and disappearing calendar anomalies in the long run are supported by the findings of Tan and Tat (1998), Wong, Agarwal and Wong (2006), Abdul Karim, Abdul Karim and Tang (2012) and Chia (2014). These studies suggest that some stock markets around the world have become increasingly efficient over long periods of time. Fifth, there is the concern of data snooping in the process of analysis. Schwert (2003) has said that researchers may reiterate and refine the 'surprising results' by using the same data. As such, this will not promote any new findings related to anomalies.

Nonetheless, anomalies stand in sharp contrast to the efficient market hypothesis (EMH). In that sense, investigating the existence of anomalies has become an alternative way to examine the EMH. We have seen that the literature on anomalies is expanding rapidly, which shows that there is a growing interest in this field. From the time of the discoveries of autocorrelation owing to the studies of Fama and French (1988) and Lo and MacKinlay (1988) until now, the continuing discoveries of anomalies have been considerably diverse and broad. There is indeed a need to identify the directions in the field and also to improve the understanding of each type of anomaly. The purpose of this chapter is to elucidate the main concepts, standard classifications, mainstream theories and empirical evidence of anomalies. The discussion in this chapter includes a number of competing theories with respect to anomalies. This will show different views regarding investor rationality and rational asset pricing.

We organize the remainder of this chapter as follows: Section 2.0: classifications for anomalies; Section 3.0: autocorrelation in stock returns; Section 4.0: calendar anomalies; Section 5.0: reversal in stock returns; Section 6.0: momentum in stock returns; Section 7.0: cross-sectional return predictability; Section 8.0: other forecasting variables; Section 9.0: conclusions.

2.0 Classifications for anomalies

Equity market anomalies that can be recognized from the literature include stock return autocorrelation, calendar anomalies, stock return reversal, the momentum effect, cross-sectional return predictability, other forecasting variables, technical anomalies, and fundamental anomalies. For the purpose of grouping, a few common classifications are used. As documented in Pattern's article titled 'Financial Market Anomalies,' in general, anomalies that arise from financial markets are divided into two broad categories: 1) cross-sectional return patterns; and 2) time series return predictability. The former is initially motivated to examine the capital asset pricing model (CAPM) through estimating cross-sectional regressions. This category of tests corresponds to the value effect, the size effect, and the momentum effect (the prior return). On the other hand, time series return predictability suggests that it is possible that stock prices contain a time-varying component such that the future prices are predictable based on their own series (stock return autocorrelation) or with predetermined observable variables (i.e. expected inflation, yield spreads of bonds with different maturities, the dividend-to-price ratio, the earnings-to-price ratio, the book-to-price ratio, etc.) and calendar turning points. Next, we noticed that the study of Dana and Cristina (2012) has sorted anomalies into three main groups: first, technical anomalies; second, fundamental anomalies; and third, anomalies on financial instrument trading. Technical anomalies can be identified through technical analysis either using simple graphical analysis or more complex analysis with the application of indicators (i.e. confirmation indicators, divergence indicators, momentum indicators and oscillators). Fundamental anomalies are concerned with both the trading of financial instruments and the elements of fundamental analysis, for example, the value effect and low price-to-book ratio. The third group consists of other anomalies on financial instrument trading, including the size effect, the effect of announcements on price, the effect of initial public offerings (IPOs) on price and the effect of insider trading.

3.0   Autocorrelation in stock returns

Basically, autocorrelation is referred to as a time series phenomenon in which the past and future returns of a stock are correlated (Lewellen, 2002). Thus, the focal point of research in this field is on autocorrelation in a stock return series. For instance, Fama (1965) shows that during the period of late 1957 to 26 September 1962, there were no large degrees of dependency in any of the series of 30 stocks that form the Dow Jones Industry Average Index. Further, autocorrelation is also concerned with the led–lag relations among different stock return series, more generally known as the cross-autocorrelation. For example, by using a large sample from the US stock market for the period spanning 6 September 1962 through 26 December 1985, Lo and MacKinlay (1988) demonstrate the presence of positive autocorrelations in the market index and size-sorted portfolio series. Also, in the case of the US stock market, Fama and French (1988) found negative autocorrelations or return reversals in the size-sorted and industrial-based portfolio series over the period 1926–1985. Many of the later studies also move in these two directions.

Looking at the Asian context, Chang, McQueen and Pinegar (1999) analyzed the monthly return data of several Asian countries, including Hong Kong, Japan,

Singapore, South Korea, Taiwan, and Thailand and the United States, using data primarily from January 1976 until December 1995. There is evidence of cross-autocorrelation in each of these countries' stock markets. The observed autocorrelation is somewhat similar to the led–lag relations introduced by Lo and MacKinlay (1988), where the monthly returns of the small stock portfolio are correlated with the lagged monthly returns of the large stock portfolio. However, there is no strong evidence of inter-Asian or Asian–US cross-autocorrelation. For the study period from January 2000 to June 2010, Hwang (2012) contributes findings of strong correlations between the selected Asian stock markets (Australia, Hong Kong, Japan, Korea, Malaysia, New Zealand, Singapore and Taiwan) with the US stock market, except in the case of China. These findings suggest that investors did not benefit from diversification during the 2008 financial crisis. To some extent, this finding indicates that financial integration potentially reduces the advantage of diversification. Meanwhile, the more recent analysis of stock return autocorrelation and cross-autocorrelation has come up with the quantile autoregressive model. Baur, Dimpfl and Jung (2012) study the stocks that comprise the Dow Jones Stock Index over the period 1 January 1987 through 18 March 2009. They find that negative returns (lower quantiles) exhibit positive dependencies. On the other hand, positive returns (upper quantiles) display negative dependencies.

4.0   Calendar anomalies

Calendar anomalies are the trading opportunities associated with calendar turning points or the so-called calendar effects. Most often, calendar effects are known as seasonality in returns. Examples of calendar effects are the day-of-the-week effect, the month-of-the-year effect, the turn-of-the-month effect and the holiday effect. Jacobs and Levy (1988) define these specific stock market anomalies as the abnormal returns, which occur at calendar turning points. The stylish fact is once calendar or seasonal regularities are discovered, they can be easily learned and exploited even by small individual investors who manage their own equity portfolios. The practicality of observing calendar anomalous patterns makes this area of research increasingly important. While a number of studies found the existence of calendar anomalies in different stock markets, the economic significance of calendar effects is still debated. It is argued that calendar effects may only be a 'chimera' delivered by intensive data mining, as they are country-specific results and may not be stable over time (Borges, 2009). It is apparent that the existence of calendar anomalies varies across different countries. A particular calendar effect may be more pronounced in some countries, but may be weaker in other countries. However, once a calendar effect is discovered, it can be easily learned and exploited for abnormal returns over a short-term investment horizon. Some common calendar effects are discussed in the following sections.

4.1   The day-of-the-week effect

The day-of-the-week effect refers to the observation that stock returns are not equal across the days of the week; usually the average return (mean return) on

Monday is negative and at its lowest, while the average return on Friday is positive and at its highest (Wong *et al.*, 2006). It is possible that certain trading days in a week will display unusually higher or lower mean returns than other trading days in a week. According to the calendar time hypothesis as proposed by French (1980), stock prices should rise higher on Monday than other, non-Monday trading days. This is because there is a three-day gap between the close of trading on Friday and the close of trading on Monday, rather than the normal one-day gap that exists between other trading days. The Monday effect is also called the weekend effect (Rogalski, 1983; Thaler, 1987). However, past empirical evidence generally suggests that Monday has a tendency to display the lowest negative mean return, while Friday is likely to have the highest positive mean return (Gao and Kling, 2005; Wong *et al.*, 2006; Lim and Chia, 2010). This finding is clearly inconsistent with French's (1980) calendar time hypothesis. One plausible explanation provided for the negative return on Monday as well as the positive return on Friday is based on the intuition of settlement delay. For instance, according to Nik Muhammad and Abdul Rahman (2010), settlement in Malaysia is made on the third trading day after a transaction. Investors enjoy an extra two days of interest-free credit from brokers if they trade Wednesday through Friday. Thus, stock prices on Monday must be lower to compensate investors who are willing to delay purchase until Monday.

4.2 The month-of-the-year effect

The month-of-the-year effect can be easily understood as the observation that stock returns are not equal across the months of the year. According to Urquhart and McGroarty (2014), the month-of-the-year effect refers to a phenomenon in which stock returns are systematically higher or lower depending on the month of the year. Specifically, the abnormally high return in January is called the January effect. There are two prominent explanations for this anomaly: Wachtel (1942) proposes the tax loss selling hypothesis, which states that investors sell the losing stocks in their portfolios at the year-end to gain a tax benefit; Haugen and Lakonishok (1988) associate the January effect with the window dressing hypothesis, which suggests that fund managers sell certain stocks at the year-end to present a more acceptable portfolio of stocks in their year-end reports (Moller and Zilca, 2008). Apart from fixed calendar events such as the January effect, there are also the effects of moving calendar events, for instance, the Muslim holy month of Ramadan in the stock markets in Islamic countries. The study of Seyyed, Abraham and Al-Hajji (2005) has documented a systematic pattern of decline in volatility during Ramadan due to a slowdown of economic activities and a decrease in speculative stock trading, implying the possibility of predictable variation in the market price of risk.

4.3 The turn-of-the-month (TOM) effect

The TOM effect describes the unusually high stock returns at the turn of the month (Wong *et al.*, 2006). Often, turn of the month refers to the last trading day of the previous month to the first three trading days of the current month (Wong *et al.*, 2006; Giovanis, 2014; Sharma and Narayan, 2014). In the study of Hansen and Lunde (2003), turn of the month is used to refer to the last four trading days of the previous month to the first four trading days of the current month. Thus, the time period of TOM effect can be slightly varied. There are at least three economically plausible explanations for the TOM effect. According to Thaler (1987), institutional investors may make seasonal adjustments in their portfolios just for 'window dressing' to clean up their portfolios before reporting dates, normally at year-end and month-end. This phenomenon may explain both the year-end and month-end effects. Ogden (1990) proposes the TOM liquidity hypothesis, which links the TOM effect with certain market activities, for example, the payments of wages, dividends and interests, which are usually undertaken towards month-end. Karadžić and Vulić (2011) relate the TOM effect to the timing of monthly cash flow received by large institutional investors, such as pension funds, which allows them to inject new funds into the stock market, causing stock prices to soar.

4.4   *The turn-of-the-year effect*

The turn-of-the-year effect, also known as the January effect, is the observation that stock returns in January are on average higher than for the other months (Wong, *et al.*, 2006). This seasonal effect is attributed to tax loss selling during the past December. In general, there will be pressure to sell small capitalization stocks in December, which leads to substantial short-term capital loss for small firms. This is because investors tend to capitalize for income tax purposes. Prices of small capitalization stocks will rebound in January as investors repurchase the stocks to re-establish their investment positions. Alternatively, Schwert (2003) defines the turn-of-the-year effect as the abnormal returns in the first two weeks in January.

4.5   *The holiday effect*

The holiday effect is the observation of a higher average return on the trading day immediately preceding a holiday (Kim and Park, 1994; Wong *et al.*, 2006). In addition, the holiday effect can be divided into two: the pre-holiday effect and the post-holiday effect. There are no fixed durations for defining pre-holiday and post-holiday. However, pre-holiday is usually defined as the last trading day before a holiday, and post-holiday as the first trading day after a holiday (Hansen and Lunde, 2003; Marrett and Worthington, 2007). Sometimes, researchers set different durations to capture the pre-holiday and post-holiday effects. For instance, Wu (2013) set a five-day duration for the pre-period, the period during and the post-period of the Chinese Lunar New Year (CLNY) or Spring Festival.

What is the logic behind the holiday effect? From the perspective of psychology, investors are more optimistic before a holiday than after a holiday (Karadžić and Vulić, 2011); thus there will be relatively more buying pressure in the market before a holiday than after a holiday. As such, we may expect a higher average return on pre-holiday trading and a lower average return on post-holiday trading, as compared to the average return on other trading days. Holidays in the Asian market context are inclusive of the national public holidays in individual countries. Due to great cultural influence, some Asian countries celebrate the same important traditional festivals as non-Asian countries, such as, New Year's Day, the CLNY Festival, Good Friday, Easter Day, the Hari Raya Puasa Festival, the Deepavali Festival, Christmas Day and Boxing Day.

4.6   *Evidence of calendar anomalies*

One strand of the literature indicates extensive evidence of calendar anomalies. Sharma and Narayan (2014) find that the TOM effect in the US stock market is heterogeneous on firm returns and return volatility. Yuan and Gupta (2014) adduce strong evidence of the holiday effect related to CLNY in several Asian markets, including China, Japan, Hong Kong, Malaysia, South Korea and Taiwan. The second strand of literature focuses on the persistence of calendar anomalies. For instance, Borges (2009) finds that the observed day-of-the-week effect and the month-of-the-year effect in a sample of 17 Western and Central European market indices are highly unstable. As the results may be attributed to data mining, he doubts the economic significance of the calendar effects studied.

The third strand of literature indicates the disappearing calendar effects. From analyzing the return data of the SES All-Singapore Index for the period 1975–1994, Tan and Tat (1998) found evidence of the weakening calendar effects (i.e. the January effect, the day-of-the-week effect, the TOM effect, and the holiday effect) in the Singapore stock market. Later, by applying the return data of the Strait Times Index and using two sub-periods: the pre-crisis period (1993–1997) and the post-crisis period (1998–2005), Wong *et al.* (2006) show that the January effect is insignificant in either the full or sub-periods; the negative Monday effect is only significant in the full and pre-crisis period but not in the post-crisis period; the pre-holiday trading days correspond with relatively higher mean daily return than other trading days, and it is only significant in the full and pre-crisis periods. The TOM effect is significant in all periods but declines across the sub-periods. In brief, the findings of both Tan and Tat (1998) and Wong *et al.* (2006) strongly suggest that the market in Singapore has become more efficient. Through the analysis based on the return data of both the Australia Morgan Stanley Capital International (MSCI) Index and the New Zealand MSCI Index for the period spanning from June 2002 to May 2014, Chia (2014) shows that the day-of-the-week effect is disappearing in the Australian and New Zealand stock markets.

The fourth strand of literature indicates calendar effects may evolve but will eventually diminish in the long run. For the period 1973–2013, Olson, Mossman and Chou (2015) produce empirical findings of the long-run disappearance of the day-of-the-week effect by employing unit root tests. According to the authors, this calendar effect may continue going up and down but will eventually disappear in the long run. Another focus of research in this area is on the changing behaviour of calendar effects. The findings in Urquhart and McGroarty (2014) show the adaptive behaviour of calendar anomalies to different market states, for example, bull markets, bear markets and market crashes.

5.0   Reversal in stock returns

The underlying idea of long-run return reversal is that stock returns display patterns of reversal around the time period of three to five years, thus it is possible to yield an abnormal return through a contrarian investing strategy. This investing strategy is based on buying the portfolio of stocks that have had very poor performance in the past (the portfolio of past losers) and selling the portfolio of stocks that have performed very well in the past (the portfolio of past winners). The anomalous pattern of return reversal was introduced in a series of published articles written by De Bondt and Thaler (1985, 1987, 1989).

5.1   Overreaction hypothesis

Irrational overreaction to news is a plausible explanation for reversal in stock returns in the long run. De Bondt and Thaler (1985, 1987) perceive that many investors are Bayesian decision makers, as they have a tendency to overreact to information. For example, they may overweight the current information of price forming, i.e. company earnings, while underweighing base rate data, or they may overreact to unexpected news. This leads to temporary stock price deviations from the fundamental values and systematic reversals in stock returns over a long period of time, i.e. around three to five years. The occurrence of return reversal is due to investors making corrections on mispricing after realizing that mistakes were made. As noted by George and Hwang (2007), the overreaction hypothesis has symmetric predictions for the portfolio of winners and the portfolio of losers. We can expect that stocks with similar past returns, for instance, those with prices near to historical low (high), may experience systematic return reversals in the long run. In other words, past loser stocks will outperform past winner stocks, and *vice versa*.

5.2   The capital gains lock-in hypothesis

As mentioned by George and Hwang (2007), another reason for stock return reversal can be explained based on the capital gains lock-in hypothesis that evolves from the study of Klein (1999). Intuitively, investors will have concerns about the payments of capital gain taxes upon realization of profits, especially from selling stocks with large embedded gains. Therefore, stocks with large accrued capital gains will trade at premiums higher than otherwise identical stocks. However, these stocks will ultimately turn over to other buyers without large embedded gains. Thus, the marginal investor's reservation price is expected to decrease gradually and, in turn, leads to a slowly dissipating reversal in stock returns.

5.3 *Evidence of return reversals*

De Bondt and Thaler (1985) analyzed the CRSP monthly return data and found that the portfolio of stocks with very poor performance in the past yielded abnormally high positive returns in January within five years of portfolio formation. This finding rejects the weak-form EMH. Later studies show that return reversals can happen over three to five years, or even a shorter period, and can be cyclical. For the period of 1955–1990, Clare and Thomas (1995) studied a sample of 1000 stocks from the UK stock market and found evidence showing that a portfolio of losers can outperform a portfolio of winners over a two-year period. Pham *et al.* (2007) show that over the study period from 2001 to 2005, there is evidence of short-term price reversals, i.e. around three days, in the markets of Australia, Japan and Vietnam. However, the profits obtained by investors from exploiting price reversals due to large price declines are less than the profits generated by passive funds. This finding is thought to favour market efficiency. Hsieh and Hodnett (2011) find that the overreaction hypothesis is valid in the case of the South African market for the period 1 January 1993 through 31 March 2009. The reversals fluctuate around the business cycle of the country.

6.0   Momentum in stock returns

The simplest explanation for momentum is continuation in stock returns (Hong, Lee and Swaminathan, 2003) or a trend in short-term returns (Forner, 2003). This term could also be defined as the sensitivity of expected stock price ratio with respect to today's price, where a positive sensitivity is called 'bullish momentum' while a negative sensitivity is known as 'bearish momentum' (Hong and Satchell, 2013). The term 'momentum effect' is used to refer to a predictable pattern in historical price data, which appears as a cross-sectional result and is different from autocorrelation in stock returns. The majority of the published empirical works on the momentum effect are based on momentum-based trading strategies, initially proposed by Jegadeesh and Titman (1993) to buy past 'winner' stocks and sell past 'loser' stocks for the earnings of positive abnormal returns over short investment horizons. Specifically, the strategies that form stock portfolios based on the past returns of stocks in the last 3 to 12 months and holding stocks for the subsequent 3 to 12 months can generate significant momentum profits. It is believed that the momentum effect is derived from the delayed price reactions to firm-specific information, such as earnings announcements; therefore momentum profits are perceived as firm-specific returns.

6.1 *The model of investor sentiment*

The proposition that investors tend to underreact to information on firm earnings is well described using the model of investor sentiment developed by Barberis, Shleifer and Vishny (BSV, 1997). Intuitively, investors tend to underreact to news, but they may overreact to the actual information of news after repeated bombardment by news of the same type. The model considers a risk-neutral[1] investor whose belief reflects the consensus representing the belief of others. There is only one security available, and the security has an equilibrium price equal to the net present value of future earnings that the investor expects. In the model, the true earning process of the stock is random walk, but the investor wrongly understood that earnings move between two regimes, neither of which is a random walk process. In the first regime, earnings are mean reverting. In the second regime, earnings trend as they rise further after an increase. The investor never alters the regime-switching model in forecast earnings. Below is the expression of the model:

$$N_t = N_{t-1} + y_t,$$

where y_t denotes the shock to earnings at time t, which can be either positive or negative shock $+y$ or $-y$. The value of y_t depends on two different regimes. In the first regime, an earnings shock is likely to reverse in the following period. In the second regime, the earnings shock may be followed by another shock in the same sign. Each regime shows the Markov process, in which the change in earnings in period t depends on the change in earnings in period $t-1$. Neither regime is random walk.

6.2   Evidence of the momentum effect

The discovery of the momentum effect is considerably new compared to return reversal. However, momentum-based investing strategies have been used by practitioners long before any academic research (Tan *et al.*, 2014). Jegadeesh and Titman (1993) was the first study that demonstrated how relative strength strategies that buy past winner stocks and sell past loser stocks (opposite to a contrarian investing strategy) will yield the momentum profits. Current research moves in two directions: in search of the evidence, which will show that momentum profits are attributed to investor underreaction to firms' earnings news, and seeking the alternative sources of momentum profits. For the period July 1987 through December 2000, Hong *et al.* (2003) verified the profitability of earnings momentum strategies in Australia, Canada, France, Germany, Hong Kong and the United Kingdom, but not in Japan, Malaysia, Singapore, South Korea or Taiwan. They find that this anomaly is less pronounced in the markets with low levels of investor protection. Alphonse and Nguyen (2013) studied a sample of 267 stocks listed on the Ho Chi Minh Stock Exchange (HOSE) for the period January 2007 through June 2012 and found that momentum profits are highest when stocks are selected based on their last one-week returns and then holding stocks for one week. Meanwhile, Cooper, Gutierrez Jr. and Hameed (2004) find that return reversal in the long run is due to time variation in risk; thus the momentum effect also corresponds with investor overreaction and different market states. Chan, Hameed and Tong (2000) found evidence of the connection between trading volume and momentum profits, but their finding is inconsistent with that of Naughton, Truong and Veeraraghavan (2008).

7.0   Cross-sectional return predictability

In this section, we focus on particular asset pricing models that can be used in testing cross-sectional return predictability. To provide the background of asset pricing models, we begin with a brief review of the development of Sharpe–Lintner CAPM. Then, we concentrate on Fama and French's three-factor model, Carhart's four-factor model and Fama and French's five-factor model.

7.1   *The Markowitz portfolio choice model and Sharpe–Lintner CAPM*

The model of portfolio choice proposed by Markowitz (1959) assumes that investors are risk averse and only consider the mean and variance of one-period investment return. They will choose mean variance–efficient portfolios in order to minimize the variance of returns and maximize the expected returns.

The Sharpe–Lintner CAPM builds on the Markowitz portfolio choice model. To better identify mean variance–efficient portfolios, Sharpe (1964) and Lintner (1965) add two assumptions to Markowitz's theory, namely, complete agreement on the distribution of returns from $t - 1$ to t; and the existence of lending and borrowing at a risk-free rate. The model is written as follows:

$$E(R_i) = R_f + \left[E(R_M) - R_f\right]\beta_{iM},$$

where R_i is the return on asset i; R_f is the risk-free return; R_M is the return on the value-weight market portfolio and β_{iM} is the beta. The CAPM describes the relation between risk and the expected return on an asset. The expected return on an asset is determined by the risk-free return, the quantity of risk contained in the asset, which is measured by the beta, and the premium per unit of beta risk, $E(R_M) - R_f$.

The asset pricing model continued to develop through research following that of Sharpe (1964) and Lintner (1965). On one side, behaviourists bring in sentiment-based pricing models, such as Hong and Stein (1999) and Shleifer (2000). On the other side, others attempt to refine the CAPM, for instance, Fama and French (1993, 1996, 2014) and Carhart (1997).

7.2   *Fama and French's three-factor model*

In the CAMP, the factors of size and value are omitted. Thus, the model does not explain the following: 1) the relation between average return and size, for instance, market capitalization; and 2) the relation between average return and value, such as the book-to-market equity ratio (B/M). In relation to this, Fama and French (1993, 1996) propose a three-factor model incorporating beta, size and value directed at improving the prediction of returns on diversified portfolios. Specifically, the three-factor model can be used to test the cross-sectional variations in average stock returns among different portfolios. This model is written as Equation (1), and Equation (2) is the regression model:

$$(R_{it}) - R_{ft} = \beta_{iM}\left[E(R_{Mt} - R_{ft})\right] + \beta_{is}E(SMB_t) + \beta_{ih}E(HML_t) \tag{2.1}$$

$$R_{it} - R_{Ft} = a_i + b_i(R_{Mt} - R_{Ft}) + s_i SMB_t + h_i HML_t + e_{it}, \tag{2.2}$$

where R_{it} is the return on portfolio i at time t; R_{ft} is the risk-free return; R_{Mt} is the return on the value-weight market portfolio; SMB_t denotes the return on a portfolio of small stocks minus the return on a portfolio of big stocks and HML_t denotes the return on a portfolio of stocks with high B/M minus the return on a portfolio of stocks with low B/M. The betas are slopes in the multiple regression of $R_{it} - R_{ft}$ on $R_{Mt} - R_{ft}$, SMB_t and HML_t (Fama and French, 2004, 2014).

The excess return on a particular portfolio can be explained by 1) excess market portfolio return, 2) the difference between the excess return on a portfolio of small stocks and the excess return on a portfolio of big stocks, and 3) the difference between the excess return on a portfolio of stocks with high B/M and the excess return on a portfolio of stocks with low B/M (Eraslan, 2013).

7.3   Carhart's four-factor model

Carhart (1997) developed a four-factor model by incorporating an additional factor into the Fama and French three-factor model. The author proposes the inclusion of a momentum factor capturing one year of momentum anomaly. Below is the regression equation of the model:

$$r_{it} = \alpha_{iT} + b_{iT}RMRF + s_{iT}SMB_t + h_{iT}HML_t + p_{iT}PR1YR_t + e_{it},$$

where r_{it} is the return on a portfolio in excess of the one-month Treasury bill return; $RMRF$ is the excess return on the value-weight market portfolio; SMB (small minus big) and HML (high minus low) represent the size factor and value factor, respectively; and PR1YR captures the excess return on one-year momentum.

7.4   Fama and French's five-factor model

To enhance the prediction of the three-factor model, Fama and French (2014) propose a five-factor model for the expected returns on diversified portfolios. The model implies that the prediction of portfolio returns is based on risk, size, value, profitability and investment patterns. The authors use the following regression model:

$$R_{it} - R_{Ft} = a_i + b_i(R_{Mt} - R_{Ft}) + s_i SMB_t + h_i HML_t + r_i RMW_t + c_i CMA_t + e_{it},$$

where there are two new variables included in the five-factor model. The first variable is RMW_t, which denotes the difference between the return on the portfolio of stocks with robust profitability and the return on the portfolio of stocks with weak profitability. The second variable added is CMA_t, which denotes the difference between the return on the portfolio of stocks representing low-investment firms and the return on the portfolio of stocks representing high-investment firms.

8.0 Other forecasting variables

The forecast power of valuation metrics over the long horizon has been studied since Fama (1970) or even earlier. Some examples of common valuation metrics are dividend yields, earnings growth, price–earnings ratios and return on equity. We also notice the use of numerous macroeconomic indicators as forecasting variables, for instance, unemployment rate, capital utilization rate, fixed capital investment, producer and consumer price indices, commodity prices, personal income, money supply, credit, interest rate spread, federal funds rate, trade balance and exchange rates. Pierdzioch, Döpke and Hartmann (2008) find that in the case of the German market over the period 1994–2005, volatility forecasts based on real-time macroeconomic data have statistical and economic value comparable to the value of forecasts using revised macroeconomic data.

9.0 Conclusion

Chapter 2 has discussed the concepts, classifications, theories and empirical evidence of different equity market anomalies. The main categories of anomalies identified from the existing literature include autocorrelation in stock returns, calendar anomalies, return reversal, momentum in stock returns, cross-sectional return predictability and other forecasting variables. In addition, the discussion in this chapter covers a number of competing theories related to anomalies. These include the rational theory of choice, the model of decision making under risk, various theories on psychology influence in individual decision making, sentiment-based pricing models, the long-run self-destruction of anomalies, the Markowitz portfolio choice model, the Sharpe–Lintner CAPM, Fama and French's three-factor model, Carhart's four-factor model and Fama and French's five-factor model. These theories reflect different views regarding investor rationality and rational asset pricing. Distinct from the EMH, behaviourists use an alternative approach based on behavioural finance to study investor investing behaviour and asset pricing. Much emphasis is given to the aspects of psychological influence in individual decision making and the role of investor sentiment in asset pricing. This approach provides strong theoretical grounds for the existence of anomalies.

Note

1 According to Hubbard (2008), risk-neutral savers judge assets only on their expected returns.

References

Abdul Karim, B., Abdul Karim, Z., and Tang, A. N. (2012). Holiday effects in Malaysia: An empirical note. *International Journal of Research in Economics and Business Management*, 1(1), 23–26.

Alphonse, P., and Nguyen, T. H. (2013). Momentum effect: Evidence from the Vietnamese stock market. *Asian Journal of Finance & Accounting*, 5(2), 183–202.

Barberis, N., Shleifer, A., and Vishny, R. W. (1997). A model of investor sentiment. Working Paper No. 5926, National Bureau of Economic Research (NBER).

Baur, D. G., Dimpfl, T., and Jung, R. C. (2012). Stock return autocorrelations revisited: A quantile regression approach. *Journal of Empirical Finance*, 19, 254–265.

Borges, M. R. (2009). Calendar effects in stock markets: Critique of previous methodologies and recent evidence in European countries. Working Paper No. WP37/2009/DE/UECE, School of Economics and Management, Technical University of Lisbon, Portugal.

Carhart, M. M. (1997). On persistence in mutual fund performance. *The Journal of Finance*, 52, 57–82.

Chan, K., Hameed, A., and Tong, W. (2000). Profitability of momentum strategies in the international equity markets. *Journal of Financial and Quantitative Analysis*, 35(2), 153–172.

Chang, E. C., McQueen, G. R., and Pinegar, J. M. (1999). Cross-autocorrelation in Asian stock markets. *Pacific-Basin Finance Journal*, 7, 471–493.

Chia, R. C.-J. (2014). The disappearing day-of-the-week effect in Australia and New Zealand stock markets: Evidence from TAR-GARCH model. *Malaysian Journal of Business and Economics*, 1(2), 51–61.

Clare, A., and Thomas, S. (1995). The overreaction hypothesis and the UK stock market. *Journal of Business Finance & Accounting*, 22(7), 961–973.

Cooper, M., Gutierrez Jr., R. C., and Hameed, A. (2004). Market states and momentum. *The Journal of Finance*, 59(3), 1345–1363.

Dana, B. E., and Cristina, S. L. (2013). Technical and fundamental anomalies, paradoxes of modern stock exchange markets. *Economic Science Series*, 22(1), 37–43.

Daniel, K., Hirshleifer, D., and Subrahmanyam, A. (DHS, 1998). Investor psychology and security market under- and overreaction. *Journal of Finance*, 53, 1839–1885.

De Bondt, W. F. M., and Thaler, R. H. (1985). Does the stock market overreact? *Journal of Finance*, 40, 793–805.

De Bondt, W. F. M., and Thaler, R. H. (1987). Further evidence on investor overreaction and stock market seasonality. *Journal of Finance*, 42, 557–581.

De Bondt, W. F. M., and Thaler, R. H. (1989). Anomalies, a mean-reverting walk down Wall Street. *Journal of Economic Perspectives*, 3(1), 189–202.

Eraslan, V. (2013). Fama and French three-factor model: Evidence from Istanbul stock exchange. *Business and Economics Research Journal*, 4(2), 11–22.

Fama, E. F. (1965). The behavior of stock-market prices. *The Journal of Business*, 38(1), 34–105.

Fama, E. F. (1970). Efficient capital markets: A review of theory and empirical work. *The Journal of Finance*, 25(2), 383–417.

Fama, E. F. (1998). Market efficiency, long-term returns, and behavioural finance. *Journal of Financial Economics*, 49, 283–306.

Fama, E. F., and French, K. R. (1988). Permanent and temporary components of stock prices. *The Journal of Political Economy*, 96(2), 246–273.

Fama, E. F., and French, K. R. (1993). Common risk factors in the returns on stocks and bonds. *Journal of Financial Economics*, *33*(1), 3–56.

Fama, E. F., and French, K. R. (1996). Multifactor explanations of asset pricing anomalies. *Journal of Finance*, *51*(1), 55–84.

Fama, E. F., and French, K. R. (2004). The capital asset pricing model: Theory and evidence. *Journal of Economic Perspectives*, *18*(3), 25–46.

Fama, E. F., and French, K. R. (2014). A five–factor asset pricing model. Fama-Miller Working Paper. Available at: http://dx.doi.org/10.2139/ssrn.2287202

Forner, C. (2003). Contrarian and momentum strategies in the Spanish stock market. *European Financial Management*, *9*(1), 67–88.

French, K. (1980). Stock returns and the weekend effect. *Journal of Financial Economics*, *8*, 55–69.

Gao, L., and Kling, G. (2005). Calendar effects in Chinese stock market. *Annals of Economics and Finance*, *6*, 75–88.

George, M. F., and Elton, G. M. (2001). Anomalies in finance what are they and what are they good for? *International Review of Financial Analysis*, *10*, 22.

George, T. J., and Hwang, C.-Y. (2007). Long-term return reversals: Overreaction or Taxes? *The Journal of Finance*, *62*(6), 2865–2896.

Giovanis, E. (2014). The turn-of-the-month effect: Evidence from Periodic Generalized Autoregressive Conditional Heteroskedasticity (PGARCH) model. *International Journal of Economic Sciences and Applied Research*, *7*(3), 1–26.

Hansen, P. R., and Lunde, A. (2003). Testing the significance of calendar effects. Working Paper No. 2003–03, Department of Economics, Brown University, USA.

Haugen, R. A., and Lakonishok, J. (1988). *The Incredible January Effect*. Homewood, IL: Dow Jones Irwin.

Hong, D., Lee, C. M. C., and Swaminathan, B. (2003). Earnings momentum in international markets. Available at: http://dx.doi.org/10.2139/ssrn.390107

Hong, H., and Stein, J. C. (1999). Differences of opinion: Rationality arbitrage and market crashes. NBER Working Paper No. 7376.

Hong, K. J., and Satchell, S. (2013). Time series momentum trading strategy and autocorrelation amplification. Cambridge Working Papers in Economics (CWPE) No. 1322, 1–37.

Hsieh, H.-H., and Hodnett, K. (2011). Tests of the overreaction hypothesis and the timing of mean reversals on the JSE Securities Exchange (JSE): The case of South Africa. *Journal of Applied Finance & Banking*, *1*(1), 107–130.

Hubbard, R. G. (2008). *Money, the Financial System, and the Economy*. 6th edition. Boston: Pearson Education, Inc.

Hwang, J.-K. (2012). Dynamic correlation analysis of Asian stock markets. *International Atlantic Economic Society*, *18*, 227–237.

Jacobs, B. I., and Levy, K. W. (1988). Calendar anomalies: Abnormal returns at calendar turning points. *Financial Analysts Journal*, *44*(6), 28–39.

Jegadeesh, N., and Titman, S. (1993). Returns to buying winners and selling losers: Implications for stock market efficiency. *The Journal of Finance*, *48*(1), 65–91.

Karadžić, V., and Vulić, T. B. (2011). The Montenegrin capital market, calendar anomalies. *Economic Annals*, *56*(191), 107–121.

Kim, C.-W., and Park, J. (1994). Holiday effects and stock returns: Further evidence. *Journal of Financial and Quantitative Analysis*, *29*(1), 145–157.

Klein, P. (1999). The capital gain lock-in effect and equilibrium returns. *Journal of Public Economics*, *71*(3), 355–378.

Lewellen, J. (2002). Momentum and autocorrelation in stock returns. *The Review of Financial Studies*, 15(2), 533–563.

Lim, S. Y., and Chia, R. C. J. (2010). Stock market calendar anomalies: Evidence from ASEAN-5 stock markets. *Economic Bulletin*, 30(2), 996–1005.

Lintner, J. (1965). The valuation of risk assets and the selection of risky investments in stock portfolios and capital budgets. *Review of Economics and Statistics*, 47(1), 13–37.

Lo, A. W., and MacKinlay, A. C. (1988). Stock market prices do not follow random walks: Evidence from a simple specification test. *Review of Financial Studies*, 1, 41–66.

Markowitz, H. (1959). *Portfolio selection: Efficient diversification of investments*. New York: .Cowles Foundation for Research in Economics at Yale University.

Marrett, G., and Worthington, A. C. (2007). An empirical note on the Holiday Effect in the Australian stock market, 1996–2006. Working Paper No. 11, 2007, School of Accounting & Finance, University of Wollongong.

Moller, N., and Zilca, S. (2008). The evolution of the January effect. *Journal of Banking & Finance*, 32, 447–457.

Naughton, T., Truong, C., and Veeraraghavan, M. (2008). Momentum strategies and stock returns: Chinese evidence. *Pacific-Basin Finance Journal*, 16, 476–492.

Nik Muhammad, N. M., and Abdul Rahman, N. M. N. (2010). Efficient market hypothesis and market anomaly: Evidence from day-of-the-week effect of Malaysian exchange. *International Journal of Economics and Finance*, 2(2), 35–42.

Ogden, J. P. (1990). Turn-of-month evaluations of liquid profits and stock returns: A common explanation for the monthly and January effects. *Journal of Finance*, 45(4), 1259–1272.

Olson, D., Mossman, C., and Chou, N. T. (2015). The evolution of the weekend effect in US markets. *The Quarterly Review of Economics and Finance*. Available at: http://dx.doi.org/10.1016/j.qref.2015.01.005

Patterns, C. S. R. Financial market anomalies. Available at: http://finance.wharton. upenn.edu/.../NewPalgraveAnomalies(May302006).pdf

Pham, V. T. L., Nguyen, D. Q. T., and To, T. D. (2007). Abnormal returns after large stock price changes: Evidence from Asia-Pacific Markets. In: Suk-Joong Kim, Michael D. Mckenzie (Eds.), *Asia-Pacific Financial Markets: Integration, Innovation and Challenges* (International Finance Review, Volume 8). Bingley, UK: Emerald Group Publishing, 205–227.

Pierdzioch, C., Döpke, J., and Hartmann, D. (2008). Forecasting stock market volatility with macroeconomic variables in real time. *Journal of Economics and Business*, 60(3), 256–276.

Rogalski, R. J. (1983). A further investigation of the weekend effect in stock returns: Discussion. *The Journal of Finance*, 39(3), 835–837.

Schumpeter, J. A. (1954). *History of Economic Analysis*. New York, NY: Oxford University Press.

Schwert, G. W. (2003). Anomalies and market efficiency. In: Constantinides, G. M., Harris, M., and Stulz, R. (Eds.), *Handbook of the Economics of Finance*. Amsterdam: Elsevier Science B. V., 939–974.

Seyyed, F. J., Abraham, A., and Al-Hajji, M. (2005). Seasonality in stock returns and volatility: The Ramadan effect. *Research in International Business and Finance*, 19, 374–383.

Sharma, S. S., and Narayan, P. K. (2014). New evidence on turn-of-the-month effects. *Journal of International Financial Markets, Institutions & Money, 29*, 92–108.

Sharpe, W. F. (1964). Capital asset prices: A theory of market equilibrium under conditions of risk. *Journal of Finance, 19*(3), 425–442.

Shleifer, A. (2000). *Inefficient Markets: An Introduction to Behavioral Finance.* Oxford, United Kingdom: Oxford University Press.

Shleifer, A., and Summers, L. H. (1990). The noise trade approach to finance. *Journal of Economic Perspectives, 4*(2), 19–33.

Tan, Y. M., Cheng, F. F., and Hassan, T. (2014). Momentum profitability in Malaysia. *Pertanika Journals* 22(S), 1–16.

Tan, R. S. K., and Tat, W. N. (1998). The diminishing calendar anomalies in the stock exchange of Singapore. *Applied Financial Economics, 8*(2), 119–125.

Thaler, R. (1987). Seasonal movements in security prices II: Weekend, holiday, turn of the month and intraday effects. *Journal of Economic Perspectives, 1*, 167–177.

Timmermann, A., and Granger, C. W. J. (2004). EMH and forecasting. *International Journal of Forecasting, 20*, 15–27.

Tversky, A., and Kahneman, D. (1986). Rational choice and the framing of decisions. *Journal of Business, 59*(4), 251–278.

Urquhart, A., and McGroarty, F. (2014). Calendar effects, market conditions and the Adaptive Market Hypothesis: Evidence from long-run U.S. data. *International Review of Financial Analysis, 35*, 154–166.

Wachtel, S. (1942). Certain observations on seasonal movements in stock prices. *The Journal of Business of the University of Chicago, 15*(2), 184–193.

Wong, W. K., Agarwal, A., and Wong, N. T. (2006). The disappearing calendar anomalies in the Singapore stock market. *The Lahore Journal of Economics, 11*(2), 123–139.

Wu, C. (2013). The Chinese New Year holiday effect: Evidence from Chinese ADRs. *Investment Management and Financial Innovations, 10*(2), 8–14.

Yuan, T., and Gupta, R. (2014). Chinese Lunar New Year effect in Asian stock markets, 1999–2012. *The Quarterly Review of Economics and Finance, 54*, 529–537.

3 The random walk hypothesis on the small and medium capitalized segment of the Indian stock market

Vinod Mishra and Russell Smyth

1.0 Introduction

A market in which futures prices cannot be predicted using past historical price data is weak-form market efficient (Fama, 1970). A market that is weak-form efficient is said to be characterized by a random walk. A random walk 'is a term loosely used in the finance literature to characterize a price series where all subsequent price changes represent random departures from previous prices' (Malkiel, 2003: 60). The implication is that if a market is characterized by a random walk, an uninformed investor purchasing a diversified portfolio will obtain, on average, a rate of return as good as that realized by an expert (assuming a comparable level of risk).

Since the early studies of Samuelson (1965) and Fama (1970), a sizeable literature has evolved that tests the efficient market hypothesis (EMH) in financial markets. Hiremath and Kumari (2014: 1) suggest, 'There is no theory that has attracted volumes of research like the EMH.' Lim and Brooks (2011) survey much of this literature. Beginning with Chaudhuri and Wu (2003, 2004) there is an increasing number of studies that have tested the EMH in emerging stock markets (see, e.g. Gough and Malik, 2005; Maghyereh, 2005; Phengpis, 2006; Lean and Smyth, 2007; Cooray and Wickremasinghe, 2008; Hasanov and Omay, 2008; Munir, Kok, Furouka and Mansur, 2012; Wang, Zhang and Zhang, 2015).

One of the most common approaches to test the EMH is to test for a unit root in stock prices. If stock prices contain a unit root, this implies that any shock to stock prices will be permanent and, hence, it is not possible to predict future prices based on movements in past prices. Such a finding would be consistent with stock prices being weak-form efficient or exhibiting a random walk. The alternative hypothesis is that stock prices are mean reverting, implying that prices will revert to their natural mean over time, thus making it possible to forecast future price movements using past data.

The starting point for testing the EMH using unit root tests is typically a traditional test with no structural breaks, such as the augmented Dickey-Fuller (ADF) unit root test, the Phillips-Perron (PP) unit root test or the stationarity test (Kwiatkowski, Phillips, Schmidt and Shin [KPSS]) (1992). Some studies, particularly the earlier ones, relied solely on these tests. Other studies used these tests to obtain benchmark results before proceeding to more advanced tests. A limitation of the ADF test is that it fails to account for one or more structural breaks in the data (Perron, 1989). There are now many studies that test for the EMH using unit root tests that allow for one or two endogenous structural breaks in the series, such as Zivot and Andrews (1992), Lumsdaine and Papell (1997), Lee and Strazicich (2003a, 2003b) and Narayan and Popp (2010; see, e.g. Chaudhuri and Wu, 2003; Narayan and Smyth, 2005, 2007; Phengpis, 2006; Lean and Smyth, 2007). Other studies have proceeded beyond the ADF test by using nonlinear unit root tests, such as that proposed by Caner and Hansen (2001; see, e.g. Narayan, 2005).

In the current study, we test the EMH for the small/medium capitalization segment of the Indian stock market by applying the Narayan, Liu and Westerlund (2015) unit root test with two structural breaks. As we employ high-frequency data, it is crucial that we use a methodology that accounts for heteroscedasticity when testing for a random walk.

The reason that we select the Narayan *et al.* (2015) unit root test with two structural breaks to test the EMH is that it has the advantage of simultaneously accounting for heteroscedasticity and structural breaks when testing for a unit root.

We focus on the Indian stock market because India is among the fastest developing economies in the world and its stock market has seen an unprecedented level of growth due to an increased level of economic activity, enhanced investor confidence and huge inflow of foreign capital. Yet, in spite of a series of financial reforms in the first half of the 1990s, India's institutional framework, regulatory policies and information disbursement mechanism are not at the same level as those evident in more developed economies. As such, the Indian stock market has been rocked by several large-scale financial scams, including the Harshad Mehta scam in 1991, the Ketan Parekh scam in 2001 and the Stayam scandal in 2009. All of this suggests that as a financial market, the Indian stock market may not exhibit a random walk (see Hiremath, 2013 for a detailed overview of the Indian stock market).

We contribute to the literature on the EMH in the following ways. First, we focus on the small and medium capitalized segment of the stock market. The small and medium capitalized segment of a stock market in a growing economy is usually perceived as an attractive investment segment with high growth potential. However, the small and medium segment also presents some real challenges for investors because of infrequent trading and high execution cost. Moreover, the information regarding the business prospects of small and medium firms may not be readily available and/or reported by media outlets and hence the prices of small/ midcapitalization stocks may or may not reflect all available information – hence the reasons for questioning whether the EMH applies to Indian markets apply *a fortiori* to the small and medium capitalized segment of the stock market. While there are many studies looking at market efficiency for the large and most liquid segment of the stock market, we know very little about the small/medium segment.

Second, we make a methodological contribution by applying the Narayan *et al.* (2015) generalized autoregressive conditional heteroscedasticity (GARCH) unit root test that accommodates both heteroscedasticity and structural breaks. As noted by Narayan *et al.* (2015) heteroscedasticity is likely to be a feature of high-frequency financial data, but it is rarely taken into account. There are very few studies that have applied the Narayan *et al.* (2015) GARCH unit root test to examine the EMH. Apart from Narayan *et al.* (2015) itself, the only other studies of which we are aware that apply this test to stock prices are Lean, Mishra and Smyth (2015) and Mishra, Mishra and Smyth (2015). We contribute to this embryonic literature through applying the Narayan *et al.* (2015) test to high-frequency data in the small and medium capitalized segment of the stock market.

Third, we contribute to the previous literature for India that has used unit root tests to examine the EMH in the Indian stock market (see, e.g. Alimov, Chakraborty, Cox and Jain, 2004; Ahmed *et al.*, 2006; Gupta and Basu, 2007; Srivastava, 2010; Jayakumar, Thomas and Ali, 2012; Mehla and Goyal, 2012; Ali, Naseem and Ali, 2013; Jayakumar and Sulthan, 2013; Kumar and Maheswaran, 2013; Kumar and Singh, 2013;). Findings from this literature have been mixed. Complicating matters, most of these studies are outdated in terms of timeframe or in terms of econometric methodology employed, or both. These considerations impair the reliability of most existing findings. One recent exception is Mishra *et al.* (2015), who apply the Lee and Strazicich (2003a, 2003b), Narayan and Popp (2010) and Narayan *et al.* (2015) tests to examine the EMH for the most liquid stocks with the largest market capitalization on the National Stock Exchange (NSE). Their main finding was that the relevant indices were mean reverting. We extend their analysis to the small and medium capitalized segment of the NSE.

The issue of whether stock prices are characterized by a random walk is important for market participants. If markets are efficient, prices reflect all information present in the market and, hence, there is no scope for making profits using either technical analysis or fundamental analysis of financial markets. However, if stock prices are found to be mean reverting, this suggests that it is possible for market traders to generate a profit through predicting future price movements based on historical data.

A second reason that the results are important is that they carry implications for the allocation of resources and regulation of the market. The stock market exists to efficiently allocate resources in the economy by converting savings into productive investments. If markets are efficient, the stock market will allocate the investment to the most efficient outcome and individual investors can invest in the market with certainty about their investment. However, if markets are not efficient then the resource allocation mechanism is undermined, suggesting a bigger role for regulators to protect the investments of market participants (see Mishra *et al.*, 2015).

2.0   Methods

For benchmarking purposes, we apply the traditional ADF, PP and KPSS unit root tests. As the methodology of these tests is well known, we do not reproduce it here. To test for a unit root in the presence of structural breaks we employ the

Narayan and Popp (2010) test. Narayan and Popp (2013) show that the Narayan and Popp (2010) test has better size and higher power, and it identifies the breaks more accurately, than either the Lumsdaine and Papell (1997) or Lee and Strazicich (2003b) tests. The Narayan and Popp (2010) test is an ADF-type unit root test for the case of innovation outliers (IOs), where the problem of spurious rejection can be avoided by formulating a data-generating process (DGP) as an unobserved components model, in which breaks are allowed to occur under both the null and alternative hypotheses. The DGP of a time series y_t has two components: a deterministic component (d_t) and a stochastic component (u_t). Narayan and Popp (2010) used two different specifications for the deterministic component; one allows for two breaks in the level, denoted as model 1 (M1) and the other allows for two breaks in the level as well as the slope of the deterministic trend component, denoted as model 2 (M2). The test equations for the two models are:

$$y_t^{M1} = \rho y_{t-1} + \alpha_t + \beta^* t + \theta_1 D\left(T_B'\right)_{1,t} + \theta_2 D\left(T_B'\right)_{2,t} + \delta_1 DU_{1,t-1}'$$
$$+ \delta_2 DU_{2,t-1}' + \sum_{j=1}^{k} \beta_j \Delta y_{t-j} + e_t, \tag{3.1}$$

with $\alpha_1 = \psi^*(1)^{-1}\left[(1-\rho)\alpha + \rho\beta\right] + \psi^*(1)^{-1}(1-\rho)\beta$, $\psi^*(1)^{-1}$ being the mean lag,

$\beta^* = \psi^*(1)^{-1}(1-\rho)\beta, \phi = \rho - 1, \delta_i = -\phi\theta_i$ and $D\left(T_B'\right)_{i,t} = 1\left(t = T_{B,i}' + 1\right), i = 1,2.$

$$y_t^{M2} = \rho y_{t-1} + \alpha^* + \beta^* t + \kappa_1 D\left(T_B'\right)_{1,t} + \kappa_2 D\left(T_B'\right)_{2,t} + \delta_1^* DU_{1,t-1}'$$
$$+ \delta_2^* DU_{2,t-1}' + \gamma_1^* DT_{1,t-1}' + \gamma_2^* DT_{2,t-1}' + \sum_{j=1}^{k} \beta_j \Delta y_{t-j} + e_t, \tag{3.2}$$

where, $\kappa_i = (\theta_i + \gamma_i), \delta_i^* = (\gamma_i - \phi\theta_i),$ and $\gamma_i^* = -\phi\gamma_i, i = 1,2.$

Since break dates $(T_{B,i}')$ are unknown and have to be estimated, Narayan and Popp (2010) used a sequential procedure, along the lines proposed by Kapetanios (2005), to derive their estimates. The unit root null hypothesis of $\rho = 1$ is tested against the alternative hypothesis of $\rho < 1$. The critical values of the test statistics, and the results of Monte Carlo simulations for the size and power of the test, are given in Narayan and Popp (2010). We test for both M1 and M2 specifications, thereby allowing for a break in the intercept only and a break in both the intercept and trend of the series.

In addition to structural breaks, high-frequency time series data is also characterized by heteroscedasticity. Narayan *et al.* (2015) relax the assumption of independent and identically distributed errors and propose a GARCH (1,1) unit root model that accommodates two endogenous structural breaks in the intercept in the presence of heteroscedastic errors. The advantage of using the Narayan and Popp (2010) and Narayan *et al.* (2015) tests together is that the latter uses the Narayan and Popp (2010) approach to identifying the structural breaks. Hence,

Narayan *et al.* (2015) is highly comparable to Narayan and Popp (2010). It simply goes one step further and allows us to examine the effect of heteroscedasticity on the results. The Narayan *et al.* (2015) test considers a GARCH (1, 1) unit root model as follows:

$$y_t = \alpha_0 + \pi y_{t-1} + D_1 B_{1t} + D_2 B_{2t} + \varepsilon_t. \tag{3.3}$$

Here, $B_{it} = 1$ for $t > T_{Bi}$; otherwise $B_{it} = 0$, T_{Bi} are structural break points where $i = 1,2$, D_1 and D_2 are break dummy coefficients and ε_t follows the first-order GARCH (1,1) model of the form:

$$\varepsilon_t = \eta_t \sqrt{h_t}, h_t = \kappa + \alpha \varepsilon_{t-1}^2 + \beta h_{t-1}. \tag{3.4}$$

Here, $k > 0$, $\alpha \geq 0$, $b \geq 0$ and η_t is a sequence of independently and identically distributed random variables with zero mean and unit variance. To estimate these equations Narayan *et al.* (2015) used joint maximum likelihood (ML) estimation. Since break dates (T_{Bi}) are unknown and have to be substituted by their estimates, a sequential procedure is used for deriving the estimates of break dates. The unit root hypothesis is tested with the ML t-ratio for p with a heteroskedastic-consistent covariance matrix.

3.0   Data

We use monthly data from the NSE of India for the period 2003 to 2014. NSE is the largest stock exchange in India, accounting for roughly 83 percent of the entire market turnover in India. NSE has the following four broad market indices capturing the small and medium segment of the market:

- *Nifty Midcap 100 Index*: This index was designed with the primary objective of capturing and benchmarking the movements in the medium capitalized segment of the Indian stock market. This index comprises 100 firms listed on NSE. It started with the base of 1 January 2003 and base value of 1000 points. The Nifty Midcap 100 Index represented about 13.86 percent of the free float market capitalization of the stocks listed on NSE as on 31 March 2015.[1]
- *Nifty Midcap 50 Index*: This index was designed to reflect the behaviour and performance of the stocks in the midcap segment of the Indian stock market, which are also part of the futures and options (F&O) segment of NSE. This index consists of 50 companies, which are also present in F&O segments (but not part of the Nifty 50 Index). It started with a base value of 1000 points on 1 January 2004.
- *Nifty Midcap LIX 15 Index*: This index was designed with the sole purpose of exposing investors to the liquid midcap stocks while ensuring that the index is easily replicable and tradable. All the stocks which are part of this index have derivatives traded on them; hence this index can be easily hedged

and investors can explore arbitrage opportunities, if any. As of 30 June 2014 this index comprised stocks from eight diversified sectors and represented approximately 8 percent of the traded value in the cash segment and around 10 percent of the traded value in the F&O segment of NSE. This index started with a base value of 1000 points on 1 January 2009.

- *Nifty Smallcap 100 Index*: The Nifty Smallcap index was designed with the objective of reflecting the behaviour and performance of the small capitalized segment of the market. This index comprises 100 tradable, exchange-listed companies, with the base date of index being 1 January 2004 and base value of 1000 points. It represents roughly 3 percent of the free float market capitalization of the stocks listed on NSE.

The first three indices on the medium capitalization segment of NSE differ from each other in terms of the selection criteria used for selecting the constituents, the methodology used for calculation and the size of market share represented by them. The currency of all of the above indices is the Indian rupee. All of the above indices are revised on a semi-annual basis incorporating the addition and deletion of companies in the index.[2]

We downloaded the monthly data for each index for the period starting from the index's base date to December 2014 (the latest full year of data available when the study was undertaken).[3] As the different indices started at different base dates, the sample period differs from index to index. A novelty of this study is that it looks at the entire history of each of the above-mentioned indices. The price data were converted to the natural logarithm before conducting the unit root tests.

Table 3.1 presents the descriptive statistics for the four indices. The average monthly value of the Nifty Midcap 100 is the highest of the four indices. The Nifty Midcap 100 also has the highest minimum and maximum values and is the most volatile, as reflected in the highest standard deviation. The Nifty Midcap LIX 15 has the lowest mean value and minimum and maximum values and is the least volatile.

Table 3.1 Descriptive statistics

Index	Sample period	Mean	SD	Min.	Max.	ARCH-LM test
Nifty Mid Cap 100	Jan 2003 – Dec 2014	5801.50	2666.56	935.69	12333.33	21.62**
Nifty Mid Cap 50	Jan 2004 – Dec 2014	2117.66	640.99	832.46	3619.35	28.84***
Nifty Mid Cap LIX 15	Jan 2009 – Dec 2014	1978.57	453.65	809.42	3035.74	20.02*
Nifty Small Cap 100	Jan 2004 – Dec 2014	3029.28	1117.25	777.02	5368.79	27.54***

Note: *, ** and *** denotes statistical significance at the 10%, 5%, and 1% levels, respectively.

4.0   Results

We began by implementing the Autoregressive Conditional Heteroskedasticity Lagrange Multiplier (ARCH-LM) test. We first filtered the data using an AR(12) model, given we have monthly data, then used the residuals to run an ARCH-LM test. The results are presented in Table 3.1. The null hypothesis of no ARCH effect is rejected at the 10 percent level for the Nifty Midcap LIX 15 and 5 percent or better for the other three indices, indicating the presence of significant time-varying volatility in the monthly returns.

Next, for benchmarking purposes, we applied the ADF and PP unit root tests and the KPSS stationarity test, without a trend. The results are reported in Table 3.2. Each of the tests suggests that each of the four indices contains a unit root. Hence, on the basis of the traditional stationarity/unit root tests, the EMH is supported for each of the four indices.

The problem with these tests, however, is that they are biased in the presence of conditional heteroscedasticity and possible structural breaks. The period studied contains several domestic and international events that previous research has shown to have caused breaks in Indian stock indices (see Mishra *et al.*, 2015). Domestic events include various natural disasters such as floods, stock market scams, high profile corruption cases and terrorist attacks as well as ongoing tension between India and Pakistan over Kashmir.

Major global events in this period were the global financial crisis and ongoing conflict in nearby Afghanistan. Both of these events have caused structural breaks in financial time series worldwide. Another related event was the Greek debt

Table 3.2 Traditional unit root tests without structural breaks

Series	ADF test	PP test	KPSS test
Nifty Midcap 100	−1.640	−4.343	1.27***
Nifty Midcap 50	−2.554	−7.437	0.77***
Nifty Midcap LIX 15	−1.323	−9.109	0.467**
Nifty Smallcap 100	−2.523	−5.660	0.924***

Notes: (1) The unit root tests were performed on the natural logarithm of each series with the assumption of an intercept in the DGP. (2) The lag lengths were selected using the Bayesian information criteria (BIC). (3) The null hypothesis for the ADF and PP tests is a unit root, whereas the null hypothesis for the KPSS test is stationarity. The critical values for each test are as follows:

Test	Critical values		
	1%	5%	10%
ADF	−3.50	−2.88	−2.57
PP	−19.94	−13.78	−11.05
KPSS	0.739	0.463	0.347

crisis, which impacted many economics in the Eurozone. Moreover, this period also coincided with major political upheavals in the Middle East (Syria and Iraq), which created a large humanitarian refugee crisis, as well as impacting the global trade in petroleum.

Indian businesses and, as a consequence, the stock markets were impacted by these events. The United States (the epicentre of the global financial crisis) is a major trading partner of India, and much of India's high-tech service industry (mainly information technology and information technology enabled services) relies on the US economy. Moreover, India is highly dependent on oil imports from the Middle East for most of its energy needs and is easily impacted by political upheavals in that region.

The results for the Narayan and Popp (2010) unit root test with two breaks in the intercept are presented in Table 3.3. Again, there is strong evidence of a random walk. The Narayan and Popp (2010) test fails to reject the unit root null for any of the four indices. Hence, while the presence of one or more structural breaks weakens the power to reject the unit root null, we can conclude that in this instance failure to find mean reversion in the ADF, PP and KPSS unit root/stationarity tests is not due to failure to take account of structural breaks.

A limitation of the Narayan and Popp (2010) test, particularly with high-frequency financial data, is that it fails to take account of heteroscedasticity. We have shown in the final column of Table 3.1 that each of the four series is characterized by heteroscedasticity. Hence, we move on to consider the Narayan *et al.* (2015) GARCH unit root test with two breaks in the intercept, which accounts for structural breaks and heteroscedasticity. The results are presented in Table 3.4. In contrast to the findings for the Narayan and Popp (2010) unit root test, there is evidence of mean reversion in three of the four indices at the 5 percent level or better. The one exception is the Nifty Midcap 50, which is characterized by a random walk.

Table 3.3 Results for Narayan and Popp (2010) unit root test with two structural breaks

Index	Test statistic	TB1	TB2
Nifty Midcap 100	−2.780	May 2006	September 2008
Nifty Midcap 50	−3.342	May 2006	September 2008
Nifty Midcap LIX 15	−2.764	July 2011	May 2013
Nifty Small Cap 100	−3.320	September 2008	March 2009

Notes: (1). The 1%, 5% and 10% critical values for Narayan and Popp (2010) test are −4.731, −4.136 and −3.825, respectively. (2) TB1 and TB2 indicate the break dates. (3) The null hypothesis for Narayan and Popp (2010) is that the series has a unit root. A failure to reject the null indicates the presence of a unit root. (4) The numbers reported are *t*-statistics for the Narayan and Popp (2010) test. (5) The unit root tests were performed on the natural logarithm of each series with the assumption of two endogenous breaks in the intercept.

Table 3.4 Results for Narayan *et al.* (2015) GARCH unit root test with two structural breaks in the intercept

Index	Test statistic	TB1	TB2
Nifty Midcap 100	–5.298**	April 2007	March 2014
Nifty Midcap 50	–1.786	February 2008	March 2009
Nifty Midcap LIX 15	–4.889**	November 2010	March 2014
Nifty Smallcap 100	–3.946**	April 2004	August 2006

Notes: (1) The 5% critical value for the unit root test statistics is –3.65, obtained from Narayan *et al.* (2015) (2) Narayan *et al.* (2015) provide critical values for the 5% level of significance only. (3) ** indicates rejection of the null hypothesis of a unit root at the 5% level of significance. (4) The null hypothesis for Narayan *et al.* (2015) is that the series has a unit root. Rejection of the null indicates mean reversion. (5) The numbers reported are *t*-statistics for the Narayan *et al.* (2015) test. (6) The unit root tests were performed on the natural logarithm of each series with the assumption of two endogenous breaks in the intercept.

5.0   Discussion

We have tested the EMH in the small and medium capitalized segment of the NSE using progressively more complicated unit root tests. Our working hypothesis was that there would be considerable evidence of inefficiencies in the small and medium capitalized segment of the stock market given that trading is thinner there than for the main indices. Our results suggest that it is only when we allow for structural breaks and heteroscedasticity in the data that we find mean reversion in 75 percent of the indices. This finding is generally consistent with previous studies that have applied the Narayan *et al.* (2015) unit root test to other stock indices. This includes the most liquid stocks with the largest market capitalization on the NSE (Mishra *et al.*, 2015) and ASEAN stock indices (Lean *et al.*, 2015). It also extends to other financial markets, such as commodity prices, including palm oil spot and futures prices (Lean and Smyth, 2015) and natural gas spot and futures prices (Mishra and Smyth, 2016).

An important result is that it is heteroscedasticity that is driving the outcomes. We can draw this conclusion because structural breaks in the Narayan and Popp (2010) and Narayan *et al.* (2015) tests are accounted for in the same way. The only difference is that one test also accounts for heteroscedasticity and the other does not. This result points to the need to account for heteroscedasticity when testing for a random walk in high-frequency financial data. This conclusion is consistent with that in other previous studies (Narayan and Liu, 2011; Lean *et al.*, 2015; Lean and Smyth, 2015; Mishra *et al.*, 2015; Mishra and Smyth, 2016).

Why does the Nifty Midcap 50 exhibit a random walk? That one of the indices contains a unit root is a somewhat surprising result, as one would expect the small and medium segment to be inefficient and mean reverting, considering most of the trading is concentrated in the large and most liquid segment of the market. The better than expected resilience and efficiency of the midcap segment could be because of the existence of speculative behaviour in this segment of the market. As most investors expect this segment to be inefficient, they probably make speculative investments in this market, hoping to make supra-normal profits. However, if a large number of investors engage in such speculative trading, the resulting market will be efficient with limited, or no, opportunities to make above-normal profits. We speculate that this could be what is happening in the midcaps market.

We briefly discuss the structural breaks in the Narayan and Popp (2010) and Narayan *et al.* (2015) unit root tests. These are graphed in Figures 3.1–3.4.

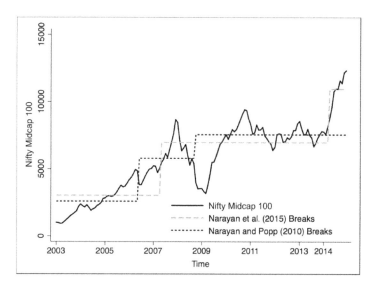

Figure 3.1 Breaks in Nifty Midcap 100 Series

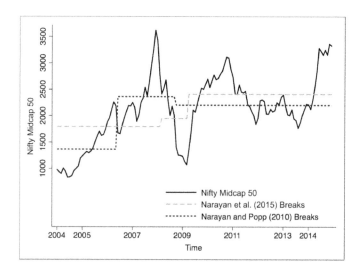

Figure 3.2 Breaks in Nifty Midcap 50 Series

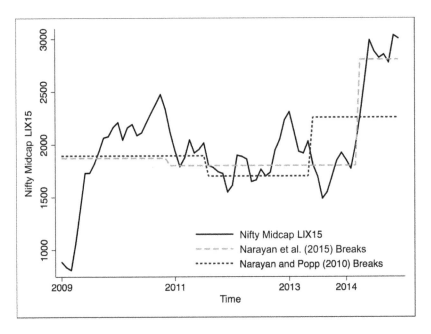

Figure 3.3 Breaks in Nifty Midcap LIX 15 Series

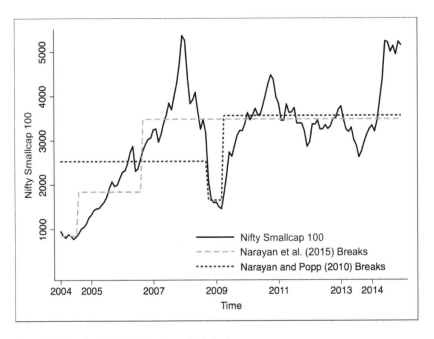

Figure 3.4 Breaks in Nifty Smallcap 100 Series

The structural breaks identified in the Narayan and Popp (2010) test for the Midcap 100 and Midcap 50 indices coincide with the Mumbai blasts in 2006 and the Mumbai terror attacks in 2008. If we look at the location of the structural breaks as identified by the Narayan *et al.* (2015) test for the same two indices, we find that most of the break dates (April 2007, Feb 2008 and March 2009) fall during the global financial crisis, which was a period of extreme volatility in stock markets.

The second break date identified by the Narayan *et al.* (2015) test for the Midcap 100 and Midcap LIX 15 corresponds to the 2014 general election in India and the associated market optimism associated with Modi's victory. The small cap segment seems to be almost always impacted by domestic events, such as the terrorist attacks in Mumbai (2006 and 2008) and the general elections (2004 and 2009). This is in line with our expectations, as investors in the stocks of small companies would be more pessimistic about corporate prospects when something catastrophic happens domestically (such as a terrorist attack), rather than when something major happens elsewhere (such as the Greek financial crisis).

6.0 Conclusion

We have tested the EMH for the small and medium capitalized segment of the Indian stock market. In so doing, we build on the contribution in Mishra *et al.* (2015) by extending their analysis to smaller, less liquid, stocks. While there is a large literature that has tested the EMH using unit root tests, no attention had been given to small and midcaps. The results from the GARCH unit root tests with two breaks in the intercept find mean reversion in three-quarters of the indices. This suggests that there is scope to potentially profit from fundamental analysis in 75 percent of the indices. In this sense, our study adds to a growing body of evidence from unit root tests that generally corroborate against the EMH in stock markets. It is fair to say that the case against the EMH has become stronger as unit root tests have become more sophisticated. With studies using high-frequency financial data, the case against the EMH from studies employing the Narayan *et al.* (2015) test is quite strong.

The implications of this conclusion are potentially far reaching. It suggests that not only are stock markets generally inefficient and that there is potential for traders to make profits through predicting future prices, but that there is a need for heavier regulation of markets to protect investors. This is particularly true for small and midcap segments of stock markets in developing countries. The more general conclusion emanating from our results is that it is not only important to accommodate structural breaks, but it is also important to consider heteroscedasticity when testing the EMH with high-frequency financial data.

We have posited that our finding that the Nifty Midcap 50 index is efficient may reflect the fact that speculative investors trade in that market in a bid to make supra-normal profits. In so doing, investors may compete away any above-normal profits and thus make the market efficient. However, one can only draw definite conclusions about this phenomenon after analyzing other aspects of this segment, such as the level of trading activity, market liquidity and volatility patterns in this segment. Hence, a natural extension of this study could be to examine the liquidity of the small and medium segment of the Indian stock market. Another avenue for future research would be to examine whether those indices that are mean reverting, and hence predictable, are also profitable through the application of trading strategies (see Narayan and Ahmed, 2014; Narayan, Ahmed, Sharma and Prabheesh, 2014).

Notes

1 The source is http://www.nseindia.com/products/content/equities/indices/cnx_midcap.htm.
2 The details of selection criteria, methodology of calculation, Index rebalancing policies and details of index governance for all of the above indices can be found at the NSE India website (http://www.nseindia.com/products/content/equities/indices/broad_indices.htm).
3 All of the data are freely available from the NSE India website (http://www.nsein dia.com).

References

Ahmad, K. M., Ashraf, S., and Ahmad, S. A. (2006). Testing weak form efficiency for Indian stock markets. *Economic & Political Weekly, 41*(1), 49–56.

Ali, S., Naseem, M. A., and Ali, N. S. (2013). Testing random walk and weak form efficiency hypotheses: Empirical evidence from the SAARC region. *Finance Management, 56,* 13840–13848.

Alimov, A. A., Chakraborty, D., Cox, R. A. K., and Jain, A. K. (2004). The random-walk hypothesis on the Bombay stock exchange. *Finance India, 18*(3), 1251–1258.

Caner, M., and Hansen, B. E. (2001). Threshold autoregression with a unit root. *Econometrica, 69*(6), 1555–1596.

Chaudhuri, K., and Wu, Y. (2003). Random-walk versus breaking trend in stock prices: Evidence from emerging markets. *Journal of Banking & Finance, 27*(4), 575–592.

Chaudhuri, K., and Wu, Y. (2004). Mean reversion in stock prices: Evidence from emerging markets. *Managerial Finance, 30*(1), 22–37.

Cooray, A., and Wickremasinghe, G. (2008). The efficiency of emerging stock markets: Empirical evidence from the South Asian region. *Journal of Developing Areas, 41*(1), 171–183.

Fama, E. F. (1970). Efficient capital markets: A review of theory and empirical work. *Journal of Finance, 25*(2), 383–417.

Gough, O., and Malik, A. (2005). Random-walk in emerging markets: A case study of the Karachi Stock Exchange. In: Motamen-Samadian, S. (Ed.), *Risk Management in Emerging Markets*. New York, NY: Palgrave Macmillan, 57–70.

Gupta, R., and Basu, P. (2007). Weak form efficiency in Indian stock markets. *International Business & Economics Research Journal, 6*(3), 57–63.

Hasanov, M., and Omay, T. (2008). Nonlinearities in emerging stock markets: Evidence from Europe's two largest emerging markets. *Applied Economics, 40*(20), 2645–2658.

Hiemstra, C., and Jones, J. D. (1994). Testing for linear and nonlinear Granger causality in the stock price-volume relation. *Journal of Finance, 49*(5), 1639–1664.

Hiremath, G. S. (2013). *Indian Stock Market.* Heidelberg: Springer.

Hiremath, G. S., and Kumari, J. (2014). Stock returns predictability and the adaptive market hypothesis in emerging markets: Evidence from India. *SpringerPlus, 3,* 428.

Jayakumar, D. S., and Sulthan, A. (2013). Testing the weak form efficiency of Indian stock market with special reference to NSE. *Advances in Management, 6*(9), 18–27.

Jayakumar, D. S., Thomas, B. J., and Ali, S. D. (2012). Weak form efficiency: Indian stock market. *SCMS Journal of Indian Management, 9*(4), 80–95.

Kapetanios, G. (2005). Unit-root testing against the alternative hypothesis of up to m structural breaks. *Journal of Time Series Analysis, 26,* 123–133.

Kumar, D., and Maheswaran, S. (2013). Evidence of long memory in the Indian stock market. *Asia Pacific Journal of Management Research and Innovation, 9*(9), 10–21.

Kumar, S., and Singh, M. (2013). Weak form of market efficiency: A study of selected Indian stock market indices. *International Journal of Advanced Research in Management and Social Sciences, 2*(11), 141–150.

Kwiatkowski, D., Phillips, P. C. B., Schmidt, P., and Shin, Y. (1992). Testing the null hypothesis of stationarity against the alternative of a unit root. *Journal of Econometrics, 54*(1), 159–178.

Lean, H. H., Mishra, V., and Smyth, R. (2015). The relevance of heteroskedasticity and structural breaks when testing for a random walk with high frequency financial data: Evidence from ASEAN stock markets. In Gregoriou, G. (Ed.), *Handbook of High Frequency Trading.* Amsterdam: Elsevier, 59–74.

Lean, H. H., and Smyth, R. (2007). Do Asian stock markets follow a random-walk? Evidence from LM unit root tests with one and two structural breaks. *Review of Pacific Basin Financial Markets and Policies, 10*(1), 15–31.

Lean, H. H., and Smyth, R. (2015). Palm oil spot and futures markets: New evidence from a GARCH unit root test with multiple structural breaks. *Applied Economics, 47,* 1710–1726.

Lee, J., and Strazicich, M. C. (2003a). Minimum LM unit toot test with one structural break. Mimeo.

Lee, J., and Strazicich, M. C. (2003b). Minimum LaGrange multiplier unit root test with two structural breaks. *Review of Economics and Statistics, 85*(4), 1082–1089.

Lim, K.-P., and Brooks, R. (2011). The evolution of stock market efficiency over time: A survey of the empirical literature. *Journal of Economic Surveys, 25*(1), 69–108.

Lumsdaine, R. L., and Papell, D. H. (1997). Multiple trend breaks and the unit-root hypothesis. *Review of Economics & Statistics, 79*(2), 212–218.

Malkiel, B. G. (2003). The efficient market hypothesis and its critics. *Journal of Economic Perspectives, 17*(1), 59–82.

Mehla, S., and Goyal, S. K. (2012). Empirical evidence on weak form efficiency in Indian stock market. *Asia Pacific Journal of Management and Innovation, 8,* 59–68.

Mishra, A., Mishra, V., and Smyth, R. (2015). The random walk hypothesis on the Indian stock market. *Emerging Markets Finance & Trade, 51,* 879–892.

Mishra, V., and Smyth, R. (2016). Are natural gas spot and futures prices predictable? *Economic Modelling, 54,* 178–186.

Munir, Q., Kok, S. C., Furouka, F., and Mansur, K. (2012). The efficient market hypothesis revisited: Evidence from the five small open ASEAN stock markets. *Singapore Economic Review, 57*(3), 1250021 (12 pages) DOI: 10.1142/S021759 081250021X.

Narayan, P. K. (2005). Are Australian and New Zealand stock prices nonlinear with a unit root? *Applied Economics, 37*(18), 2161–2166.

Narayan, P. K., and Ahmed, H. A. (2014). Importance of skewness in decision making: Evidence from the Indian stock exchange. *Global Finance Journal, 25,* 260–269.

Narayan, P. K., Ahmed, H. A., Sharma, S. S., and Prabheesh, K. P. (2014). How profitable is the Indian stock market? *Pacific Basin Finance Journal, 30,* 44–61.

Narayan, P. K., and Liu, R. (2011). Are shocks to commodity prices persistent? *Applied Energy, 88,* 409–416.

Narayan, P. K., Liu, R., and Westerlund, J. (2015). New evidence on the weak-form efficient market hypothesis. Working Paper, Centre for Financial Econometrics, Deakin University.

Narayan, P. K., and Popp, S. (2010). A new unit root test with two structural breaks in level and slope at unknown time. *Journal of Applied Statistics, 37,* 1425–1438.

Narayan, P. K., and Popp, S. (2013). Size and power properties of structural break unit root tests. *Applied Economics, 45,* 721–728.

Narayan, P. K., and Smyth, R. (2005). Are OECD stock prices characterised by a random-walk? Evidence from sequential trend break and panel data models. *Applied Financial Economics, 15*(8), 547–556.

Narayan, P. K., and Smyth, R. (2007). Mean reversion versus random-walk in G7 stock prices: Evidence from multiple trend break unit root tests. *Journal of International Markets, Financial Institutions and Money, 17*(2), 152–166.

Perron, P. (1989). The great crash, the oil price shock, and the unit root hypothesis. *Econometrica, 57*(6), 1361–1401.

Phengpis, C. (2006). Are emerging stock market price indices really stationary? *Applied Financial Economics, 16,* 931–939.

Samuelson, P. A. (1965). Proof that properly anticipated prices fluctuate randomly. *Industrial Management Review, 6,* 41–49.

Srivastava, A. (2010). Are Asian stock markets weak form efficient? Evidence from India. *Asia Pacific Business Review, 6,* 5–11.

Wang, J., Zhang, D., and Zhang, J. (2015). Mean reversion in stock prices of seven Asian markets: Unit root and stationarity test with Fourier functions. *International Review of Economics and Finance, 37,* 157–164.

Zivot, E., and Andrews, D. W. K. (1992). Further evidence on the great crash, the oil-price shock, and the unit-root hypothesis. *Journal of Business and Economic Statistics, 10*(3), 251–270.

4 Stock market index price prediction using predetermined variables

A case study of Malaysia

Qaiser Munir and Sook Ching Kok

1.0 Introduction

The EMH states that security prices fully reflect the available information (Fama, 1970, 1991). The weak-form EMH asserts that security prices already fully reflect the information contained in the history of past trading Stock market efficiency in the weak-form sense has been widely studied and the methodologies being used are various. These include the tests used for assessing the stochastic properties of stock prices and the tests under the rubric of return predictability (Fama, 1991). On return predictability in particular, one strand of the literature attempts to predict the movements of stock prices using predetermined variables, most often by employing the data of macroeconomic variables and commodity prices.

This focused area of study has long been established; for example, Campbell (1987) associates stock returns with the term structure of interest rates in the United States; Fama and French (1989) relate the expected returns of stocks and bonds to business cycle conditions in the United States; and Campbell and Hamao (1989) find that dividend-to-price ratio and interest rates can help to forecast excess returns in the US and Japan stock markets. Nevertheless, this research area has gained growing interest recently that is mainly motivated by increased financial market integration; economic cyclical changes, i.e. economic boom, economic downturn, bull market and bear market; commodity price fluctuations; and the outbreaks of financial crises, i.e. asset price bubbles, stock market crash, currency crisis, banking crisis and twin crisis. For instance, Zhu, Li and Li (2014) look into the time-varying dynamic relationship between the Asia Pacific stock market returns and crude oil prices before and in the aftermath of the September 2008 global financial crisis. Choudhry, Hassan and Shabi (2015) analyze the nonlinear co-movement between stock market returns, stock market volatility and gold returns in the United States, the United Kingdom and Japan by incorporating the effects of the recent global financial crisis. Cho, Choi, Kim and Kim (2016) find that there are capital movements induced by flight to quality in global down markets during 1996–2009, where there was a tendency of capital outflow from emerging markets to developed countries. This leads to a positive correlation between stock returns and currency returns in emerging markets and to the inverse in developed countries. Basically, researchers are in search of possible systematic relationships and time-varying dynamic linkages between stock prices and other variables. If the evidence of a significant relationship can be found, it would be against the EMH but in favour of stock price forecasting. Some recent related studies are Pan, Fok and Liu (2007), Gay, Jr. (2008), Basher, Haug and Sadorsky (2012), Park and Shin (2013), Ghosh and Kanjilal (2014), Zhu *et al*. (2014), Akgül, Bildirici and Özdemir (2015), Choudhry *et al*. (2015), and Cho *et al*. (2016).

The purpose of this study is to investigate the co-movement between the Malaysia stock market index (FTSE) Kuala Lumpur Composite Index (KLCI) prices with three variables, namely, crude oil prices, gold prices and exchange rates, for the period spanning January 1994 to December 2014. First, the literature on emerging markets is relatively scanter than is that on the markets in developed countries. We address this issue by emphasizing the case of the Malaysia market. Second, the relationship between stock market prices and exchange rates is essential in international portfolio management, as investing in foreign stock markets must involve currency conversion (Cho *et al*., 2016). Third, crude oil plays an important role in economic development and financial markets, and the relationship between crude oil prices and stock market prices has significant implications for portfolio selection, risk management and international asset allocation (Zhu *et al*., 2014). Especially in Malaysia, the domestic demand for crude oil has increased following its recent rapid economic growth lately. Nonetheless, the country remains as a net exporter of crude oil in 2013, primarily to Australia, India, Thailand and Japan (International Monetary Fund, 2015). Therefore, the relationship between crude oil prices and stock market prices in the country warrants attention. Fourth, commodities like crude oil and gold have drawn much attention because of their price fluctuations (Akgül *et al*., 2015). Fifth, gold investment gains momentum for inflation hedging (Munir and Kok, 2014). On the other hand, equities are considered as a hedge against inflation (Bodie, 1976). In addition, gold may be used for portfolio hedging, as indicated by the findings of Choudhry *et al*. (2015). In that sense, the relationship between gold prices and stock market prices is feasible.

This chapter consists of five sections. Section 2.0 is a literature review; Section 3.0 discusses data and methodology; Section 4.0 presents the estimated results; Section 5.0 concludes.

2.0   Literature review

There is less literature on emerging markets than on the markets in developed countries. In certain studies, the significant relationship between stock prices, macroeconomic variables and commodity prices cannot be validated. Gay, Jr. (2008) investigates if there are significant relationships between stock market indices with exchange rates and oil prices in the emerging markets of Brazil, Russia, India and China. The study covers a period spanning from 1999 to 2006 and employs the monthly data on stock market index prices, exchange rates (monthly average foreign exchange per US dollar [USD]) and oil prices. The analysis is carried out using the Box-Jenkins autoregressive integrated moving average (ARIMA) model. Exchange rates and oil prices are included as independent variables, while the stock market index series is the dependent variable. The study outcome indicates that there is no evidence of a significant relationship between the two macroeconomic variables and stock market indices in all the selected markets. Thus, the markets are efficient in the weak-form sense.

The majority of past studies have found evidence of significant relationships between stock prices, macroeconomic variables and commodity prices. A typical economic relationship is the short-run causal relationship. Pan *et al.* (2007) analyze the relationship between exchange rates and stock market index prices for Hong Kong, Japan, Korea, Malaysia, Singapore, Taiwan and Thailand over the period of January 1988 through October 1998. Considering that the sample used is focused on the East Asian countries, the analysis has taken into account the impact from the Asian financial crisis in 1997. The exchange rate data employed are expressed in local currency per USD. The data of daily stock market indices and exchange rates are transformed to natural logarithms. Based on the results from Granger causality tests, variance decomposition analysis and impulse response analysis, the study confirms a causal link from exchange rates to stock market index prices in four countries, Hong Kong, Japan, Malaysia and Thailand, for the pre-crisis period. Similarly, the causality running from exchange rates to stock market index prices during the crisis is significant in all countries except for Malaysia.

Ghosh and Kanjilal (2014) analyze both the long-run and short-run relationships between the stock market index in India and crude oil prices. The co-movement of Indian stock market and oil prices (Brent crude oil prices) is analyzed by incorporating the rupee–dollar exchange rates, in order to capture the possible feedback effect arising from the impact of oil prices on stock market. The period of study is divided into three phases, Phase I (2 January 2003 through 1 July 2007), Phase II (2 July 2007 through 29 December 2008) and Phase III (30 December 2008 through 29 July 2011). Phase II is the period with the most volatile oil prices. The results of threshold cointegration tests by Gregory and Hansen (1996) and Hatemi-J (2008) indicate long-run cointegration among stock market index, oil prices and exchange rates in the third sub-period. The transmission between oil prices and the stock market index is asymmetric, as indicated by the presence of the threshold effect. The effect of oil prices on the Indian stock market is significant in the Phase II and Phase III periods. The stock market index is Granger caused by oil prices in Phase II with a significant feedback effect, since there is also causality running from the stock market index to exchange rates. In Phase III, oil prices Granger caused the stock market index without feedback effect. Oil prices may be affecting the Indian stock market through fiscal deficits, inflation and the depreciation of the rupee, but is not affecting the decreases in the present values of listed companies.

Zhu *et al.* (2014) employ the daily data of 10 Asian Pacific stock market indices (Australia, China, Hong Kong, India, Indonesia, Japan, South Korea, Malaysia, Singapore and Taiwan) and the daily crude oil prices (West Texas Intermediate

[WTI] Index, measured in USD per barrel) for the period of 4 January 2000 through 30 March 2012 to study the relationship between oil prices and stock market index returns. The methodology used is based on copula models with tail dependence parameters, which allow for capturing the asymmetric dependence structure between the variables. The findings suggest that the dependence between the variables is generally weak in the pre-global financial crisis period: 4 January 2000 through 23 September 2008, but increases significantly in the post-crisis period: 24 September 2008 through 30 March 2012.

Basher *et al.* (2012) employ a structural vector autoregression (SVAR) model to investigate the dynamic relationship among oil prices (dollars per barrel based on the WTI crude oil spot prices), exchange rates (the trade-weighted exchange rate index on the USD against the most widely traded currencies), interest rates (the yield spread between the three-month Eurodollar London interbank borrowing rate and the three-month US Treasury bill rate), oil supply, global real economic activity and emerging market index prices (MSCI emerging stock market index denominated in the USD). The data used are on a monthly basis and expressed in natural logarithms. The period of study is from January 1988 to December 2008. One of the main findings is that positive shocks to oil prices have a tendency to lower the stock prices in emerging markets in the short run. The logic behind is this that the increase in the factor of production costs and the rise in interest rates due to inflationary pressure are likely to reduce the future cash flows of non–oil-related listed companies, hence decreasing the present values of listed companies.

Park and Shin (2013) have proposed and demonstrated the application of a semi-supervised learning (SSL) algorithm in analyzing the complex interrelation between stock prices and economic factors (i.e. exchange rates, interest rates, oil prices and the stock market index prices of other countries). An experiment was carried out by using stock prediction method to forecast the prices of 200 companies that consisted of KOSPI200 and the prices of 16 stock market indices (i.e. Dow Jones average [Dow], Japanese Stock Market Index [NIKKEI], Korea Composite Stock Price Index [KOSPI] and so forth) from January 2007 to August 2008. The data used in the experiment were daily data. The method was found to be able to reflect the cyclical and reciprocal influences of economic factors to stock price prediction.

Cho *et al.* (2016) analyze pairwise correlations between stock market index returns and currency using a sample of 12 emerging markets (Brazil, Chile, Czech Republic, Hungary, Israel, Korea, Mexico, New Zealand, Philippines, Poland, South Africa and Turkey) and nine developed countries (Australia, Canada, Germany, Japan, Norway, Sweden, Switzerland, the United Kingdom and the United States) throughout the period 1996–2009. In emerging markets, domestic stock returns and currency returns are generally positively correlated. In developed countries, the correlations are negative and weaker than the evidence from emerging markets. The authors plausibly explain the results based on a mechanism that there are outflows of capital from emerging markets to developed countries in global down markets, causing appreciations of developed country currencies and depreciations of emerging market currencies. Hence, there is a positive correlation between domestic stock returns and currency returns in emerging markets, and the inverse occurs in developed countries. This finding has implications for the use of currency-hedging strategies when investing in the equity markets.

The relationship between gold and the stock market has drawn considerable research attention lately. Akgül *et al.* (2015) analyze the nonlinear linkage between gold prices (USD/oz.) and the S&P 500 Stock Price Index over the period of April 1986 through November 2013 by using monthly data. The methodology used is based on the Markov-Switching Bayesian VAR models and by adding crude oil prices (Brent-$/barrel) as an exogenous variable. The results indicate that there are three regimes in the period analyzed, namely, the growth regime, pre-crisis regime and crisis regime. It is found that crude oil changes can affect both stock market index prices and gold prices in all three regimes. The stock market index gives a negative response to gold price shocks in the first period when in the growth regime. The response becomes positive in the first period when in the pre-crisis regime. When entering the crisis regime, the response is negative in the first period but positive in the second period. Turning to the response of gold prices to the index shocks, in both the pre-crisis regime and crisis regime, the response is negative in the second period. In the growth regime, gold prices give a positive response to the index changes. Investors and policy makers may consider the changing behaviour of the linkages among the variables in their decision making.

Choudhry *et al.* (2015) focus on the nonlinear co-movement between stock market returns, stock market volatility and gold returns for the United States (S&P 500), the United Kingdom (FTSE 100) and Japan (Nikkei 225) by incorporating the effect of the most recent global financial crisis. Two sub-periods are used: the pre-crisis period of January 2000 through June 2007 and the crisis period of July 2007 through March 2014. The data used are on a daily basis obtained from Thompson Financial Datastream. The results of both the bivariate nonlinear test of Hiemstra and Jones (1994) and the multivariate nonlinear test of Bai, Wong and Zhang (2010) suggest that there is limited evidence of a bidirectional causality or feedback effect between gold returns and stock returns, as well as between gold returns and stock volatility in the pre-crisis period, implying that gold was a safe haven before the crisis. However, the results indicate strong evidence of the feedback effect in the crisis period, suggesting gold has lost its ability to act as a safe haven during the crisis. Thus, it may be unfeasible to use gold for portfolio hedging during financial crises.

3.0 Data and methodology

3.1 Data set

We employ the monthly data of FTSE KLCI index prices, crude oil prices (Brent-$/barrel), gold prices (USD/oz.) and exchange rates (ringgit Malaysia per USD). All the data are available online at http://www.investing.com/indices/.

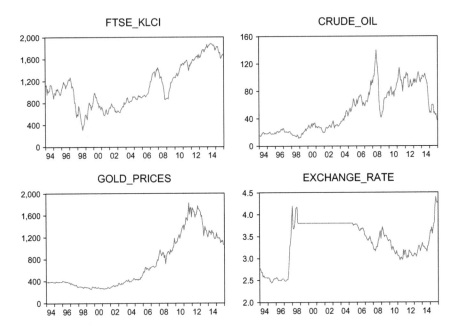

Figure 4.1 Plots of the variables

3.2   *Descriptive statistics*

Table 4.1 summarizes the descriptive statistics of the data used in this study. We present descriptive statistics for the monthly data, n = 264 for the total period of January 1994 until December 2015. The mean for FTSE_KLCI series is 6.943, which means on average that FTSE_KLCI is 6.943 monthly. The average values of other parameters such as CRUDE_OIL, GOLD_PRICES, and EXCHANGE_RATE, are 3.735, 6.360 and 1.212, respectively.

Skewness gives a measure of how symmetric the observations are around the mean. For a normal distribution, the value of the skewness is 0. A distribution skewed to the right has a positive skewness, while distribution that skewed to the left has a negative skewness. GOLD_PRICES is the only variable that has a positive skewness, in which the right tail of the distribution is longer than the left, while other variables show a negative skewness, in which the left tail of the graph is longer.

Kurtosis is a degree of the zero peakedness or flatness of a distribution relative to normal distribution. A Kurtosis value of 0 represents a normally distributed data. Positive kurtosis indicates a relatively peaked distribution, while negative kurtosis indicates a relatively flat distribution. The variables studied have a positive kurtosis, which implies that the distributions of the variables have a relatively peaked distribution. Jarque-Bera is a test statistic for testing whether the series is normally distributed. The test statistic measures the difference of the skewness

Table 4.1 Descriptive statistics

	FTSE KLCI	Crude oil	Gold prices	Exchange rate
Mean	6.943	3.735	6.360	1.212
Median	6.922	3.789	6.061	1.253
Maximum	7.540	4.942	7.511	1.481
Minimum	5.713	2.418	5.544	0.891
Std. Dev.	0.369	0.670	0.633	0.148
Skewness	−0.267	−0.063	0.376	−0.796
Kurtosis	2.615	1.598	1.589	2.550
Jarque-Bera	4.769	21.783	28.135	30.093
Probability	0.092	0.093	0.090	0.089
Observations	264	264	264	264

and kurtosis of the series with those from the normal distribution. The normality test, based on Jarque-Bera statistics, indicates that the hypothesis of normality is not rejected at the 5 percent significance level for all variables, showing that the variables are normally distributed.

3.3 Methodology

In this study, the test for cointegration is carried out using the autoregressive distributive lag (ARDL) model approach of Pesaran, Shin and Smith (2001), where we estimate unrestricted error correction with FTSE_KLCI as a dependent variable. Haug (2002) has argued that the ARDL approach to cointegration provides better results for small sample data sets, such as in our case, as compared to traditional approaches to cointegration, i.e. Engle and Granger (1987); Johansen and Juselius (1990). Another advantage of ARDL bounds testing is that the unrestricted model of ECM seems to take satisfactory lags that capture the data-generating process in a general-to-specific framework of specification (Laurenceson and Chai, 2003). This method avoids the classification of variables as $I(1)$ and $I(0)$ by developing bands of critical values which identify the variables as being stationary or nonstationary processes. Unlike other cointegration techniques (e.g. Johansen's procedure), which require pre-testing for unit roots and require that the underlying variables to be integrated are in the same order, the ARDL model provides an alternative test for examining a long-run relationship regardless of whether the underlying variables are purely $I(0)$ or $I(1)$, even fractionally integrated. Therefore, the previous unit root testing of the variables is unnecessary. Moreover, traditional cointegration methods may also suffer from the problem of endogeneity, while the ARDL method can distinguish dependent and explanatory variables. The estimates obtained from the ARDL method of cointegration analysis are unbiased and efficient, since they avoid the problems that may arise in the presence of serial correlation and endogeneity. Note also that the ARDL procedure allows for uneven lag orders, while Johansen's VECM does not. However, Pesaran and Shin (1999) contend, 'appropriate modification of the orders of ARDL model is sufficient to simultaneously correct for residual serial correlation and problem of endogenous variables'.

A two-step procedure is used in estimating the long-run relationship. In the first step, we investigate the existence of a long-run relationship predicted by theory among the variables in question. The short- and long-run parameters are estimated in the second stage, when the long-run relationship is established in the first step. Suppose that at the first stage, the theory predicts that there is a long-run relationship among variables. Without having any prior information about the direction of the long-run relationship among the variables, the following models are estimated:

$$\Delta FTSE\_KLCI_t = \alpha_0$$
$$+ \sum_{i=1}^{p} \beta_i \Delta FTSE\_KLCI_{t-i} + \sum_{i=1}^{p} \delta_i \Delta CRUDE\_OIL_{t-i} + \sum_{i=0}^{p} \sigma_i \Delta GOLD\_PRICES_{t-i}$$
$$+ \sum_{i=0}^{p} \gamma_i \Delta EXCH\_RATE_{t-i} + \Phi_1 FTSE\_KLCI_{t-1} + \Phi_2 CRUDE\_OIL_{t-1} \tag{4.1}$$
$$+ \Phi_3 GOLD\_PRICES_{t-1} + \Phi_4 EXCH\_RATE_{t-1} + e_t$$

The above model (1) shows the unrestricted version of ARDL specification. The F-statistic is used for testing the existence of long-run relationships. The null hypothesis for testing the nonexistence of the first long-run relationship can be written as H_0: $\Phi_1 = \Phi_2 = \Phi_3 = \Phi_4 = 0$.

The F-test has a nonstandard distribution which depends upon (i) whether variables included in the ARDL model are to be $I(0)$ or $I(1)$, (ii) the number of regressors and (iii) whether the ARDL model contains an intercept and/or a trend. Two sets of critical values are reported in Pesaran *et al.* (2001): one set is calculated assuming that all variables included in the ARDL model are $I(1)$ and the other is estimated considering the variables are $I(0)$. If the computed F values fall outside the inclusive band, a conclusive decision could be drawn without knowing the order of integration of the variables.

$$\Delta FTSE\_KLCI_t = \alpha_1$$
$$+ \sum_{t=1}^{m} X_i \Delta FTSE\_KLCI_{t-i}$$
$$+ \sum_{i=0}^{n} K_i \Delta CRUDE\_OIL_{t-i} \tag{4.2}$$
$$+ \sum_{i=0}^{0} V_i \Delta GOLD\_PRICES_{t-i} + \sum_{i=0}^{p} \pi_i \Delta EXCH\_RATE_{t-i} + \lambda ECM_{t-i}$$
$$+ \vartheta_t,$$

where ECM_{t-i} is the error correction term resulting from the verified long-run equilibrium relationship, and λ is a parameter indicating the speed of adjustment to the equilibrium level after a shock. The sign of $ECM_{t-}i$ must be negative and significant to ensure convergence of the dynamics to the long-run equilibrium. The value of the coefficient, λ, which signifies the speed of convergence to the equilibrium process, usually ranges from -1 and 0. While -1 signifies perfect and instantaneous convergence, 0 means no convergence after a shock in process. Moreover, Pesaran and Pesaran (1997) argue that it is extremely important to ascertain the constancy of the long-run multipliers by testing the above error correction model for the stability of its parameters. The commonly used tests for this purpose are the cumulative sum (CUSUM) and the cumulative sum of squares (CUSUMQ), both of which were introduced by Brown, Durbin and Evans (1975).

4.0 Estimated results

4.1 Unit root tests without structural break

Before proceeding with the estimation, it is essential to conduct unit root tests to examine the stationarity property and the order of integration of the variables employed in this study. The reason is to ensure that no incorrect inferences are made due to spurious regression. For this, all the series used are tested using the augmented Dickey-Fuller (ADF), the Dickey-Fuller generalized least square (DF-GLS) and the Phillip Perron (PP) unit root tests as well as the Kwiatkowski-Phillips-Schmidt-Shin (KPSS) stationarity test. The KPSS test is often suggested to confirm the results from the ADF and PP tests.

The results of ADF, DF-GLS, PP, KPSS and Elliott, Rothenberg and Stock are reported in Table 4.2. We present the results, which contain a constant term and both constant and linear trend for the series in levels and first differences. These tests possess different null hypotheses, where the null hypothesis of the ADF, PP and DF-GLS is that a time series contains a unit root while the KPSS test has the null hypothesis of stationarity. The rationale of using more than one traditional unit root test is to ensure the robustness of our results. The lag length selection of ADF, DF-GLS and ERS are based on the Schwarz Bayesian information criterion (SIC) with a maximum of nine lags, while PP and KPSS use the Bartlett kernel for spectral estimation method with a Newey–West bandwidth automatic selection.

In the level form, the test statistics obtained are clearly less than the critical values, even at the 10 percent level of significance, except for CRUDE_OIL in the ADF test, where it is significant at the 5 percent level when the only constant is included. Overall, the null hypothesis of a unit root cannot be rejected for the variables, implying that the series have a unit root. Based on the KPSS test result, we can confirm that all series have a nonstationary property, as the null of stationarity is rejected at least at the 5 percent level of significance and mostly at the 1 percent level of significance.

In the first difference, all variables in the unit root tests are stationary around a constant and trend, mostly at the 1 percent of significance. The result of the KPSS test indicates that almost all variables are stationary around a constant and

Table 4.2 Results of traditional unit root tests

| | Test statistics | | | | |
	ADF	DF-GLS	PP	KPSS	Conclusion
A: Level					
Model Specification: Constant					
FTSE_KLCI	−1.442	−1.480	−1.414	1.307*	I(0)
CRUDE_OIL	−1.629**	−0.553	−1.701	1.855*	I(0)
GOLD_PRICES	−0.389	0.274	−0.295	1.816*	I(0)
EXCH_RATE	−1.458	−0.298	−1.435	0.413*	I(0)
Model Specification: Constant, Linear Trend					
FTSE_KLCI	−2.762	−1.788	−2.678	0.325*	I(0)
CRUDE_OIL	−0.997	−1.414	−1.418	0.224*	I(0)
GOLD_PRICES	−1.623	−0.981	−1.565	0.348*	I(0)
EXCH_RATE	−1.545	−1.455	−1.546	0.332**	I(0)
B: First Difference					
Model Specification: Constant					
ΔFTSE_KLCI	−13.967*	−13.572*	−13.911*	0.116	I(1)
ΔCRUDE_OIL	−14.357*	−6.294*	−14.357*	0.204	I(1)
ΔGOLD_PRICES	−18.589*	−18.479*	−18.659*	0.327	I(1)
ΔEXCH_RATE	−12.944*	−5.649*	−12.919*	0.135	I(1)
Model Specification: Constant, Linear Trend					
ΔFTSE_KLCI	−13.980*	−13.806*	−13.916*	0.042	I(1)
ΔCRUDE_OIL	−14.426*	−13.288*	−14.426*	0.087	I(1)
ΔGOLD_PRICES	−18.569*	−18.617*	−18.641**	0.331***	I(1)
ΔEXCH_RATE	−12.919*	−12.138*	−12.895*	0.102	I(1)

Notes: Δ denotes the first difference operator. Asterisks (*), (**), (***) denote the statistical significance at the 1, 5 and 10 percent levels, respectively.

trend, except for GOLD_PRICES, where the null hypothesis of stationarity can be rejected at the 10 percent level of significance when the trend is included. As a whole, the results of traditional unit root tests suggest that all the variables used in this study are integrated of order one, that is $I(1)$.

4.2   Unit root test with structural break

A common problem with the conventional unit root tests, such as the ADF, DF-GLS and PP tests, is that they do not allow for the possibility of a structural break. In order to capture the effect of any possible structural shift over the estimation period, the Zivot and Andrews (1992) unit root test is used. This test treats the presence of any structural break in the series under study as endogenous. The break date is selected where the *t*-statistic from the ADF test of the unit root is at a minimum (most negative). Consequently, a break date will be chosen where the evidence is least favourable for the unit root null. Zivot and Andrews have presented two versions of the sequential trend break model, model A and model C. Model A allows for a change in intercept, while model C allows for a change in both intercept and slope.

The result of the Zivot and Andrew (1992) unit root test is presented in Table 4.3. In level, the result in model A suggests that we can reject the null of a unit root for all the variables at the 1 and 5 percent levels of significance. In first difference, all variables are stationary in model A (break in intercept). While in model C, we fail to reject the unit root hypothesis for CRUDE_OIL and EXCH_RATE in level, but in first difference, all variables are stationary (break in intercept and trend).

At the same time, the test also identifies endogenously the point of the single most significant structural break (TB) in every variable examined in this paper. The break dates are also reported in Table 4.3. In a one-break case, Dolmas, Beldav and Slotje (1999) justify using model C over model A because model C encompasses model A. The break dates in the first difference are our concern since the variables are stationary.

Table 4.3 Results of Zivot and Andrews (1992) unit root test

	Model A: break in intercept			Model C: break in intercept and trend			
	t-*statistic*	k	TB	t-*statistic*	k	TB	Conclusion
Level							
FTSE_KLCI	−5.158*	7	1998M03	−5.499*	7	1998M03	I(1)
CRUDE_OIL	−2.637*	1	2003M11	−3.389	1	2012M08	I(0)
GOLD_PRICES	−3.150*	1	2005M09	−1.897*	1	2008M11	I(1)
EXCH_RATE	−4.771**	1	1997M07	−3.742	1	1997M07	I(0)
1st Difference							
FTSE_KLCI	−5.151*	8	1998M09	−5.996*	8	1998M09	I(1)
CRUDE_OIL	−14.717*	0	199M12	−14.799*	0	1998M12	I(1)
GOLD_PRICES	−19.821*	0	2011M09	−19.787*	0	2011M09	I(1)
EXCH_RATE	−13.427*	0	1998M02	−14.917*	0	1998M02	I(1)

Notes: The 1%, 5% and 10% critical values obtained from estimating model A are −65.34, −4.80 and −4.11, respectively. The 1 percent, 5 percent, and 10 percent critical values obtained from estimating model C are −5.57, − 5.08 and −4.82, respectively. *, ** and *** denote rejection of the null hypothesis of nonstationary at the 1, 5 and 10 percent significance levels, respectively. TB is the estimated break year, and *k* stands for the endogenously selected lag order for the minADF test. The lag is selected using the Akaike information criteria (AIC).

The structural breaks for the FTSE_KLCI, CRUDE_OIL, GOLD_PRICES and EXCH_RATE variables are identified as on September 1998, December 1998, September 2011 and February 1998, respectively. These break dates may correspond to important historical events, for instance, the break date in the year 1998 may correspond to the Asian financial crisis of 1997–1998, and the break date in September 2011 coincides with the September 2001 terrorist attack in the United States. Having all the variables stationary at first difference, we can proceed to investigate the long-run relationship with respect to the main variable using the ARDL bound test for cointegration.

4.3   *The cointegration test – the ARDL bound testing approach to the cointegration test*

This study employs the ARDL approach to cointegration proposed by Pesaran and Shin (1999 and Pesaran *et al.*, 2001) to examine the long-term relationship between FBM KLCI and crude oil prices, gold prices and exchange rates. The most critical aspect of the ARDL approach is that is does not assume all the variables are integrated of the same order. The variables can be integrated of order one $I(1)$, or they can be stationary $I(0)$ or a mixture of both. In addition, this procedure is more appropriately used in testing the long-run relationship between the variables when the data are from a small sample size and the long-run and short-run parameters of the model can be estimated simultaneously.

The long-run relationship between the variables is tested using F-statistics to determine the significance of the lagged levels of the variables in the unrestricted error correction model. Specifically, the F-test is used to determine the existence of a cointegrating relationship between the variables. The F-test has a nonstandard distribution which relies on whether the variables included in the model are integrated of order $I(0)$ or $I(1)$, the number of independent variables, whether the ARDL model contains an intercept and/or trend and also relies on sample sizes. The null hypothesis in this test is that there is no long-run relationship between the variables. The alternative hypothesis states that there is a long-run relationship between the variables.

The results reported in Table 4.4 show that there is evidence of cointegration between FTSE KLCI with all other variables used in this study. This is supported by the computed F-statistic, which is statistically significant at the 1 percent level, as the computed value is higher than the critical values. In particular, the F-statistic value is 4.994. Accordingly, we strongly reject the null hypothesis of no long-run relationship between the variables in both models. The optimal lag length for both models is 3, which was chosen based on the Akaike information criteria (AIC). This result suggests that the stock market index prices can be predicted from these variables.

Before presenting the ARDL long-run results, it is important that the residuals of the model are serially independent. A serially correlated model will give inconsistent parameter estimates due to the lagged values of the dependent variable that appears as a regressor in the model. We present the result of the residual diagnostic using correlogram q-statistics in Table 4.5. The estimated model passes the diagnostic test of serial correlation, as all the p-values are not significant,

Table 4.4 Results of ARDL bound testing cointegration approach

Dependent variable/ Independent variables	F-statistic value	Optimal lag length	Conclusion
(FTSE KLCI/ Crude oil, gold prices, exchange rate)	4.994*	3	There is a long-run relationship
Bound critical values by Pesaran *et al.* (2001)			
	I(0)	I(1)	
1%	3.65	4.66	
5%	2.79	3.67	
10%	2.37	3.2	

Notes: * denotes rejection of null hypothesis of no cointegration at the 1 percent significance level.

Table 4.5 Serial correlation diagnostic test

Autocorrelation	Partial correlation		AC	PAC	Q-Stat	Prob*
.|. |	.|. |	1	0.072	0.072	1.316	0.251
.|. |	.|. |	2	0.032	0.027	1.585	0.453
.|. |	.|. |	3	−0.022	−0.026	1.711	0.635
*|. |	*|. |	4	−0.124	−0.122	5.711	0.222
.|. |	.|. |	5	0.010	0.029	5.738	0.333
.|. |	.|. |	6	−0.048	−0.045	6.354	0.385
.|* |	.|* |	7	0.074	0.076	7.792	0.351
*|. |	*|. |	8	−0.076	−0.101	9.309	0.317
.|* |	.|* |	9	0.102	0.119	12.05	0.211
.|. |	.|. |	10	0.073	0.051	13.46	0.199
.|. |	.|. |	11	−0.057	−0.056	14.328	0.215
.|. |	.|. |	12	0.003	−0.018	14.330	0.280

Notes: AC denotes autocorrelations, PAC denotes partial autocorrelations, Q-Stat denotes Ljung-Box Q-statistics.

indicating that the null hypothesis of no serial correlation can be accepted. In other words, the test strongly suggests that there is no evidence of autocorrelation in the model's residuals.

4.4 Multivariate bound test cointegration approach for long-run and short-run estimates

Having found the long-run relationship among the variables, the next step is to estimate the long-run marginal effects of CRUDE_OIL, GOLD_PRICES and

EXCH_RATE on FTSE_KLCI. The long-run estimation results are shown in Table 4.6. Based on the AIC, the selected model for the regression is ARDL (1, 1, 0, and 10).

As reported in Table 4.6, all coefficients in the model are significant except for EXCH_RATE, and all have mixed signs. Based on the result, CRUDE_OIL has a long-run negative effect on FTSE_KLCI and is significant at the 1 percent level. The elasticity of coefficient implies that a 1 percent increase in CRUDE_OIL leads to a 187.59 percent decrease in FTSE_KLCI. On the other hand, GOLD_PRICES is found to have a long-run positive effect on FTSE_KLCI, and it is significant at the 5 percent level. The elasticity implies that a 1 percent change in GOLD_PRICES will result in a positive long-run change of 136.56 percent in FTSE_KLCI. Similarly, EXCH_RATE also has a positive long-run impact to FTSE_KLCI but is not significant. Specifically, a 1 percent increase in EXCH_RATE will cause a long-run increase of 126.68 percent in FTSE_KLCI, and the elasticity is not statistically significant.

The final step of the ARDL model is the error correction to estimate the short-run parameter with the speed of adjustment. The short-run estimation results are shown in Table 4.7. As can be seen from the results, the error correction (ECM_{t-1}) coefficient is negative, as expected, and is very significant, ensuring that the models will converge to the long-run equilibrium regardless of the regressor used. The ECM_{t-1} measures the speed at which the endogenous variable adjusts to

Table 4.6 Results of ARDL long-run estimation

	Coefficient	St. error	t-Statistic	Prob.
DEPENDENT: FTSE KLCI				
Crude oil	−1.8759	0.5935	−3.1606	0.0063
Gold prices	1.3656	0.6089	2.2424	0.0259
Exchange rate	1.2668	1.2999	0.9745	0.3308
Intercept	0.1035	3.1586	0.0328	0.9739

Table 4.7 Results of ARDL short-run estimation

	Coefficient	St. error	t-Statistic	Prob.
DEPENDENT: FTSE_KLCI				
ΔCrude oil	**0.0796	0.0381	2.0896	0.0377
ΔGold prices	0.0210	0.0729	0.2886	0.7731
ΔExchange rate	*−1.0182	0.1522	−6.6892	0.0000
ECM_{t-1}	*−0.0480	0.0095	−5.0343	0.0000

Note: Asterisks * and ** denote significant level at 1% and 5%, respectively.

changes in the explanatory variables before converging to its equilibrium level. In sum, following Bannerjee and Mestre (1998), the results confirm that there exists a stable long-run relationship between the variables shown by the significance of the error correction term.

The coefficient of the error correction term is negative (–0.0480) and very significant, as expected. The coefficient suggests an adjustment of approximately 4.80 percent towards the long-run equilibrium after one year. In other words, the short-run disequilibrium is corrected in the long-run equilibrium at a rate of 4.80 percent in the following period.

4.5 Diagnostic tests

We also use diagnostic tests to check the adequacy of model specification, and the results are summarized in Table 4.8. The diagnostic tests used are the Lagrange multiplier test of residual correlation; the heteroscedasticity test, which is based on the regression of squared residuals on square fitted values; and the normality test, which is based on a test of skewness, kurtosis of residuals and the Jarque-Bera test of normal distribution. The null hypothesis of no serial correlation in the Breusch-Godfrey statistics cannot be rejected even at the 10 percent level of significance. In other words, there is no serial correlation in the model. Similarly, the heteroscedasticity test suggests that the null hypothesis of no heteroscedasticity cannot be rejected at the 10 percent significance level, implying that there is no heteroscedasticity in the model. The Jarque-Bera statistic for the model is insignificant, indicating that the null hypothesis of normality is accepted. This means that the model is normally distributed (see Figure 4.2). The diagnostic tests suggest that the estimation of long-run coefficients and ECM are free from serial correlation, heteroscedasticity and nonnormality even at the 10 percent level of significance.

Further, the other issue, related to the adequacy of the ARDL model, addressed is the stability of the long-run coefficients that are used to form the error correction term in conjunction with the short-run dynamics. Some of the problems of instability encountered from inadequate modelling of the short-run dynamics arise from its being a long-run relationship. Therefore, it is important to incorporate the short-run dynamics in testing for constancy of long-run parameters. In view of this, we applied the CUSUM test proposed by Brown *et al.* (1975) to the residuals of each model. The CUSUM test shows that if the cumulative sum goes outside the two critical lines, then the model is not free from instability. Figure 4.3

Table 4.8 Diagnostic tests

	F-*test*	p-*value*
Breusch-Godfrey serial correlation LM test	0.8597	0.4246
Breusch-Pagan Godfrey heteroscedasticity test	1.8923	0.1100
Jarque-Bera	4.1647	0.1246

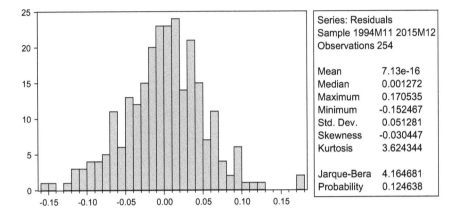

Figure 4.2 Normality test

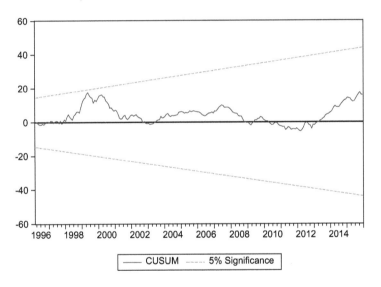

Figure 4.3 CUSUM test

shows that the plot of the CUSUM statistics stay within the critical bounds of the 5 percent level of significance, implying that the null hypotheses of all coefficients in the model are stable and cannot be rejected.

4.6 *The bivariate bound test cointegration approach*

The results reported in Table 4.9 show that there is evidence of cointegration between FTSE_KLCI and GOLD_PRICES. This is supported by the computed F-statistic, which is found to be statistically significant at the 1 percent level, and the fact that the computed F-statistic value 5.810 is higher than the critical

Table 4.9 Results of ARDL bound testing cointegration approach

Dependent variable/ Independent variable	F-statistic value	Optimal lag length	Conclusion
(FTSE KLCI/ Gold prices)	5.810*	1	There is a long-run relationship
(FTSE KLCI/ Exchange rate)	1.647	1	There is no long-run relationship
(FTSE KLCI/ Crude oil)	1.857	1	There is no long-run relationship
Bound critical values by Pesaran *et al.* (2001)			
	I(0)	*I*(1)	
1%	4.94	5.58	
5%	3.62	4.16	
10%	3.02	3.51	

Note: * denotes rejection of the null hypothesis of no cointegration at the 1 percent significance level.

values. This result strongly rejects the null hypothesis of no long-run relationship between the stock market index prices and gold prices. The optimal lag length for the model is one which is chosen based on the AIC. There is no evidence of cointegration between the stock market index prices either with CRUDE_OIL or with EXCH_RATE. Their corresponding F-statistics are insignificant even at the 10 percent level. The computed F-statistic values are lower than the critical values. Thus, the null hypothesis of no long-run relationship between the variables in both models cannot be rejected. The optimal lag length for both models is one chosen based on the AIC.

5.0   Conclusion

In this study, we investigated the co-movement between FTSE KLCI with crude oil prices, gold prices and exchange rates over the period of January 1994 through December 2015. The methodology used is based on the ARDL bound testing cointegration approach of Pesaran *et al.* (2001). Before proceeding with the cointegration test, the stationarity property and the order of integration of the variables used were examined by using the unit root and stationarity tests (ADF, DF-GLS, PP and KPSS tests) without structural break and the Zivot and Andrew (1992) one structural break unit root test. As a whole, the results of traditional unit root tests suggest that all the variables used in this study are integrated of order one, that is $I(1)$. Based on the result of the one structural break unit root test in model C, we failed to reject the unit root null for CRUDE_OIL and EXCH_RATE in level, but in the first difference, all variables were stationary (break in intercept and trend). The break dates identified in 1998 and 2011 may correspond to the Asian financial crisis in 1997–1998 and the September 2001 terrorist attack in the United States.

Having all the variables stationary at first difference, we proceeded with the ARDL bound cointegration test to identify whether the variables were cointegrated in the long run or not. Our results from the multivariate cointegration test between FTSE_KLCI and GOLD_PRICES, CRUDE_OIL and EXCH_RATE suggest that there is a long-run relationship between their variables. In other words, the movement of the stock market index can be predicted based on the macroeconomic variables used in this study. Thus the empirical evidence is not in favour of weak-form EMH.

Contrastingly, our finding from the bivariate cointegration test is that there exists a long-run cointegration between FTSE_KLCI and GOLD_PRICES in the case of Malaysia. This implies that the two series tend to move in the same direction over the long-term horizon. This finding is not in favour of the weak-form EMH, since the historical data on gold prices can predict the movements of stock market index prices. In addition, this finding does not support the view that gold investment serves for portfolio hedging in relation to equity investment. In addition, as ARDL bound test cointegration also provides results for the vector error correction coefficient, we confirm that the variables have a short-run relationship, as the coefficient of the error correction term is negative (–0.0480) and very significant, as expected.

There is no evidence of co-movement between FTSE_KLCI with crude oil prices and exchange rates. In other words, there is no support provided for a significant relationship between the stock market index prices with any of the two variables. In that sense, our finding is partly consistent with the finding of Pan *et al.* (2007). The study found evidence of unidirectional causality running from exchange rates to FTSE_KLCI in the period before the Asian financial crisis, but there was no significant causal relationship during the crisis. However, our finding that there is no significant relationship between FTSE_KLCI and crude oil prices is inconsistent with the finding of Zhu *et al.* (2014). The study found weak evidence of the dependence between FTSE_KLCI and crude oil prices in the pre-global financial crisis period, but the dependence increased significantly in the post-crisis period. Variations in the findings can be explained by the longer time span of data employed in the present study, from January 1994 to December 2014, as compared with the duration January 2000 through March 2012 chosen by Zhu *et al.* (2014). As Zhu *et al.* (2014) found that the relationship was considerably weak before the global financial crisis but that its significance increased in the post-crisis period, there is reason to believe that the crisis shock had an important influence on the relationship. This can be a direction for future research.

References

Akgül, I., Bildirici, M., and Özdemir, S. (2015). Evaluating the nonlinear linkage between gold prices and stock market index using Markov-Switching Bayesian VAR models. *Procedia – Social and Behavioral Sciences, 210*, 408–415.

Bai, Z., Wong, W. K., and Zhang, B. (2010). Multivariate linear and nonlinear causality tests. *Mathematics and Computers in Simulation, 81*(1), 5–17.

Bannerjee, A. D., and Mestre, R. (1998). Error-correction mechanism test for cointegration in single equation framework. *Journal of Time Series Analysis, 19,* 267–283.

Basher, S. A., Haug, A. A., and Sadorsky, P. (2012). Oil prices, exchange rates and emerging stock markets. *Energy Economics, 34,* 227–240.

Bodie, Z. (1976). Common stocks as a hedge against inflation. *The Journal of Finance, 31*(2), 459–470.

Brown, R. L., Durbin, J., and Evans, M. (1975). Techniques for testing the constancy of regression relations over time. *Journal of the Royal Statistical Society, 37,* 149–163.

Campbell, J. Y. (1987). Stock returns and the term structure. *Journal of Financial Economics, 18*(2), 373–399.

Campbell, J. Y., and Hamao, Y. (1989). Predictable stock returns in the United States and Japan: A study of long-term capital market integration. NBER Working Paper Series No. 3191, National Bureau of Economic Research, Cambridge.

Cho, J.-W., Choi, J. H., Kim, T., and Kim, W. (2016). Flight-to-quality and correlation between currency and stock returns. *Journal of Banking & Finance, 62,* 191–212.

Choudhry, T., Hassan, S. S., and Shabi, S. (2015). Relationship between gold and stock markets during the global financial crisis: Evidence from nonlinear causality tests. *International Review of Financial Analysis, 41,* 247–256.

Dolmas, J., Beldav, R., and Slotje, D. (1999). The U.S. productivity slowdown: A peak through the structural break window. *Economic Inquiry, 37,* 226–241.

Engle, R. F., and Granger, C. J. (1987). Co-integration and error correction representation, estimation, and testing. *Econometrica, 55,* 251–276.

Fama, E. F. (1991). Efficient capital markets: II. *The Journal of Finance, 46*(5), 1575–1617.

Fama, E. F., and French, K. R. (1989). Business conditions and expected returns on stocks and bonds. *Journal of Financial Economics, 25,* 23–49.

Gay, Jr., R. D. (2008). Effect of macroeconomic variables on stock market returns for four emerging economies: Brazil, Russia, India, and China. *International Business & Economics Research Journal, 7*(3), 1--8.

Ghosh, S., and Kanjilal, K. (2014). Co-movement of international crude oil prices and Indian stock market: Evidences from nonlinear cointegration tests. *Energy Economics.* Available at: http://dx.doi.org/10.1016/j.eneco. 2014.11.002

Gregory, A. W., and Hansen, B. E. (1996). Tests for cointegration in models with regime and trend shifts. *Oxford Bulletin of Economics and Statistics, 58,* 555–560.

Hatemi-J, A. (2008). Tests for cointegration with two unknown regime shifts with an application to financial market integration. *Empirical. Economic, 35*(3), 497–505.

Haug, A. A. (2002). Temporal aggregation and the power of cointegration tests: A Monte Carlo study. *Oxford Bulletin of Economics and Statistics, 64*(4), 399–412.

International Monetary Fund, Malaysia Selected Issues, March 2015. IMF Country Report No. 15/59, International Monetary Fund, Washington, DC.

Johansen, S., and Juselius, K. (1990). Maximum likelihood estimation and inference on cointegration – With application to the demand for money. *Oxford Bulletin of Economics and Statistics, 52*(2), 169–211.

Laurenceson, J., and Chai, C. H. (2003). *Financial Reform and Economic Development in China.* UK: Edward Elgar Publishing.

Munir, Q., and Kok, S. C. (2014). Does Malaysian gold bullion coin prices follow mean reversion or random walk? *Journal of Applied Economic Sciences, IX, 1*(27), 76–87.

Pan, M.-S., Fok, R. C.-W., and Liu, Y. A. (2007). Dynamic linkages between exchange rates and stock prices: Evidence from East Asian Markets. *International Review of Economics and Finance, 16*, 503–520.

Park, K., and Shin, H. (2013). Stock price prediction based on a complex interrelation network of economic factors. *Engineering Applications of Artificial Intelligence, 26*, 1550–1561.

Pesaran, M. H., and Pesaran, B. (1997). *Working with Microfit 4.0: Econometric Analysis*. Oxford: Oxford University Press.

Pesaran, M. H., and Shin, Y. (1999). An autoregressive distributed lag modelling approach to cointegration analysis. In: Strom, S. (Ed.), *Econometrics and Economic Theory in the 20th Century: The Ragnar Frisch Centennial Symposium*. Cambridge: Cambridge University Press, 371–413.

Pesaran, M. H., Shin, Y., and Smith, R. J. (2001). Bounds testing approaches to the analysis of level relationships. *Journal of Applied Economics, 16*, 289–326.

Zhu, H.-M., Li, R., and Li, S. (2014). Modelling dynamic dependence between crude oil prices and Asia-Pacific stock market returns. *International Review of Economics and Finance, 29*, 208–223.

Zivot, E., and Andrews, K. (1992). Further evidence on the great crash, the oil price shock, and the unit root hypothesis. *Journal of Business and Economic Statistics, 10*(10), 251–270.

5 A re-examination of the calendar anomalies during the Asian financial crisis

Some empirical evidence from the closure test principle and the EGARCH–mean model

Ricky Chee-Jiun Chia and Shiok Ye Lim

1.0 Introduction

The Asian financial crisis was a remarkable financial crisis that hit many East Asia economies and prompted large financial bailouts. The financial crisis started in Thailand in July 1997 with slumping currency, devalued stock market and other asset prices. Indonesia, South Korea, Hong Kong, Malaysia and the Philippines were also hurt by the slump due to financial contagion. The financial crisis also put pressure on the United States, as its market was severely hit in October 1997. The movement of the major Asian indices and the Chicago Board Option Exchange (CBOE) Volatility Index (VIX), which is often referred to as the fear index, are plotted in Figure 5.1. As seen in Figure 5.1, the financial markets were calm from June to early October 1997, with major indices in a decreasing trend. However, the crisis changed the trend, the markets became extremely volatile and stock prices of a few markets dropped significantly towards the end of October 1997.

In highly volatile markets, market return is expected to behave differently, and many of the documented calendar anomalies will reverse or disappear in action. Thus, in this study, we test whether the well-documented day-of-the-week effect behaves differently during crises for the affected Asian stock markets. The day-of-the-week effect is a well-documented calendar anomaly in which stock market returns tend to display systematic patterns at certain times of the day (Lakonishok and Maberly, 1980; Gibbons and Hess, 1981; Rogalski, 1984; Jaffe and Westerfield, 1985; Lakonishok and Smidt, 1988). Specifically, when the characteristics or the pattern of stock behaviour for some days of the week are consistently different from others, calendar anomaly or calendar effect is said to exist. There is an extensive literature on calendar anomalies, and previous studies have shown that the average return on Monday is significantly less than the average returns of other days, and this anomaly is known as the Monday effect.

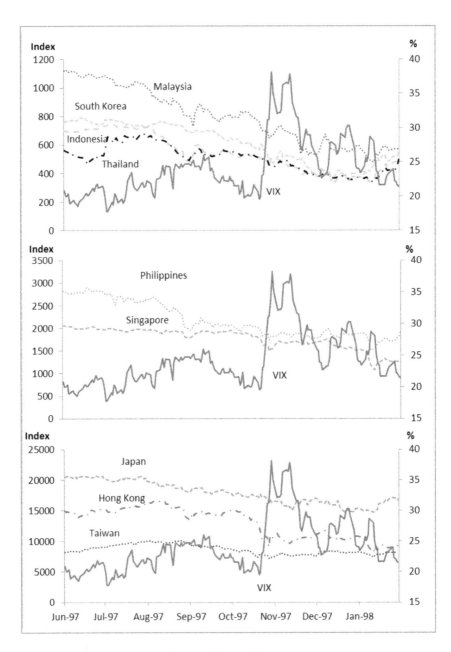

Figure 5.1 Historical values of Asian indices and VIX

In testing the day-of-the-week effect, French (1980) developed the traditional model using the regression equation with dummy variables as given by the following equation:

$$R_t = \alpha_1 + \sum_{i=2}^{5} \alpha_i \delta_{it} + \varepsilon_t, \tag{5.1}$$

where R_t is the return of the stock index on day t, and the dummy variables δ_{it} take a value of 1 if the return occurs on the ith day and 0 if the return occurs on days other than the ith day ($\delta_2 t$ represents Tuesday, $\delta_3 t$ Wednesday, $\delta_4 t$ Thursday, and $\delta_5 t$ Friday). The coefficient α_1 measures the mean return (in percentage) for Monday, and the coefficients α_2 through α_5 measure the difference between the mean return for each of the other days of the week as compared to the Monday. ε_t is the error term for the equation. This model was adopted by numerous studies of daily seasonality in stock markets, among them are Lakonishok and Levi (1982), Connolly (1989), Galai and Levy (2005) and Joshi (2006) in investigating the day-of-the-week effect. The null hypothesis of $\alpha_2 = \alpha_3 = \alpha_4 = \alpha_5$ for this model implies that there is equality of average daily rates of return. If there is no day-of-the-week effect in stock returns, the coefficients for the dummy variables are not significantly different from zero.

Generally, several explanations have been given for the day-of-the-week effect, such as trading behaviour, the settlement effect, earning announcements, negative information releases and bid–ask-spread biases. Alexakis and Xanthakis (1995) explained the daily seasonal effect based on human behaviour patterns. For example, if bad news is released after markets close on Friday, this will allow the market to absorb the shock over the weekend. Thus, the impact of bad news will reflect on Monday's returns. On the other hand, positive Monday returns are also reported in the literature. The study of Lyroudi, Subeniotis and Komisopoulos (2002) offered a possible explanation, positing that the fact of positive Monday returns may relate to the positive economic news which was revealed during the weekend. This favourable news may influence the majority of the investors positively, causing them to buy on the coming Monday.

Besides the Monday effect, previous studies also found significant return on other trading days. Chen, Kwok and Rui (2001) explained that the negative returns on Tuesday may be due to the settlement procedure. They opined that the market of the United States led Europe and the Asia Pacific region by one day but not *vice versa*. Their result suggested that the flow of information is primarily from the United States to Europe and the Asia Pacific. In other words, the negative information from the Americas' markets may affect Europe's and the Asia Pacific's financial markets on the next trading day and lead the markets to perform negatively. Hui (2005) and Lucey (2006) also found that the information arrival hypotheses appears to be more relevant than the other hypotheses in explaining the day-of-the-week effect.

Before the Asian financial crisis, the Monday effect was well documented in Asian stock markets by numerous studies. Among them, the study of Ho and Kok

(1995) found evidence of a negative Monday effect in the Kuala Lumpur Composite Index (KLCI) second board–selected companies for the period between 1992 and 1995. Kohers, Kohers, Pandey and Kohers (2004) also found that during the 1980s, the pattern of significant negative Monday returns was clearly evident in the vast majority of developed markets, including Japan's in the Asian region. Kok and Wong (2004) studied the Monday effect in the pre-crisis and post-crisis periods. They found a significant negative Monday effect in Malaysia, Singapore and Thailand during the pre-crisis period. However, after the crisis, the negative Monday effects only appeared in Thailand but not other markets. Hui (2005) also selected the post-crisis period (January 1998 to June 2001) to test for the day-of-the-week effect in Hong Kong, Singapore, Taiwan and Japan. Only Singapore had a significant low return on Monday and high returns on Friday during the sample period.

From the literature, it is obvious that studying the seasonal effect during crisis periods is rare. An inaugural study, which reported the behaviour of the stock market during crisis periods, was conducted by Al-Rjoub and Alwaked (2010). They examined the January effect during the financial crises in the US market and found evidence of a new behaviour as part of the January effect during crises. In particular, they found that the average January returns were consistently negative during crises. However, for the daily seasonal effect, to the best of our knowledge, none of the studies in the literature has examined the day-of-the-week effect during the Asian financial crisis. Therefore, we hope to contribute to the calendar anomalies literature and help investors have a better understanding of Asian stock markets' behaviour and thereby develop investment and hedging strategies for hard times.

A few years after the Asian financial crisis, major stock markets in Asia grew impressively. This is mainly due to after-crisis restructuring, and nowadays the markets have become more diversified and sophisticated. As such, the size of equity markets or market capitalization has grown at an average of 163.41 percent of the gross domestic product (GDP) for the region from 1997 to 2005 – although the figure for Japan is not included. Furthermore, the percentage change in market capitalization in billions of dollar in Asian markets excluding Japan is significantly higher than is that in the developed markets. Relatively speaking, the Asian stock markets are as significant as developed markets. Looking at the external headwinds and contagion risks, it is hardly predictable whether the Asian markets will be severely hit by external factors. Thus, this is the right time to revisit the issue of calendar anomaly during financial crises to provide insight for investors.

There are increasing empirical findings on the day-of-the-week effect in the stock market (Wong, Hui and Chan, 1992; Arsad and Coutts, 1996; Lucey, 2000; Brooks and Persand, 2001; Apolinario et al., 2006; Berument and Dogan, 2012; Compton, Kunkel and Kuhlemeyer, 2013; Chia, 2014; Floros and Salvador, 2014). However, researchers, especially those in the early stages, have assumed that variance, a measure of uncertainty, is constant through time and have employed linear regression models in examining the anomalies.

Recent research further investigated volatility, and evidence showed that variance changes over time, where a high (low) return is associated with a corresponding high (low) return for a given day.

In terms of methodology, generalized autoregressive conditional heteroscedasticity (GARCH) models are generally used to account for the time-varying volatility of the stock returns in the calendar effect. According to Engle (1993), finding certain patterns in volatility may be useful in several ways, including the use of predicted volatility patterns for hedging and speculative purposes and in the valuation of certain assets, especially the stock index option. For example, risk-aderse investors may adjust their portfolio by reducing their investment in those assets whose volatility is expected to increase. Additionally, it is important to know whether a high (low) return is associated with the corresponding high (low) return for a given day. This may allow investors to adjust their investment portfolio by taking into account the day-of-the-week variations in volatility.

Nonetheless, the GARCH model has ignored information on the direction of returns. It only takes into account the magnitude of returns. There is some convincing evidence that the direction does affect volatility. Particularly, according to Engle (2001), it is commonly observed that the negative returns are followed by a higher volatility than are the positive returns. Therefore, it is worthwhile to examine the asymmetric GARCH model, including the exponential GARCH model of Nelson (1991) and the threshold GARCH model of Zakoian (1994). There are a few studies that have employed the asymmetric GARCH models to examine the asymmetric behaviour in the Asian stock market returns. For example, Holden, Thompson and Ruangrit (2005) examined the calendar effects and its asymmetric behaviour on stock returns in Thailand from 1995 to 2000. Recent studies which take into consideration asymmetric behaviour include Syed Khalid Wafa, Liew and Chia (2007), Chia, Liew and Syed Azizi Wafa (2008), Chia and Liew (2010) and Chia and Lim (2011).

In addition to the GARCH family's models, this study will utilize the approach of the closure test principle, which was proposed by Alt, Fortin and Weinberger (2011) to examine stock market anomalies. This closed test procedure differs from the traditional approaches where the null hypotheses are tested in such a way that the probability of committing a type 1 error is always kept smaller than or equal to a given significance level for each combination of true null hypotheses.

As a conclusion, this study focuses on the Asian stock markets (Thailand, Indonesia, Hong Kong, Taiwan, Singapore, Malaysia, Philippines, South Korea and Japan) during the Asian financial crisis and examines the day-of-the-week effect by taking into account both the mean and its volatility. We believe that the EGARCH–mean models may provide some important evidence on asymmetric behaviour in the Asian stock markets during crisis periods. If the same pattern of effect is identified during a crisis, then it will give investors the opportunity to use the same trading strategies. If there is evidence of any new behaviours in the day-of-the-week effect during crises, this can be a precaution to investors.

2.0   Data

This study uses daily closing values of Asian stock markets (in Thailand, Indonesia, Hong Kong, Taiwan, Singapore, Malaysia, Philippines, South Korea and Japan) from 1 June 1997 to 31 January 1998 (eight months).[1] The daily returns are calculated as the first difference in the natural logarithms of the stock market index:

$$R_t = \log(I_t) - \log(I_{t-1}) \times 100, \tag{5.2}$$

where I_t and I_{t-1} are the values for each index for period t and $t-1$, respectively. In the case of a day following a nontrading day, the return is calculated using the closing price indices of the previous trading day.

3.0   Empirical method

This study employs the following EGARCH–mean specification on the conditional volatility to test the daily seasonality in stock markets:

$$R_t = \alpha_1 + \sum_{i=2}^{5} \alpha_i \delta_{it} + \alpha_6 R_{t-1} + \alpha_7 \sigma_t^2 + \varepsilon_t \tag{5.3}$$

$$\log \sigma_t^2 = \beta_1 + \sum_{j=1}^{p} \gamma_j \log \sigma_{t-j}^2 + \sum_{i=1}^{q}\left[\pi_i\left(\left|\frac{\xi_{t-i}}{\sigma_{t-i}}\right| - \sqrt{\frac{2}{\pi}}\right) + \psi_i \frac{\xi_{t-i}}{\sigma_{t-i}}\right] + \sum_{i=2}^{5} \beta_i \delta_{it}. \tag{5.4}$$

In Equation (3), also known as the return equation, R_t is the logarithmic return of the market index at day t; R_{t-1} is the logarithmic return of the market index on day $t-1$; $\delta_{2t}, \delta_{3t}, \delta_{4t}$ and δ_{5t} are dummy variables which take on the value 1 if the corresponding return for day t is a Tuesday, Wednesday, Thursday or Friday, respectively, and 0 otherwise. Meanwhile, $\alpha_1, \alpha_2, \ldots, \alpha_7$ are the parameters to be estimated in Equation (3). Among them, α_1 measures the mean return (in percentage) on Monday; whereas $\alpha_2, \ldots, \alpha_5$ capture the difference of the average return of the stock index for Tuesday, Wednesday, Thursday and Friday, respectively, as compared to Monday's mean return. A lagged value of the return variable with its coefficient, α_6, is introduced in Equation (3) to avoid serial correlation error terms in the model, which may yield misleading inferences. Also, in Equation (3), the Monday dummy variable is excluded to avoid the dummy variable trap. Furthermore, α_7 measures the reward-to-risk ratio, ε_t is the error term with zero mean and conditional variance σ_t^2.

Equation (4) is the variance equation, where the left-hand side of the equation is the logarithm of the conditional variance. This implies that the leverage effect is exponential, rather than quadratic, and that forecasts of the conditional variance are guaranteed to be nonnegative. In this case, the presence of leverage effects can be tested by the hypothesis that $\psi_i > 0$, whereas the impact is asymmetric if $\psi_i \neq 0$.

Referring to our case, the closure principle is applied to the mean equation and variance equation. Apart from the global and primary null hypotheses, we have to add all possible intersections into the set of hypotheses. The complete set of hypotheses is listed in Table 5.1 below.

Table 5.1 All primary, intersection and global hypotheses

Primary	Intersection		Global
H_{0i}	H_{0ij}	H_{0ijk}	H_0
$\alpha_2 = 0$	$\alpha_2 = \alpha_3 = 0$	$\alpha_2 = \alpha_3 = \alpha_4 = 0$	$\alpha_2 = \alpha_3 = \alpha_4 = \alpha_5 = 0$
$\alpha_3 = 0$	$\alpha_2 = \alpha_4 = 0$	$\alpha_2 = \alpha_3 = \alpha_5 = 0$	
$\alpha_4 = 0$	$\alpha_2 = \alpha_5 = 0$	$\alpha_2 = \alpha_4 = \alpha_5 = 0$	
$\alpha_5 = 0$	$\alpha_3 = \alpha_4 = 0$	$\alpha_3 = \alpha_4 = \alpha_5 = 0$	
	$\alpha_3 = \alpha_5 = 0$		
	$\alpha_4 = \alpha_5 = 0$		

Source: Alt *et al.* (2011)

The closed test procedure started with testing for the global null hypothesis. The closure principle states that if the global null hypothesis cannot be rejected, then none of the null hypotheses stating pairwise equality can be rejected. On the other hand, if the global null hypothesis is rejected, then there is a need to check all the primary null hypotheses, H_{0i}, and the corresponding sets of intersection hypotheses, H_{0ij} and H_{0ijk}. An adjusted p-value for H_{0i} is then introduced, which is defined as the maximum of all p-values corresponding to all the hypotheses contained in the given primary hypothesis. A given primary hypothesis is rejected if the adjusted p-value is smaller than 10 percent.

4.0 Empirical results and discussions

A number of points emerge from the analysis of descriptive statistics. The returns of those selected Asian markets deteriorated during the crisis period, as evidenced by the negative mean returns. Among them, the Malaysian market has the lowest mean return of -0.17 percent. The descriptive statistics in Table 5.2 also report the standard deviation (Std. Dev.), skewness and kurtosis for the respective stock indices. In addition, Jarque-Bera normality test statistics together with the corresponding p-value are presented in Table 5.2. Overall, the descriptive statistics provide us an overview of the volatility and the distribution of the stock returns. In finance, standard deviation represents the risk associated with stock price variation. The stock market of Hong Kong has the highest value of standard deviation, followed by South Korea, Malaysia, Indonesia and then Thailand. Generally, this means that investing in these markets incurs higher risk than does investing in others. Moreover, none of the stock markets passes the Jarque-Bera normality test. The rejection of the null hypothesis of the normality test implies that daily returns are not normally distributed during the period of study.

The results of the mean returns and variance equations of the asymmetric exponential GARCH–mean (EGARCH–M) model for the day-of-the-week effect are presented in Table 5.3. The estimated value of α_7 shows a nonsignificant negative

Table 5.2 Descriptive statistics for daily returns

	Thailand	Indonesia	Hong Kong	Taiwan	Singapore	Malaysia	Philippines	South Korea	Japan
Mean	-0.0322	-0.0910	-0.1204	-0.0034	-0.1228	-0.1684	-0.0924	-0.0764	-0.0517
Std. Dev.	1.1971	1.2514	1.3996	0.7669	0.9063	1.2930	1.0236	1.3746	0.7917
Skewness	0.9904	-0.1631	0.1439	-0.4290	-0.3007	0.5706	-0.1147	0.1593	0.1908
Kurtosis	4.6134	6.5829	9.9009	5.0128	8.9904	6.4888	6.1428	4.9707	5.4119
Jarque-Bera	47.3191	93.8387	345.8649	34.7079	262.7906	97.6874	71.9927	28.8938	43.2318
Probability	0.0000	0.0000	0.0000	0.0000	0.0000	0.0000	0.0000	0.0000	0.0000

Table 5.3 Estimated exponential GARCH–mean results

EGARCH–mean results for the day-of-the-week effect (return equation)

Parameter	Thailand	Indonesia	Hong Kong	Taiwan	Singapore	Japan	Malaysia	Philippines	South Korea	Japan
(p,q)	(2,5)	(1,2)	(5,3)	(4,2)	(3,2)	(2,2)	(2,1)	(3,1)	(3,1)	(2,2)
Constant, α_1	-1.1585 (0.0005)*	-0.1174 (0.1659)	-0.0621 (0.5509)	0.1562 (0.1641)	0.0703 (0.2455)	-0.1738 (0.2141)	-0.3885 (0.0053)*	-0.4747 (0.0009)*	-0.1888 (0.0406)**	-0.1738 (0.2141)
Tuesday, α_2	-0.0756 (0.7739)	0.1892 (0.4538)	-0.1003 (0.5597)	-0.2786 (0.0148)**	-0.1063 (0.3255)	0.0293 (0.8637)	0.1261 (0.6827)	0.2343 (0.2120)	-0.1332 (0.3360)	0.0293 (0.8637)
Wednesday, α_3	0.4302 (0.1202)	0.0230 (0.8694)	0.1067 (0.3678)	-0.0964 (0.4224)	-0.2603 (0.0013)*	0.2163 (0.1570)	0.1272 (0.4563)	0.3066 (0.0465)**	0.2705 (0.0126)**	0.2163 (0.1570)
Thursday, α_4	0.2376 (0.3825)	-0.1921 (0.1793)	0.1511 (0.2860)	-0.2312 (0.0817)***	-0.2545 (0.0113)**	0.0437 (0.7765)	-0.0818 (0.6945)	-0.2457 (0.1918)	0.0506 (0.6379)	0.0437 (0.7765)
Friday, α_5	0.1177 (0.6469)	0.0543 (0.7734)	0.0157 (0.9205)	0.0004 (0.9966)	-0.1052 (0.1941)	-0.0293 (0.8545)	0.2629 (0.1851)	0.4405 (0.1190)	0.3660 (0.0007)*	-0.0293 (0.8545)
Return (–1), α_6	-0.0303 (0.8085)	0.4180 (0.0000)*	0.0539 (0.3656)	0.0533 (0.4347)	0.2114 (0.0022)*	-0.1676 (0.0103)**	0.2187 (0.0057)*	0.2886 (0.0000)*	0.1149 (0.1155)	-0.1676 (0.0103)**
α_7	1.0085 (0.0023)*	0.1296 (0.0885)***	-0.0265 (0.6851)	-0.0754 (0.6002)	-0.0565 (0.5711)	0.1042 (0.5500)	0.1519 (0.1180)	0.2893 (0.0578)***	-0.0398 (0.4416)	0.1042 (0.5500)

EGARCH–mean results for the day-of-the-week effect (variance equation)

Parameter	Thailand	Indonesia	Hong Kong	Taiwan	Singapore	Japan	Malaysia	Philippines	South Korea	Japan
Constant, β_1	-1.3972 (0.0069)*	-0.6284 (0.0000)*	0.4255 (0.4808)	0.1887 (0.4577)	0.0283 (0.9559)	-0.0032 (0.9942)	0.4349 (0.4419)	0.1923 (0.8119)	0.2836 (0.2863)	-0.0032 (0.9942)
γ_1	0.3692 (0.0000)*	0.9620 (0.0000)*	0.5854 (0.0004)*	0.9294 (0.0000)*	0.8610 (0.0000)*	-0.0406 (0.4183)	1.6397 (0.0000)*	2.5874 (0.0000)*	0.3153 (0.0000)*	-0.0406 (0.4183)

(*Continued*)

Table 5.3 (Continued)

Parameter	Thailand	Indonesia	Hong Kong	Taiwan	Singapore	Japan	Malaysia	Philippines	South Korea	Japan
γ_2	-0.9484 (0.0000)*	—	-0.1878 (0.4365)	-0.4721 (0.0001)*	0.7903 (0.0000)*	0.9838 (0.0000)*	-0.6693 (0.0000)*	-2.4355 (0.0000)*	-0.2598 (0.0000)*	0.9838 (0.0000)*
γ_3	—	—	0.8386 (0.0000)*	-0.1464 (0.1824)	-0.7463 (0.0000)*	—	—	0.8162 (0.0000)*	0.9496 (0.0000)*	—
γ_4	—	—	-0.0933 (0.6869)	0.5779 (0.0000)*	—	—	—	—	—	—
γ_5	—	—	-0.4268 (0.0215)**	—	—	—	—	—	—	—
π_1	0.3565 (0.0194)**	0.3062 (0.0000)*	0.3277 (0.0813)***	0.3109 (0.0418)**	0.6759 (0.0011)*	0.3454 (0.0000)*	-0.0831 (0.0000)*	0.0500 (0.0331)**	0.9669 (0.0000)*	0.3454 (0.0000)*
π_2	0.3492 (0.0200)**	-0.5470 (0.0000)*	0.2737 (0.1021)	0.4982 (0.0009)*	-0.4733 (0.0666)***	0.0590 (0.7054)	—	—	—	0.0590 (0.7054)
π_3	0.3488 (0.0494)**	—	-0.1724 (0.4240)	—	—	—	—	—	—	—
π_4	0.2039 (0.0770)***	—	—	—	—	—	—	—	—	—
π_5	0.1894 (0.1905)	—	—	—	—	—	—	—	—	—
ψ_1	0.1392 (0.1614)	-0.1492 (0.3362)	-0.1773 (0.1935)	-0.3351 (0.0049)*	-0.2336 (0.0052)*	-0.1155 (0.0000)*	-0.1538 (0.0000)*	-0.0228 (0.0018)*	-0.0713 (0.4084)	-0.1155 (0.0000)*
ψ_2	0.1294 (0.1211)	-0.3123 (0.0362)**	-0.3593 (0.0091)*	-0.0319 (0.0031)*	-0.0401 (0.6784)	-0.0447 (0.0000)*	—	—	—	-0.0447 (0.0000)*
ψ_3	0.2678 (0.0139)**	—	-0.0626 (0.6906)	—	—	—	—	—	—	—

ψ_4	0.2179 (0.0069)*	—	—	—	—	—	—	—	—	—
ψ_5	0.0938 (0.2896)	—	—	—	—	—	—	—	—	—
Tuesday, α_2	0.0240 (0.9531)	1.6937 (0.0000)*	-1.0771 (0.2067)	-1.6451 (0.0012)*	0.2189 (0.7838)	-0.6440 (0.2048)	0.2535 (0.7598)	0.2693 (0.8180)	-0.8082 (0.1230)	-0.6440 (0.2048)
Wednesday, α_3	0.0567 (0.8630)	0.2127 (0.3606)	-1.8264 (0.0251)**	-1.0888 (0.0004)*	-1.4026 (0.0459)**	-0.6244 (0.3281)	-1.5109 (0.0231)**	-0.5178 (0.5707)	-1.3102 (0.0328)**	-0.6244 (0.3281)
Thursday, α_4	-0.0177 (0.9403)	0.5570 (0.0615)***	-0.1178 (0.8920)	-0.4198 (0.4030)	0.3798 (0.6316)	-0.4580 (0.5452)	0.2595 (0.7010)	0.7217 (0.4099)	-2.0210 (0.0011)*	-0.4580 (0.5452)
Friday, α_5	0.0162 (0.9739)	1.1619 (0.0000)*	-1.5685 (0.0649)***	-1.8857 (0.0000)*	-0.7646 (0.3022)	-0.0962 (0.8649)	-0.8984 (0.3963)	-1.6923 (0.3214)	-1.0328 (0.0267)**	-0.0962 (0.8649)

EGARCH–mean results for the day-of-the-week effect (diagnostic checking)

ARCH-LM statistic (p-value)

5 Lags	0.5660	0.8064	0.6381	0.9117	0.4154	0.7858	0.7830	0.9376	0.0243	0.7858
10 Lags	0.6066	0.8046	0.9125	0.7824	0.2751	0.6814	0.7052	0.2042	0.0128	0.6814

Ljung-Box Q^2 statistic (p-value)

5 Lags	0.5130	0.7570	0.5620	0.8800	0.3330	0.7510	0.7960	0.9370	0.0180	0.7510
10 Lags	0.6610	0.7740	0.8950	0.9570	0.1330	0.6160	0.6220	0.1370	0.0590	0.6160

Notes: *, ** and *** denote significance at the 1%, 5% and 10% levels, respectively. Numbers in parentheses depict the p-Value. The highest order of p and q considered in this study is 5. The selection of appropriate orders of p and q in this study were determined by the smallest Schwarz information criterion (SIC; Clare, Ibrahim and Thomas, 1998).

risk premium in the Hong Kong, Taiwan, Singapore and South Korea stock markets. On the other hand, the risk premium is positive in the Thailand, Indonesia, Malaysia, Philippines and Japan stock markets. However, only the Indonesia and Philippines markets have a significant positive risk premium. The leverage effect terms, ψ_j, are mostly statistically different from zero in most of the markets. Thus, this amounts to evidence of asymmetrical market reactions towards positive and negative news, which reflects the presence of an asymmetrical stock market in this study. Moreover, the diagnostic test results show that there is no remaining ARCH effect in all the estimated EGARCH–M models, except for the South Korea market.

Further, the closure test principle was applied to all the selected markets in this study. For the mean equation, the p-values for the hypotheses of pairwise equality of Monday returns with other day-of-the-week returns are presented in Table 5.4. For each primary hypothesis, the first value is the adjusted p-value, while the other values are traditional p-values. For example, in testing the hypotheses that Monday returns are equal to Tuesday returns (MON = TUE) in the Thailand stock market, the adjusted p-value is 0.7947, which is the maximum of the p- values for all the hypotheses of H_{02}. The adjusted p-values for all the hypotheses, H_{0i}, are summarized in Table 5.5. In determining the Monday effect from the closed test results, we followed the definition of the Monday effect as defined by Alt *et al.* (2011). The term 'weak Monday effect' is used when Monday returns are statistically different from at least one other day of the week, while the 'strong Monday effect' refers to the case where Monday returns are statistically different from all other days of the week. Referring to Table 5.5, Thailand does not have the Monday effect, as the Monday returns are not different from all other weekdays. Overall, from the nine selected Asian stock markets, only those of Taiwan, Singapore and South Korea demonstrate a weak Monday effect.

Table 5.6 and Table 5.7 present the closure test results for the variance equation of the EGARCH–mean model. In a similar manner, we determined the adjusted p-values for the complete set of hypotheses for the variance equation. In the following, we will use the term 'weak Monday volatility' when Monday volatility is distinguishable from at least one other day of the week. On the other hand, if Monday volatility is statistically different from all other days of the week, then this can be concluded to be 'strong Monday volatility'. Referring to Table 5.7, Indonesia, Taiwan, Malaysia and South Korea have weak Monday volatility. However, no significant result is found for the other countries.

5.0   Conclusion

This study examined the existence of a daily pattern of the day-of-the-week effect in selected Asian stock markets during the Asian financial crisis by using the asymmetric exponential GARCH–mean model with the closure test principle of Alt *et al.* (2011). Generally, a weak Monday effect is found in the Taiwan, Singapore and South Korea stock markets. When the time-varying volatility in the market returns are taken into account by the EGARCH–M model, Taiwan, Singapore,

Table 5.4 Adjusted p-value and traditional p-values for the complete set of hypotheses of the EGARCH–mean mean equation

		Thailand	Indonesia	Hong Kong	Taiwan	Singapore	Malaysia	Philippines	South Korea	Japan
MON = TUE										
Adjusted p-value	$H_{02}: \alpha_2 = 0$	0.7947	0.8956	0.7863	0.0710	0.3651	0.7876	0.5197	0.3375	0.9601
Traditional p-values	$H_{02}: \alpha_2 = 0$	0.7743	0.4549	0.5606	0.0160	0.3271	0.6832	0.2566	0.3375	0.8639
	$H_{023}: \alpha_2 = \alpha_3 = 0$	0.1487	0.7489	0.3138	0.0384	0.0067	0.7388	0.5197	0.0001	0.3238
	$H_{024}: \alpha_2 = \alpha_4 = 0$	0.4619	0.2065	0.3670	0.0508	0.0413	0.7876	0.0459	0.3224	0.9601
	$H_{025}: \alpha_2 = \alpha_5 = 0$	0.7947	0.7506	0.7863	0.0042	0.3651	0.4174	0.1541	0.0000	0.9339
	$H_{0234}: \alpha_2 = \alpha_3 = \alpha_4 = 0$	0.2332	0.3666	0.3802	0.0710	0.0059	0.7224	0.0888	0.0003	0.4609
	$H_{0235}: \alpha_2 = \alpha_3 = \alpha_5 = 0$	0.2794	0.8956	0.5071	0.0117	0.0167	0.6249	0.2306	0.0000	0.3358
	$H_{0245}: \alpha_2 = \alpha_4 = \alpha_5 = 0$	0.6618	0.3306	0.5699	0.0036	0.0939	0.3556	0.0121	0.0000	0.9549
	$H_{02345}: \alpha_2 = \alpha_3 = \alpha_4 = \alpha_5 = 0$	0.3553	0.4869	0.5356	0.0086	0.0081	0.5055	0.0269	0.0000	0.4864
MON = WED										
Adjusted p-value	$H_{03}: \alpha_3 = 0$	0.4571	0.9563	0.6509	0.5655	0.0167	0.7388	0.5197	0.0247	0.4864
Traditional p-values	$H_{03}: \alpha_3 = 0$	0.1223	0.8696	0.3693	0.4237	0.0016	0.4574	0.4729	0.0136	0.1590
	$H_{023}: \alpha_2 = \alpha_3 = 0$	0.1487	0.7489	0.3138	0.0384	0.0067	0.7388	0.5197	0.0001	0.3238
	$H_{034}: \alpha_3 = \alpha_4 = 0$	0.2984	0.3686	0.5030	0.2160	0.0020	0.5668	0.1042	0.0247	0.2878
	$H_{035}: \alpha_3 = \alpha_5 = 0$	0.2844	0.9563	0.6291	0.5655	0.0062	0.4172	0.1347	0.0038	0.1853
	$H_{0234}: \alpha_2 = \alpha_3 = \alpha_4 = 0$	0.2332	0.3666	0.3802	0.0710	0.0059	0.7224	0.0888	0.0003	0.4609
	$H_{0235}: \alpha_2 = \alpha_3 = \alpha_5 = 0$	0.2794	0.8956	0.5071	0.0117	0.0167	0.6249	0.2306	0.0000	0.3358
	$H_{0245}: \alpha_2 = \alpha_4 = \alpha_5 = 0$	0.4571	0.5004	0.6509	0.1191	0.0033	0.3570	0.0201	0.0029	0.3295
	$H_{02345}: \alpha_2 = \alpha_3 = \alpha_4 = \alpha_5 = 0$	0.3553	0.4869	0.5356	0.0086	0.0081	0.5055	0.0269	0.0000	0.4864

(Continued)

Table 5.4 (Continued)

		Thailand	Indonesia	Hong Kong	Taiwan	Singapore	Malaysia	Philippines	South Korea	Japan
MON = THU										
Adjusted p-value	$H_{04}: \alpha_4 = 0$	0.6830	0.5004	0.6509	0.2160	0.0939	0.7876	0.2199	0.6386	0.9601
Traditional p-values	$H_{04}: \alpha_4 = 0$	0.3839	0.1812	0.2877	0.0837	0.0123	0.6950	0.2199	0.6386	0.7769
	$H_{024}: \alpha_2 = \alpha_4 = 0$	0.4619	0.2065	0.3670	0.0508	0.0413	0.7876	0.0459	0.3224	0.9601
	$H_{034}: \alpha_3 = \alpha_4 = 0$	0.2984	0.3686	0.5030	0.2160	0.0020	0.5668	0.1042	0.0247	0.2878
	$H_{045}: \alpha_4 = \alpha_5 = 0$	0.6830	0.3198	0.5420	0.0615	0.0430	0.2078	0.0085	0.0014	0.8645
	$H_{0234}: \alpha_2 = \alpha_3 = \alpha_4 = 0$	0.2332	0.3666	0.3802	0.0710	0.0059	0.7224	0.0888	0.0003	0.4609
	$H_{0245}: \alpha_2 = \alpha_4 = \alpha_5 = 0$	0.6618	0.3306	0.5699	0.0036	0.0939	0.3556	0.0121	0.0000	0.9549
	$H_{0345}: \alpha_3 = \alpha_4 = \alpha_5 = 0$	0.4571	0.5004	0.6509	0.1191	0.0033	0.3570	0.0201	0.0029	0.3295
	$H_{02345}: \alpha_2 = \alpha_3 = \alpha_4 = \alpha_5 = 0$	0.3553	0.4869	0.5356	0.0086	0.0081	0.5055	0.0269	0.0000	0.4864
MON = FRI										
Adjusted p-value	$H_{05}: \alpha_5 = 0$	0.7947	0.9563	0.9207	0.9966	0.3651	0.6249	0.2306	0.0038	0.9549
Traditional p-values	$H_{05}: \alpha_5 = 0$	0.6476	0.7738	0.9207	0.9966	0.1961	0.1870	0.0540	0.0009	0.8547
	$H_{025}: \alpha_2 = \alpha_5 = 0$	0.7947	0.7506	0.7863	0.0042	0.3651	0.4174	0.1541	0.0000	0.9339
	$H_{035}: \alpha_3 = \alpha_5 = 0$	0.2844	0.9563	0.62A91	0.5655	0.0062	0.4172	0.1347	0.0038	0.1853
	$H_{045}: \alpha_4 = \alpha_5 = 0$	0.6830	0.3198	0.5420	0.0615	0.0430	0.2078	0.0085	0.0014	0.8645
	$H_{0235}: \alpha_2 = \alpha_3 = \alpha_5 = 0$	0.2794	0.8956	0.5071	0.0117	0.0167	0.6249	0.2306	0.0000	0.3358
	$H_{0235}: \alpha_2 = \alpha_3 = \alpha_5 = 0$	0.6618	0.3306	0.5699	0.0036	0.0939	0.3556	0.0121	0.0000	0.9549
	$H_{0345}: \alpha_3 = \alpha_4 = \alpha_5 = 0$	0.4571	0.5004	0.6509	0.1191	0.0033	0.3570	0.0201	0.0029	0.3295
	$H_{02345}: \alpha_2 = \alpha_3 = \alpha_4 = \alpha_5 = 0$	0.3553	0.4869	0.5356	0.0086	0.0081	0.5055	0.0269	0.0000	0.4864

Table 5.5 Closed *F*-test results (mean equation)

Primary hypothesis	Mon = Tue (adjusted p-value)	Mon = Wed (adjusted p-value)	Mon = Tue (adjusted p-value)	Mon = Fri (adjusted p-value)
Thailand	0.7947	0.4571	0.6830	0.7947
Indonesia	0.8956	0.9563	0.5004	0.9563
Hong Kong	0.7863	0.6509	0.6509	0.9207
Taiwan	0.0710***	0.5655	0.2160	0.9966
Singapore	0.3651	0.0167**	0.0939***	0.3651
Malaysia	0.7876	0.7388	0.7876	0.6249
Philippines	0.5197	0.5197	0.2199	0.2306
South Korea	0.3375	0.0247**	0.6386	0.0038*
Japan	0.9601	0.4864	0.9601	0.9549

Notes: *, ** and *** indicate significance at the 1%, 5% and 10% levels. If the Monday return is different from all the other days of the week, it can be concluded to be a strong Monday effect. If the Monday return is different from at least one other day of the week, it can be concluded to be a weak Monday effect.

Table 5.6 Adjusted p-value and traditional p-values for the complete set of hypotheses of the EGARCH–mean variance equation

		Thailand	Indonesia	Hong Kong	Taiwan	Singapore	Malaysia	Philippines	South Korea	Japan
MON = TUE										
Adjusted p-value	$H_{02}: b_2 = 0$	0.9986	0.0000	0.4169	0.0015	0.8910	0.9281	0.9522	0.1250	0.6281
Traditional p-values	$H_{02}: b_2 = 0$	0.9532	0.0000	0.2087	0.0015	0.7841	0.7602	0.7776	0.1250	0.2067
	$H_{023}: b_2 = b_3 = 0$	0.9848	0.0000	0.0833	0.0000	0.0614	0.0002	0.8443	0.0781	0.4061
	$H_{024}: b_2 = b_4 = 0$	0.9897	0.0000	0.4169	0.0000	0.8910	0.9281	0.1109	0.0050	0.4485
	$H_{025}: b_2 = b_5 = 0$	0.9979	0.0000	0.1830	0.0000	0.3641	0.1976	0.9260	0.0306	0.4405
	$H_{0234}: b_2 = b_3 = b_4 = 0$	0.9986	0.0000	0.1224	0.0000	0.0770	0.0000	0.1093	0.0109	0.5546
	$H_{0235}: b_2 = b_3 = b_5 = 0$	0.9585	0.0000	0.1547	0.0000	0.0880	0.0003	0.9522	0.0202	0.6126
	$H_{0245}: b_2 = b_4 = b_5 = 0$	0.9946	0.0000	0.2842	0.0000	0.4446	0.2740	0.1948	0.0057	0.6266
	$H_{02345}: b_2 = b_3 = b_4 = b_5 = 0$	0.9881	0.0000	0.1914	0.0000	0.0759	0.0001	0.1898	0.0095	0.6281
MON = WED										
Adjusted p-value	$H_{03}: b_3 = 0$	0.9986	0.3620	0.1914	0.0006	0.1337	0.0382	0.9522	0.0781	0.7987
Traditional p-values	$H_{03}: b_3 = 0$	0.8632	0.3620	0.0266	0.0006	0.0476	0.0244	0.7488	0.0344	0.3296
	$H_{023}: b_2 = b_3 = 0$	0.9848	0.0000	0.0833	0.0000	0.0614	0.0002	0.8443	0.0781	0.4061
	$H_{034}: b_3 = b_4 = 0$	0.9850	0.0000	0.0609	0.0000	0.0434	0.0382	0.3215	0.0041	0.6051
	$H_{035}: b_3 = b_5 = 0$	0.9594	0.0000	0.0744	0.0000	0.1337	0.0072	0.9114	0.0096	0.6169
	$H_{0234}: b_2 = b_3 = b_4 = 0$	0.9986	0.0000	0.1224	0.0000	0.0770	0.0000	0.1093	0.0109	0.5546
	$H_{0235}: b_2 = b_3 = b_5 = 0$	0.9585	0.0000	0.1547	0.0000	0.0880	0.0003	0.9522	0.0202	0.6126
	$H_{0245}: b_3 = b_4 = b_5 = 0$	0.9873	0.0000	0.1075	0.0000	0.0675	0.0128	0.3560	0.0042	0.7987
	$H_{02345}: b_2 = b_3 = b_4 = b_5 = 0$	0.9881	0.0000	0.1914	0.0000	0.0759	0.0001	0.1898	0.0095	0.6281

MON = THU

	Hypothesis									
Adjusted p-value	$H_{04}: b_4 = 0$	0.9986	0.0634	0.8922	0.8910	0.4043	0.9281	0.3560	0.0109	0.8040
Traditional p-values	$H_{04}: b_4 = 0$	0.9404	0.0634	0.8922	0.6323	0.4043	0.7016	0.1384	0.0014	0.5461
	$H_{024}: b_2 = b_4 = 0$	0.9897	0.0000	0.4169	0.8910	0.0000	0.9281	0.1109	0.0050	0.4485
	$H_{034}: b_3 = b_4 = 0$	0.9850	0.0000	0.0609	0.0434	0.0000	0.0382	0.3215	0.0041	0.6051
	$H_{045}: b_4 = b_5 = 0$	0.9964	0.0000	0.1509	0.3233	0.0000	0.5387	0.2941	0.0024	0.8040
	$H_{0234}: b_2 = b_3 = b_4 = 0$	0.9986	0.0000	0.1224	0.0770	0.0000	0.0000	0.1093	0.0109	0.5546
	$H_{0245}: b_2 = b_4 = b_5 = 0$	0.9946	0.0000	0.2842	0.4446	0.0000	0.2740	0.1948	0.0057	0.6266
	$H_{0345}: b_3 = b_4 = b_5 = 0$	0.9873	0.0000	0.1075	0.0675	0.0000	0.0128	0.3560	0.0042	0.7987
	$H_{02345}: b_2 = b_3 = b_4 = b_5 = 0$	0.9881	0.0000	0.1914	0.0759	0.0000	0.0001	0.1898	0.0095	0.6281

MON = FRI

	Hypothesis									
Adjusted p-value	$H_{05}: b_5 = 0$	0.9979	0.0000	0.2842	0.4446	0.0000	0.5387	0.9872	0.0306	0.8651
Traditional p-values	$H_{05}: b_5 = 0$	0.9740	0.0000	0.0669	0.3038	0.0000	0.3975	0.9872	0.0281	0.8651
	$H_{025}: b_2 = b_5 = 0$	0.9979	0.0000	0.1830	0.3641	0.0000	0.1976	0.9260	0.0306	0.4405
	$H_{035}: b_3 = b_5 = 0$	0.9594	0.0000	0.0744	0.1337	0.0000	0.0072	0.9114	0.0096	0.6169
	$H_{045}: b_4 = b_5 = 0$	0.9964	0.0000	0.1509	0.3233	0.0000	0.5387	0.2941	0.0024	0.8040
	$H_{0235}: b_2 = b_3 = b_5 = 0$	0.9585	0.0000	0.1547	0.0880	0.0000	0.0003	0.9522	0.0202	0.6126
	$H_{0235}: b_2 = b_4 = b_5 = 0$	0.9946	0.0000	0.2842	0.4446	0.0000	0.2740	0.1948	0.0057	0.6266
	$H_{0345}: b_3 = b_4 = b_5 = 0$	0.9873	0.0000	0.1075	0.0675	0.0000	0.0128	0.3560	0.0042	0.7987
	$H_{02345}: b_2 = b_3 = b_4 = b_5 = 0$	0.9881	0.0000	0.1914	0.0759	0.0000	0.0001	0.1898	0.0095	0.6281

Table 5.7 Closed *F*-test results (variance equation)

Primary hypothesis	Mon = Tue (adjusted p-value)	Mon = Wed (adjusted p-value)	Mon = Tue (adjusted p-value)	Mon = Fri (adjusted p-value)
Thailand	0.9986	0.9986	0.9986	0.9979
Indonesia	0.0000*	0.3620	0.0634***	0.0000*
Hong Kong	0.4169	0.1914	0.8922	0.2842
Taiwan	0.0015*	0.0006*	0.4043	0.0000*
Singapore	0.8910	0.1337	0.8910	0.4446
Malaysia	0.9281	0.0382**	0.9281	0.5387
Philippines	0.9522	0.9522	0.3560	0.9872
South Korea	0.1250	0.0781***	0.0109**	0.0306**
Japan	0.6281	0.7987	0.8040	0.8651

Notes: *, ** and *** indicate significance at the 1%, 5% and 10% levels. If the Monday volatility is different from all other days of the week, it can be concluded to be a strong Monday volatility. If the Monday volatility is different from at least one other day of the week, it can be concluded to be a weak Monday volatility.

Malaysia and South Korea are found to have weak Monday volatility. However, there is no significant Monday volatility found in the other markets. Lastly, the leverage effect terms in most of the Asian markets are found to be significant, which reflects the presence of asymmetrical behaviour in these markets. The findings of this study show that a strong Monday effect and its volatility apparently disappears in the Asian stock markets during the crisis period. This study provides an alert to investors in the Asian markets that crises will change the pattern of stock movement and only a weak Monday effect remained in some markets.

Note

1 The selection of the crisis period is based on the study by Jang and Sul (2002).

References

Alexakis, P., and Xanthakis, M. (1995). Day of the week effect on the Greek stock market. *Applied Financial Economics*, 5(1), 43–50.

Al-Rjoub, S. A. M., and Alwaked, A. (2010). January effect during financial crisis: Evidence from the US. *European Journal of Economics, Finance and Administrative Sciences*, 24, 29–35.

Alt, R., Fortin, I., and Weinberger, S. (2011). The Monday effect revisited: An alternative testing approach. *Journal of Empirical Finance*, 18(3), 447–460.

Apolinario, R. M. C., Santana, O. M., Sales, L. J., and Caro, A. R. (2006). Day of the week effect on European stock markets. *International Research Journal of Finance and Economics*, 9(2), 53–70.

Arsad, Z., and Coutts, J. A. (1996). The weekend effect, good news, bad news and the Financial Times Industrial Ordinary Shares Index: 1935–9. *Applied Economics Letters*, 3(12), 797–801.

Berument, M. H., and Dogan, N. (2012). Stock market return and volatility: Day-of-the-week effect. *Journal of Economics and Finance*, 36(2), 282–302.

Brooks, C., and Persand, G. (2001). Seasonality in Southeast Asian stock markets: Some new evidence on day-of-the-week effects. *Applied Economics Letters*, 8(3), 155–158.

Chen, G., Kwok, C. C. Y., and Rui, O. M. (2001). The day-of-the-week regularity in the stock markets of China. *Journal of Multinational Financial Management*, 11(2), 139–163.

Chia, R. C. J. (2014). The disappearing day-of-the-week effect in Australia and New Zealand stock markets: Evidence from TAR-GARCH Model. *Malaysian Journal of Business and Economics*, 1(2), 51–61.

Chia, R. C. J., and Liew, V. K. S. (2010). Evidence on the day-of-the-week effect and asymmetric behavior in the Bombay stock exchange. *The IUP Journal of Applied Finance*, 16(6), 17–29.

Chia, R. C. J., Liew, V. K. S., and Syed Azizi Wafa, S. K. W. (2008). Day-of-the-week effects in selected East Asian stock markets. *Economics Bulletin*, 7(5), 1–8.

Chia, R. C. J., and Lim, S. Y. (2011). Stock market anomalies in South Africa and its neighbouring countries. *Economics Bulletin*, 31(4), 3123–3137.

Clare, A. D., Ibrahim, M. S. B., and Thomas, S. H. (1998). The impact of settlement procedures on day-of-the-week effects: Evidence from the Kuala Lumpur stock exchange. *Journal of Business Finance and Accounting*, 25(3–4), 401–418.

Compton, W., Kunkel, R. A., and Kuhlemeyer, G. (2013). Calendar anomalies in Russian stocks and bonds. *Managerial Finance*, 39(12), 1138–1154.

Connolly, R. A. (1989). An examination of the robustness of the weekend effect. *The Journal of Finance and Quantitative Analysis*, 24(2), 133–169.

French, K. R. (1980). Stock returns and the weekend effect. *Journal of Financial Economics*, 8(1), 55–70.

Engle, R. F. (1993). Statistical models for financial volatility. *Financial Analysts Journal*, 49(1), 72–78.

Engle, R. F. (2001). GARCH 101: The use of ARCH / GARCH models in applied econometrics. *Journal of Economics Perspectives*, 15(4), 157–168.

Floros, C., and Salvador, E. (2014). Calendar anomalies in cash and stock index futures: International evidence. *Economic Modelling*, 37, 216–223.

Galai, D., and Levy, H. K. (2005). Day-of-the-week effect in high moments. *Financial Markets, Institutions & Instruments*, 14(3), 169–186.

Gibbons, M. R., and Hess, P. (1981). Day of the week effect and assets returns. *The Journal of Business*, 54, 579–596.

Ho, P. C., and Kok, K. L. (1995). Day-of-the-week effect of the Malaysian second board stock market. *Malaysian Management Review*, 1–10.

Holden, K., Thompson, J., and Ruangrit, Y. (2005). The Asian crisis and calendar effects on stock returns in Thailand. *European Journal of Operational Research*, 163(1), 242–252.

Hui, T. K. (2005). Day-of-the-week effects in US and Asia-pacific stock markets during the Asian financial crisis: A non-parametric approach. *The International Journal of Management Science*, 33, 277–282.

Jaffe, J., and Westerfield, R. (1985). The weekend effect in common stock returns: The international evidence. *Journal of Finance*, 40(2), 433–454.

Jang, H., and Sul, W. (2002). The Asian financial crisis and the co-movement of Asian stock markets. *Journal of Asian Economics, 13*(1), 94–104.

Joshi, N. K. (2006). Day-of-the-week effect: Is it an industry – Specific phenomenon? *Economic Journal of Nepal, 29*(1), 1–12.

Kohers, G., Kohers, N., Pandey, V., and Kohers, T. (2004). The disappearing day-of-the-week effect in the world's largest equity markets. *Applied Economics Letters, 11*(3), 167–171.

Kok, K. L., and Wong, Y. C. (2004). Seasonal anomalies of the stocks in ASEAN equity markets. *Sunway College Journal, 1*, 1–11.

Lakonishok, J., and Levi, M. (1982). Weekend effects on stock returns: A note. *Journals of Finance, 37*(3), 883–889.

Lakonishok, J., and Maberly, E. (1980). The weekend effect: Trading patterns of individual and institutional investors. *Journal of Finance, 45*(1), 231–243.

Lakonishok, J., and Smidt, S. (1988). Are seasonal anomalies real? A ninety year perspective. *The Review of Financial Studies, 1*(4), 403–425.

Lucey, B. M. (2000). Anomalous daily seasonality in Ireland? *Applied Economics Letters, 7*(10), 637–640.

Lucey, B. M. (2006). Investigating the determinants of the Wednesday seasonal in Irish equities. *Research in International Business and Finance, 20*(1), 62–76.

Lyroudi, K., Subeniotis, D., and Komisopoulos, G. (2002). Market anomalies in the A.S.E: The day of the week effect. EFMA 2002 London Meetings. Available at: http://ssrn.com/abstract=314394 or http://dx.doi.org/10.2139/ssrn.314394

Nelson, D. B. (1991). Conditional heteroskedasticity in asset returns: A new approach. *Econometrica, 59*(2), 347–370.

Rogalski, R. J. (1984). New findings regarding day-of-the-week returns over trading and non-trading periods: A note. *Journal of Finance, 39*(5), 1603–1614.

Syed Khalid Wafa, S. A. W., Liew, V. K. S., and Chia, R. C. J. (2007). Calendar anomalies in the Malaysian stock market. *The ICFAI Journal of Applied Finance, 13*(6), 5–18.

Wong, K. A., Hui, T. K., and Chan, C. Y. (1992). Day-of-the-week effect: Evidence from developing stock markets. *Applied Financial Economics, 2*(1), 49–56.

Zakoian, J. M. (1994). Threshold heteroskedastic models. *Journal of Economic Dynamics and Control, 18*(5), 931–944.

6 The mean reversion effect and the contrarian strategy

Tamara Teplova and Evgeniya Mikova

1.0 Introduction

With the development of stock market analysis and the beginning of academic studies of stock prices' behaviour, different trading rules have been offered to investors – when to buy and when to sell. For instance, one of the rules is based on the tracking of short-term and long-term moving average returns. Stocks should be bought when the short-term moving average return line crosses the long-term moving average ones. Another possible indicator for rule building is the estimation of the relation between average returns at different time intervals. In the paper by Park (2010) the decision indicator was based on the comparison of a 50-day-to–200-day moving average ratio. The author showed that periods over the 6-month holding earned a 1.45 percent per month return. Furthermore, Park's moving average ratio strategy earns a profit also with 1 day, 5 days and 20 days in the formula for ratio calculating.

Many financial analysts and practitioners use the comparison of the current stock price and its 52-week high and low. Such trading rules assume that the past price dynamics may suggest to investors which stocks they should buy and which they should sell. From the efficient market hypothesis (EMH) standpoint, the profitability of these rules should be equal to zero. However, in practice the rules work in certain periods, and strict empirical research has confirmed that in some cases it is possible to construct trading strategies by analyzing the past stock price and return behaviour. While technical analysis indicators and various trading rules are very popular, they do not always withstand harsh statistical tests. The problem of detecting the right design of a profitable investment strategy that would demonstrate a statistical significance is still unsolved. The academic marketplace allows us to add our thoughts in this widely discussed topic. The academic marketplace allows us to estimate the aptness of the discussions. For instance, Jegadeesh (2000) in the same journal volume (*Journal of Finance* 55, 2000) argued that trading rules proposed by Andrew Lo in his seminal paper Lo, Mamaysky and Wang (2000) are actually not statistically profitable. Many attempts were made to revise the results both in terms of transaction costs (Lesmond, Schill and Zhou, 2004) and the expansion of the sample by the inclusion of long-term time horizons and national markets.

An interesting anomaly in financial assets pricing, including the stock market, is the mean reversal. The idea of reversal (or the contrarian strategy) is to capture relative past performance (raw cumulative return or more sophisticated measures).

Understanding the possible deviations in prices and asset returns from their fair level practices on financial market actively uses a contrarian strategy. We analyze the stock selection portfolio strategy with investing in long and short positions at the same time. One portfolio is in the buy (long trading) position and the second is in the sell (short trading) position. In the contrarian strategy, an investor is given the recommendation to purchase the past relative 'losers' and to sell the past relative 'winners'.

2.0   Profitability evidence of long-run and short-term contrarian strategies

The study of the possibility of profiting from a long position on portfolios with past losers (by buying them) and from a short position on past winners (short sales) has generated a separate research direction in the academic literature, which can be called the 'contrarian effect'. The contrarian effect is based on the empirically observed tendency for rising asset prices to decrease in the three- to five-year interval and on the contrary situation of past falling stocks, which demonstrate a significant return growth in the future.

The contrarian effect implies that there is a systematic excess of asset portfolio returns which earlier fell behind the market (demonstrated relatively worse results from investment; in the literature, such portfolios are called 'losers') over the portfolio with the assets which have performed better than the market in their past (called 'winner' portfolios). The systematic deviations and the ability to get a positive profit from opening investment positions in the antiphase (by selecting past losers for purchase and past winners for sale) are fixed in two periods:

1   In the long-term (LT) time horizon when the profit can be earned only after three to five years since the formation of the portfolio (so-called long-run reversal, LT contrarian effects). In the literature, the long-run effect is often taken at intervals of more than 12 months. Empirical observations confirmed this effect in the late 1980s.

2   In short-term (ST) intervals, within one or two months (one to four weeks), including the intervals within one day (intraday and ST contrarian effects). Active study of these ST effects started only in the early 1990s (Jegadeesh (1990), Jegadeesh and Titman (1993), Lehmann (1990)).

The profitability of the 'against the current', or contrarian, strategy is based on the fulfilment of the following condition: asset prices should seek the so-called average value over time. A contrarian strategy takes advantage of the negative autocorrelation of asset returns. This means that relatively high and low asset prices are temporary, and they will return to some 'trending' or fair value in the future. It turns out that in a situation when the observed return of an asset is below its average level (most likely because of the market underestimation) the asset is attractive for purchase. Investors can expect the growth of the asset price and the return of its profitability to the 'fair' level. Many papers are devoted to the research of this substantial mean reversion effect (De Bondt and Thaler (1985), Jegadeesh (1991), Balvers and Gilliand (2000), Chou, Wei and Chung (2007), Liew (2013) and Shi et al. (2015)).

The first work, which documented the effect in the long-term periods, is the study of De Bondt and Thaler (1985). This paper opened a line of the information efficiency paradigm's criticism for the US stock market even in its weak form. Moreover, this paper laid down the principal basics of reversion and momentum effects testing, which was actively used in the subsequent studies. For example, in the following studies the authors used the zero-cost (zero financing, long–short) strategy with shorting a portfolio (winners in contrarian and losers in momentum). In a follow-up study the authors used equal weights of stocks in two portfolios (win and lose) and long–short portfolios. Traditionally, research considers the monthly investment results (or the raw cumulative investment result in percentages).

The authors examined the equal observation periods (windows) for the cumulative stock returns and the investment (holding). So the windows in this basic strategy design coincided with most of the subsequent work and assumed equal periods for ranking and investment windows ($J = K$). For instance, in the early works (Lo and MacKinlay (1990), Jegadeesh and Titman (1993) and Conrad and Kaul (1998)) the authors assumed that this relationship (equal ratio) between the period of portfolio formation and investment is optimal. Note that it was later revealed that the combination of investment and ranking windows matters in different markets. As an example, in Jegadeesh and Titman (2001), a strategy that provides the maximum profitability involves 6 months of observation and 12 months of investing.

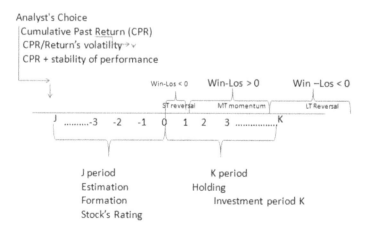

Figure 6.1 The estimation (J) and holding (K) periods. Analyst's choice for effect testing

De Bondt and Thaler (1985) found that a portfolio constructed from losers and based on the data of the past three to five years brought more profit in the next three to five years than a portfolio created from relative winners over the same period. According to their calculations, the arbitrage portfolio (formed on the basis of the opening of 36 months long and short positions [36/36 months is the strategy design]) can annually produce up to 8 percent return. De Bondt and Thaler (1985) concluded that the best ranking and investment period is equal to three years. According to the authors' estimation, by holding such a portfolio, an investor can earn 24.6 percent in three years (this return estimation is higher than the average return for the US market data for which the results were obtained). Moreover, past losers ensured a greater contribution to this profitability growth (19.6 percent).

The authors used the monthly data for ordinary stocks listed on the New York Stock Exchange (NYSE) from 1926 to 1980. Every three years starting in January, they formed two portfolios of 35 stocks: relative winners (with the highest return over the past three years) and losers (with the lowest return for the past three years). The analysis of these two portfolios' profitability at the end of the respective years (1932, 1935, 1938 and so on) as well as the difference in the portfolios' return (loser minus winner) has shown interesting results (16 observations):

- For the 36-month period of the portfolios' holding, the loser portfolio was ahead of the market by an average of 19.6 percent (the return for three years), while the portfolio of winners turned out to be worse than the market by 5 percent (Figure 6.2). Consequently, the three-year yield for the arbitrage portfolio was 24.6 percent. The authors evaluated this statistically significant result as a LT mean reversal effect (the investment period was 3 years).
- The one-month investment period (Figure 6.2) gave an arbitrage portfolio return of 8 percent (it is worth noting that this was not the annual return but the cumulative one, so in this case the return was for the one-month period), while the losers portfolio overtook the market by 6–7 percent. However, it should be mentioned that the arbitrage portfolio was created at the end of the calendar year, which could distort the assessment because of the traditionally observed 'January effect'. Thus, the displacement of the investment return estimation possibly had an upward tendency.

The second work of these authors, also based on the US market (De Bondt and Thaler, 1987), demonstrated the importance of such anomalies in financial assets pricing as a January effect, a value and size effect in profitability of the contrarian strategy. These findings made the researchers think again about the explanation of the observed effects and perhaps about the exaggerated role of the behavioural motives in the anomalies explanation.

Jegadeesh (1990) and Lehmann (1990) found evidence supporting the existence of a short-term price reversal over a period of one week to one month. The first explanation of this phenomenon the authors saw was in transaction costs.

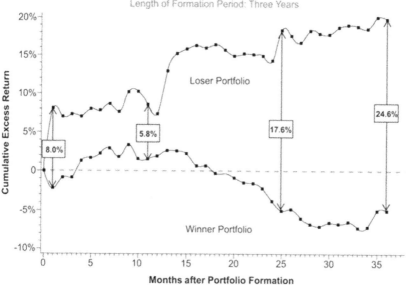

Average of 16 Three-Year Test Periods between January 1933 and December 1980
Length of Formation Period: Three Years

Figure 6.2 Results of the first paper in testing the reversal effect in the US market: De Bondt and Thaler (1985)

Jegadeesh and Titman (1993) illuminated ST abnormal profits due to short-term price pressure or lack of liquidity in the market rather than overreaction.

Research on the US market since the end of the 1990s has generated a lot of papers on foreign markets, including Asia. Primarily there are interesting works exploring the largest capital markets. Baytas and Cakici (1999) report the presence of a long-run contrarian effect in seven non-US markets.

In 1999, Schiereck, De Bondt and Weber published a paper on the LT effect analysis of the German stock market. The authors analyzed the period from 1961 to 1986 on the Frankfurt Stock Exchange (FSE). From the total sample, the authors built portfolios by tracking the relative best and worst 20 stocks' monthly returns in a three-year interval (by the cumulative yield). They showed that the peak of cumulative return was achieved in the 48-month investment period. The profitability was 19.28 percent in this window. Thus, Schiereck, De Bondt and Weber (1999) concluded that the three-year period of the portfolio formation and the four-year investing (holding) period provided the best result for the contrarian strategy on the German market.

Another interesting Asian market, which is considered a developed one, is the stock market in Japan. It is the third largest world market by capitalization ($13 trillion); more than 85 percent of the total market capitalization is concentrated in the Tokyo Stock Exchange (TSE).

Regarding the Japanese market, the most interesting results were obtained from the short-term reversal effect (STR). Chang, McLeavey and Rhee (1995) and Chou *et al.* (2007) find the ST price contrarian effect in the Japanese market. Chang *et al.* (1995) documented that the ST strategy is observed in the Japanese market and remains profitable after taking into account the systematic risk of size. The seasonality effect does not affect the profitability of the reversal strategy. Contrary to the empirical results obtained on the US stock market, there is a strong asymmetry of marginal (best and worst) portfolio returns in the sample (winners and losers).

In the paper by Chou *et al.* (2007), as well as in the work of De Bondt and Thaler (1985), the authors used a monthly return of 1854 common stocks of Japanese companies in various industries with more than 275 observations. The total return was considered (with the inclusion of the dividend yield) on the basis of the adjusted close prices. All stocks were ranked according to the cumulative return from maximum to minimum and divided into 10 portfolios with approximately the same number in each of them. The first portfolio included the 10 percent of the stocks with the highest cumulative return (equal weights of stocks in the portfolio); the tenth portfolio included the 10 percent with the lowest cumulative return. The periods of the arbitrage portfolio formation and holding varied from 1 to 36 months.

Chou *et al.* (2007) obtained the following results on the Japanese market:

1   For any choice of arbitrage portfolio formation and investment period, the presence of a positive statistically significant profitability is observed, reflecting the superiority of the recent 'losers' over the recent relative 'winners' and the lack of a momentum effect for medium-term (within a year) investment. The maximum monthly return of the ST reversal strategy is achieved when selecting a one-month formation period. During the one-month investment period, the strategy return is 2.4 percent (similar results were obtained earlier in the work by Chang *et al.* (1995)).

2   On the Japanese stock market, there is a LT reversal to the average return. The effectiveness of the reversal strategy is higher when the portfolio formation period is longer (i.e. in this case, there is a direct correlation between the formation period and the monthly return in contrast to the ST strategy). Therefore, the maximum monthly return of the arbitrage portfolio is achieved by the formation period of 36 months (as well as the investment period) and is about 0.87 percent.[1]

For the emerging Asian markets there are interesting studies which cover China's stock market. The Chinese market is unique because it is one of the largest (it is the second in terms of capitalization [\$53 trillion], second only to the US market), but on the other hand it is a relatively young (it started to function from the 1990s) and a fast-growing market, with the particularly expressed degree of stock's overvaluation. Investors in the Chinese market have limited investment choices, with a low rate of bank deposits and a closed (actually nontraded) bonds

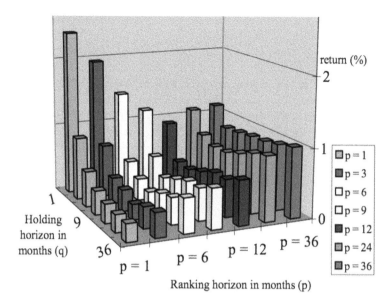

Figure 6.3 Various combinations of testing windows and reversal results by Chou *et al.* (2007). Average monthly contrarian profits (in %) in the Japanese market

market. The Chinese stock market is characterized by the higher than global multiples average values (the global price-earnings ratio is in the range 16–21, while for the Chinese market it is more than 40). The stock market crisis of summer 2015, which had a more than 30 percent index fall, and the unprecedented support measures by the government have shown this market to be highly fragile. The Chinese market is characterized by a certain isolation (with a separate market for foreign investors – the B Market, with quotes in dollars – and one for domestic investors – the A Market [the Shanghai Stock Exchange (SSE) and the Shenzhen Stock Exchange (SZSE)], with quotes in the local currency) and a relatively short observation period, which can bring the correction in the obtained results. A number of studies have been done at different time periods and at different samples of shares (A and B), so the findings are ambiguous (Kang, Liu and Ni (2002), Du and Nie (2007), Li, Qiu and Wu (2010) and Chen, Jiang and Li (2011)).

In the Kang *et al.* (2002) paper a STR effect was investigated in the eight-year period (from 1993 to 2000) and on a relatively small sample (in 1993 the sample consisted of only 48 stocks, in 1994 of 163, in 1995 of 268). The authors examined the returns for one-week periods (not for the traditionally monthly data) and 20th percentile portfolios (the stock sample was divided into five parts, depending on the cumulative return level). The formation and investment periods for the arbitrage portfolio ranged from 1 week to 26 weeks (0.5 years). Although the authors concluded that there is a ST reversal effect on the Chinese stock market, not all estimates for formation and investment periods for arbitrage portfolio were statistically significant. The maximum average return corresponds with the selection of a strategy with a one-week period of formation and investment for an arbitrage portfolio and is 1.8 percent.

In a more resent study, Chen *et al.* (2011) investigated STR effect on the 'A shares' China market during the period from 1995 to 2010 under different market states (SHSE and SZSE, including those having been delisted; 238 stocks at beginning of observation). Authors with overlapping methodologies documented statistically significant profits from contrarian strategies (four- to eight-week formatting and investment periods), especially during the period after 2007, when China (along with other markets) experienced an economic downturn following the worldwide financial crisis. Our calculations showed that the pre-crisis time interval from 2007 to 2010 was the 12-week period of portfolio formation and occurred within a one-month (1–4 weeks) period of investment to generate the weekly return arbitrage strategy (Lose–Win) of 0.6 percent. In the long-run analysis (1995–2010), the weekly return was slightly less than –0.3 percent.

Another interesting emerging Asia market for research is the Indian market (Sehgal and Balakrishnan (2002), Avramov, Goyal and Chordia (2006), Dhankar and Maheshwari (2014), and Kaur (2014)). It is unique because of the large number of shares on the stock exchange listings, high capitalization and the phenomenal growth rate of the whole economy and the stock index. Let us go through the results of the three works that deal with contrarian strategies on the Indian stock market.

Sehgal and Balakrishnan (2002) examined the stocks from the CRISIL-500 index for 10 years (from 1989 to 1999). The authors divided the sample into five groups and looked at 20 percentiles in the formation of the relative best and the worst portfolios (with equal weights of stocks in it). They concluded that there was a long-term reversal effect on the Indian capital market. The maximum yield of the arbitrage portfolio was observed during the 36-month investment period and 12-month formation period. The average annual return from this strategy was estimated by the authors at 6.48 percent. The losers' (P1) and the winners' (P5) portfolio return were, respectively, 27.24 percent and 12.11 percent.

The authors also showed that in the medium-term period the momentum effect was observed in the Indian market (see chapter 7, 'Momentum effect: pricing paradox or new beta strategy'). The maximum arbitrage (long–short) portfolio's return was achieved in the 12-month period of its formation and investment (the authors also introduced a short-term lag period, taking into account the possible STR effect).

In the next paper, Dhankar and Maheshwari (2014) considered a longer period (from 1997 to 2013). The stock sample was formed on the basis of the Indian National Stock Exchange (NSE) and included 328 of the most liquid shares. As in the previous work on the Indian market, the testing methodology was based on the 20 percentile and monthly steps for portfolio formation. The formation and investment period of the arbitrage portfolio ranged from 18 to 36 months.

The statistical significance was observed only in the long-term ranking and investment periods (36/24 and 36/36 in months), and the losers return exceeded

Table 6.1 Dhankar and Maheshwari (2014) results for the Indian stock market (1997–2013)

Average monthly returns of momentum and the contrarian strategy for different formation (F) and holding (H) periods

Formation periods in months	Portfolio	Holding period return in month (H)						
		H = 3	H = 6	H = 9	H = 12	H = 18	H = 24	H = 36
F = 18	Winner	-0.0004	-0.0206	-0.0013	-0.0246	-0.1132	-0.0704	-0.1367
	Loser	-0.01870	0.03287	0.04894	0.09106	0.05920	0.02842	0.03008
	Loser–Winner	-0.01820	0.05348	0.05030	0.11575	0.17244	0.10244	0.16678
	t-values	-0.458	0.993	0.670	1.458	1.780	1.242	1.499
F = 24	Winner	-0.00590	0.02095	0.03030	0.04093	-0.0185	-0.0907	-0.0505
	Loser	-0.0422	0.00813	0.00173	0.02403	0.01766	-0.0258	0.01882
	Loser–Winner	-0.03620	-0.01280	-0.02850	-0.01690	0.03626	0.06482	0.06935
	t-value	-0.930	-0.259	-0.365	-0.240	0.456	0.752	0.792
F = 36	Winner	-0.03450	-0.06690	-0.05920	-0.09420	-0.20750	-0.14841	-0.27710
	Loser	-0.08420	-0.04750	-0.07650	-0.03360	-0.01850	0.04167	0.08010
	Loser–Winner	-0.04970	0.01947	-0.01720	0.06059	0.18898	0.19008	0.35724
	t-values	-0.793	0.390	-0.217	0.597	1.610	2.454*	2.699*

the winners portfolio's return for the whole period by 29–35.7 percent (about 0.9 percent per month). At the same time, the authors did not spot any STR effect.

The peculiarity of the third paper by M. Kaur (2014) is the comparison of effects across economy sectors in a relatively short time period from 2005 to 2010. The author examined and compared results from contrarian strategy on 225 stocks of industrial companies and 112 stocks of service companies. Kaur (2014) showed that in the short and the medium term, the momentum effect was not observed. The mean reversal effect existed in the two industry samples for an investment period of 3 months and more (10 percent significance level). The highest statistically significant profitability in the industrial sector was observed during the portfolio formation and holding (investment) period of 9 months, on the service market (112 stocks of service companies) during the 9-month formation period and the 6-month investment period.

Beside the works on the Malaysia market (Arifin and Power (1996) and Hameed and Ting (2000) find the reversal effect in the Malaysian stock market), other notable papers dealing with emerging Asian markets are represented in academic journals. We consider the results for other Asian markets in comparison with our calculations in the period from 2002 to 2015.

3.0   Nature of mean reversal effect and lack of LT reversal factor after risk control

The nature of the reversal effect had dual explanation as a momentum effect. We suggest two main branches of explanations for the nature of the reversal effect: irrational (or behavioural) and rational.

It should be noted that empirical studies of these effects' nature disclosure prevail in the developed capital markets. In most papers on emerging markets, authors reveal the presence of ST and LT reversal and factors that may increase the abnormal return of the long–short strategy. Certainly, understanding the factors reveals the essence of the investigated effects.

The irrational explanation attempts to disclose the appearance of the reversal effect belonging to the realm of behavioural economics. Overreaction and under-reaction have become extremely important concepts in behavioural finance. The 'parents' of the reversal effect interpret this pattern as the result of irrational investor behaviour and cognitive biases. One of the theories suggested by Kahneman and Tversky (1979, 1982) – the overreaction concept – may be the driving source or reversal in stock returns. Overreaction postulates that investors tend to overweight recent information and underweight past events when revising their prospects.

Another feature of investor behaviour may be excessive optimism or pessimism. Typically, these conditions are linked with the situation in the economy, or with the expectation of significant events. For example, in the United States before the presidential elections, practitioners record growing trading activity and rising stock prices (mini-bubble). Analysts attribute this situation to increased waiting. Such behaviour leads to excessive optimism about good news and extreme

pessimism about dramatic events. Investors are able to overreact to both negative and positive news, pushing the prices of stocks away from their fundamental
values. However, there comes a time when investors are aware of overbought
shares and the direction of price changes, creating the reversal effect. Investors
realize that they have overreacted to news, and the greater the overreaction, the
greater the subsequent reversal effect. The impacts of macroeconomic factors on
momentum and contrarian profits are well explained by the superposition of the
effects on business cycles. T-bill yield, dividend yield, default spread and term
structure spread may be considered as sources of abnormal return of long–short
portfolios. Chordia and Shivakumar (2002) documented that during recession periods of business cycle momentum returns are negative (reversal effect is
detected) and statistically insignificant.

Traditionally slow investor's reaction to the news is seen as the basis of the
inertia in the stock's dynamic. The representativeness bias refers to making a decision based on stereotypes. Conservatism bias supposes that investors are too slow
with changing their opinions and are opposed to new information. Such underreaction to new information causes the positive serial returns correlations and the
subsequent effect on portfolio returns from past winners and losers (momentum
effect). Daniel, Hirschleifer and Subrahmanyam (1998) develop a theory that
argues that price momentum results from delayed overreactions induced by investor overconfidence and biased self-attribution.

The second approach attempts to relate the reversal effect to rational explanation concerning higher premium for risk, data-snooping or microstructure effects.

STR anomalies traditionally relate to microstructure biases. In particular, a
growing body of literature suggests that the STR effect is due to a lack of liquidity
as in a bid–ask spread (Kaul and Nimalendran, 1990; Conrad and Kaul, 1993).
The greater the spread, the greater the potential transaction costs. Empirically,
Avramov *et al.* (2006) find that the reversal effect occurs from positions in small,
high turnover and illiquid stocks. Liquidity suppliers get compensation for providing trading volume, causing prices to revert. The consensus of analysts is that
when investors exploit momentum investing they are able to skip one week or
one month to avoid a STR effect. Some academics argue that long-run and STR
effects are attributable to transaction costs. After taking into account the impact of
trading costs, the reversal effect becomes an illusion (Keim and Madhavan, 1997).
Lesmond *et al.* (2004) revisits the seminal papers of Jegadeesh and Titman (1993,
2001) through the inclusion of transaction costs and by utilizing four different
methods. Lesmond *et al.* (2004) documented that the profitability of momentum
and reversal investing is in doubt after a consideration of transaction costs.

One more potential explanation of the reversal effect may be based on rational
basis – risk differentials. Several studies attempt to propose a risk-based explanation for the long-run reversal effect. Zarowin (1990) and Chopra, Lakonishok
and Ritter (1992) find evidence that after controlling for size effect, the returns
of the losers are reduced. It should be noted that the losers' betas increase after
a period of abnormal (dramatic) loss (a similar situation with betas decrease for
winners) and we cannot use the last beta to assess the current and future risk. The

contrarian strategy is based on picking the riskier losers when the expected market risk premium is high. So the investor realizes an abnormal return, but that excess profit is a normal compensation for the risk.

An important paper by Fama and French (1996) created a turning point in the study of the long-run reversion effect. The authors have shown that their three-factor model (market risk, value effect and size) fully explains the long-run reversals.

A more recent study assumes that downside risk may be the more probable candidate to explain contrarian profits and develops the direction of earlier proposals (Chan, 1988; Ball and Kothari, 1989).

Additionally, like any financial anomaly, the reversal effect can be the result of data snooping and errors in statistical tests. Data snooping occurs when a given set of data is used more than once for inference or when model selection of the possible explanation of getting abnormal return is the result of data mining. In financial economics, there are examples of exposing previously shown results (see arguments by Jegadeesh (2000) and Asness, Frazzini, Israel and Moskowitz (2014)).

4.0   Short-term and long-run mean reversion and profitability of contrarian strategy in the eight Asian markets

Since only a few studies consider Asian markets for the reversal and due to the controversy of the results, there is an academic and a practical interest in comparing the results of different markets, when testing is implemented with the same principles.

The ambiguity of the results may be associated with different principles of portfolio construction and hypotheses testing. Therefore, for the Asian sample, we consider different design investment strategies: equal or nonequal weights, different percentiles, inclusion or not of those companies that have stopped listing and so on. There is an academic and a practical interest in comparing the results of different markets, when testing is implemented with the same principles.

We show below the results of testing for eight countries: China, India, Malaysia, Philippines, Taiwan, Korea, Indonesia and Thailand. The period of formation of portfolios is from 2002 to the end of 2015. The size of the samples used in the different markets and the principles of its formation are shown in Table 6.2. Table 6.3a summarizes the descriptive statistics for our sample. In Table 6.3b we show the sample sectors' structure. A number of studies have highlighted the importance of the industry to generate momentum and reversal effects. As can be seen from Table 6.3b, the sectoral structure of our sample is sufficient enough.

The problem with data on emerging capital markets is that the number of shares available for the formation of portfolios significantly changes over the years. We have taken into account this feature, and the appearance of new shares on the stock exchange, and we have modelled the possibility for investors to include these stocks in a portfolio, if stocks show relatively better or worse performance.

Table 6.2 Markets for contrarian strategy and samples

Market	Sampling at the end of the period (not less than)	Principle of sampling	The total number of portfolios in the strategy, which is considered for abnormal return calculation
China, (B shares)	102	The largest companies in the listing (for foreign investors)	288
India	190	The largest companies covering at least 85% of the market capitalization	323
Malaysia	42	MSCI Index	305
Indonesia	29	MSCI Index	273
Taiwan	96	MSCI Index	294
Korea	105	MSCI Index	305
Philippines	45	MSCI Index	282
Thailand	32	MSCI Index	303

In different years, the number of stocks in the sample changed. For example, the Shanghai Composite Index included 1044 securities in 2015 and less than 100 in 2002.

For the first step test we consider weekly return from Friday to Friday, when every week we are forming two portfolios with past relative winners and losers. The ranking period (observe the raw cumulative return for the period of portfolio formation) and investment were made equal. We used a 10th percentile (i.e. top return decile of stocks in national market were selected on win portfolios; similarly, 10 percent of the west stocks in the losers portfolio are selected).

Robustness check was realized through a change in the day of the week (analysis of calendar effects). Thus, the first step was compared with the monthly return of all the portfolios considered within eight strategies (e.g. 4/4 means 4 weeks for observation [ranking] and 4 weeks for investment), and the second step examined 40 strategies (8 strategies for each day of the week).

We used the overlapping methodology for portfolio constructing.

The following strategies are analyzed in weeks: 4/4, 12/12, 24/24, 36/36, 48/48, 96/96, 144/144 and 192/192. This corresponds to the periods of 1 month, 3 months, 6 months, 9 months, 1 year, 2 years, 3 years and 4 years.

An arbitrage portfolio (as a zero-cost strategy) was formed as the difference between the return of the portfolio Win and portfolio Los (Win–Los). It is the model's abnormal returns (see Table 6.4 and so on). Thus, the effect of the reversal was recorded (we recognize its existing) when we receive a statistically significant negative return for portfolios in a strategy (for example, the strategy 4/4 on Malaysia market examined 305 portfolios in the time interval from 2002 to 2015).

Table 6.3a Descriptive statistics for Eight market samples

Countries	Min capitalization, mln. $	Max capitalization, mln. $	Median capitalization, mln. $	Min EV/EBITDA	Max EV/EBITDA	MedianEV/EBITDA
Malaysia	361,820,000	8,841,000,000	1,249,630,000	4,910,000	45,310,000	12,750,000
Taiwan	215,290,000	98,118,930,000	1,952,680,000	1,260,000	50,750,000	9,270,000
Philippines	51,150,000	6,798,170,000	618,760,000	5,700,000	25,210,000	11,490,000
Korea	355,430,000	115,000,900,000	2,172,350,000	1,850,000	74,590,000	10,570,000
India	59,120,000	32,994,940,000	1,065,650,000	2,230,000	77,950,000	15,750,000
Indonesia	222,130,000	12,107,650,000	1,592,190,000	2,510,000	34,680,000	9,790,000
Thailand	460,290,000	15,162,930,000	2,338,270,000	1,830,000	47,040,000	12,260,000
China-B	138,480,000	16,253,280,000	1,667,660,000	0.49*	50.09*	2.34*

*For China we used the P/BV ratio instead of the EV/EBITDA ratio.

Table 6.3b Descriptive statistics for Eight market samples. Sector structures

Countries	Financial	Utilities	Basic materials	Commu- nications	Consumer, noncyclical	Diversified	Energy	Industrial	Consumer, cyclical	Technology	Total
Malaysia	21%	5%	2%	12%	19%	7%	12%	10%	12%	0%	100%
Taiwan	20%	0%	5%	5%	2%	0%	1%	26%	16%	25%	100%
Philippines	36%	13%	4%	9%	11%	7%	0%	4%	16%	0%	100%
Korea	17%	2%	9%	8%	13%	1%	4%	21%	21%	5%	100%
India	18%	5%	10%	4%	22%	1%	6%	16%	12%	5%	100%
Indonesia	28%	3%	0%	21%	28%	0%	7%	10%	3%	0%	100%
Thailand	25%	3%	9%	9%	13%	6%	16%	9%	9%	0%	100%
China-B	12%	3%	8%	3%	10%	0%	3%	28%	31%	2%	100%

The results of the first step of our study (Friday–Friday) are shown in Tables 6.2–6.9 for eight markets. For the Chinese market a statistically significant return on the contrarian strategy is fixed since 3 months (10 percent significance level) and the maximum monthly return (1.16–1.17 percent) is observed on the windows at 9 months and 1 year (Table 6.4).

Our results (Table 6.4) are partially different from those earlier mentioned empirical studies regarding the discovery of a reversal effect in the Chinese stock market. The majority of papers find evidence of a short-term (not exceeding three months) reversal effect and a long-term (longer than 1–1.5 years) one. In our study we suggest the statistically significant intermediate-term and long-term reversal.

Kang *et al.* (2002) find that STR effect is statistically significant in China using weekly data for the period of 1993 to 2000. They reported statistically significant reversal effect with formation periods of previous 1-, 2-, 4-, 8- and 12-week returns and holding period not longer than 16 weeks. Li *et al.* (2010) find evidence of abnormal returns for STR effect in the Chinese stock market for the formation and holding periods of 1 to 3 months with return of about 12 percent per annual on average for the period from 1994 to 2007. Using longer formation and holding periods, reversal effect is not observed. Du and Nie (2007) suggest substantial profitability of contrarian strategy using long-term holding and formation periods (18–36 months).

The best statistical result (Table 6.5) is observed on the windows 9 and 12 months (the opening of the investment strategy on Monday that gives 1.25 percent per month in the strategy 12/12). (1-Monday,. . . 5-Friday)

For the Indian market by 1 month, the strategy shows a negative abnormal return (Table 6.6), but the statistical significance is not large (less than 20 percent). The 323 portfolio reversal effect was observed only for the amount of 169 (52 percent). At 3 and 6 months there is a momentum effect (the strategy of

Table 6.4 China market (B shares) and abnormal return. Intermediate-term and long-term reversal

Abnormal month returns	t-stat	p-value	$J = \kappa$	Amount of negative portfolios
−0.002	0.40	0.686	1 month	134
−0.004	1.65	0.100	3 months	143
−0.007	3.65	0.000	6 months	166
−0.012	5.65	0.000	9 months	166
−0.012	6.30	0.000	1 year	189
−0.002	2.85	0.005	2 years	169
0.001	2.22	0.027	3 years	112
−0.001	1.70	0.090	4 years	127

Table 6.5 China market (B shares) ranking strategies on weekdays

Day of the week	Abnormal month returns	t-stat	p-value	J = κ, months	Amount_ of_negative
1	−0.0125	6.47	0.000	12	184
4	−0.0124	6.92	0.000	12	200
1	−0.0123	5.60	0.000	9	161
3	−0.0122	6.57	0.000	12	197
5	−0.0118	6.30	0.000	12	189
5	−0.0117	5.65	0.000	9	166
4	−0.0116	5.62	0.000	9	166
2	−0.0111	6.31	0.000	12	193
2	−0.0107	5.34	0.000	9	170

Table 6.6 Contrarian abnormal return in the Indian stock market

Abnormal month returns	t-stat	p value	J = κ, months	Amount of negative
−0.005	1.34	0.183	1	169
0.011	3.56	0.000	3	118
0.004	1.30	0.194	4	104
−0.001	0.39	0.699	6	104
0.000	0.15	0.884	1 year	111
−0.004	1.87	0.063	2 year	142
−0.007	3.90	0.000	3 year	213
−0.010	4.75	0.000	4 year	187

opening a long position on the past relative winners and short selling on the past relative losers brings about 0.36–0.08 percent per month. The best strategy design is 3/3 months). The statistically significant reversal effect in the intervals of 2–4 years (Table 6.3) with a maximum monthly returns on the two windows in the 4 years (1 percent per month from 0 percent significance – 187 portfolios showed negative profitability for Win–Los).

Our finding is consistent with previous studies. In agreement with the previous paper we find the presence of short-term and long-term reversal effect on the Indian stock market. Sehgal and Balakrishnan (2002) were the first who confirmed the presence of the long-term return reversal effect in the Indian stock market. Kaur (2014) explores contrarian strategy on the Indian stock market from April 2005 to March 2010. He discovered strong return contrarian effect across a variety of formation and holding periods (from 1 till 12 months). There is no momentum effect observed in the Indian stock market. In strategies with equal ranking and investment windows, we also document the lack of a momentum effect. Maheshwari and Dhankar (2015) find a phenomenon when stock returns exhibit reversal effect over a time horizon of more than 36 months in line with our results (longer horizons in the Indian market increased profitability of contrarian strategy).

The reversal effect is recorded in the Malaysian stock market for 2 years windows (Table 6.7). With high statistical significance monthly return of contrarian strategy is 0.33 percent (184 portfolios from 305 available to analyze portfolios provide a positive result of this strategy). Within one year, we document the momentum effect (0.4–0.9 percent per month). The best statistical result of the momentum strategy is fixed on the window at 4 months and gives 0.7 percent monthly abnormal return (only 89 portfolios show negative results of investing).

According to the literature on the Malaysian stock market, Arifin and Power (1996) found some evidence of short-run reversal effect, especially in the first two weeks after portfolio formation date, using weekly data from a very short horizon: 1990 to 1994. Hameed and Ting (2000) suggest a strong positive relationship between the short-term contrarian profits and the level of trading activity. Our sample includes highly liquid Malaysian stocks and so the result is indicative.

According to the Indonesian stock market (Table 6.8), although a negative return on Win–Los portfolios is fixed already since the 2-year windows, but the statistical significance observed in the 3 year portfolio's design. The monthly return of contrarian strategy is 1.2 percent with 140 portfolios with the 'correct result' from 273 portfolios. Maximum return can be earned by the investor while investing for 4 years (7.4 percent per month return).

Within 1–3 months and 9 months our results show the statistical significance of the momentum strategy (1.66–0.1 percent per month return) for Indonesian stock market (Table 6.8).

Bismark and Pasaribu (2011) exploring data on Indonesian stock market within the shortest period of time (from 2003 to 2007) concluded that the reversal

Table 6.7 LT reversal in the Malaysian stock market

Abnormal month returns	t-stat	p-value	J = K, months	Amount of negative
0.009	2.66	0.008	1	135
0.007	3.34	0.001	3	119
0.007	*3.69*	*0.000*	*4*	*89*
0.006	3.36	0.001	6	111
0.004	2.44	0.015	1 year	125
−0.003	3.33	0.001	2 year	184
0.002	3.39	0.001	3 year	142
0.000	0.34	0.731	4 year	174

Table 6.8 The Indonesian stock market. Short-term and intermediate momentum effect and long-term reversal

Abnormal month (Win–Los) returns	t-stat	p-value	J = K	Amount of negative
0.017	2.13	0.034	1 month	129
0.012	2.24	0.026	3 months	110
0.001	0.15	0.882	6 months	95
0.009	1.86	0.063	9 months	94
0.003	0.79	0.431	1 year	104
−0.003	0.69	0.490	2 years	123
−0.012	3.04	0.003	3 years	140
−0.074	11.28	0.000	4 years	204

Table 6.9 The Taiwan stock market. Intermediate momentum effect and long-term reversal

Abnormal month (Win–Los) return	t-stat	p-value	J = K	Amount of negative
0.008	1.85	0.065	1 month	124
0.013	*4.30*	*0.000*	*3 months*	*96*
0.001	0.18	0.858	6 months	121
−0.003	1.20	0.231	9 months	135
−0.004	2.30	0.022	1 year	145
0.002	2.69	0.008	2 years	124
0.005	5.87	0.000	3 years	126
0.000	0.34	0.731	4 years	154

pattern does not occur in Indonesia Stock Exchange (BEI) in all periods (quarterly, semiannually, and yearly) in particular stocks incorporated in the LQ-45. Our sample is smaller and includes the largest liquid stocks, a longer time period of analysis revealed the LT (3–4 years) reversal effect.

According to the Taiwan stock market (Table 6.9) the mean reversal effect is observed on the two windows to one year. The abnormal return is 0.43 percent per month with 12/12 strategy's design (145 portfolios from 294 corresponds to the expectations of the strategy). Up to 3 months, there is a momentum effect (1.3 percent is an abnormal monthly return for 3 months investment and formations windows).

On the stock market of Korea (Table 6.10) contrarian strategy is profitable if the windows exceed 2 years. For strategies 2, 3 and 4 years, the strategy brings abnormal return not less than 0.8 percent per month. The maximum efficiency

Table 6.10 Momentum and LT contrarian strategies in the Korean stock market

Abnormal month (Win–Los) return	t-stat	p-value	J = K	Amount of negative
0.000	0.10	0.920	6 months	151
0.004	1.50	0.133	9 months	147
0.004	*1.77*	*0.078*	*1 year*	*138*
−0.008	6.62	0.000	2 years	189
−0.017	13.88	0.000	3 years	223
−0.025	23.50	0.000	4 years	293

Table 6.11 Pronounced LT reversal effect in the Philippines stock market

Abnormal month (Win–Los) return	t-stat	p-value	J = K	Amount of negative
−0.001	0.21	0.830	1 month	138
−0.002	0.44	0.657	3 months	139
−0.003	1.09	0.278	6 months	137
−0.003	1.05	0.293	9 months	148
−0.006	2.77	0.006	1 year	175
−0.009	3.49	0.001	2 years	171
−0.019	9.12	0.000	3 years	195
−0.009	3.43	0.001	4 years	152

of this trading (arbitrage) strategy fixed at 4 years – monthly return is 2.5 percent (293 portfolios from 305 (93 percent) provide a positive return of this strategy). ST reversal effect can be recognized in the period of 1 month (0.4 percent) with statistical significance within 10 percent.

With a window of more than 1 year, in the stock market of the Philippines also observed a positive investment result for the contrarian strategy (Table 6.11). Maximum return is observed at 3 years (1.8 percent per month). Statistically significant return on strategies with design from 1 to 4 years is not less than 0.6 percent per month. As in China, viewed eight strategies with the same ranking and investment windows (more than 1 year) give a positive result for the contrarian strategy, but up to 1 year period, this result is statistically not significant.

In the market of Thailand (Table 6.12), a statistically significant result for contrarian strategy provides for 3 and 4 years. The best result on the windows of 4 years/4 years with abnormal return is 1.07 percent per month. From 303 portfolios, this strategy provides a positive result in 61 percent (185 out of 303 portfolios). Within one year there is revealed a momentum effect (1.3–1.8 percent per month).

Table 6.12 The Thailand stock market. Pronounced LT reversal effect and medium-term momentum effect

Abnormal month (Win–Los) return	t-stat	p-value	J = K	Amount of negative
−0.005189	1.002528	0.316891	1 month	162
0.002539	0.879421	0.379872	3 months	149
0.006964	2.457653	0.014547	6 months	109
0.013381	*6.105984*	*0*	*9 months*	*78*
0.018413	*8.460292*	*0*	*1 year*	*73*
0.003627	2.084482	0.037956	2 years	136
−0.006626	5.026679	0.000001	3 years	185
−0.010742	7.659352	0	4 years	185

Table 6.13 Taiwan stock market. Ranking strategies to maximize contrarian strategy's return

day	Abnormal (Win–Los) return	t-stat	p-value	J = K, months	Amount of negative
1	−0.005462	2.92588	0.003701	12	149
3	−0.004496	2.501264	0.012894	12	163
5	−0.004261	2.300818	0.022104	12	145
4	−0.004235	2.304644	0.021867	12	147
2	−0.003559	1.939132	0.053398	12	142

The robustness check we provide through changing the day of the week for opening investment position (1 – from Monday to Monday, 2 – from Tuesday to Tuesday, and so on, Friday – Day 5).

We repeat this, as a change in the investment decision of the day of the week changes the conclusion when there is abnormal return (positive return on contrarian strategy) in the Asian markets.

Strategies with the best results of investing in the market of Taiwan are shown in Table 6.13. The Chinese market strategy indicates the maximum return at the opening position on Monday.

5.0 Summary and conclusion

In summary, our results (Table 6.13) show that a short-term (one-month) reversal effect is not revealed in the stock return dynamics on eight Asian markets. There is a general tendency to long-run mean -reversion on periods of two to three years (the average estimation for the markets). Contrarian profits are higher during the crisis period of 2008–2010.

Compilation of the results of previous studies and our findings allowed us to make some important recommendations for investors, enabling them to boost the profitability of contrarian strategy. For those readers of the chapter who are going to make money on the contrarian strategy we document that profitability of contrarian effect depends on market state. The contrarian strategy following a bear market generates higher abnormal return than those following a bullish ("up") market. So, this strategy should be used as a shelter when the market is in decline. Contrarian effect is significant in both bullish and bearish states. The ST contrarian effect disappears in bullish market states.

It is consensus opinion that between reversal effect and size the inverse relationship is observed: the smaller the company's size, the more pronounced the effect. In particular, Chopra *et al.* (1992) concluded that larger arbitrage portfolio return (Loser–Winner) is provided for smaller firms. A similar conclusion was that significant contrarian effect persists after controlling the size and came to work on the Asian markets: Chinese (Kang *et al.*, 2002), Japanese (Chang *et al.*, 1995). We are warned that the small companies are generally less liquid, which affects transaction costs. Therefore, when applying contrarian strategy on small companies, the investor has to take into account the influence of transaction costs.

More liquid assets are more likely to show reverse effect. It is related to the tendency of high liquid stocks to respond on news rapidly (see Hameed and Ting (2000) on Malaysian stock market).

There is a positive relationship between the seasonality effect and the reversal effect. So the contrarian strategy is able to be statistically and economically significant in January. In December, the end of the year investors optimize their portfolios for minimizing tax payments and selling losers. Moreover portfolio managers sell (buy) assets that have underperformed (outperformed) during the year in order to make their portfolio look more appealing (so-called window dressing). In January market investors and portfolio managers begin their histories from scratch that allows them to take higher risk and buy previous losers (see DeBondt and Thaler, 1987; Zarowin, 1990; Ahmad and Hussain, 2001 regarding to Chinese New Year Effect).

Note

1 T-statistics of the returns estimates are adjusted for possible heteroscedasticity and autocorrelation.

Reference

Ahmad, Z., and Hussain, S. (2001). KLSE long run overreaction and the Chinese new-year effect. *Journal of Business Finance & Accounting, 28*(1–2), 63–105.
Arifin, M. N., and Power, D. M. (1996). Some evidence of short-run market overreaction for the Kuala Lumpur stock exchange. *Capital Market Review, 4*, 21–32.

Asness, C. S., Frazzini, A., Israel, R., and Moskowitz, T. J. (2014). Fact, fiction and momentum investing. *Journal of Portfolio Management*, Fall (40th Anniversary Issue).

Avramov, D., Goyal, A., and Chordia, T. (2006). Autocorrelations in individual stock returns. *Journal of Financial Economics*, 81(2), 339–377.

Balvers, R. J., Yangru, W., and Gilliland, E. (2000). Mean reversion across national stock markets and parametric contrarian investment strategies, *Journal of Finance*, 55, 745–772.

Baytas, A., and Cakici, N. (1999). Do markets overreact: International evidence. *Journal of Banking and Finance*, 23(7), 1121–1144.

Bismark, R., and Pasaribu, F. (2011). Overreaction anomaly in Indonesian stock exchange. *Journal of Economics and Business*, 5(2), 87–115.

Chan, K. C. (1988). On the contrarian investment strategy. *Journal of Business*, 61(2), 147–163.

Chang, R. P., McLeavey, D. W., and Rhee, S. G., (1995). Short-term abnormal returns of the contrarian strategy in the Japanese stock market. *Journal of Business Finance and Accounting*, 22(7), 1035–1048.

Chen, Q., Jiang, Y., and Li, Y. (2011). State of market and the contrarian strategy: Evidence from China's stock market. *Journal of Chinese Economic and Business Studies*, 10(1), 89–108.

Chopra, N., Lakonishok, J., and Ritter, J. R. (1992). Measuring abnormal performance: Do stocks overreact? *Journal of Financial Economics*, 31(2), 235–268.

Chordia, T., and Shivakumar, L. (2002). Momentum, business cycle and time-varying expected returns. *Journal of Finance*, 57(2), 985–1019.

Chou, P. H., Wei, K. C., and Chung, H. (2007). Sources of contrarian profits in the Japanese stock market. *Journal of Empirical Finance*, 14(3), 261–286.

Conrad , J., and Kaul, G. (1998). An anatomy of trading strategies. *Review of Financial Studies*, 11(3), 489–519.

Conrad, J., and Kaul, G. (1993). Long-term market overreaction or biases in computed returns? *The Journal of Finance*, 48(1), 39–63.

Dhankar, Raj S., and Maheshwari, S. (2014). A study of contrarian and momentum profits in Indian stock market. *International Journal of Financial Management*, 4(2), 40–54.

Du, X.-Q., and Nie, Z.-P. (2007). Medium-term and long-term momentum and contrarian effects on China during 1994–2004. *Journal of Modern Accounting and Auditing*, 3(2), 63–69.

Fama, E. F. and French, K. R. (1996). Multifactor explanations of asset pricing anomalies. *The Journal of Finance*, 51(1), 55–84

Hameed, A., and Ting, S. (2000). Trading volume and short-horizon contrarian profits: Evidence from the Malaysian market. *Pacific-Basin Finance*, 8(1), 67–84.

Daniel, K., Hirshleifer, D., and Subrahmanyam A. (1998). Investor psychology and security market under- and over-reactions, *Journal of Finance*, 53, 1839–1886.

DeBondt, W., and haler, R., 1987. Further evidence of overreaction and stock market seasonality. *Journal of Finance* 42, 557–581.

De Bondt, W. F.M., and Thaler, R (1985). Does the stock market overreact? *The Journal of Finance*, 40(3), 793–805.

Jegadeesh, N. (1990). Evidence of predictable behavior of security returns. *Journal of Finance*, 45(3), 881–898.

Jegadeesh, N. (1991). Seasonality in stock price mean reversion: Evidence from the U.S. and the U.K. *Journal of Finance*, 46(4), 1427–1444.

Jegadeesh, N. (2000). Discussion on foundation of technical analysis. *Journal of Finance, 55*(4), 1765–1770.

Jegadeesh, N., and Titman, S. (1993). Returns to buying winners and selling losers: Implications for stock market efficiency. *Journal of Finance, 48*(1), 65–91.

Jegadeesh N., and Titman S. (2001). Profitability of momentum strategies: an evaluation of alternative explanations. *Journal of Finance, 56,* 699–720.

Kahneman, D., and Tversky, A. (1979). Prospect theory: An analysis of decision under risk. *Econometrica, 47,* 263–291.

Kahneman, D., and Tversky, A. (1982). The psychology of preferences. *Scientific American, 246,* 160–173.

Kang, J., Liu, M., and Ni, X. (2002). Contrarian and momentum strategies in the China stock market: 1993–2000. *Pacific-Basin Finance Journal, 10*(3), 243–265.

Conrad, J., Kaul, G., and Nimalendran, M. (1991). Components of short-horizon individual security returns. *Journal of Financial Economics, 29*(2), 365–384.

Kaur, M. (2014). Contrarian effect and industry type in the Indian stock market. *PARIPEX Indian Journal of Research, 3*(5), 35–37.

Keim, D. B., and Madhavan, A. (1997). Transactions costs and investment style: an inter-exchange analysis of institutional equity trades, *Journal of Financial Economics, 46,* 265–292.

Lehmann, B. (1990). Fads, martingales and market efficiency, *Quarterly Journal of Economics, 105,* 1–28.

Lesmond, D. A., Schill, M. J. and Zhou, C. (2004). The illusory nature of momentum profits. *Journal of Financial Economics, 71*(2), 349–380.

Li, B., Qiu, J., and Wu, Y. (2010). Momentum and seasonality in Chinese stock markets. *Journal of Money, Investment and Banking, 17,* 24–36.

Lo, A. W., and Mackinlay, A. C. (1990). Data-snooping biases in tests of financial asset pricing models, *Review of Financial Studies* 3, 431–468.

Lo, A. W., Mamaysky, H., and Wang, J. (2000). Foundation of technical analysis: Computations algorithms, statistical inference and empirical implementation. *Journal of Finance, 55*(4), 1705–1765.

Maheshwari, S., and Dhankar, Raj S. (2015). The long-run return reversal effect: A re-examination in the Indian stock market. *The Journal of Business Inquiry, 14*(2), 59–78.

Park, S.-C. (2010). The moving average ratio and momentum. *Financial Review, 45*(2), 415–447.

Schiereck, D., De Bondt, W., and Weber, M. (1999). Contrarian and momentum strategies in Germany. *Financial Analysts Journal, 55*(6), 104–116.

Sehgal, S., and Ilango, B. (2002). Contrarian and momentum strategies in the Indian capital market. *VIKALPA, 27*(1), 13–19.

Shi, H.-L., Jiang, Z.-Q., and Zhou, W.-X. (2015). Profitability of contrarian strategies in the Chinese stock market. *PLoS One, 10*(9), 1–22.

Zarowin, P. (1990). Size, seasonality and stock market overreaction. *Journal of Financial and Quantitative Analysis, 25*(1), 113–125.

7 The momentum effect
Pricing paradox or new beta strategy

Tamara Teplova and Evgeniya Mikova

1.0 Introduction

The efficient markets hypothesis (EMH) postulates (Fama, 1970) that market prices fully reflect all available information and fundamental analysis (market, industry or stock specific and past performance) cannot be exploited to earn abnormal returns. Prices should react quickly and correctly to the news; they should neither overreact nor underreact to information, and so no price trends or reversals should be observed in the financial assets market. The predictability of stock returns is considered as one of the challenges facing EMH. The most striking evidence against the EMH is the existence of intermediate (from three months to one year) momentum in stock return (the tendency of past relative winners to continue to outperform past relative losers).

Appealing to the roots of the momentum effect and momentum style of investing, Jegadeesh and Titman discovered in 1993 that their work was following well-known papers by De Bondt and Thaler (1985, 1987). Jegadeesh and Titman (1993) documented the pattern that the portfolios consisting of the stocks that have demonstrated relatively high return in the past (within the time periods from 3 months up to one year, the authors covered 16 combinations of selection and investment windows; 3/3, 3/6, 3/9, etc.) retain their leading positions in terms of profit – they continue to outperform the stocks with relatively worse results for the past 3–12 months by 1 percent per month on the US stock market. Such pattern for winners to keep winning and for losers to keep losing is preserved in average up to one year.

2.0 Time series and cross-section momentum effect

Since 1980 practitioners and academics have extrapolated the concept of inertial motion or momentum to financial markets. Technical analysts consider momentum oscillators to help identify trend lines and obtain the signal for overbought and oversold conditions in a security. Another large group of investigations deals with different investment strategies based on the momentum effect (trend-follow effects on single asset or cross-section momentum for portfolios). Strategy is based on 'momentum rule' when investors buy past winners and sell past losers.

This strategy will generate abnormal returns in the medium run, which cannot be explained by conventional risk measures (e.g. the standard deviation or the market beta). Grinblatt *et al.* (1995) find that about 77 percent of mutual funds in their sample use momentum strategies in their investment portfolios. This strategy proved to be profitable at the level of national stocks indices (e.g. Cenedese, Payne, Sarno and Valente, 2013) and for stock's portfolio formation (Rouwenhorst, 1998, 1999), among currencies (Menkhoff, Sarno, Schmeling and Schrimpf, 2012), commodities, bonds and other assets (Asness, Moskowitz and Pedersen, 2013).

Stock price momentum strategy can be implemented on single asset (trend-following strategy) or on a cross-section of the same class of assets by creating only long, only short or simultaneously long–short momentum portfolios based on relative past stocks' performance. The trend-following style uses different indicators (past average returns, moving average ratios and so on) to obtain signals to buy or sell the security by comparing past performance with the current ones.

The cross-section momentum effect is observed among portfolios of the same class of assets (bonds, stocks, currency) and based on their past relative performance (e.g. prior returns or different measures of risk and return). Trading strategies involving selecting the 'right' stocks based on past returns have become one of the traditional measures for testing stock market efficiency (with autocorrelation tests and delays in stock reactions in various corporate events [(reports publication and other news)]).

Now there is accumulating evidence for the momentum and mean reversal effects that challenge the validity of the weak form of EMH and that has attracted the attention of both academics and practitioners. Many papers have been devoted to both disclosure and documenting such puzzling anomalies, such as profits evaluation of trading strategies and search for an adequate explanation of the observed evidence. Although momentum strategies became a well-organized investment style in many markets (Chan, Jegadeesh and Lakonishok (1996), Asness, Frazzini, Israel and Moskowitz (2014), Asness et al. (2015)) and the existence of momentum is a well-established empirical fact, the debate remains regarding its efficacy and its use as a practical investment tool. Money managers and the academic community is still out on whether momentum is a behavioural or risk-based factor.

The crucial question for the momentum strategy – 'what theory?' 'it has no theory.' There is much debate regarding the explanation behind momentum as other robust return premia, such as size and value effects. The study of such stock pricing anomalies is an important area of financial economics.

3.0   Steps in understanding the effect: from US to national markets

The first empirical paper examines the US market (Jegadeesh and Titman (1993), Asness (1994)). In general strategies that include buying winning stocks (stocks with high returns over the previous three months to one year) and selling losing stocks (stocks with low returns over the same period, the so-called formation period), earn profits of about 1 percent per month for the following months within the year.

Current research is increasingly expanding the time horizon of the analysis. For example Geczy and Samonov (2013) considered the behaviour of prices from 1801 to 2012.

National capital markets deserve special consideration. Hurn and Pavlov (2003) obtained momentum profits evidence from the Australian market, Ismail (2012), and Sakr, Ragheb, Ragab and Abdou (2014) provided evidence on the Egyptian market, Martin and Malabika (2015) on the Indian. Mixed results were obtained for the Chinese market: the existence of reversal rather than relative strength (momentum) effects (Wang, 2004). Teplova and Mikova (2015a) investigated the cross-section momentum effect in the Japanese stock market over the period January 1997 to December 2013, sub-periods before August 2008 and during the crisis September 2008–2009. The authors have shown the conditional nature of momentum and identified the characteristics of companies and their stocks and market states, allowing investors to earn positive momentum profit in the Japanese market (the statistically significant positive monthly return of zero-cost portfolios is not less than 1 percent). This study highlights the limitation of standard notions on momentum profits.

Some papers measured momentum profits internationally. Rouwenhorst (1998) found evidence supporting the existence of momentum strategies in 12 European markets during the period 1980–1995. Additional evidence has been found by Hameed and Kusnadi (2002) from Pacific Basin stock markets. Griffin *et al.* (2003) analyzed samples from all the continents. The results showed that momentum profits are significant in all regions except Asia. Emerging markets showed weaker profits compared to developed ones. Results in developed markets are quite stable (excluding Japan). Asness (2011) showed that for Japan market the momentum strategy gives zero historical momentum premium. Results for the Japanese market differ with the common understanding of the momentum in the developed capital markets (Liu and Lee, 2001; Fama and French, 2012; Asness *et al.*, 2013; Teplova and Mikova, 2015b).

The results of emerging markets seem somehow mixed. Perhaps this is due to the relatively short empirical horizon of testing (no history of stock trading since the beginning of the 20th century), and the small number of liquid shares. For instance, there are only 48 stocks in the sample for year 1993 in Kang *et al.* (2002)'s study (for first year of portfolio formation). In some papers the authors ascertain the momentum effect, in some cases – no. Hameed and Yuanto (2002) studied momentum strategies in six Asian countries and they did not find conclusive evidence of the momentum effect.

The work by Hart *et al.* (2002) presents the testing of 32 emerging capital markets; however the statistical significance (*t*-statistic) of benefits of the momentum investment is proved for six markets only. Thus, the research with cross-country comparison (Chan *et al.*, 2000; Abinzano *et al.*, 2010; Chao *et al.*, 2012; Cakici *et al.*, 2013) showed that the cross-section portfolio momentum effect is more evident in the developed capital markets exactly, and the market tensions are not able to fully explain the gain difference between countries. It may be noted among Asian markets work in Taiwan (Wang, 2014).

4.0   Nature of the momentum effect

Most theories explaining the phenomenon of momentum profits fall into one of two categories: risk-based and behavioural. Academic community and practices does not have a single opinion on which of these explanations is better. The Nobel Prize committee 2013 year couldn't decide and split the prize between the two camps: rational (Eugene Fama) and irrational (Robert Shiller). Israel and Moskowitz (2013) take up issue of degradation effect in time. Authors looked at a host of out-of-sample periods for momentum (after the original momentum studies were published) to see if there was any degradation in its returns. Interestingly, they did not find any evidence of degradation. This conclusion emphasize that we are talking about systematic effects, which should be included in the pricing model.

As momentum strategies generate high returns with insignificant overall market risk, the momentum return is either evidence for market inefficiency or a compensation for another (unrecognized) risk factor. We give brief comments on two alternative positions and show the common ground.

The basic explanation of the majority of anomalies in asset pricing is the attempt to connect the observed excess returns with the compensation for taking higher risk by investor. In particular, Daniel and Moskowitz (2013) make a conclusion that the momentum returns distribution (on the formed portfolios) is strongly left-skewed (it is referred to a long fat left tail), which denotes low possibility of achieving extremely negative returns that is unwillingly for rational investors. In the US stock market, within the period of 1929–2010, or 978 months, it was 13 times when the momentum strategy generates losses exceeding 20 percent per month. In some papers there were attempts to find a correlation between the cross-sectional momentum factor and momentum profits (Brennan, Chordia and Subrahmanyam, 1998) or the industry momentum factor (Grundy and Martin, 2001). The momentum effect was also tested by factors of liquidity and trading costs (Frazzini et al, 2013, Lee and Swaminathan, 2000, Lee and Swaminathan, 2000), value and size, by conditional and unconditional constructions and by downside risk measures. However, it could be said with certainty that currently (Van der Hart, De Zwart and Van Dijk, 2005) there is no model supported by theoretical background. Out-of-sample empirical evidences are capable to explain the existence of the momentum effect.

The behavioural models typically explain momentum as either an underreaction or delayed overreaction phenomenon (Shefrin and Statman, 1985). Overreaction and underreaction have become extremely important concepts in behavioural finance. Underreaction case postulates that information travels slowly into prices because of investors being too conservative, being inattentive, facing liquidity issues, or displaying the disposition effect (sell winners too quickly and hold onto losers too long). So, cognitive biases drive the momentum effect. Overreaction is observed in cases when investors chase profits, providing a feedback mechanism that drives prices higher and higher.

According to Chan *et al.* (1996), Grinblatt and Han (2005) and Daniel, Hirshleifer and Subrahmanyam (1998), the conservatism and representativeness biases can explain the medium-term momentum effect. The disposition effect also can drive price momentum (Grinblatt and Han (2002)). Conservatism bias supposes that investors are too slow to change their opinions and are opposed to new information. Such underreaction to new information causes the positive serial returns correlations or a momentum effect. The representativeness bias refers to making a decision based on stereotypes. In other words, investors neglect the laws of probability and behave as if recent events are typical of the return-generating process. Hong and Stein (1999) propose a model describing the interaction between two types of investor: news watchers and noisy (momentum) traders. The former group makes forecasts based on fundamental analysis, ignoring the past price changes, whereas the latter condition their demand on past prices. Hong and Stein (1999) assume that fundamental information distributed gradually among news watchers results in an initial underreaction of the entire market, causing the momentum to begin. Momentum traders interpret this as a signal, pushing the price of past winners (losers) above (below) the fundamental value. The growing mispricing stimulates news watchers to take action in order to prevent it. Overreaction produces a long-term reserve on stock price. Therefore the Hong and Stein (1999) model explains both short-term continuation and long-term reversal.

Trying to empirically test the disposition effect on the Egypt stock market behaviour and momentum is represented by recent Sakr *et al.* (2014).

In contrast to previous theories based on underreaction, Daniel *et al.* (1998) develop a theory which argues that price momentum results from delayed overreactions induced by investor overconfidence and biased self-attribution.

Behavioural explanation of momentum effect is that it reflects slow diffusion of information. So this effect should be more pronounced in small firms (stocks). Lesmond, Schill and Zhou (2014) point out that the majority of momentum portfolio abnormal returns are from stocks that are 'small, high beta, and off-NYSE'. Therefore, academic interest is testing in large companies in emerging markets, that stocks are sufficiently liquid. Below we show the evaluating strategy's profits for large companies in Japan and Indian stock markets.

As already stated above, adherents to the rational financial theories try to relate the momentum profits to risk-based explanations (Conrad and Kaul, 1993; Fama and French, 1996). By rational explanation can be referred the evidence of errors in data mining. Data-snooping bias is one possible explanation for the abnormal return of momentum strategy. Another possible explanation is related to the underestimation of transaction costs and short-selling constraints (Korajczyk and Sadka, 2004).

Business risks that affect firm investment and economic growth impact the long-term cash flows and firm's dividends that generate momentum patterns. High- momentum stocks face greater cash flow risk because of their growth prospects due to their investment opportunities, causing them to face a higher cost of capital (greater discount rate).

For example, Conrad and Kaul (1993) showed that the momentum effect is driven by cross-section variations in expected returns rather than time series variations. This contribution requires searching for a convenient asset pricing model that can fully explain unconditional cross-section variation. Berk, Green and Nike (1999) confirmed that the momentum effect can be explained by a time-varying systematic risk inherent in each company (time-varying beta). Some recent risk-based models that deliver momentum: Berk, Green and Naik (1999), Johnson (2002), Zhang (2004), Sagi and Seasholes (2007), Asness *et al.* (2013).

The asymmetry of the reaction to the news and risk-taking explanation allow to hypothesize asymmetry in the upside and downside risks: the past winners and the past losers are differently exposed to the upside and downside market risks (winners systematically have higher relative downside market betas and lower relative upside market betas than losers).

Fama and French (1996) attempted to explain the momentum effect by traditional asset pricing models (CAPM and 3FF model) but had to admit that significant abnormal returns from the momentum strategy still existed even after controlling for market risk, size and value factors.

Four-factor Carhart (1997) model developing three-factor model Fama and French (3FF) and can be represented as follows:

$$E(r_{it}) - r_{0t} = \alpha_i + \beta_{i1}(r_{pt} - r_{0t}) + b_{i2}SMB_t + b_{i3}HML_t + b_{i4}WML + e_{it},$$

where WML – a new factor (the fourth), introduced Carhart to explain differences in returns; r_{0t} – risk-free rate; $E(r_{it})$ – expected i- asset return at time t; r_{pt} – market return; $(r_{pt} - r_{0t})$ – risk premium for the market portfolio (MRP) as the portfolio average risk in the market (the first factor FF3 model); α – constant; b_{i1}, b_{i2}, b_{i3} – sensitivity coefficients of ith stock return of a change in risk premium (first risk factor – market risk, sensitivity to the market dynamic – beta as a traditional measure of the market risk), second risk factor – the size (the size' risk premia) and belongs to a group of stocks – value or growth (the third factor).

The SMB (small minus big) – a size factor introduced into the model as the average premium for the size; HML (high minus low) – the third factor, showing the difference in the average return of the portfolios with high and low book-to-market value stock's ratio (B/M); i.e. the unsystematic part of the return of the ith stocks (not explained by the model), 'white noise.'

A recent study by Fama and French (2012) has tested four-factor Carhart model (1997) in global capital markets, including emerging markets (25 portfolios were analyzed on the criteria of the 'size-momentum' and 'size-BV / MV'). The authors used data on 23 markets, grouped in four regions: North America, Japan, Europe and the Asia Pacific region (sample was formed in the interval from November 1989 to March 2011). Interestingly, the authors obtained evidence of the significance of the momentum factor. Thus, the momentum strategy can be considered as one of the beta strategies.

Since the significance of momentum profit is not absolute for different markets, the academics are seeking more adequate expression of this risk premium. Another possible explanation derives from Cooper, Gutierrez and Hameed's (2004) study based on the conditional nature of momentum. Momentum nature can be attributed to asymmetric recognition of the information on the different periods of economic growth. Momentum payoffs can be low or negative following periods of decline in aggregate market valuations (or 'DOWN – market' state, bearish periods) and momentum profits should be strong following 'UP' states. We hypothesize that the state dependence on momentum profits may explain a glaring exception in the momentum literature about the Japan market (Teplova and Mikova, 2015b).

Jegadeesh and Titman (1993, 2001), and Grundy and Martin (2001) find an interesting seasonality in price momentum profits in the US stock market. They document that the Winners outperform the Losers in all months except January, and the momentum portfolio earns significantly negative returns in January and significantly positive returns in months other than January. So, in the US market, momentum strategies exhibit an interesting pattern of seasonality in January. The January effect refers to the most popular seasonal anomaly exhibited by stocks generating abnormal returns (predominantly for small cap stocks). This pattern occurs in the last trading days in December and then continues to rally during the first weeks in January of the following year. The strategy based on the January effect implements buying small firms with negative annual returns in the prior period and selling at the beginning of the year.

Momentum strategies exhibit an interesting pattern of seasonality in January. Jegadeesh and Titman (2001) examine the momentum effect in January and on an entire sample except for January. The obtained results confirm the January seasonality: the average non-January return is 1.48 percent per month and –1.55 percent in January. Another reason for the seasonal momentum profits can be attributed to the company's reporting (Sias, 2007).

The lack of momentum investing in emerging markets may be due to institutional market structure (no foreign investors) or some cultural features. For instance, investors in emerging markets may be more irrational or have greater cognitive bias than those in developed markets. We can see different behaviour by month/year or market state dependence (Cooper *et al.*, 2004). Recent research has documented that foreign investors tend to be momentum investors (Choe *et al.*, 1999; Grinblatt and Keloharju, 2000). Studies based on the US market (Brockman and Yan, 2009) show that institutional investors trade aggressively to exploit mispricing and block ownership is associated with more informative stock prices. We assume that differences in the ownership structure and the presence of foreign investors should be reflected in the behaviour of stock prices.

Peculiarities of the stock prices behaviour of Japanese companies can be explained by the specificity of the financial structure of the country (Teplova and Mikova, 2015a). Japan is not rich in resources such as crude oil, iron ore, timber, cotton, sugar or coffee beans, the best way to grow and create value was to mobilize its human resources, support relationship-based systems and add value to imported technologies and ideas. These conditions have created a specific Japanese management system and corresponding financial structure and relationship (so-called Japanese or relationship-based or main-bank financial system), which takes an intermediate position between the German and arm's-length Anglo-Saxon financial systems (Demirguc-Kunt and Levine, 2001). Stock ownership in Japan is much less dispersed than in the United States with a different share of institutional and foreign investors. The corporate control market plays a negligible role. More than half of all publicly-listed firms have no outside directors on Japanese boards (in the United States, all companies whose stocks are traded on the NYSE, have to have a majority of independent directors on their boards). Until now, only a few of Japan's major firms were family-controlled but insider ownership has surged from around 6 percent in 1999 to 11 percent in 2006–2013. The average share of foreign investors in the sample of 1,756 listed Japanese companies in the middle of the 2000s is 24 percent. The share of institutional investors in Japan is less than in the United States (23 percent vs. 61 percent in 2010) and the share of institutional investors not affiliated with the listed companies is also much less than in the United States.

The Japanese model is characterized by a high percentage of banks and various corporations in the structure of shareholders. Although official statistics are lacking, long-term block holding through cross-shareholding and ownership of listed subsidiaries among listed companies and banks, portfolio relationships of parent and sub-firms, are popular in Japan. Interestingly, Japanese companies are interested in long-term, preferably affiliated ('stable') shareholders. Cross-shareholding used to be a prominent feature of Japan's stock market until the late 1990s to mid-2000s. In the 2000s firms began unwinding on a massive scale, but a recent survey in 2008 shows that cross ownership has increased. Cross-holding practice (*keiretsu* affiliation) and bank-lending relations, closed decision making within the group began to lose its influence in 2000s, but still persists in Japanese companies in form of 'stable shareholders' (as those who almost never sell out stocks and consistently support management).

Group affiliation in Japan is supported by the system of the corporate governance, which differs from the United States. For example, the procedure for disclosure in Japan is significantly different from that of the United States. In Japan, financial information is provided every six months, and in the United States it is every quarter; Japan reports the amount of total compensation to managers and directors, and in the United States, for each person. Lists of major owners in Japan report the 10 largest shareholders, while in the United States all shareholders with shareholdings of more than 5 percent are listed.

In Figure 7.1 we show the results of testing the momentum effect in the Japanese stock market (1125 publicly-listed companies) over the period January 1997 to December 2013, sub-periods before August 2008 and during crisis September 2008–2009. The traditional algorithm of forming long–short strategies does not allow us to conclude that the effect is present (Figure 7.1). During the whole analyzed period the momentum effect is observed only using nonoverlapping portfolios. Reducing the sample to the largest companies (580) it provides the

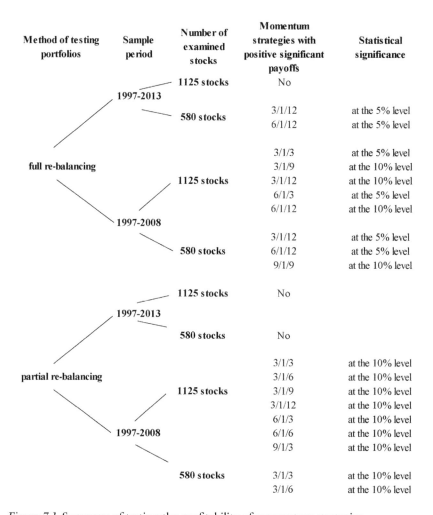

Method of testing portfolios	Sample period	Number of examined stocks	Momentum strategies with positive significant payoffs	Statistical significance
	1997-2013	1125 stocks	No	
		580 stocks	3/1/12	at the 5% level
			6/1/12	at the 5% level
full re-balancing		1125 stocks	3/1/3	at the 5% level
			3/1/9	at the 10% level
			3/1/12	at the 10% level
			6/1/3	at the 5% level
			6/1/12	at the 10% level
	1997-2008	580 stocks	3/1/12	at the 5% level
			6/1/12	at the 5% level
			9/1/9	at the 10% level
	1997-2013	1125 stocks	No	
		580 stocks	No	
partial re-balancing		1125 stocks	3/1/3	at the 10% level
			3/1/6	at the 10% level
			3/1/9	at the 10% level
			3/1/12	at the 10% level
			6/1/3	at the 10% level
			6/1/6	at the 10% level
	1997-2008		9/1/3	at the 10% level
		580 stocks	3/1/3	at the 10% level
			3/1/6	at the 10% level

Figure 7.1 Summary of testing the profitability of momentum strategies

presence of a medium-term momentum effect using any way of testing with 3 months formation period, 3–6 months holding period and skipping one month with a payoff of monthly 1 percent.

Additionally, in the Japanese stock market we find evidence that the momentum effect is statistically significant during the period before crisis whereas momentum strategies do not show a positive return after periods of financial and economic crisis. We argue that momentum becomes more pronounced after market gains. Optimistic sentiment among investors can drive the momentum effect. Therefore investors should strengthen their position in momentum strategy during UP markets.

Integration in the strategy effects the calendar (seasonality patterns in Japanese stocks returns) and has increased the momentum profits. We suggest taking the opposite positions in recent losers and winners for one month before the beginning of the year what can lead to more profitable results (Table 7.1).

Momentum profit's decomposition technique allows investors to select the components of abnormal return associated with a rational explanation and irrational explanation. Below we show a possible method, which develops works by Lehmann (1990), Lo and MacKinlay (1990), and Conrad and Kaul (1998). For this decomposition the stocks sample breaking into two portfolios is implemented by the weighted relative strength (WRS) portfolio procedure (50 percentile).

Profits (to be more exact, return over corresponding time interval) of momentum strategy are decomposed into three components, two of them (C and O) connected with irrational factors (contradictory to EMH), and one (S) may rationally explain the effect of statistically significant profit in arbitrage (long–short) portfolio. Rational component S is a variation of expected mean returns of stocks in a considered sample. Irrational components, connected with failure of random walk hypothesis, are an observed autocorrelation in cross-sectional series of stocks' return (C) and autocorrelation of returns (O).

Thus, general decomposition takes on the following form:

$$E(\pi_t) = -C + O + S$$

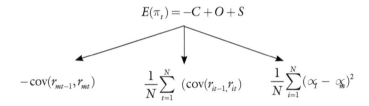

$$-\mathrm{cov}(r_{mt-1}, r_{mt}) \qquad \frac{1}{N}\sum_{t=1}^{N}(\mathrm{cov}(r_{it-1}, r_{it})) \qquad \frac{1}{N}\sum_{i=1}^{N}(\alpha_i - \alpha_m)^2$$

This equation may be interpreted as: the presence of the momentum effect (positive returns on arbitrage, i.e. self-financed, portfolio) may be caused by three sources: 1) positive autocorrelation of sample stocks' return (i.e. an asset profitability for some past period accounts for its future return, a share's price may be forecast on the basis of its past values), 2) negative correlation of a considered stock return with those of other stocks in a sample (i.e. the reason for a stock return growth may be negative or diminishing returns of other securities, their loss against which stocks of the company considered become more attractive), 3) cross-sectional variation of expected return, i.e. differences in mean returns and, therefore, differences in risks. This risk difference and corresponding difference in returns is what actually allows an investor, forming his portfolio in a certain way, to gain abnormal returns. Conrad and Kaul (1998) for the US stock market assert relative significance of rational component. For the Russian stock market Teplova and Mikova (2015a) showed that the component responsible for rational explanations is statistically significant and its weight prevails in most momentum strategies with investment periods not exceeding 9 months. For longer investment periods bigger weight goes to time series predictable component dealing with the possibility to predict future profits by past returns. With the increase of investment period in strategies the significance of component C (first-order autocovariance of the return) grows and, respectively, component O (the average of the first-order

Table 7.1 Returns on price momentum portfolios by calendar month across the 16 investment strategies

Date	Jan.	Feb.	Mar.	Apr.	May	Jun.	Jul.	Aug.	Sept.	Oct.	Nov.	Dec.
03/1/03	-4.0%	0.1%	0.1%	0.2%	-0.2%	2.1%	3.7%	1.1%	3.4%	0.1%	-2.1%	2.5%
03/1/06	-3.3%	-0.1%	0.1%	-0.1%	-2.3%	1.6%	3.1%	0.8%	3.1%	0.1%	-1.4%	2.0%
03/1/09	-3.3%	-0.1%	0.1%	-0.1%	-2.3%	1.6%	3.1%	0.8%	3.1%	0.1%	-1.4%	2.0%
03/1/12	-2.2%	-0.1%	0.3%	0.6%	-1.9%	0.5%	1.9%	1.0%	2.4%	-0.3%	0.0%	1.4%
06/1/03	-4.0%	-0.2%	0.4%	-0.3%	-3.5%	2.1%	4.1%	1.0%	4.1%	0.0%	-2.0%	2.7%
06/1/06	-3.2%	-0.4%	0.6%	0.0%	-3.4%	1.4%	3.0%	0.9%	3.6%	0.2%	-0.8%	2.5%
06/1/09	-2.5%	-0.5%	0.8%	0.6%	-2.8%	0.7%	2.3%	1.3%	3.2%	-0.1%	0.0%	2.1%
06/1/12	-2.3%	-0.7%	0.5%	0.7%	-2.4%	0.5%	1.9%	1.5%	2.7%	-0.8%	0.1%	1.4%
09/1/03	-3.8%	-0.7%	0.8%	0.2%	-4.2%	1.7%	3.3%	1.7%	4.5%	0.6%	-1.5%	2.8%
09/1/06	-3.1%	-0.6%	1.0%	0.7%	-3.5%	1.0%	2.7%	1.9%	4.1%	0.0%	-0.5%	2.2%
09/1/09	-2.7%	-0.9%	0.6%	0.8%	-2.9%	0.5%	2.1%	2.0%	3.4%	-0.7%	-0.1%	1.5%
09/1/12	-2.4%	-1.1%	0.0%	0.7%	-2.3%	0.3%	1.5%	1.7%	2.8%	-1.1%	-0.3%	1.0%
12/1/03	-3.4%	-0.8%	1.1%	0.9%	-3.9%	1.0%	2.7%	2.2%	4.4%	-0.3%	-1.4%	2.4%
12/1/06	-2.8%	-1.2%	0.6%	0.8%	-3.2%	0.6%	2.3%	2.1%	3.7%	-0.9%	-0.7%	1.4%
12/1/09	-2.5%	-1.4%	-0.2%	0.7%	-2.6%	0.2%	1.6%	1.9%	3.1%	-1.1%	-0.5%	1.0%
12/1/12	-2.0%	-1.5%	-0.7%	0.6%	-2.1%	-0.2%	1.2%	1.6%	2.5%	-1.1%	-0.6%	0.6%

autocovariances of the N individual stocks in the arbitrage portfolio) diminishes. The dominance of rational or irrational part depends on momentum or reversal effects (accordingly the windows). Irrational component is dominated within reversal effect and *vice versa*.

5.0   Statistical control for momentum effect testing, data mining, data snooping and errors in data processing

Accumulated literature devoted to investigating the momentum effect focus on descriptions of various approaches on how to form and how to test the strategy. One of the important features unifying all the approaches is an increase of sample to make the achieved results statistically significant: whether the strategy is profitable or not.

The most typical mistake of the researchers in investing the process of seeking patterns in vast amounts of unstructured data was finding the patterns, which disappeared shortly after, while testing on other data series. This can be explained by the fact that in any data set it is possible to find hidden patterns. The patterns that must be of interest in the investment canon are those which occur with acceptable frequency, but not the random ones. It appears that, while working with a large set of data (for example, time data series of stock prices or returns of financial assets), it is highly possible to achieve profitable results. However, these patterns may be unsustainable, ephemera; that is why it is necessary to be strictly adhered to the statistical tests. Carefulness in evaluation of statistical reliability of the achieved results is the cornerstone of the given research.

Thus, the existence of excess return of investment strategies may represent a result of incorrect data mining (Lovell (1983), Chatfield (1995), and Hand (1998)). Besides, the question is how adequate the statistical testing of the achieved results is in the case of abnormal return distribution or of using overlapping portfolios. Such problem arises every time at testing the historical data for anomaly. Each subsequent testing of the historical data for seeking patterns brings us closer to the fact that, eventually, we will find the criterion ensuring the desired outcome. Thus, the repeated operation with the analogous retrospective database influences the subsequent test results. Malkiel (2003) wrote: 'Given enough time and massaging of data series, it is possible to tease almost any pattern out of most data series.'

The consequence of data snooping can be misleading results. One of the most effective (and frequently used) tests is the verification of the hypothesis on out of sample. Thus, Jegadeesh and Titman (2001) repeated their research of the momentum testing on the US stock market on out of sample, within the later period of time, having avoided the data-snooping bias. The paper confirmed their previous conclusions on the profitability of the momentum strategy with the same parameters of the portfolio design. However, macroeconomic factors have a significant influence on the momentum effect. It is still relevant to test for the robustness of the conclusions within a single business cycle period and of investors behaviour.

There are many examples of disproving the patterns revealed earlier. For instance, responding to the work by Robert Levi (Jensen and Bennington, 1970) the authors retested Levi's strategy on the sample far exceeding the original one and demonstrated the fact that the momentum strategy does not exceed the 'buy-and-hold' long-term investment strategy, and accounted the results achieved by R. Levi for the result of data mining.

There are few researches accumulated in the field of studying the influence of data-snooping effect on the results of testing the momentum strategy and the methods of how to avoid it. We succeeded in finding some works dedicated to explore whether the data-snooping bias is substantial in momentum strategy testing or not. One of the works describes the analysis of the momentum investment profitability on the US stock market within the period from 1963 to 2002, where the statistical significance of the achieved results is checked following the White reality check (White, 2000; Ericsson and Gonzalez, 2003). In this work, the null hypothesis is rejected and the conclusion is made that the momentum effect exists taking into account the data-snooping effect, though not all the strategies become statistically significant already.

Merton (1987) was one of the first to ask a question of the correctness of using standard t-statistics as a valid significance measure while testing the null hypothesis on the basis of the data series which had already been tested before. Merton applied to the fact that the achieved results of investigation could influence the choice of the hypothesis being tested.

Halbert White (White, 2000) offered the methodology of hypotheses testing which checks the predictive superiority of the best strategy/model over the benchmark, taking into account the data-snooping effect, by way of comparing the return of the strategies being tested to the benchmark. The zero return may appear for the benchmark to which the best strategies returns are compared, what is in line with the idea of the zero-cost portfolio (Ericsson and Gonzalez, 2003). Null hypothesis postulates that the strategy with the best results in terms of the average does not surpass the benchmark. The best strategy is defined on the basis of the statistical analysis on the full set of strategies, and then the desired p-value may be achieved through the comparison of the best strategy results with approximation of asymptotic distribution of strategies on the whole set of investment strategies. Given that the asymptotic distribution of critical statistics is atypical, White suggested approximating it. There are two ways of generating distribution: through Monte Carlo simulation or bootstraping. The second variant is preferable, because it has no restrictions on its application.

The bootstrap approach is necessary in emerging markets because there is a short observation period (for example, for the Chinese market – from 1990-s) and accordingly, a small sample of the results of arbitrage investment portfolios of the specific strategy's design. Moreover, the return of portfolios within the strategy of the specific design does not exhibit a normal distribution. Normality may be a poor approximation in practice when we consider the weekly return of individual stocks and arbitrage portfolios of investors.

6.0   Investigation of the importance of strategy's design: two criteria for strategies selection (the criterion of a mean return and risk)

After the publication of the pioneering study, there was a chain of practical tests of momentum strategy in different markets. Tests show different results depending on the choice of portfolio formation rules, the length of formation and investment periods. Any factor investing requires the selection of investment strategy's design. However construction of momentum strategy is considered by investors as the most complex task since it involves the determination of the range of portfolio elements (ranking and investment periods, principles of including winners and losers in a portfolio, etc.) in a manner of national capital market. The profitable momentum strategies are traditionally selected through the consideration of multiple possible combinations of elements of the strategy's design (usually searching is based on two or three windows; the formation period or the period over which the past returns are measured and investment periods during which investors hold portfolio and skipping window between formation and investment periods; Jegadeesh and Titman, 1993 – 16 strategies with searching of two windows: 3/{3.6.9.12}, 6/{3.6.9.12}, 9/{3.6.9.12}, 12/{3.6.9.12}, less frequently – in accordance with percentiles of stock selection for a portfolio). The strategy ranking criteria used in this well-known process is a positive mean return under control of the t-statistic and the corresponding p-value. However, such a method can potentially provide great losses to investor, especially if the analyzed time period is quite short and, consequently, there are few observed portfolios of the same design for testing (the probabilistic return distribution on these portfolios is most likely to be far beyond the norm) that leads to achieve not sustainable results sensitive to time period.

Likewise, increasing sample time period to select a profitable design is not the best way, as at different stages of financial market development (growth, downturn, recession) the strategies of various design demonstrate their advantages (Ilmanen, 2011).

Researchers and investors should distinctly pay attention to the methods of testing the factor investing as well as the elements of strategy's design.

Novy-Marx (2012) concluded that momentum in US stocks is better measured by past cumulative returns from 7 to 12 months ago and that using the most recent six months of returns is not valuable. Goyal and Wahal (2012) replicated Novy-Marx's results in 36 international markets and find that in 35 out of 36 countries (the only exception being the United States), Novy-Marx's (2012) conclusion is not confirmed. The first tests of momentum builds profit at equal windows of formation and investing (holding).

Siganos (2010) investigated the optimal number of issuers whose stocks investors need to include in the momentum strategy portfolios. The author made a conclusion that 20 winners stocks and 20 losers stocks are enough for gaining profit from the momentum strategy, inclusive of all the expenses. So, the percentile that include stocks in the portfolio is another design element of the momentum strategy.

Next, we compare the momentum profits (monthly returns) on strategies for different designs on the two largest Asian markets – India and China. We are interested in the opportunity to build a profitable strategy through a combination of momentum effects and short-term reversal. Let's briefly describe the sequence of actions. Across the ranked stocks (our sample) in ascending order by the past return we choose two groups of stocks – in relation to the best and the worst ones (it is a selection within the given J time period – ranking or formation). These stocks will form our two portfolios of winners and losers. The method of dividing the sample into two portfolios may be implemented in various ways – for example, into two equal parts or into two parts when the first portfolio takes all the stocks with more than the mean return in the sampling, and the others are lower with weights depending on the difference between the return of the stock i and mean of the sample. The most popular method assumes constructing portfolios using the given percentile (top 10 percent of the best and 10 percent of the worst ones or top-20 percent or any other). The return of two momentum portfolios could be either equally weighted or value-weighted. In our research, we use the quantile method of forming a portfolio with different number of stocks in portfolios: q = 10 percent, 20 percent, 30 percent and 50 percent. We consider the percentile of 50 percent to be a particular case of relative strength strategy (RSS) (dividing all the stocks into two portfolios).

One more key element of constructing momentum strategy is determination of investment period. Traditionally, the investment period is medium-term and does not exceed 12 months. Jegadeesh and Titman analyze 16 different combinations with varying formation and investment periods (3, 6, 9 and 12 months). The most common practice among researchers and investors is to skip the short-term gap (from one week to several months) between the formation and investment periods (Jegadeesh, 1990; Lehmann, 1990; Lo and MacKinlay, 1990). We continue to use this trading rule to test the influence of the skipping period for profitability of strategy.

For testing the return predictability, the researcher could exploit either non-overlapping or overlapping portfolios. To increase the number of observations and therefore the power of the tests, we form overlapping portfolios and repeat the process of stock ranking and constructing portfolios within the initial time horizon with a shift of one week. Jegadeesh and Titman (1993, 2001) used each month rebalancing, Gutierrez and Kelley (2008) – one week. In any given month t, the strategies hold a series of portfolios that are selected in the current month as well as in the previous K – 1 months, where K is the holding period. (Jegadeesh and Titman, 1993). The return of overlapping portfolio is calculated as average of K arbitrage portfolios' returns where the return of arbitrage portfolio is estimated as the difference between the returns of winner and loser portfolios.

The following Table 7.2 summarizes the possible design elements of the strategy and the choice of an analyst for testing the momentum effect.

Our first task is searching for parameters of the momentum strategy design's elements that ensure statistically significant profitable results for arbitrage portfolios in national markets (India, 200 largest stocks and China, 284 largest in

Table 7.2 Design elements for momentum profit maximization

Formation period (J)	• 1–12 months (Jegadeesh and Titman, 1993) • performance 12 to seven months prior to portfolio formation (Novy-Marx, 2012)
Holding period (K)	• 1–12 months (Jegadeesh and Titman, 1993)
Skipping period (M)	• 1 week – 2 months
Momentum indicator, i.e. the criterion for ranking the stocks	• Past cumulative return (raw return) • Technical indicators (Park's ratio)
Criterion of selection the stocks in two portfolios	• Percentile (10%, 20%, 30%) • By half (R. Levy)
Weighting Methods	• Equally weighted • Value-weighted
The method of portfolio formation	Weighted relative strength strategy (WRSS, Lo and Mac Kinlay (1990), Conrad and Kaul (1998). The division of the sample into two portfolios to include all stocks with weights proportional to the deviation from the average market return Relative strength strategy or quantile (RSS, Rouwenhorst, 1998; Chordia and Shivakumar, 2002) The selection of the percentile to form portfolios of stocks consisted of winners and losers

'B shares' market, period from 2002 to December 2015). Our aim is to rank the models (as independent strategies varying in design elements) for gaining the maximum investment return (on the monthly return criterion).

Our second task is to find those design elements that will ensure minimal risk for strategy (control of statistical significance and the number of portfolios with negative results). The strategy with the best design (that earns the maximum return or demonstrates the minimum risk) is also checked by White's (2000) Bootstrap Reality Check. We use White's Bootstrap *p*-value for verification of the null hypothesis postulating that the chosen model specification does not exceed the benchmark in the results (risk-free return in national market).

Results for the two markets (India and China) show that the best strategies (maximum average monthly abnormal return) should be based on the 10th percentile. In the Indian market maximum return does not exceed 1.5 percent per month.

Design elements of the best strategy that gives 1.55 percent monthly return is: ranking period – 8 months, short-term waiting period (lag for investing) – 0 weeks, and holding period – 1 month, percentile – 10 percent. Although this strategy shows the acceptable *t*-statistics, but bootstrap *p*-value equal to 0,81. The number of negative returns in this strategy –32 from 89 (35.96 percent). In Table 7.3 empirical results are shown (ranking, skipping and investment periods in weeks).

Table 7.3 Top 10 momentum strategies in the Indian market

Abnormal monthly return	T-stat	p-value	Ranking per	skipping	Invest per	percent	Amount of negative
0.01547	2.586589	0.011335	32	0	4	0.1	32
0.014949	2.756071	0.007111	24	8	4	0.1	33
0.014565	2.582542	0.011459	24	6	4	0.1	35
0.014474	1.989174	0.049788	4	5	4	0.1	44
0.014354	2.643357	0.009718	24	7	4	0.1	31
0.014298	2.51388	0.013761	28	3	4	0.1	32
0.013949	2.462433	0.015748	28	2	4	0.1	32
0.013095	2.28194	0.024905	28	4	4	0.1	31
0.012892	2.250394	0.026917	24	5	4	0.1	31
0.012744	2.249317	0.026988	28	1	4	0.1	36

Table 7.4 Momentum windows and design elements for negative returns. Indian market

Abnormal monthly return	T-stat	p-value	Ranking per	skipping	Invest per	percent	Amount of negative
−0.007114	1.875916	0.063982	8	7	8	0.2	50
−0.00704	1.856104	0.066786	8	8	8	0.2	53
−0.006859	1.596813	0.113892	8	8	8	0.1	50

Risk criteria for ranking strategies gives different results from mean return ones (Table 7.5). Best strategy on *t*-statistic base gives lower monthly return (0.9 percent) and has the following elements: a ranking period of 5 months, a waiting period of 1 week, an investment period of 5 months and a percentile of 20 percent. The number of negative returns is 28 (31.46 percent).

Shorter ranking periods in strategies design give negative momentum abnormal returns. Examples of strategies with negative monthly average profits are shown in Table 7.4.

For short skipping periods (0–2 weeks) the profitability of momentum strategies is reduced (Table 7.5), but the statistical significance of the momentum findings is at its maximum.

In the Chinese market ranking and holding periods of 1 year form the reversal effect (negative abnormal return in Win–Los portfolios). Table 7.6 shows three time windows (in weeks).

Reduction of the investment period from 12 months to 9 months allows investors to earn using the momentum strategy (Table 7.7). Increasing the skipping period from one to three weeks leads to a drop in profits, but does not eliminate

Table 7.5 Best statistical results. Indian Market

Abnormal monthly return	t-stat	p-value	Ranking per	skipping	Invest per	percent	Amount of negative
0.009004	4.614353	0.000013	20	1	20	0.2	28
0.008785	4.560122	0.000016	20	0	24	0.2	32
0.007436	4.492051	0.000021	20	0	24	0.3	30
0.005967	4.433996	0.000027	20	1	20	0.5	31
0.007387	4.418222	0.000028	16	0	24	0.3	30
0.005726	4.400218	0.00003	20	0	24	0.5	31
0.007024	4.380176	0.000033	16	1	24	0.3	31
0.005855	4.341115	0.000038	20	2	20	0.5	30
0.008638	4.294776	0.000045	20	2	20	0.2	27
0.008743	4.274311	0.000048	20	0	20	0.2	26

Table 7.6 Top 10 strategies with reversal effect in the Chinese stock market (B)

Abnormal monthly return	t-stat	p-value	Ranking per	skipping	Invest per	percent	Amount of negative
−0.009607	5.896069	0	48	8	48	0.5	63
−0.009053	4.844551	0.000006	48	8	48	0.3	55
−0.008918	5.403814	0.000001	48	7	48	0.5	61
−0.00873	4.937569	0.000004	48	8	44	0.5	57
−0.008154	4.839723	0.000006	48	6	48	0.5	54
−0.008121	3.777363	0.000293	48	8	44	0.3	51
−0.00801	4.452696	0.000026	48	7	44	0.5	57
−0.007794	4.449434	0.000026	48	8	40	0.5	54
−0.007762	4.086534	0.000099	48	7	48	0.3	50
−0.007738	4.850059	0.000006	48	8	36	0.5	55

Table 7.7 LT reversal and momentum effects in the Chinese stock market

Abnormal monthly return	t-stat	p-value	Ranking per	skipping	Invest per	percent	Amount of negative
−0.007794	**4.449434**	**0.000026**	**48**	**8**	**40**	**0.5**	**54**
0.009172	**3.892639**	**0.000197**	**48**	**0**	**36**	**0.1**	**24**
0.008633	3.718297	0.000359	48	1	36	0.1	23
0.008076	3.52331	0.000689	48	2	36	0.1	24
0.006774	3.064223	0.002924	48	3	36	0.1	27
0.005491	2.879541	0.005038	48	0	36	0.2	27

the momentum effect. When skipping the window over 4 weeks we again see a manifestation of the reversion effect (on the strategies 48 / 4–8 / 32–48 weeks). Changing the percentile for the selection of stocks in two portfolios does not alter this conclusion. If the period of investment is in the range of 1–6 months, percentile and skipping periods are significant for catching the momentum effect. For example, at the 50th percentile and 48/8/20 weeks design momentum return becomes not statistically significant. All other percentile and shorter skipping periods provide a significant effect (monthly return around 0.3 percent)

It should be noted that the profitability of the momentum strategy is higher than in the Indian stock market (about 3.5 percent in a month using a technique with the skipping period). High return strategies are shown in Table 7.8. Table 7.8 demonstrates that the investor should be guided by the 10th percentile and the relatively short time of portfolios holding. The ranking period should be significantly bigger than the investment period (the same conclusion can be drawn for the Indian market).

The strategy with maximum results of investment gives the average monthly return of 3,66 percent and has the following design elements: the ranking period is 11 months, the skipping period is 5 weeks, the investment period is 1 month and the percentile is 10 percent. The bootstrap p-value is equal to 0,104. The total number of portfolios in the best strategy is 86. The number of portfolios with negative returns is 32 (37,21 percent).

With increasing investments periods (Table 7.9) profitability of momentum return decreases (to 1 percent monthly) and this positive result demonstrates statistical significance.

The criterion of high statistical significance and low drawdowns leads to another strategies ranking and design selection. Abnormal return in best strategy

Table 7.8 Top 10 momentum strategies in the Chinese stock market

Abnormal monthly return	t-stat	p-value	Ranking per	skipping	Invest per	percent	Amount of negative
0.036568	4.179065	0.000071	44	5	4	0.1	32
0.036054	4.270548	0.000051	44	6	4	0.1	34
0.03584	4.073865	0.000103	48	4	4	0.1	33
0.035641	4.089544	0.000098	48	3	4	0.1	32
0.035447	3.96812	0.000151	44	4	4	0.1	31
0.03536	3.969159	0.00015	48	2	4	0.1	31
0.034675	4.250467	0.000054	44	7	4	0.1	31
0.034201	3.602858	0.000529	40	2	4	0.1	33
0.033986	3.564255	0.000602	40	1	4	0.1	31
0.033893	5.532342	0	44	3	8	0.1	26

Table 7.9 Relatively low momentum returns on long windows

Abnormal monthly return	t-stat	p-value	Ranking per	skipping	Invest per	percent	Amount of negative
0.012359	5.736475	0	36	0	48	0.1	18
0.012014	5.307298	0.000001	40	0	48	0.1	18
0.011606	5.500753	0	36	1	48	0.1	18
0.01144	5.098452	0.000002	40	1	48	0.1	20
0.011266	5.097308	0.000002	44	0	48	0.1	22
0.010855	4.889747	0.000005	40	2	48	0.1	19
0.010845	4.839831	0.000006	16	0	48	0.1	26
0.010807	5.179916	0.000001	36	2	48	0.1	18
0.010728	5.920313	0	32	0	48	0.1	19
0.010653	3.830174	0.000244	12	0	48	0.1	29

with risk criterion is 2,72 percent and has the following parameters: the formation period – 11 months, skipping period – 3 weeks, the investment period – 4 months. Bootstrap *p*-value equals to 0,268. Number of portfolios with negative returns – 18 (20,93 percent).

Thus, the investor should take into account the strategy design to catch the momentum profit. For the general case we can say that the maximum abnormal return can be earned at the 10th percentile technique for filling the portfolio and a relatively short (within a year) period of investment (portfolio's holding).

7.0   Summary and conclusion

This chapter is devoted to one of the most revealing anomalies in financial asset pricing behaviour – the momentum effect. The momentum effect is an attractive case for academics as well as for practitioners. Despite the fact that the momentum effect has been exploited by investors for more than 20 years this pattern continues to persist. Traditionally many anomalies tend to disappear when investors begin to construct profitable investment strategies eliminating market inefficiency by their trades. The momentum effect has become popular in the investment canoe; as a result, the world's largest providers of geared exchange traded product, ProShares and Vanguard, have launched momentum exchange traded funds (ETFs). Moreover a number of works (Khandani and Lo, 2007; Kaniel, Saar and Titman, 2008) put emphasis on practical applicability of the results obtained in tests.

Some papers aim to find tweaks increasing the profitability of the momentum strategy. In particular, it is the general consensus of academics that the momentum effect depends on the state of the stock market and business cycle. It is assumed that momentum strategies work best in trending markets. Markets without a clear direction or with higher volatility are not suitable for such strategies. Momentum crashes (Daniel and Moskowitz, 2013) occur when market changes direction and volatility is high. As shown by the tests on the markets of India and China, even the best strategies on risk ranking demonstrate the drawdown with a negative result of investment.

This chapter suggests a new approach for investors to construct momentum strategy and choose the most profitable design. Investors can construct a wide variety of momentum strategy's designs combining parameters of ranking period, skipping window, investment period and the portion of stocks that will contain winner and loser portfolios. How can one choose the best design? This new approach is based on implementing two possible criteria for the selection of the best strategy: 1) to maximize mean return of the strategy, 2) to minimize the risk and taking into account the number of drawdowns under bootstrap reality check. Thus, the investor should take into account the strategy design to catch the momentum profit. For the general case we can say that the maximum abnormal return can be earned at the 10th percentile technique for filling portfolio and relatively short (within a year) period of investment (portfolio's holding).

In this chapter we also cover the nature of the momentum effect. In search of the momentum effect explanation research in this field falls into two basic trends of rational and irrational nature, the latter pertaining to the field of behavioural finance. Among works with rational arguments we should note those containing hypotheses and proofs of: 1) existence of risk premium (through asset pricing models) and possible existence of differences in mean unconditional returns of stocks; 2) problems with data processing, so-called noise effects: data-snooping bias, data selection bias etc.; 3) problems in market microstructure: limitations on opening short sales, high transactional costs (Lesmond, 2005) etc.

Hypotheses allegedly explaining the momentum effect through the behavioural finance postulate that abnormal arbitrage portfolio returns are connected with investors' irrational behaviour prone to excess self-confidence in assessing stocks and their unwillingness to admit mistakes, as well as with 'disposal effect' and refusal to fix losses, and over- or underreaction to latest news, etc.

As the result of the momentum effect's dual nature an idea emerged to conduct profit decomposition of this strategy into two components, reflecting return time series predictability (which corresponds to irrational explanation of profit existence and contradicts EMH), and higher risk premium connected with difference in mean returns of sample securities (this is rational argumentation built through selection of respective risk factors).

Depending on the results, investigators tends to search the most appropriate asset pricing model or behavioural theory.

Reference

Abinzano, I., Muga, L., and Santamaria, R. (2010). Do managerial skills vary across fund managers? Results using European mutual funds. *Journal of Financial Services Research*, 38. No.1, 41–67.

Asness, C. S. (1994). Variables that explain stock returns. Ph.D. Dissertation, University of Chicago.

Asness, C. S. (2011). Momentum in Japan: The exception that proves the rule. *The Journal of Portfolio Management, 37*(4), 67–75.

Asness, C. S., Frazzini, A., Israel, R., and Moskowitz, T. J. (2014). Fact, fiction and momentum investing. *Journal of Portfolio Management*, Fall 2014 (40th Anniversary Issue).

Asness, C., Ilmanen, A., Israel, R., and Moskowitz, T. (2015). Investing with style. *Journal of Investment Management, 13*(1), 27–63.

Asness, C., Moskowitz, T., and Pedersen, L. (2013). Value and momentum everywhere. *Journal of Finance, 68*(1), 929–985.

Berk J., Green, R., and Naik, V. (1999). Optimal investment, growth options, and security returns. *Journal of Finance*, 54, 1553–1608.

Brennan, M., Chordia, T., and Subrahmanyam, A. (1998). Alternative factor specifications, security characteristics, and the cross-section of expected stock returns," *Journal of Financial Economics* 49, 345–373.

Brockman, P., Chung, D. Y., and Yan, X. (2009). Block ownership, trading activity, and market liquidity, *Journal of Financial and Quantitative Analysis*, 44, issue 06, 1403–1426.

Cakici, N., Fabozzi, F. J., and Tan, S. (2013). Size, value, and momentum in emerging market stock returns. *Emerging Markets Review*, 16(0), 46–65.

Carhart, M. M. (1997). On persistence in mutual fund performance. *Journal of Finance, 52*(1), 57–82.

Cenedese, G., Payne, R., Sarno, L., and Valente, G. (2013). What do stock markets tell us about exchange rates? Bank of England Working Paper No. 537, Bank of England.

Chan K., Hameed A., and Tong, W. (2000). Profitability of momentum strategies in the international equity markets. *Journal of Financial and Quantitative Analysis*, 35(02),153–172.

Chao, S., Hardle, W. K., and Wang, W. (2012). Quantile regression in risk calibration, SFB 649 Discussion Paper 2012-006, Humboldt University, Berlin, German.

Chan, L. K. C, Jegadeesh, N., and Lakonishok, J. (1996). Momentum strategies. *Journal of Finance, 51*(5), 1681–1713.

Chatfield, C. (1995). Model uncertainty, data mining and statistical inference. *Journal of the Royal Statistical Society*, 158, Series A, 419–466.

Choe, H., Kho, R., and Stulz, R. M. (1999). Do foreign investors destabilize stock markets? The Korea experience in 1997. *Journal of Financial Economics*, 54(2), 227–264.

Chordia, T., and Shivakumar, L. (2002). Momentum, business cycle and time-varying expected returns. *Journal of Finance* 57, 985–1019.

Conrad, J., and Kaul, G. (1988). Time-variation in expected returns, *Journal of Business*. 61, 409–425.

Conrad, J., and Kaul, G. (1993). Long-term market overreaction or biases in computed returns? *Journal of Finance, 48*(1), 39–63.

Cooper, M., Gutierrez, Jr. R., and Hameed, A. (2004). Market states and momentum. *Journal of Finance, 59*(3), 1345–1365.

Daniel, K., Hirshleifer, D., and Subrahmanyam, A. (1998). Investor psychology and security market under- and overreactions. *Journal of Finance, 53*(6), 1839–1885.

Daniel, K., and Moskowitz, T. (2013). Momentum crashes, Swiss Finance Institute Research Paper, 13–61, Geneva, Switzerland.

De Bondt, W. F. M., and Thaler, R. (1985). Does the stock market overreact. *Journal of Finance*, *40*(3), 793–805.

De Bondt, W. F. M., and Thaler, R. (1987). Further evidence on investor overreaction and stock market seasonality. *The Journal of Finance*, 42(3), 557–81.

Demirguc-Kunt, A., and Levine, R. (2001). *Financial Structures and Economic Growth: A Cross-Country Comparison of Banks, Markets, and Development.* Cambridge, MA: MIT Press.

Ericsson, J., and González, A. (2003). Is momentum due to data-snooping? Working Paper. Stockholm School of Economics.

Fama, E. F. (1970). Efficient capital markets: A review of theory and empirical work. *Journal of Finance*, *25*(2), 383–417.

Fama F., and French, K. R. (1996). Multiple explanations of asset pricing anomalies. *Journal of Finance*, 51, 55–84.

Fama, E. F., and French, K. R. (2012). Size, value, and momentum in international stock returns. *Journal of Financial Economics*, *105*(3), 457–472.

Frazzini, A., Israel, R., and Moskowitz, T. J. (2013). Trading costs of asset pricing anomalies. *Journal of Finance*, *68*(3), 929–985.

Geczy, C., and Samonov, M. (2013). 212 years of price momentum (The World's Longest Anomalies). *Journal of Financial Economics*, *108*(2), 275–301.

Goyal, A., and Wahal, S. (2015). Is momentum an echo? *The Journal of Financial and Quantitative Analysis*, *50*(6), 1237–1267.

Grinblatt, M., and Keloharju, M. (2000). The investment behavior and performance of various types of investors: A study of Finland's unique data set, *Journal of Financial Economics*, *55*(1), 43–67.

Griffin, J., Ji, X., and Martin, S. (2003). Momentum investing and business cycle risk: Evidence from pole to pole. *Journal of Finance*, *58*(6), 2515–2547.

Grinblatt, M., and Han, B. (2002). The disposition effect and momentum. NBER Working Paper No. 8734.

Grinblatt, M., and Han, B. (2005). Prospect theory, mental accounting, and momentum. *Journal of Financial Economics*, *78*(2), 311–339.

Grinblatt, M., Titman, S., and Wermers, R. (1995). Momentum investment strategies, portfolio performance, and herding: A study of mutual fund behavior. *American Economic Review*, *8*(1), 1088–1105.

Grundy, B., and Martin, J. (2001). Understanding the nature of the risks and the sources of the rewards to momentum investing. *Review of Financial Studies*, *14*(1), 29–78.

Gutierrez, R. C., and Kelley, E. K. (2008). The long-lasting momentum in weekly returns. *The Journal of Finance*, *63*, 415–447.

Hameed, A., and Kusnadi, Y. (2002). Momentum strategies: Evidence from Pacific Basin stock markets. *Journal of Financial Research*, *25*(3), 383–397.

Hand, D. J. (1998). Data mining: statistics and more. *American Statistician 52*, 112-118.

Hart, J., Slagter, E., and Dijk, D. (2002). Stock selection strategies in emerging markets, *Journal of Empirical Finance 21*, 104–121.

Hong, H., and Stein, J. C. (1999). A unified theory of under-reaction, momentum trading, and overreaction in asset markets. *Journal of Finance*, *54*(6), 2143–2184.

Hurn, S., and Pavlov, V. (2003). Momentum in Australian stock returns. *Australian Journal of Management, 28*(2), 141–155.

Ilmanen, A. (2011). *Expected Returns: An Investors Guide to Harvesting Market Rewards.* Chichester, UK: Wiley.

Ismail, E. (2012). Do momentum and contrarian profits exist in the Egyptian stock market? *International Research Journal of Finance and Economics, 87,* 48–72.

Israel, R., and Moskowitz, T. J. (2013). The role of shorting, firm size, and time on market anomalies. *Journal of Financial Economics, 108*(2), 275–301.

Jegadeesh, N. (1990). Evidence of predictable behavior of security returns. *Journal of Finance, 45*(3), 881–898.

Jegadeesh, N., and Titman, S. (1993). Returns to buying winners and selling losers: Implications for stock market efficiency. *Journal of Finance, 48*(1), 65–91.

Jegadeesh, N., and Titman, S. (2001). Profitability of momentum strategies: An evaluation of alternative explanations. *Journal of Finance, 56*(2), 699–720.

Jensen M. C., and Benington G. A. (1970). Random walks and technical theories: Some additional evidence, *Journal of finance.* 25(2), 469–482.

Kaniel, R., Saar, G., and Titman, S. (2008). Individual investor sentiment and stock returns, *Journal of Finance, 63,* 273–310.

Johnson, T. C. (2002). Rational momentum effects, *Journal of Finance, 57*(2), 585–608.

Kang, J., Liu, M., and Ni, S. X. (2002). Contrarian and momentum strategies in the China stock market: 1993–2000, *Pacific-Basin Finance Journal, 10*(3), 243–265

Khandani, A., and Lo, A. (2007). What happened to the quants in August 2007? *Journal of Investment Management, 5,* 29–78.

Korajczyk, R. A., and Sadka, R. (2004). Are momentum profits robust to trading costs? *Journal of Finance, 59*(3), 1039–1082.

Lee, C., and Swaminathan, B. (2000). Price momentum and trading volume. *Journal of Finance, 55*(5), 2017–2070.

Lehmann, B. (1990). Fads, martingales, and market efficiency. *Quarterly Journal of Economics, 105*(1), 1–28.

Lesmond, D. A., Schill, M. J. and Zhou, C. (2004). The illusory nature of momentum profits, *Journal of Financial Economics, 71,* 349–380.

Liu, C., and Lee, Y. (2001). Does the momentum strategy work universally? Evidence from the Japanese stock market, *Asia-Pacific Financial Markets, 8,* 321–339.

Lo, A. W., and Mac Kinlay, A. C. (1990). Data-snooping biases in tests of financial asset pricing models, *Review of Financial Studies* 3, 431–468.

Lovell, M. C. (1983). Data mining. *Review of Economics and Statistics, 65,* 1–12.

Malkiel, B. (2003). The efficient market hypothesis and its critics, *Journal of Economic Perspectives, 17*(1), 59–82.

Martin, B., and Malabika, D. (2015). Price momentum strategies: Evidence from Indian equity market. *Journal of Applied Finance, 21*(1), 5–21.

Menkhoff, L., Sarno, L., Schmeling, M., and Schrimpf, A. (2012). Currency momentum strategies. *Journal of Financial Economics, 106*(3), 660–684.

Merton, R. C. (1987). A simple model of capital market equilibrium with incomplete information. *The Journal of Finance, 42*(3), 483–510.

Novy-Marx, R. (2012). Is momentum really momentum? *Journal of Financial Economics, 103*(3), 429–453.

Rouwenhorst, K. G. (1998). International momentum strategies. *Journal of Finance, 53*(1), 267–284.

Sakr, A. M., Ragheb, M. A., Ragab, A. A., and Abdou, R. (2014). Return anomalies "Disposition effect and momentum": Evidence from the Egyptian stock market. *International Journal of Economics and Finance, 6*(2), 181–196.

Sagi, Jacob S., andSeasholes, Mark S. (2007). Firm-specific attributes and the cross-section of momentum, *Journal of Financial Economics, 84,* 389–434.

Shefrin, H., and Statman, M. (1985). The disposition to sell winners too early and ride losers too long. *Journal of Finance, 40*(3), 777–790.

Sias, R. (2007). Window-dressing, tax-loss selling, and momentum profit seasonality. *Financial Analysts Journal, 63*(2), 48–54.

Siganos, A. (2010). Can small investors exploit the momentum effect? *Financial Markets and Portfolio Management,* 24(2), 171–192.

Teplova, T., and Mikova, E. (2015a). Decomposition of cross-sectional momentum and contrarian strategy returns: Behavior or rational explanation on Russia capital market. 16th International Conference in Moscow, NRU HSE, April.

Teplova, T., and Mikova, E. (2015b). New evidence of determinants of price momentum in the Japanese stock market. *Research in International Business and Finance, 34,* 84–109.

Van der Hart, J., De Zwart, G., and Van Dijk, D. (2005). The success of stock selection strategies in emerging markets: Is it risk or behavioral bias? *Emerging Markets Review, 6*(3), 238–262.

Wang, C. (2004). Relative strength strategies in China's stock market: 1994–2000. *Pacific-Basin Finance Journal, 12*(2), 159–177.

Wang, H. C. J. (2014). Causes of short-term momentum anomaly in daily returns: Evidence from Taiwan. *Actual Problems of Economics, 154*(4), 366.

White, H. (2000). A Reality Check For Data Snooping, Econometrica, 68, No 5, 1097-1126.

Zhang, H. (2004). Dynamic Beta, Time-Varying Risk Premium, and Momentum, Yale School of Management Working Papers, New Haven, CT.

8 Momentum returns, market states and financial crises

Evidence from China and Hong Kong

*Muhammad A. Cheema and
Gilbert V. Nartea*

1.0 Introduction

Momentum refers to the tendency for past winners to continue winning while past losers continue losing. The momentum effect has been a popular issue in recent finance literature and is considered most prominent among all the stock market anomalies (Fama and French, 2008). Jegadeesh and Titman (1993) report that the momentum trading strategy of buying recent winners and selling recent losers generates an abnormal return of 1 percent per month (12 percent per year) in the US market over the period 1965 to 1989.

The presence of the momentum effect in US stock markets has led to a number of studies that document statistically significant and economically large momentum returns in international stock markets, e.g. Rouwenhorst (1998) for European countries, Rouwenhorst (1998) for emerging markets, Chan, Hameed and Tong (2000) for the stock market indexes of 23 countries, Chui, Wei and Titman (2000) for eight Asian countries except Japan, Schiereck and Weber (1995) for the German market, Bacmann and Dubois (2000) for the Swiss market, Bacmann, Dubois and Isakov (2001) for the G-7 countries and Hameed and Kusnadi (2002) for six Asian markets.

Behavioural explanations of the momentum anomaly are considered more reliable because the Fama-French and other risk factors fail to explain momentum returns. Behavioural theories assume that investor irrationality and psychological biases are responsible for momentum returns. The behavioural factors that the extant literature relate to the momentum effect are investor conservatism, representative heuristic, biased self-attribution, overconfidence and bounded rationality (for example, see among others, Barberis, Shleifer and Vishny, 1998; Daniel, Hirshleifer and Subrahmanyam, 1998, 2002; Hong and Stein, 1999; Hong and Stein, 2007). The behavioural model of Barberis *et al.* (1998) explains momentum returns as the result of investor underreaction to new public information and overreaction to their beliefs. They argue that this tendency for investors to overreact to their beliefs cause prices to continue in the same direction; underreaction to new public information takes time to stop the continuity of prices. They show that underreaction to new information and overreaction to their prior beliefs results from investors' cognitive biases including representativeness and conservatism.

In the representativeness bias, investors assume that the extraordinary growth (reduction) of the firm will continue in the future and, as a result, take prices away from their fundamental values. The conservatism bias, on the other hand, leads to underreaction to new information.

Daniel *et al.* (1998) argue that investor overconfidence is responsible for overreaction in stock prices, which results in momentum returns. Cooper, Gutierrez and Hameed (2004) extend Daniel *et al.* (1998) overreaction theory to predict differences in momentum returns across UP and DOWN market states. They argue that, since in aggregate investors hold long positions, investor overconfidence must be higher after an UP market because the UP market brings in gains. They further explain that investors will attribute the rise in stock prices to their skills leading to a further boost in their overconfidence that generates momentum returns. So, they argue that the large rise in investor overconfidence is a result of the UP market state, and hence it is the market state that explains momentum returns. Using NYSE- and AMEX-listed stocks, they find significant positive momentum returns in the UP market state. Daniel and Moskowitz (2013) extend the Cooper *et al.* (2004) study and report losses to the momentum trading strategy when the market is under stress. Daniel and Moskowitz (2013) find that major losses to the momentum trading strategy occur after a severe market downturn and in the months when the market starts to rise. Daniel and Moskowitz (2013) argue that their results are loosely consistent with behavioural findings (see Loewenstein, 2000; Loewenstein, Weber, Hsee and Welch, 2001; Sunstein and Zeckhauser, 2008). These behavioural findings suggest that investors are more fearful in extreme situations and ignore probabilities. We suggest that their fear drives the loser stocks below fundamental levels; consequently, when the market improves, loser stocks over perform. Given that the market state can explain momentum returns in the United States, it is worth testing the market state explanation in markets outside the United States to show that this relationship is not due to data snooping.

This study is motivated by the following issues: first, there are very few studies on the profitability of momentum trading strategies in the Hong Kong and Chinese stock markets and the empirical evidence provided in those studies about the profitability of momentum trading strategy is mixed. The mixed evidence about the profitability of momentum in China and Hong Kong is due to the use of different holding and formation periods (from 1 week to 2 years), size of sample data sets, and the differential use of the Shanghai and Shenzhen stocks. For example, Kang, Liu and Ni (2002), Wang and Chin (2004), Naughton, Truong and Veeraraghavan (2008), Wang (2008), and Cheema and Nartea (2014) report that momentum strategies are profitable , but Wang (2004), Chen, Kim, Yao and Yu (2010), Cakici, Chan and Topyan (2011), Wu (2011), and Pan, Tang and Xu (2013) report insignificant momentum returns. Hameed and Kusnadi (2002) find insignificant momentum returns for the Hong Kong Stock Exchange (HKSE) in their study of six Asian markets; however, Cheng and Wu (2010) find significant momentum returns for the HKSE and they argue that Hameed and Kusnadi's (2002) findings might be the result of including small and illiquid stocks in their sample. Secondly, there are no studies on the profitability of the momentum trading strategy in China and Hong Kong during the Global Financial crisis. Therefore, we want to test the impact of the Global Financial crisis on the profitability of momentum returns because the literature provides evidence that crises can affect the profitability of this trading strategy.

Using the two mainland Chinese stock markets – Shanghai Stock Exchange (hereafter SSE), and Shenzhen Stock Exchange (hereafter SZSE) – as well as the HKSE, we find positive and large momentum returns in a normal market environment (before 2007) since it appears that investors underreact to public information, whereas we find negative momentum returns from 2007 to 2010 with past losers earning more than past winners. However, we do not find any evidence that lagged market returns can explain momentum returns for China and Hong Kong. The rest of the chapter is organized as follows: Section 2.0 discusses the data and methodology, Section 3.0 presents the momentum returns for all datasets and Section 4.0 presents the momentum returns in the UP and DOWN market states using 36-, 24- and 12-month lagged market returns and Section 5.0 concludes the study.

2.0 Data and model

2.1 Sample and descriptive statistics

We use all stocks listed on the SSE, Shenzhen Stock Exchange (SZSE) and HKSE from the China Securities Market (CSMAR) and DataStream from November 1994 to November 2010. We exclude the period before 1994 since only a limited number of stocks were traded during that period. We also exclude all financial institutions, closed-end funds and real estate stocks. We also exclude stocks with monthly returns greater than 100 percent to avoid any possible data recording errors and to ensure that our results are not driven by stocks with extreme returns. At the beginning of the sample period, there were 155, 95 and 455 stocks from the SSE, SZSE and HKSE, respectively. At the end of the sample period, the number of stocks in the sample increased to 745, 690 and 815, for SSE, SZSE and HKSE, respectively.

Table 8.1 reports the summary statistics for the monthly value-weighted market returns for All China, HKSE, SSE and SZSE and monthly RF rates for All China and HKSE.[1] Panel A reports that the average monthly (mean) value-weighted market return for the full sample for All China, HKSE, SSE and SZSE is 1.58 percent, 0.75 percent, 1.50 percent and 1.83 percent, respectively. In Panel A, Table 8.1, the average monthly RF rates for All China and HKSE are 0.32 percent and 0.40 percent, respectively. The summary statistics in Panel A show that in the long run, market returns are larger for stock markets than for RF rates, consistent with risk-based theories. Panels B and C report the summary statistics before and during the global financial crisis (GFC), respectively. The average monthly (mean) value-weighted market returns before the GFC are 1.98 percent for All China, 0.91 percent for HKSE, 1.94 percent for SSE and 2.12 percent for SZSE. However, the average monthly (mean) value-weighted market returns during the GFC are very small and even negative for All China and SSE. The summary statistics

Table 8.1 Summary statistics (market return, risk-free return)

This table reports the summary statistics for the value-weighted market return (RET) of All China, HKSE, SSE and SZSE. It also reports summary statistics for the risk-free (RF) rate for All China and HKSE. Panel A reports the summary statistics for the full sample (November 1994-November 2010), panel B reports the summary statistics before the Global Financial crisis (November 1994-Septmber 2007) and panel C reports the summary statistics during the financial crisis (October 2007-November 2010). The average monthly mean, median, 25%, 75% and 90% of the values are given in percent.

Panel A: Summary statistics for the full sample (1994–2010)

Variable	N	Mean	StdDev	Median	25%	75%	90%
All China-RET	193	1.58	9.67	1.34	−4.86	6.45	13.31
HKSE-RET	193	0.75	7.72	1.28	−3.61	4.55	9.53
SSE-RET	193	1.50	9.43	1.38	−4.87	5.94	12.58
SZSE-RET	193	1.83	10.56	1.16	−4.93	7.17	13.59
All CHINA-RF	193	0.32	0.22	0.19	0.19	0.39	0.73
HKSE-RF	193	0.40	0.19	0.50	0.25	0.54	0.58

Panel B: Summary statistics before the global financial crisis (1994–2007)

Variable	N	Mean	StdDev	Median	25%	75%	90%
All China-RET	155	1.98	9.16	0.90	−4.80	6.45	14.18
HKSE-RET	155	0.91	7.55	1.33	−3.44	4.85	9.53
SSE-RET	155	1.94	8.84	1.21	−4.60	5.94	13.11
SZSE-RET	155	2.12	10.22	0.84	−4.81	6.27	13.59
All CHINA-RF	155	0.34	0.24	0.19	0.19	0.46	0.87
HKSE-RF	155	0.46	0.14	0.52	0.32	0.56	0.58

Panel C: Summary statistics during the global financial crisis (2007–2010)

Variable	N	Mean	StdDev	Median	25%	75%	90%
All China-RET	38	−0.25	11.71	2.69	−7.68	8.50	13.42
HKSE-RET	38	0.17	8.68	0.38	−5.24	3.85	12.92
SSE-RET	38	−0.47	11.63	2.48	−7.98	7.38	13.90
SZSE-RET	38	0.43	12.18	2.45	−7.49	9.27	16.57
All CHINA-RF	38	0.24	0.07	0.19	0.19	0.32	0.34
HKSE-RF	38	0.15	0.16	0.04	0.04	0.29	0.38

results provide evidence that the GFC affected the Chinese and Hong Kong markets. Therefore, we expect to find different results before and during the GFC.

2.2 Methodology

First, we calculate momentum returns for each market based on the methodology proposed by Jegadeesh and Titman (1993). We use the conventional 6-month formation period for the momentum trading strategy. A month is skipped between the formation and holding period to mitigate the bid–ask bounce effect. At the end of each month t, all stocks are ranked in ascending order by their past 6-month returns ($t-6$ to $t-1$). These rankings are used to form equally weighted decile portfolios, where the top decile portfolio (P1) is called the losers decile, and the bottom (P10) is the winners decile. We buy (sell) the winners (losers) decile and define the return of the momentum trading strategy as P10-P1. The portfolios are held for K months ($K = 3, 6, 9$ and 12). Following Jegadeesh and Titman (1993), the portfolio monthly return for a K-month holding period is based on an equal-weighted average of portfolio returns from strategies implemented in the current month and the previous $K-1$ months.

We also calculate value-weighted momentum returns to ensure that these returns are not the result of small stocks. To calculate value-weighted momentum returns, we follow the same procedure as for equally weighted momentum returns except that we invest money in stocks according to their market capitalization instead of equal money in all stocks.

Finally, we investigate if market states affect momentum returns by following Cooper *et al.* (2004) who employ UP and DOWN market states. We employ value-weighted market returns for All China, SSE composite index, the SZSE composite index and the Hang Seng Index as proxies for the market for All China, SSE, SZSE and HKSE over 36 months before the portfolio formation date to define the market state. If the lagged 36-month value-weighted market return is positive (negative), then the market state is defined as UP (DOWN). A longer horizon is expected to capture major changes in market states but, on the other hand, it reduces the number of observations for UP and DOWN market states (see Cooper *et al.*, 2004). As a robustness test, we apply 24-month and 12-month market states against these momentum returns. Following Cooper *et al.* (2004), we use buy-and-hold momentum returns to investigate the relationship between momentum returns and market. Buy-and-hold momentum returns are calculated at the end of 6-month holding periods instead of revising portfolio weights every month. Since the buy-and-hold returns are overlapping, we use robust Newey–West t-statistics.

Following Cooper *et al.* (2004), the momentum returns followed by UP and DOWN market states are adjusted for CAPM and Fama-French risk factors to ensure that momentum returns remain significant and cannot be explained by the risk factors.[2]

$$MR_{t,6\times6} = \alpha + \sum_{m=1}^{n}\beta_m f_{i,t} + e_t \tag{8.1}$$

$MR_{t,6\times6}$ is the raw momentum returns following UP and DOWN market states generated at time t with a 6-month formation and 6-month holding period. The notation $f_{i,t}$ ($I = 1,2$) are risk factors (1 = CAPM, 2 = Fama-French) used in this study at time t, β_m ($m = 1,2,\ldots,n$) is the loading for risk factors, α is the coefficient estimate for constant and e_t is the residual, with $(e_t) = 0$, Cov $(e_t, f_t) = 0$ and $e_t \approx (0, \sigma^2)$. We use the excess returns of the value-weighted market returns over RF return as the sole factor for the CAPM risk adjustment. We use the excess returns of value-weighted market returns; the small-minus-big return factor and the high-book-to-market-minus-low-book-to-market return factors for the Fama-French risk adjustment.

3.0 Momentum returns for different markets

Table 8.2 presents the average monthly returns of the winners (P10), losers (P1) and winners minus losers (P10-P1) during the period November 1995 to November 2010.[3]

Table 8.2 Equal-weighted and value-weighted momentum returns

At the beginning of each month t, All China, SSE, SZSE and HKSE stocks are allocated into deciles based on their lagged 6-month returns ($t - 6$ to $t - 1$) and portfolios are formed one month after the lagged returns used for forming these portfolios are measured (panels A and B). We then form an equal-weighted and value-weighted (panels A and B only) zero-cost portfolio selling (buying) the decile of stocks with the lowest (highest) 6-month lagged returns. These portfolios are held for K months (K = 3, 6, 9 and 12 months). The average monthly returns of portfolio P1 (losers), P10 (Winners) and momentum returns (P10-P1) are reported in percent and t-statistics provided in parentheses. The sample period is November 1994 to November 2010.

Panel A: Equal-weighted momentum returns

Market	#Months	184	181	178	175
	K =	3	6	9	12
All China	P1 (Losers)	1.36	1.37	1.50	1.62
		(3.64)	(4.03)	(4.80)	(5.59)
	P10 (Winners)	1.92	1.95	1.91	1.84
		(5.59)	(6.16)	(6.54)	(6.93)
	P10-P1	0.56	0.58	0.41	0.22
		(3.04)	(3.80)	(3.29)	(2.12)
HKSE	P1 (Losers)	0.39	0.13	0.25	0.41
		(0.92)	(0.34)	(0.78)	(1.50)
	P10 (Winners)	1.15	0.73	0.67	0.61
		(3.28)	(2.45)	(2.50)	(2.51)
	P10-P1	0.76	0.60	0.43	0.20
		(4.12)	(3.58)	(3.36)	(1.67)

(*Continued*)

Table 8.2 (Continued)

Panel A: Equal-weighted momentum returns

Market	#Months	184	181	178	175
	K =	3	6	9	12
SSE	P1 (Losers)	1.27	1.32	1.39	1.48
		(3.42)	(3.80)	(4.52)	(5.17)
	P10 (Winners)	2.06	2.15	2.12	2.02
		(6.09)	(6.88)	(7.51)	(7.94)
	P10-P1	0.80	0.83	0.73	0.53
		(3.88)	(4.78)	(4.74)	(4.08)
SZSE	P1 (Losers)	1.68	1.68	1.76	1.81
		(4.11)	(4.49)	(5.10)	(5.75)
	P10 (Winners)	1.71	1.71	1.82	1.80
		(4.74)	(5.14)	(5.61)	(6.00)
	P10-P1	0.02	0.04	0.06	−0.01
		(0.13)	(0.27)	(0.53)	(−0.06)

Panel B: Value-weighted momentum returns

Market	#Months	184	181	178	175
	K =	3	6	9	12
All China	P1 (losers)	0.97	0.90	0.99	1.15
		(2.78)	(2.85)	(3.42)	(4.32)
	P10 (Winners)	1.66	1.67	1.63	1.58
		(4.90)	(5.25)	(5.47)	(5.77)
	P10-P1	0.69	0.77	0.64	0.43
		(3.68)	(4.93)	(4.99)	(3.93)
HKSE	P1 (losers)	−0.84	−0.25	0.33	0.66
		(−2.20)	(−0.68)	(1.08)	(2.43)
	P10 (Winners)	0.98	0.79	0.80	0.78
		(3.06)	(2.84)	(3.14)	(3.16)
	P10-P1	1.82	1.04	0.48	0.12
		(7.18)	(4.27)	(2.52)	(0.72)
SSE	P1 (losers)	0.85	0.80	0.84	0.93
		(2.57)	(2.60)	(3.00)	(3.66)
	P10 (Winners)	1.72	1.72	1.69	1.62
		(5.20)	(5.60)	(5.96)	(6.17)
	P10-P1	0.87	0.92	0.85	0.69
		(4.34)	(5.43)	(5.88)	(5.42)
SZSE	P1 (losers)	1.36	1.33	1.48	1.57
		(3.29)	(3.70)	(4.45)	(5.24)
	P10 (Winners)	1.72	1.70	1.74	1.70
		(4.80)	(5.13)	(5.38)	(5.62)
	P10-P1	0.36	0.37	0.26	0.13
		(1.63)	(2.38)	(2.08)	(1.26)

Panel A of Table 8.2 presents equally weighted momentum returns for all markets. The average monthly equally weighted momentum returns for All China (SSE and SZSE) are positive for different holding periods of 3 (0.56 percent per month), 6 (0.58 percent per month), 9 (0.41 percent per month) and 12 months (0.22 percent per month) and statistically significant for all the holding periods. The average monthly equally weighted momentum returns for HKSE are positive and significant for 3- (0.76 percent per month), 6- (0.60 percent per month) and 9-month (0.43 percent per month) holding periods, but small and insignificant for the 12-month (0.20 percent per month) holding period. Momentum returns for SSE are positive and statistically significant for the 3- (0.80 percent per month), 6- (0.83 percent per month), 9- (0.73 percent per month) and 12-month (0.53 percent per month) holding periods. In contrast, there is no evidence of a momentum effect for equally weighted portfolios in the SZSE since average monthly momentum returns for different holding periods are not statistically different from zero.

Panel B of Table 8.2 reports the value-weighted returns for all markets. We find large momentum returns for the Chinese and Hong Kong markets. The value-weighted momentum returns for All China are larger than equally weighted momentum returns and statistically significant for all holding periods. This indicates that momentum returns are not driven by small stocks. For HKSE, the value-weighted momentum returns are larger and significant for the 3- 6- and 9-month holding periods than for the corresponding equally weighted returns, but small and insignificant for the 12-month holding period. Momentum returns for the SSE are somewhat larger and statistically significant when we use value-weighted returns. Interestingly, momentum returns for the SZSE increase when we use value-weighted returns and becomes statistically significant for 6- and 9-month holding periods.

The equal-weighted and value-weighted results in Table 8.2 show that the momentum trading strategy is profitable both in the SSE and HKSE markets. However, momentum returns for SZSE are small and insignificant (equally weighted). The value-weighted momentum returns are higher than equal-weighted momentum returns for all markets in the sample. These higher value-weighted momentum returns are consistent with those shown in Korajczyk and Sadka (2005), and McLean (2010). This study also finds evidence consistent with Korajczyk and Sadka (2005), and McLean (2010) that the momentum winner effect for Chinese stocks is stronger in the equal-weighted portfolio, but the momentum loser effect is stronger in the value-weighted portfolios. The results reported in Table 8.2 are consistent with studies documenting a momentum effect in China (see for example Kang *et al.*, 2002; Naughton *et al.*, 2008; Wang, 2008). There are, however, studies that report insignificant momentum returns in China. For example Wang (2004), Chen *et al.* (2010), Cakici *et al.* (2011), Wu (2011), and Pan *et al.* (2013) all report insignificant equally weighted momentum returns using A shares for both the SSE and SZSE. If we include only A shares of both SSE and SZSE, then we get the similar results. In sum, we find that there is no evidence of a momentum effect in A- and B shares of SZSE using equally weighted returns but the effect is stronger and significant for both A- and B shares in SSE.

Table 8.3 reports the average monthly returns of the winners (P10), losers (P1) and winners minus losers (P10-P1) before (November 1995- December 2006)

Table 8.3 Momentum returns and financial crises

At the beginning of each month t, All China, SSE, SZSE and HKSE stocks are allocated into deciles based on their lagged 6-month (t-6 to t-1) returns and portfolios are formed one month after the lagged returns used for forming these portfolios are measured. We then form an equal-weighted and value-weighted zero-cost portfolio selling (buying) the decile of stocks with the lowest (highest) 6-month lagged returns. These portfolios are held for 6 months. The average monthly returns of portfolio P1 (losers), P10 (Winners) and momentum returns (P10-P1) are reported in percent and *t*-statistics provided in parentheses. The sample period is November 1994 to November 2010.

Panel A: Equal-weighted momentum returns before the global financial crisis

Market	P1 (Losers)	P10 (Winners)	P10-P1	%>0	#Months
All China	0.50 (1.73)	1.56 (5.97)	1.07 (6.10)	69.70	134
HKSE	−0.38 (−1.05)	0.73 (2.45)	1.11 (6.60)	80.30	134
SSE	0.44 (1.62)	1.85 (6.89)	1.41 (6.06)	76.52	134
SZSE	0.92 (2.49)	1.23 (4.41)	0.31 (2.11)	58.33	134

Panel B: Value-weighted momentum returns before the global financial crisis

Market	P1 (Losers)	P10 (Winners)	P10-P1	%>0	#Months
All China	0.27 (1.10)	1.46 (5.30)	1.19 (7.62)	80.60	134
HKSE	−0.80 (−2.26)	0.86 (2.29)	1.67 (6.98)	79.85	134
SSE	0.14 (0.65)	1.59 (6.24)	1.45 (8.43)	80.60	134
SZSE	0.62 (1.82)	1.33 (4.94)	0.72 (4.67)	70.90	134

Panel C: Equal-weighted momentum returns from 2007 to 2010

Country	P1 (Losers)	P10 (Winners)	P10-P1	%>0	#Months
All China	3.81 (4.11)	3.03 (3.21)	−0.78 (−3.69)	31.91	47
HKSE	1.50 (1.53)	0.68 (0.90)	−0.82 (−2.25)	61.97	47
SSE	3.83 (4.11)	2.99 (3.25)	−0.84 (−4.52)	25.31	47
SZSE	3.81 (4.17)	3.07 (3.13)	−0.74 (−2.76)	34.30	47

Table 8.3 (Continued)

Panel D: Value-weighted momentum returns from 2007 to 2010

Country	P1 (Losers)	P10 (Winners)	P10-P1	%>0	#Months
All China	2.72 (2.81)	2.29 (2.39)	−0.43 (−1.24)	42.55	47
HKSE	1.32 (1.38)	0.59 (0.89)	−0.73 (−1.26)	44.68	47
SSE	2.69 (2.77)	2.08 (2.23)	−0.61 (−1.79)	53.19	47
SZSE	3.35 (3.60)	2.76 (2.72)	−0.59 (−1.46)	42.55	47

and during (January 2007- November 2010) the GFC.[4] Panels A and B report equally weighted and value-weighted returns before 2007, respectively. Panels C and D show equally weighted and value-weighted returns for the period January 2007 to November 2010. Columns one and two report loser and winner portfolios, respectively; column three presents the momentum returns (P10-P1). The next column titled '% > 0' is the percentage of momentum returns that are positive over the sample period. The last column reports the number of months used to calculate momentum returns.

Panel A of Table 8.3 presents equally weighted momentum returns for all markets before the GFC. The equally weighted momentum returns for All China (SSE and SZSE) before the GFC are almost twice larger (1.07 percent per month) than the entire sample period and are statistically significant with 69.70 percent of the months greater than zero. The equally weighted returns for HKSE are also large, positive and significant (1.11 percent per month) before the GFC. The SSE returns are also high (1.41 percent per month) before the GFC. Interestingly, the SZSE returns are also large (0.31 percent per month) before the GFC and statistically significant. Panel B of Table 8.3 reports the value-weighted returns for all markets before the GFC. We find large, significant value-weighted momentum returns for both the Chinese and Hong Kong markets.

Panel C of Table 8.3 reports the equally weighted momentum returns for all markets during the GFC (2007–2010). We find negative and significant momentum returns for all markets. Panel D of Table 8.3 reports the value-weighted returns for all markets during the GFC; there are negative momentum returns for all markets, but they are statistically insignificant. The negative momentum returns during the GFC are consistent with the findings of Chordia and Shivakumar (2002) that the profitability of momentum is related to the business cycle. Negative momentum returns during a financial crisis are broadly consistent with Daniel and Moskowitz (2013) who report worst momentum returns during recessions and financial crises, especially in the months when market conditions improved.

These results are also consistent with the small and negative value-weighted market returns shown in Table 8.1 for All China and SSE during the GFC.

Panels C and D of Table 8.3 show that, from 2007, the momentum trading strategy underperformed and experienced large losses because loser stocks outperformed winner stocks. Figure 8.1 also shows losers outperforming winners, especially during the GFC years and, to a lesser degree, during and after the 1997 Asian financial crisis. It is evident from Figure 8.1 that, before 2007, past winners generally outperform past losers but, after 2007, there were many months when losers outperformed winners, especially in the months when the market started rising.

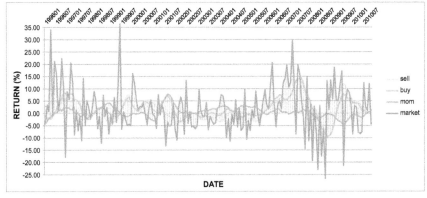

(a) Momentum Returns for All China

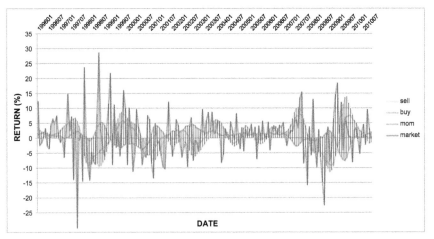

(b) Momentum Returns for HKSE

Figure 8.1 Momentum returns for All China, HKSE, SSE and SZSE

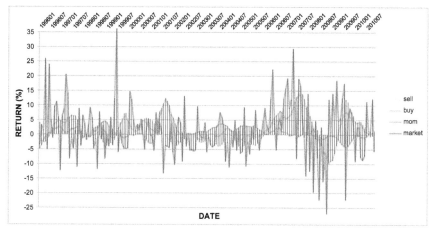

(c) Momentum Returns for SSE

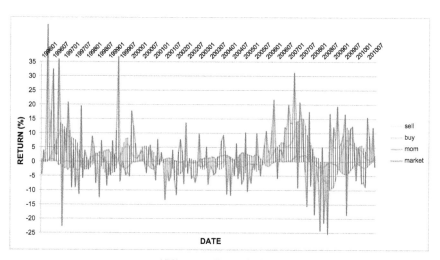

(d) Momentum Returns for SZSE

Figure 8.1 (Continued)

The sub-period analysis in Table 8.3 shows higher and significant momentum returns in all markets before the GFC. However, the momentum trading strategy fails to earn profits during the GFC. The results in Table 8.3 are consistent with Daniel and Moskowitz's (2013) study, which argues that the momentum trading strategy is large and significant during normal environments and turns into losses during market downturns or crises.

To summarize, our results provide evidence of large momentum returns in mainland Chinese markets, but they come mainly from SSE stocks.[5] The difference in momentum returns across SSE and SZSE appears to be related to firm size since we find (see Table 8.2) that value-weighted returns for SSE and SZSE are higher. Higher value-weighted returns indicate that large-cap companies generate higher momentum returns, consistent with Korajczyk and Sadka (2005), and McLean (2010). Note that SSE is dominated by large-cap companies, whereas SZSE is dominated by small companies. Momentum returns for HKSE stocks are also positive and statistically significant except for 12-month holding period. The sub-period analysis shows higher and significant momentum returns in all markets before the GFC. However, we find negative momentum returns following the GFC, and it is evident that the momentum trading strategy fails to earn profits during the GFC. Our results suggest that consistent momentum returns happen in normal environments where the market supposedly underreacts to public information. The presence of consistent momentum returns in a normal environment is in line with Daniel and Moskowitz's (2013) findings because it takes time for information to be adjusted into prices. On the other hand, after 2007, we find negative momentum returns and it appears that the worst returns for the momentum trading strategy occur in the months when the market conditions improve (see Figure 8.1). Figure 8.1 shows that the winner portfolio generally performs well in a normal environment and the loser portfolio performs well when the market emerges from severe crises. This trend is somewhat consistent with some other behavioural findings (see Loewenstein, 2000; Loewenstein *et al.*, 2001; Sunstein and Zeckhauser, 2008). During market downturns, we suggest that investors are fearful and focus more on losses especially if they already hold a loser stock. So there is a greater tendency for loser stocks to decline more than winner stocks during market downturns. When the market conditions improve, we suggest that these loser stocks experience large gains because their losses were the result of fear instead of bad performance. The strong gains of loser stocks then result in losses for the momentum trading strategy.

4.0   Market state effects on momentum returns

In this section, following Cooper *et al.* (2004), we examine the effect of the market state on momentum returns. The monthly average raw returns of the momentum trading strategy, as well as the CAPM and Fama-French adjusted returns (i.e. alphas) following UP and DOWN market states are shown in Table 8.4. Panel A reports the results when the market state is defined based on the past 36 months, whereas panels B and C report the results when the market state is defined based on the past 24 and 12 months, respectively. Panel A shows that during the period November 1995 to November 2010, using 36 months to define UP and DOWN markets, the UP market raw momentum returns, CAPM, and Fama-French alphas for All China are 0.34 percent, 0.37 percent and 0.35 percent per month, respectively, but statistically insignificant. Following DOWN market states, the raw momentum returns, CAPM and Fama-French alphas are 1.57 percent, 1.55 percent and 1.85 percent, respectively. When we define market state based on the past 24 months (panel B), the returns for All China in the DOWN market state

Table 8.4 Momentum returns and market states

At the beginning of each month t, All China, SSE, SZSE and HKSE stocks are allocated into deciles based on their six-month lagged returns, and portfolios are formed one month after the lagged returns used for forming these portfolios were measured. These portfolios are held for another six months. Holding period returns are then calculated. Positive (negative) returns of the value-weighted market returns for All China, VW SSE index, VW SZSE Index and Hang Seng Index over months $t - m$ ($m = 36$, 24 and 12 months) are used to define UP (DOWN) market states for each market. Monthly average momentum returns (winner minus loser), CAPM alphas, and Fama–French alphas over the sample period are reported below. Panels A, B, and C report momentum returns following 36-, 24- and 12- month UP and DOWN markets over the period from 1995 to 2010, respectively. Panels D and E and report momentum returns following 24-month UP and DOWN markets over the period from 1995 to 2006, and 2007 to 2010, respectively. All the returns are reported in percentages, and the numbers in the parentheses represent robust Newey and West t-statistics.

Panel A: Momentum returns following 36-month UP and DOWN markets

	All China		HKSE		SSE		SZSE	
	Up	Down	Up	Down	Up	Down	Up	Down
N	136	45	151	30	137	44	127	54
Momentum returns	0.34	1.57	0.54	0.51	0.65	1.97	−0.18	0.67
(t-statistic)	(1.04)	(3.71)	(1.03)	(1.06)	(1.07)	(4.56)	(−0.43)	(1.66)
CAPM alpha	0.37	1.55	0.51	0.50	0.66	1.59	−0.17	0.75
(t-statistic)	(1.01)	(3.58)	(1.08)	(1.06)	(1.08)	(4.46)	(−0.57)	(1.74)
Fama–French alpha	0.35	1.85	0.83	0.52	0.72	1.61	−0.14	1.01
(t-statistic)	(1.03)	(3.70)	(2.01)	(1.21)	(1.26)	(4.69)	(−0.56)	(2.01)

Panel B: Momentum returns following 24-month UP and DOWN markets

	All China		HKSE		SSE		SZSE	
	Up	Down	Up	Down	Up	Down	Up	Down
N	117	64	134	47	118	63	113	68
Momentum returns	0.48	0.93	054	0.53	0.77	1.31	−0.15	0.42
(t-statistic)	(1.18)	(2.92)	(1.32)	(0.86)	(1.73)	(2.98)	(−0.38)	(1.26)
CAPM alpha	0.55	0.90	0.53	1.01	0.79	1.65	−0.14	0.48
(t-statistic)	(1.10)	(2.88)	(1.60)	(1.64)	(1.86)	(3.02)	(−0.36)	(1.31)
Fama–French alpha	0.51	0.89	0.82	0.78	0.90	1.58	−0.13	0.55
(t-statistic)	(1.14)	(2.99)	(2.06)	(1.67)	(1.92)	(3.13)	(−0.39)	(1.56)

(Continued)

Table 8.4 (Continued)

Panel C: Monthly momentum returns following 12-month UP and DOWN markets

	All China		HKSE		SSE		SZSE	
	Up	Down	Up	Down	Up	Down	Up	Down
N	111	70	126	55	115	66	103	78
Momentum returns	0.84	0.33	0.38	0.88	1.20	0.55	0.15	−0.03
(*t*-statistic)	(2.06)	(1.08)	(0.99)	(1.20)	(2.50)	(1.59)	(0.57)	(−0.13)
CAPM alpha	0.85	0.42	0.37	1.10	1.20	0.69	0.13	0.13
(*t*-statistic)	(2.05)	(1.19)	(1.12)	(1.67)	(2.48)	(1.60)	(0.51)	(0.47)
Fama–French alpha	0.82	0.54	0.66	1.23	1.25	0.79	0.17	0.22
(*t*-statistic)	(2.03)	(1.27)	(1.71)	(1.97)	(2.55)	(1.86)	(0.62)	(0.79)

Panel D: Momentum returns following 24-month UP and DOWN markets before 2007

	All China		HKSE		SSE		SZSE	
	Up	Down	Up	Down	Up	Down	Up	Down
N	80	54	98	36	83	51	69	65
Momentum returns	1.08	1.19	0.89	1.26	1.55	1.66	0.09	0.56
(*t*-statistic)	(2.16)	(4.16)	(2.13)	(2.02)	(2.47)	(4.97)	(0.27)	(1.79)
CAPM alpha	1.20	1.16	0.87	1.48	1.59	1.65	0.12	0.65
(*t*-statistic)	(2.29)	(4.01)	(2.13)	(2.07)	(2.59)	(5.32)	(0.36)	(1.81)
Fama–French alpha	1.06	1.19	1.00	2.06	1.56	1.58	0.01	0.71
(*t*-statistic)	(2.16)	(4.10)	(2.19)	(2.32)	(2.51)	(5.11)	(0.27)	(2.03)

Panel E: Momentum returns following 24-month UP and DOWN markets from 2007 to 2010

	All China		HKSE		SSE		SZSE	
	Up	Down	Up	Down	Up	Down	Up	Down
N	36	11	35	12	34	13	43	4
Momentum returns	−0.83	−0.32	−0.14	−2.53	−1.11	−0.04	−0.53	−1.80
(*t*-statistic)	(−2.01)	(−0.61)	(−0.39)	(−1.69)	(−2.08)	(−0.11)	(−1.40)	(−2.05)
CAPM alpha	−0.84	−0.36	−0.14	−3.57	−1.12	−0.09	−0.62	−1.31
(*t*-statistic)	(−2.02)	(−0.82)	(−0.40)	(−1.60)	(−2.04)	(0.24)	(−1.59)	(−1.71)
Fama–French alpha	−0.69	−0.53	0.05	−3.61	−1.10	−0.26	−0.42	−1.21
(*t*-statistic)	(−1.61)	(−0.59)	(0.10)	(−1.25)	(−2.14)	(−0.32)	(−0.97)	(−1.31)

are larger (significant) than for UP market state (insignificant). However, when market state is defined based on the past 12 months (panel C), we find that the raw momentum returns, as well as the CAPM and Fama-French alphas following UP markets are large and statistically significant whereas those following DOWN markets are small and insignificant. In sum, we find positive momentum returns following both UP and DOWN markets, but the magnitude of momentum returns is larger and significant only for the 36- and 24-month DOWN market states and the 12-month UP market state. We conclude that there is no relationship between market state and momentum returns for China.

The raw, CAPM and Fama-French adjusted momentum returns for HKSE in panels A and B following 36- and 24-month (both UP and DOWN) market states are similar but statistically insignificant except the Fama-French alpha. However, the raw, CAPM and Fama-French adjusted momentum returns for the HKSE reported in panel C following the 12-month DOWN market states are larger than the corresponding values for UP market states, but they are insignificant except for the Fama-French alpha. We do not find any relationship between market states and momentum returns for HKSE stocks since the raw and CAPM-adjusted momentum returns following UP and DOWN market states are insignificant.

These results show that the DOWN market state explains momentum returns better for SSE if 36- and 24-month lagged market returns are used to define the DOWN market state. However, we find larger momentum returns following the UP market state when we use 12-month lagged market returns to define the market state. We conclude that there is no reliable relationship between market state and momentum returns for SSE. The momentum returns for the entire sample of SZSE stocks are statistically not different from zero except the Fama-French alpha following the 36-month DOWN market state. We conclude that market state cannot explain momentum returns for SZSE since there is no evidence of a relationship between momentum returns and 36-, 24- and 12-month market states.

In summary, it appears that momentum returns do not depend on market state since we report significant momentum returns for All China, HKSE and SSE stocks regardless of the market state before the GFC.[6] However, momentum returns for SZSE are insignificant before the GFC. Interestingly, momentum returns become negative for all markets from 2007 until 2010 regardless of the market state. Therefore, momentum returns seem to follow worldwide business cycle expansions and recessions since momentum returns are totally different before and after 2007.

5.0   Conclusion

The momentum trading strategy first found profitable by Jegadeesh and Titman (1993), remains most prominent among all the anomalies found in the finance literature. The momentum effect is robust across international markets and time periods and though a few empirical studies link momentum returns with market states none has done so for the markets of China and Hong Kong. Given that China and Hong Kong are the world's fastest growing emerging markets and China expected to be the largest economy of the world by 2041, it is imperative for the global investment community to gain a deeper understanding of its financial markets. Also, the impact of the GFC on momentum returns has not been tested. The literature suggests a relationship between momentum returns and economic activity; therefore, it is important to test the relationship between momentum returns and the GFC.

In this chapter, we investigate the impact of market state and the GFC on momentum returns in the Chinese and Hong Kong markets. We report positive and significant momentum returns for All China, HKSE and SSE and small insignificant momentum returns for SZSE. The difference in momentum returns between SSE and SZSE appears to be related to firm size since SZSE is dominated by small companies. However, we find large momentum returns before the GFC and negative momentum returns from 2007 until 2010 for all markets. There is a dramatic impact of the GFC on momentum returns since the loser portfolio generates higher returns than the winner portfolio from 2007 until 2010 and hence negative momentum returns. Before the GFC, all markets seem to under-react to public information resulting in consistent momentum returns. However, during the GFC, it appears that investors were fearful and avoided loser stocks resulting in a decrease in the price of loser stocks beyond their fundamental level. Any improvement in market conditions after a severe downturn returns the prices of loser stocks back to their fundamental level; hence, losers generate higher returns than winners. Our results indicating the worst momentum returns during the GFC are in line with Daniel and Moskowitz (2013), who also find the worst momentum returns during recessions and stock market crises. Our results also appear to be consistent with some behavioural findings.[7] These behavioural findings imply that individuals are fearful in extreme situations and appear to focus more on losses and, therefore, probabilities are largely ignored. Research is needed to examine whether the empirical results documented for China and Hong Kong are fully consistent with these behavioural findings.

In the finance literature, there are largely two possible explanations for the momentum anomaly, one is risk-based, and the other is behaviour-based. We find that momentum returns cannot be explained by risk factors because momentum returns remain almost the same after controlling for the Fama-French risk factors. Among the behavioural explanations, Daniel *et al.* (1998) overreaction theory is well known, where investor overconfidence results in overreaction that generates momentum returns. Cooper *et al.* (2004) extend Daniel *et al.* (1998) theory to predict differences in momentum returns across market states suggesting that if investor overconfidence is responsible for momentum returns, then overconfidence would be greater following UP market states. Cooper *et al.* (2004) find positive significant momentum returns following UP market states (36, 24 and 12 months) in the US market.

However, unlike Cooper *et al.* (2004), we find no systematic relationship between market state and momentum returns in China and Hong Kong, which highlights the fact that we cannot simply generalize the findings in mature markets to new and emerging markets. Nonetheless, we find a strong relationship between momentum returns and economic activity because there are large momentum returns before the GFC.

This study contributes to the literature because it is the first study that finds a strong relationship between momentum returns and economic activity for Chinese and Hong Kong stocks. The results of this study have important implications because they provide supplementary evidence that investors could have increased their returns by using the momentum strategy because it was profitable before the GFC. Also, the results suggest that from 2007–2010 investors could have earned greater returns over the next 3 to 12 months by buying previous loser stocks because loser stocks outperform winners during economic downturns.

Notes

1 The risk-free rate for All China (SSE and SZSE) is the monthly rate charged by People's Bank of China to financial institutions. The risk-free rate for Hong Kong refers to the monthly interbank rate.
2 Momentum returns with 6-month formation and holding periods are adjusted for risk factors.
3 We also calculate CAPM- and Fama-French risk adjusted momentum returns that are very similar to raw momentum returns. To save space, we only report raw momentum returns.
4 Although the Global Financial Crisis officially started in late 2007, for convenience we define the 2007–2010 period as "the Global Financial Crisis". However, our results are robust if we define "the Global Financial Crisis period" from 2008 to 2010.
5 Value-weighted momentum returns for SZSE are smaller than SSE and HKSE but statistically significant for 6- and 9-month holding periods. However, equal-weighted momentum returns for SZSE are insignificant for all the holding periods.
6 To save the space, we only report momentum returns following 24-month UP and DOWN market before and after the Global Financial Crises.
7 See Loewenstein (2000), Loewenstein *et al.* (2001), and Sunstein and Zeckhauser (2008).

References

Bacmann, J. F., and Dubois, M. (2000). La performance des stratégies contraires et momentum sur le marché suisse. *Financial Markets and Portfolio Management, 14*, 252–266.

Bacmann, J. F., Dubois, M., and Isakov, D. (2001). *Industries, business cycle and profitability of momentum strategies: An international perspective*. Paper presented at the EFMA 2001 Lugano Meetings.

Barberis, N., Shleifer, A., and Vishny, R. (1998). A model of investor sentiment. *Journal of financial economics, 49*(3), 307–343.

Cakici, N., Chan, K., and Topyan, K. (2011). Cross-sectional stock return predictability in China. Available at: http://dx.doi.org/10.2139/ssrn.2038497

Chan, K., Hameed, A., and Tong, W. (2000). Profitability of momentum strategies in the international equity markets. *Journal of Financial and Quantitative Analysis, 35*(2), 153–172.

Cheema, M. A., and Nartea, G. V. (2014). Momentum returns and information uncertainty: Evidence from China. *Pacific-Basin Finance Journal, 30*, 173–188.

Chen, X., Kim, K. A., Yao, T., and Yu, T. (2010). On the predictability of Chinese stock returns. *Pacific-Basin Finance Journal, 18*(4), 403–425.

Cheng, J. W., and Wu, H. (2010). The profitability of momentum trading strategies: Empirical evidence from Hong Kong. *International Review of Economics & Finance, 19*(4), 527–538.

Chui, A. C. W., Wei, K. C., and Titman, S. (2000). Momentum, legal systems and ownership structure: An analysis of Asian stock markets. University of Texas at Austin Working Paper.

Cooper, M. J., Gutierrez, R. C., and Hameed, A. (2004). Market states and momentum. *The Journal of Finance, 59*(3), 1345–1365.

Daniel, K. D., Hirshleifer, D., and Subrahmanyam, A. (1998). Investor psychology and security market under-and overreactions. *The Journal of Finance, 53*(6), 1839–1885.

Daniel, K. D., Hirshleifer, D., and Subrahmanyam, A. (2002). Overconfidence, arbitrage, and equilibrium asset pricing. *The Journal of Finance, 56*(3), 921–965.

Daniel, K. D., and Moskowitz, T. J. (2013). Momentum crashes. Swiss Finance Institute Research Paper No. 13–61; Columbia Business School Research Paper No. 14–6; Fama-Miller Working Paper.

Fama, E. F., and French, K. R. (2008). Dissecting anomalies. *The Journal of Finance, 63*(4), 1653–1678.

Hameed, A., and Kusnadi, Y. (2002). Momentum strategies: Evidence from Pacific Basin stock markets. *Journal of Financial Research, 25*(3), 383–397.

Hong, H., and Stein, J. C. (1999). A unified theory of underreaction, momentum trading, and overreaction in asset markets. *The Journal of Finance, 54*(6), 2143–2184.

Hong, H., and Stein, J. C. (2007). Disagreement and the stock market. *The Journal of Economic Perspectives, 21*(2), 109–128.

Jegadeesh, N., and Titman, S. (1993). Returns to buying winners and selling losers: Implications for stock market efficiency. *The Journal of Finance, 48*(1), 65–91.

Kang, J., Liu, M.-H., and Ni, S. X. (2002). Contrarian and momentum strategies in the China stock market: 1993–2000. *Pacific-Basin Finance Journal, 10*(3), 243–265.

Korajczyk, R. A., and Sadka, R. (2005). Are momentum profits robust to trading costs? *The Journal of Finance, 59*(3), 1039–1082.

Loewenstein, G. (2000). Emotions in economic theory and economic behavior. *The American Economic Review, 90*(2), 426–432.

Loewenstein, G. F., Weber, E. U., Hsee, C. K., and Welch, N. (2001). Risk as feelings. *Psychological Bulletin, 127*(2), 267.

McLean, R. D. (2010). Idiosyncratic risk, long-term reversal, and momentum. *Journal of Financial and Quantitative Analysis, 45*(04), 883–906.

Naughton, T., Truong, C., and Veeraraghavan, M. (2008). Momentum strategies and stock returns: Chinese evidence. *Pacific-Basin Finance Journal, 16*(4), 476–492.

Pan, L., Tang, Y., and Xu, J. (2013). Weekly momentum by return interval ranking. *Pacific-Basin Finance Journal, 21*(1), 1191–1208.

Rouwenhorst, K. G. (1998). International momentum strategies. *The Journal of Finance, 53*(1), 267–284.

Rouwenhorst, K. G. (1999). Local return factors and turnover in emerging stock markets. *The Journal of Finance, 54*(4), 1439–1464.

Schiereck, D., and Weber, M. (1995). Zyklische und antizyklische Handelsstrategien am deutschen Aktienmarkt. *Zeitschrift für betriebswirtschaftliche Forschung, 47*, 3–24.

Sunstein, C., and Zeckhauser, R. (2008). Overreaction to fearsome risks. Harvard Law School Program on Risk Regulation Research Paper No. 08–17.

Wang, C. (2004). Relative strength strategies in China's stock market: 1994–2000. *Pacific-Basin Finance Journal, 12*(2), 159–177.

Wang, C., and Chin, S. (2004). Profitability of return and volume-based investment strategies in China's stock market. *Pacific-Basin Finance Journal, 12*(5), 541–564.

Wang, D. (2008). Are anomalies still anomalous? An examination of momentum strategies in four financial markets. Working Paper No. WP-775, University of Navarra.

Wu, Y. (2011). Momentum trading, mean reversal and overreaction in Chinese stock market. *Review of Quantitative Finance and Accounting, 37*(3), 301–323.

9 The profitability of technical trading rules

Empirical application on Asian stock markets

Andrei Anghel and Cristiana Tudor

1.0 Introduction and related literature

One of the most influential papers discussing technical trading rules was the 1961 paper of Sidney Alexander, 'Price Movements in Speculative Markets: Trends or Random Walks.' Fama and Blume (1966) highlighted some shortcomings of this study. Among them, the author did not take into account large price jumps or what we now call 'fast markets' and 'price slippage': simply put, some of the prices of Alexander's trades were simply unobtainable in the real world. Other perceived weaknesses of that study were not taking into account brokerage fees or dividends, although we do not agree with this line of reasoning. Despite these criticisms and others, the method described by Sidney Alexander kept capturing researchers' attention for years. Also unabated by controversial research on the subject, Alexander's filters remained one of the standard tools in technical analysis packages provided on many trading platforms by brokerage houses all over the world. The filter was a simple rule that decided when to go long and when to short the market; it was designed in such a way that the strategy would benefit if the market was trending and the filter was somehow calibrated to profit from this 'abnormal' behaviour of the market. The calibration was required to filter out market noise – variations that did not exceed a certain level – and retain only those movements of the prices that were large enough to indicate that some (important) piece of information had started to unfold.

This basic idea allowed a number of different variations of the aforementioned filters, and many others that predate them, to flourish. With the advent of computing power the rules became even more numerous due to their relative ease in implementation. All these rules and filters are collectively known as technical trading rules. Bootstrapping was singled out as a convenient way of testing technical trading rules on data generated using some algorithm. What was previously only a simple rule of thumb was now rigorously tested to see whether it actually revealed something relevant and new about markets. Brock, Lakonishok and LeBaron (1992) proposed using bootstrapping on some of the simplest trading rules and found out that technical rules – in particular simple moving averages – were actually uncovering something interesting about markets that could not otherwise be explained using the popular random walk theory, the $AR(1)$ process or GARCH (M or exponential) models.

However, what was initially a blessing for the advent of technical rules – computing power – soon became a threat, as the rules could be thought of as the result of aggressive data mining. Also called data snooping, this is the process of testing and retesting filters, rules and combinations of them up to the point when some apparently significant relation had to emerge, even if only luck was to be considered. The authors of this paper found several studies where an impressive number of trading rules – up to 39.832 in one of them – were investigated (see, for example, Hsu and Kuan, 2005). Such extensive testing of rules would erode its significance by itself, had the authors not used an adapted test for significance when testing a high number of models. This test was 'the reality check for data snooping' proposed by White (2000), which allows the researcher to decide with a certain degree of confidence whether the best model which he has uncovered using a large number of specifications has no predictive superiority over a given benchmark model, such as the buy-and-hold policy.

We attempt to check the superiority of the simplest and most famous rule – the simple moving average. We use various configurations and four Asian stock markets and the results are entirely presented here, in order to protect our research from known biases, such as data mining or survivorship bias, as much as possible.

The remainder of the paper is organized as follows. In Section 2.0, the data and methodology are presented. The empirical results are reported in Section 3.0, while Section 4.0 concludes the study.

2.0 Data and method

We begin by examining simple moving average (SMA, from this point forward) strategies in relation to a simple 'buy-and-hold' strategy on four Asian stock market indexes (i.e. NIKKEI for Japan, HANGSENG for Hong Kong, Shanghai Stock Exchange (SSE) composite for China and BSE SENSEX for India) for a 23-year period ranging from December 1990 (May 1997 for BSE Sensex) to May 2013.

These daily returns observations are indexed from R to T, so that $T = R + n - 1$. We follow White (2000) and compute daily returns as:

$$y_{t+1} = \frac{Index_{t+1}}{Index_t} - 1.$$

Excess returns over a given benchmark produced by a technical trading rule is written as:

$$\hat{f}_{t+1} = (1 + y_{t+1} S_1 (X_{1,t}, \beta_1^*)) / (1 + y_{t+1} S_0 (X_{0,t}, \beta_0^*)) - 1.$$

Here S_1 and S_0 are 'signal functions' with only two permissible values, 1 for long and –1 for short. We thus simplified the Brock *et al.* (1992) framework, which contains a third value of 0 (zero) for neutral positions. The signal functions convert indicators $X_{1,t+1}$ or $X_{0,t+1}$ and parameters β_1^* or β_0^* into market position.

Average excess returns for a particular technical trading rule will be:

$$\bar{f} = n^{-1}\sum_{t=R}^{T}\hat{f}_{t+1}.$$

This framework accommodates most if not all the trading strategies based on technical indicators. The nominator in the above equation represents strategy to be tested (SMA, in this case), while the denominator represents the benchmark strategy. Since we only want to investigate SMAs as a trading rule, the indicators $X_{1,\,t+1}$ are simple values, and parameters are the lengths of the two averages (n_1 for shorter MA and n_2 for longer MA). Since we chose:

$$n_1 \in \{1;2;3;4;5;6;7;8;9;10\}$$
$$n_2 \in \{25;50;75;100;150;200;250,300;350;500\}.$$

We thus obtain length($n1$) × length($n2$) = 100 combinations for the parameter β_l^*, l from 1 to 100. Simply put, we will test 100 trading strategies based on a SMA. A formal definition of the SMA trading rule is as follows:

$$short\,SMA_t = 1/n_1\sum_{t-n_1}^{t}X_t$$
$$long\,SMA_t = 1/n_2\sum_{t-n_2}^{t}X_t.$$

The function S_1 will simply convert into market positions (long or short) the heuristics behind the SMA trading strategy, which states that whenever the short and 'faster' SMA crosses the long SMA from below, you should buy, and when it crosses from above, you should sell. Since we want to test our strategies against the simple buy-and-hold strategy, the S_0 function is a special case that only yields value 1 (always 'long' on the market).

Having said this, we first proceed by computing average excess returns over the buy-and-hold policy for our 100 different strategies. We look for abnormal, statistically significant excess returns under the assumption of normality. We thus emulate the analysis of Alexander (1961), though on a different strategy (i.e. SMA).

Secondly, we want to test the apparent superiority of the best trading rule by using the nonparametric bootstrapping method as described by Brock *et al.* (1992). The classic diagnosis on the statistical significance of excess returns involves investigating the null hypothesis that excess return is less than or equal to zero versus the alternative hypothesis that the same return is greater than zero. Under the assumption of the normal distribution, the t-test is:

$$t-statistic = \frac{\mu_{exces}}{\sigma_{exces}/\sqrt{N-1}},$$

where N is the number of days (observations) of the data set.

But, as expected, our return series violate the normality assumption. Thus we are dealing with a clear case of leptokurtic distribution, and the null hypothesis of normality could lead to serious inference errors. A partial solution is to follow Brock *et al.* (1992) and test the significance of the difference between average returns corresponding to N_{long} long positions and average returns corresponding to N_{short} short positions. In this case the *t*-test would be:

$$t-statistic = \frac{\mu_{long} - \mu_{short}}{\left(\dfrac{\sigma^2}{N_{long}} + \dfrac{\sigma^2}{N_{short}}\right)^{1/2}}.$$

In this research we will not proceed to testing under the assumption of normal distribution of returns. Instead, for the technical trading rules mentioned before, we describe how to implement a method to estimate *p*-values using the bootstrapping method together with an assumption about the distribution of returns (random walk in our study). The theoretical foundation for the bootstrapping methodology is detailed in Efron (1979), while the theory on estimating *p*-values for similar trading rules under different null distributions (i.e. random walk, AR (1), GARCH-M and EGARCH) is described in Brock *et al.* (1992).

Here, we proceed thus to test whether such trading rules manage to generate a return above normal, where normality is described by the null hypothesis that stock returns follow the random walk with a drift model. If the estimated *p*-values turn out to be sufficiently small, we can conclude that it is likely that the trading rules benefit from certain (unidentified) features of the return distribution not captured by the null model.

After computing excess return, the bootstrapping method allows us to compare the returns produced by a particular technical trading rule with returns taken from the empirical distribution, where the empirical distribution is constructed by applying the same trading rule to simulated time series with replacement (1000 times) under the null of a random walk. So, we sample with replacement from the original return series, and the length of the simulated series equals the original series.

Once sampling has been carried out, the next step is to build recursive series of prices or simulated quotations (we use the symbol '*' for simulated prices or returns). For logarithmic returns, the value X^* at time *t*, based on *T* returns sampled with replacement from the original series, will be equal to:

$$X_t^* = X_{t-1}^*(y_t^* + 1),$$

where y_t^* is the *t*th return from the sample $t = R . . . T$.

The next step is to calculate the average return $\bar{f}_b^*$ obtained by applying the technical trading rules on simulated time series, where $b = 1 . . . B$ is the number of the simulation from the total of *B* simulations performed. In this study, $B = 1000$. Therefore, the estimated *p*-value results from comparing the average real return $\bar{f}$ with the quantiles of average simulated returns $\bar{f}^* = \bar{f}_b^*$, $b = 1 . . . B$. Therefore:

$$bootstrap\ p-value = \frac{\sum_{b=1}^{B} 1_{\{\bar{f} < \bar{f}_b^*\}}}{B}.$$

Finally, we want to test the apparent superiority of the best trading rule by taking into account biases that data mining could introduce. We employ the reality check for data snooping introduced by White (2000).

White (2000) introduces the reality check test applied to the best model selected from a large sample of previously tested models. His algorithm consists in firstly computing the performance of the benchmark, which can be expressed either as average return (as we have used bellow) or RMSE (root mean squared error, as in the original article) or the Sharpe ratio, etc. Thus the first step consists in computing $\bar{f}_1$ – the average excess performance of rule 1, followed by computing $\bar{f}_1^* = \bar{f}_{1,b}^*$, $b = 1...B$, which is a vector of length B containing the average excess performances on simulated (bootstrapped) time series, all for rule 1. B represents the number of simulations or bootstrapped samples. Basically, up to this point the procedure is identical to the (naïve) p-value computation.

Next, White sets $\bar{V}_1 = \bar{f}_1$ and $\bar{V}_{1,b}^* = \bar{f}_{1,b}^* - \bar{f}_1$, $b = 1...B$, so that we can test whether rule 1 is better than the benchmark by comparing $\bar{V}_1$ with the quintiles of $\bar{V}_{1,b}^*$. Similarly for rule 2 he sets:

$$\bar{V}_2 = max\{\bar{f}_2, \bar{V}_1\}$$
$$\bar{V}_{2,b}^* = max\{(\bar{f}_{2,b}^* - \bar{f}_2), \bar{V}_{1,b}^*\},$$

where $b = 1...B$. In order to test whether the best of rules 1 and 2 is better than the benchmark, we compare $\bar{V}_2$ with the quintiles of $\bar{V}_{2,b}^*$.

Thus there is a recursive process of testing whether the best of k rules is better than the benchmark, where $k = 3...l$ and l is the number of rules that we intend to test (100 in this study). It can generally be resumed as comparing

$$\bar{V}_k = max\{\bar{f}_k, \bar{V}_{k-1}\}$$

with the quintiles

$$\bar{V}_{k,b}^* = max\{\bar{f}_{k,b}^* - \bar{f}_k, \bar{V}_{k-1,b}^*\},$$

where $b = 1...B$. The process continues for each of the l rules that we want to test, and finally we can draw a conclusion about the best of these rules. Formally, reality check p-value could be expressed as:

$$RC\ p-value = \frac{\sum_{b=1}^{B} 1_{\{\bar{V}_i < \bar{V}_{i,b}^*\}}}{B}.$$

3.0   Empirical results

Table 9.1 summarizes our findings on the excess return for each of the rules applied on the four Asian stock indexes. Results show that the returns of the 100 SMA rules over their benchmark indicate consistent gains at least in some

Table 9.1 Annual excess return for SMA ($n1$, $n2$) rules (in percentages)

$n2$	25	50	75	100	150	200	250	300	350	500
$n1$										
Nikkei										
1	1.10%	5.70%	4.90%	5.30%	5.00%	5.20%	1.60%	2.90%	1.70%	1.20%
2	0.60%	6.50%	5.90%	5.70%	5.20%	4.90%	2.00%	2.00%	2.70%	1.10%
3	1.30%	5.70%	6.50%	6.00%	5.70%	3.90%	1.00%	1.30%	2.80%	1.30%
4	2.80%	6.00%	5.80%	4.60%	5.60%	3.60%	1.50%	2.30%	3.20%	0.90%
5	4.50%	4.40%	6.10%	4.00%	5.40%	3.80%	2.20%	1.20%	1.80%	1.50%
6	5.30%	5.00%	6.20%	4.00%	6.60%	3.80%	1.50%	2.50%	2.10%	1.80%
7	4.90%	4.10%	4.90%	3.60%	6.40%	3.60%	0.80%	1.90%	2.30%	0.60%
8	2.80%	3.30%	4.80%	3.50%	5.80%	4.50%	1.20%	1.20%	1.80%	1.10%
9	2.70%	1.70%	3.70%	3.50%	6.80%	4.60%	0.60%	1.20%	2.60%	0.90%
10	3.10%	1.80%	2.30%	4.20%	7.50%	4.20%	0.20%	1.20%	2.90%	0.80%
HANGSENG										
1	1.50%	0.90%	1.00%	0.80%	-1.00%	-3.30%	-3.90%	-5.30%	-3.80%	-5.10%
2	0.50%	1.40%	-0.20%	1.00%	-2.80%	-2.50%	-2.90%	-5.40%	-3.30%	-4.90%
3	-1.80%	2.00%	-2.00%	-1.60%	-3.10%	-1.80%	-1.90%	-4.00%	-3.10%	-6.00%
4	-6.40%	0.50%	-0.50%	-3.20%	-2.60%	-1.90%	-2.80%	-4.50%	-3.90%	-6.70%
5	-6.20%	-0.50%	-0.80%	-3.50%	-2.70%	-2.10%	-3.00%	-5.00%	-3.30%	-6.70%
6	-4.60%	0.30%	-1.50%	-3.50%	-2.60%	-1.90%	-2.30%	-4.10%	-3.50%	-6.70%
7	-4.60%	0.70%	-1.60%	-3.00%	-3.20%	-0.40%	-3.30%	-4.60%	-3.50%	-6.30%
8	-2.90%	-0.50%	-1.80%	-2.40%	-3.50%	-0.70%	-3.60%	-5.10%	-5.00%	-7.10%
9	-2.40%	-1.30%	-2.20%	-4.40%	-3.70%	-1.90%	-4.20%	-4.20%	-5.10%	-7.30%
10	-1.30%	-0.80%	-2.80%	-4.70%	-3.70%	-1.60%	-3.70%	-4.20%	-4.80%	-8.10%

(*Continued*)

Table 9.1 (Continued)

n2	25	50	75	100	150	200	250	300	350	500
SSE COMPOSITE										
1	18.00%	9.30%	2.10%	-1.60%	-5.10%	-11.50%	-12.30%	-9.80%	-10.40%	-15.40%
2	19.20%	9.10%	3.60%	-3.90%	-3.80%	-8.10%	-13.20%	-9.50%	-11.60%	-17.00%
3	15.80%	8.70%	3.10%	-2.40%	-4.30%	-8.20%	-12.40%	-10.30%	-12.50%	-16.00%
4	11.60%	7.10%	-0.50%	0.00%	-2.60%	-9.40%	-15.50%	-14.00%	-13.60%	-15.90%
5	8.30%	6.30%	0.30%	-1.00%	-5.80%	-10.70%	-13.40%	-13.00%	-15.20%	-17.30%
6	5.40%	4.80%	0.80%	-0.10%	-6.00%	-10.70%	-11.10%	-13.20%	-16.30%	-15.20%
7	6.40%	5.80%	0.30%	1.40%	-4.70%	-11.20%	-12.80%	-13.40%	-14.90%	-15.00%
8	3.70%	6.70%	1.50%	-0.70%	-5.40%	-9.50%	-13.80%	-14.60%	-16.60%	-14.80%
9	0.00%	3.50%	1.00%	0.60%	-3.70%	-7.20%	-14.10%	-13.80%	-16.70%	-16.50%
10	1.20%	1.30%	-2.40%	0.90%	-3.40%	-6.50%	-14.50%	-15.50%	-16.10%	-15.50%
BSE SENSEX										
1	8.00%	5.20%	6.60%	5.80%	-0.70%	-2.00%	-3.60%	-4.60%	-2.60%	-3.30%
2	1.40%	-0.20%	4.10%	3.90%	1.20%	-4.30%	-3.20%	-4.00%	-2.30%	-3.30%
3	-0.60%	-2.00%	0.10%	2.00%	-1.40%	-2.80%	-2.30%	-3.40%	-3.90%	-4.30%
4	-4.30%	1.40%	-2.30%	0.00%	-2.90%	-2.40%	-2.00%	-3.90%	-4.70%	-4.90%
5	-2.90%	-0.40%	-2.80%	-0.20%	-2.20%	-3.00%	-1.20%	-2.40%	-4.90%	-4.70%
6	-2.30%	-0.80%	-3.90%	0.30%	-2.00%	-2.60%	-2.30%	-2.10%	-3.90%	-4.70%
7	-1.40%	-3.10%	-4.30%	1.20%	-2.10%	-3.00%	-0.60%	-2.50%	-2.40%	-4.00%
8	0.10%	-3.20%	-4.40%	0.10%	-2.40%	-3.10%	-1.00%	-3.40%	-2.80%	-3.00%
9	-2.10%	-2.90%	-3.00%	-0.40%	-3.30%	-2.40%	-1.10%	-3.60%	-2.40%	-2.90%
10	-3.00%	-4.00%	-3.20%	-1.00%	-3.70%	-1.10%	-1.30%	-4.10%	-2.30%	-3.50%

cases for each market, and consistently for Japan. Daily returns have been annualized by multiplication with 220. Higher excess returns achieved with technical trading rules are most visible for the SSE composite.

Whether the returns in excess of their respective benchmark produced by following trading rules (presented above) are due to chance or these technical trading rules are able to truly uncover some market anomalies and thus consistently beat the buy-and-hold strategy could only be established using some formal testing. We start by estimating standard bootstrapping p-values, which are presented in Table 9.2.

Reported bootstrapped p-values in Table 9.2 suggest that these technical strategies might do a better job in explaining market returns than the null model (i.e. the random walk with a drift) on all Asian markets with the exception of Japan, where all p-values exceed 10 percent. However, this conclusion would hold

Table 9.2 Bootstrap p-values for excess returns of SMA rules vs. random walk for the four Asian markets (H0: excess return for SMA $[n1, n2] \leq 0$)

n2	25	50	75	100	150	200	250	300	350	500
n1	Nikkei									
1	40%	16%	18%	17%	19%	19%	36%	29%	35%	39%
2	42%	14%	15%	16%	18%	20%	34%	34%	30%	38%
3	39%	17%	13%	15%	16%	24%	40%	39%	30%	39%
4	31%	16%	15%	21%	17%	25%	37%	32%	27%	41%
5	21%	21%	14%	23%	18%	23%	33%	40%	34%	37%
6	17%	18%	14%	23%	13%	24%	37%	29%	32%	35%
7	19%	23%	18%	26%	13%	24%	41%	34%	32%	42%
8	30%	27%	19%	25%	15%	20%	38%	39%	34%	40%
9	30%	34%	23%	25%	12%	19%	42%	39%	28%	41%
10	28%	34%	31%	22%	11%	21%	45%	39%	27%	41%
	HangSeng									
1	4%	3%	4%	5%	9%	18%	20%	29%	20%	28%
2	5%	4%	5%	5%	15%	14%	16%	31%	18%	28%
3	9%	2%	11%	10%	16%	12%	12%	22%	17%	37%
4	28%	4%	7%	15%	15%	13%	17%	24%	21%	43%
5	27%	6%	8%	17%	15%	13%	17%	27%	17%	43%
6	19%	5%	9%	17%	15%	12%	13%	22%	18%	42%
7	20%	5%	9%	15%	17%	8%	18%	24%	18%	40%
8	14%	7%	9%	13%	19%	9%	19%	26%	27%	45%
9	13%	7%	11%	21%	20%	13%	21%	21%	28%	48%
10	9%	7%	13%	22%	19%	12%	19%	21%	27%	53%

(*Continued*)

Table 9.2 (Continued)

n2	25	50	75	100	150	200	250	300	350	500
	SSE composite									
1	0%	0%	2%	7%	15%	47%	52%	39%	46%	78%
2	0%	1%	2%	12%	12%	28%	58%	38%	52%	84%
3	0%	1%	2%	9%	13%	28%	52%	41%	57%	80%
4	0%	1%	6%	5%	9%	34%	69%	64%	64%	79%
5	0%	1%	4%	6%	17%	41%	57%	58%	72%	84%
6	1%	2%	3%	5%	18%	42%	46%	59%	77%	78%
7	1%	1%	4%	3%	13%	43%	55%	61%	68%	77%
8	2%	1%	3%	6%	16%	36%	59%	68%	79%	76%
9	5%	2%	4%	4%	11%	25%	61%	64%	79%	82%
10	4%	4%	8%	4%	10%	22%	63%	73%	75%	78%
	BSE sensex									
1	1%	1%	2%	1%	9%	12%	18%	22%	15%	18%
2	5%	9%	3%	3%	5%	22%	16%	20%	13%	18%
3	8%	13%	9%	5%	10%	15%	13%	18%	19%	23%
4	19%	5%	13%	8%	16%	13%	12%	21%	24%	26%
5	13%	9%	15%	8%	13%	15%	9%	15%	24%	26%
6	12%	10%	20%	7%	12%	15%	13%	14%	20%	25%
7	10%	17%	23%	5%	13%	16%	8%	15%	15%	21%
8	7%	17%	22%	8%	13%	16%	9%	18%	16%	15%
9	12%	15%	17%	9%	17%	14%	9%	19%	14%	15%
10	16%	18%	19%	9%	19%	10%	10%	20%	14%	18%

only if the particular technical trading rule that produces excess return had been discovered completely by chance.

However, since data mining and survivorship bias could contribute to this apparent significance, we compute next the reality check (RC) p-value for the SMA rules, which will help reach a conclusion about the efficiency of the four Asian markets.

In Figure 9.1 we present the RC p-value as it is recursively generated when each added rule (until 100) is tested using a bootstrapping procedure.

The overall results are presented in Table 9.3, along with the best technical trading rule for each market, the excess annual return it produced over the buy-and-hold strategy, its corresponding bootstrapped p-value and finally the RC p-value, which validates (or not) the robustness of the returns.

Among the four Asian equity markets, only in Shanghai, China (RC p-value of 5.8 percent corresponding to an annual excess return of 19.22 percent achieved

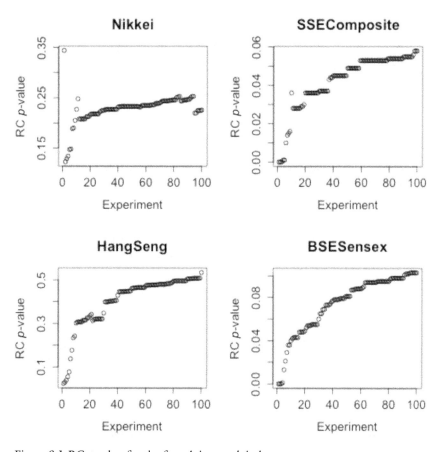

Figure 9.1 RC *p*-value for the four Asian stock indexes

Table 9.3 Best technical trading rules, excess returns and *p*-values (bootstrap and RC) for the four Asian equity markets

	Stock index	Best technical trading rule	Excess Return (Annual)	Naïve p-value	Reality check p-value
1	Nikkei	SMA (10,150)	0.075062296	0.105	0.226
2	SSE composite	SMA (2,25)	0.192217438	0	0.058*
3	HangSeng	SMA (3,50)	0.019852109	0.024	0.535
4	BSE Sensex	SMA (1,25)	0.080103627	0.009	0.103

*significant at 10%.

by the SMA (2,25) technical trading rule) and marginally India (RC p-value of 10.3 percent corresponding to an annual excess return of 8.01 percent achieved by the SMA(1,25) technical trading rule) does technical trading seem to be able to achieve superior (and statistically significant) results. For Japan and Hong Kong excess returns did not remain significant, and hence we conclude that the two markets are efficient.

4.0 Conclusion

The continued use of technical analysis tools such as SMAs seems to have little justification on closer scrutiny. The good track record that they have enjoyed in the past might be explained by aggressive data mining or might be the pervasive effect of a survivorship bias manifested among trading rules in a similar way that it manifests among hedge funds and their trading strategies.

Prior studies that employed the same tests that we have used in this paper did find, however, some use for technical strategies, including the simple cases that we have analyzed here. Not only did those rules manage to explain market dynamics better than the traditional random walk model, but they were even capable of consistently surpassing the buy-and-hold benchmark. However, we could only confirm these findings without any doubt for one out of the four analyzed Asian equity markets in our study (i.e. China). Such results, which seem to contradict the efficient markets theory, are not singular. For example, Fama (1965b) affirms that some historical information about past prices is useless when trading on the New York Stock Exchange, but definitely is more relevant for stocks listed on the Amsterdam Exchange. The unanswered question is why American traders do not move into the second market to take advantage of such inefficiencies. Here we add another market that seems to behave inefficiently and propose a method to take advantage of such behaviour. We think that a plausible cause for the existence of such pockets of inefficiency is that information and knowledge necessary to exploit such traits are actually heterogenic distributed on various markets. A lucky time frame chosen here might also be the culprit, although this was our only trial. Finally, the fact that we have tested our rules on indices rather than on individual stocks could also have affected our results, although we don't think it would invalidate our conclusions. Fama (1965b), Fisher (1966) and again Fama and Blume (1966) mention the effect of nonsynchronous trading, which signifies the situation in which some stock, due to its low trading liquidity or some other factor, could not fully adjust to some new, systemic information and is thus forced to gradually adjust its pricing during several trading sessions. This would mean that an index containing that stock would be trending as well, although the trending of that particular stock could not be exploited due to the same low liquidity. Our take on this particular case is that although full indexing might not actually be able to replicate the excess returns that we showed above, investing via futures written on indices or possibly via ETFs could still be done. Of course, besides trading commissions, now interest rates should be taken into account, as well as bid–ask spreads. Thus a final conclusion regarding the profitability of such rules should definitely take into account the actual, real opportunities that exist out there.

Finally, the tests that we have employed in this study, particularly White's RC, might be a bit too drastic and thus prone to type II errors. By presenting the results of all tested strategies, and by choosing the strategies to test as 'randomly' as possible (the only condition for our n_2 parameter was to be a 'round, beautiful' number), we are convinced that we did try to avoid both the traps of data mining and survivorship bias. The adjustment for the initial *p*-values is thus probably too large in our opinion. This supposition might be relatively simple to confirm on subsequent research by using some other test, such as the test for superior predictive ability proposed by Hansen (2005) or a Monte Carlo derived test.

References

Alexander, S. (1961). Price movements in speculative markets: Trends or random walks. *Industrial Management Review*, 2(2), 7–26.

Brock, W., Lakonishok, J., and LeBaron, B. (1992). Simple technical trading rules and the stochastic properties of stock returns. *Journal of Finance*, 47(5), 1731–1764.

Efron, B. (1979). Bootstrap methods: Another look at the Jackknife. *The Annals of Statistics*, 7(1), 1–26.

Fama, E. F. (1965). Tomorrow on the New York stock exchange. *The Journal of Business*, 38(3), 285–299.

Fama, E. F. (1970). Efficient capital markets: A review of theory and empirical work. *The Journal of Finance*, 25(2), 383–417.

Fama, E. F. (1991). Efficient capital markets: II. *The Journal of Finance*, 46(5), 1575–1617.

Fama, E. F., and Blume, M. E. (1966). Filter rules and stock market trading. *The Journal of Business*, 39(1), Part 2, 226–241.

Fisher, L. (1966). Some new stock-market indexes. *Journal of Business*, 39(1), 191–225.

Hansen, P. (2005). A test for superior predictive ability. *Journal of Business & Economic Statistics*, 23(4), 365–380.

Park, C.-H., and Irwin, S. H. (2004). The profitability of technical analysis: A review. AgMAS Project Research Report 2004–04. Available at: http://chesler.us/resources/academia/AgMAS04_04.pdf, descărcată la [2015-08-09]

White, H. (2000). A reality check for data-snooping. *Econometrica*, 68(5), 1097–1126.

10 Technical trading and market efficiency in Asian equity markets

Piyapas Tharavanij

1.0 Introduction

This chapter explores the issue of equity market efficiency and its implication on technical trading. According to the efficient market hypothesis (EMH) (Fama, 1970), which states that all available and relevant information must already be incorporated in security prices, technical trading rules, which use only historical trading data, cannot generate positive abnormal returns. If investors could make money from applying technical trading rules, this would indicate that the market is inefficient.

However, even from a theoretical perspective, the EMH has been increasingly challenged. Grossman and Stiglitz (1980) theoretically demonstrate that in a competitive market, no one has an incentive to obtain costly information if the market-clearing price reflects all available information. Therefore, the market cannot be fully efficient. More recently, behavioural models, such as noisy rational expectations models (Brown and Jennings, 1989), noise trader risks (DeLong, Shleifer, Summers and Waldmann, 1990; Shleifer and Summers, 1990), feedback models (DeLong, Shleifer and Summers, 1990) and herding models (Froot, Scharftstein and Stein, 1992) challenge the EMH. These models assert that price adjusts sluggishly to new information due to noise, feedback mechanism or herding behaviour. In these models, there exist profitable trading opportunities based on past trading data that are not being exploited.

To resolve this conflict, researchers have undertaken numerous empirical studies of technical trading rules in mature markets. Some studies find that trading rules do deliver superior returns, for example, Brock, Lakonishok and LeBaron (1992), Sullivan, Timmermann and White (1999), Lo, Mamaysky and Wang (2000) and Kavajecz and Odders-White (2004). Other studies conclude that trading rules cannot be used to trade profitably especially after taking transaction costs into account. Bessembinder and Chan (1998) show that transaction costs outweigh the predictive power of trading rules. Ready (2002) argues that the apparent success of trading rules in previous studies is a spurious result of data snooping. Interestingly, even studies which support profitability of technical trading also point out that the profitability of technical analysis has declined over time and tends to disappear (Sullivan *et al.*, 1999). More recently, Bajgrowiczy and Scaillet (2012) find that the early success of technical trading strategies are mainly due to the data-snooping bias.

In emerging markets, there is some evidence showing that technical analysis is profitable. Bessembinder and Chan (1995) find that technical rules were successful in predicting stock price movement in the emerging markets of Malaysia, Thailand and Taiwan. However, they had less explanatory power in the more mature markets of Hong Kong and Japan. Ratner and Leal (1999) find that Taiwan, Thailand and Mexico emerge as markets where technical trading strategies may be profitable, though they find no strong evidence of profitability in other markets. Lento (2006) examines the effectiveness of nine technical trading rules in eight Asian Pacific equity markets. The TSEC, Straits Times, Hang Seng, Jakarta, KOSPI and the BSE emerge as equity markets where technical trading rules may be profitable even after taking transaction costs into account. Ming-Ming and Siok-Hwa (2006) examine the profitability of trading rules based on a moving average and a trading range breakout on nine Asian market indices. Their results give strong support for moving average rules in the China, Thailand, Taiwan, Malaysian, Singaporean, Hong Kong, Korean and Indonesian stock markets. Yu, Nartea, Gan and Yao (2013) find that technical trading rules can slightly beat a buy-and-hold strategy even after transaction costs in Thailand.

2.0 Theories

This part provides an overview of theories related to profitability of technical analysis. We begin with the EMH, which states that asset prices incorporate all available and relevant information, making it impossible to make risk-adjusted profits by trading on past trading data. However, Grossman and Stiglitz (1980) later theoretically demonstrate that the market cannot be fully efficient because no one would have an incentive to obtain costly information if the market-clearing price reflects all available information.

Later on, behavioural models, such as noisy rational expectation models (Brown and Jennings, 1989) and information role of volume (Blume, Easley and O'Hara, 1994), noise trader risks (DeLong, Shleifer, Summers *et al.*, 1990; Shleifer and Summers, 1990), positive feedback models (DeLong *et al.*, 1990) and herding models (Froot *et al*, 1992) were developed to challenge the EMH. These models explain how profitable trading opportunities based on past trading data can still exist. Basically, these types of models show that price adjusts slowly to new information due to noise trading, feedback trading or herding behaviour. We will discuss each theory in detail in turn.

2.1 The efficient market hypothesis (Fama, 1970)

The EMH states that asset prices incorporate all available and relevant information (Fama, 1970). As such, a security price is a fair price. Later, Jensen (1978) extends the concept and proposes three relevant information subsets. Firstly, the market is weak-form efficient if asset prices reflect just historical trading data. Hence, trading strategies based on past trading data cannot generate positive abnormal returns. However, it is still possible that traders earn positive abnormal returns if they possess superior fundamental analyses or have access to relevant nonpublic information.

Secondly, the market is semi–strong-form efficient if asset prices fully adjust to publicly available information, such as earnings, macroeconomic figures, trading data, etc. In this case, no trading strategies based on publicly available information (past trading data included) could generate positive abnormal returns. Nevertheless, traders with relevant nonpublic information may still earn abnormal returns from trading based on that information.

Lastly, the market is strong-form efficient if asset prices fully reflect all relevant information even when that information is not publicly available. This is the extreme case in which traders cannot expect to earn any positive abnormal returns regardless of their information or analytical abilities.

The implication for technical analysis, which studies only historical trading data, is that any attempt to apply it to make positive abnormal returns is ultimately futile if the stock market is at least weak-form efficient. Another key implication is that if that particular stock has a positive expected return, then technical trading rules cannot have greater expected profits than a buy-and-hold (BH) investment strategy.

2.2   Impossibility of informationally efficient market theory (Grossman and Stiglitz, 1980)

Grossman and Stiglitz (1980) show that if obtaining and processing information is costly, then the market price cannot incorporate all available relevant information because otherwise there would be no incentive to obtain and process costly information in the first place. They conclude that the market cannot be fully efficient.

However, Grossman and Stiglitz's model does still support the weak form of the efficient market hypothesis where there is no profits from looking at trading history. The reason is that their model assumes rational expectations among uninformed traders. What is not supported by their model is the strong form of the efficient market hypothesis because prices are unable to fully reflect all private information. As a result, informed traders would be more successful than uninformed ones.

2.3   The noisy rational expectation equilibrium model (Brown and Jennings, 1989) and the information role of volume (Blume et al., 1994)

Brown and Jennings (1989) develop a rational expectation model, in which the current price does not fully reveal private information because of supply uncertainty, which they call 'noise'. As a result, historical prices can help predict future prices.

Noise in the current equilibrium price makes it impossible for the price to reveal perfectly the private information from earlier periods. As a result, historical prices together with current prices allow more accurate inferences about past and present signals than do current prices alone. Because current prices do not fully reveal past prices, i.e. technical analysis provides information to agents forming their demands, the implication is that technical analysis does have value. Past price levels enable traders to make more precise inferences about the signal.

Later, Blume *et al.* (1994) developed an equilibrium model to show the importance of volume. Their model assumes that the source of 'noise' is the quality of information. Volume provides information about the quality of traders' information that cannot be conveyed by prices alone. Technical analysis is valuable because the price and volume statistics together can be more informative than observing the price alone.

2.4 Noise trader risks (DeLong et al., 1990; Shleifer and Summers, 1990)

The noise trader approach thinks of financial markets as consisting of two types of investors: first, 'noise traders' and, second, 'arbitrageurs' or 'rational investors.' Noise traders are not fully rational and their demand for risky assets depends on their beliefs or sentiments not being fully justified by fundamentals and being subject to systematic biases such as overconfidence, trend extrapolation and putting too much weight on the newest information. They may also respond to pseudo-signals that investors believe convey information about future returns, though these signals do not actually convey such information in a fully rational model (Black, 1986). An example of such pseudo-signals is advice of financial gurus or trading rumours. The 'technical analysis' is another example of a pseudo-signal without a fundamental rationalization. In contrast, rational investors or arbitrageurs are investors who form rational expectations of asset returns.

Friedman (1953) argues that investors trading on noise and not information (noise traders) might lose their money when asset prices move back to fundamental values as a result of arbitrage activities performed by rational investors (arbitrageurs), leading to a decrease in their wealth and effect on demand. In the long run, they should have no effect on demands. However, DeLong, Shleifer, Summers, *et al.* (1990) and Shleifer and Summers (1990) argue that when arbitrage is risky and therefore limited, investor demand would also depend on noise or sentiment. As a result, asset prices would move in response to both changes in fundamentals and to changes in investor sentiment. Arbitrageurs would partially counter shifts in asset demands by changes in investor sentiment, but would not eliminate the effects on prices completely. Consequently, prices vary more than is warranted by changes in fundamentals.

Shleifer and Summers (1990) posit that there are two types of risk that limit arbitrage. The first is fundamental risk. It results from the fact that arbitrageurs might not know the fundamental values with certainty or be able to detect price changes that reflect deviations from fundamentals. There is always a chance that realized fundamental values say actual dividends differ from expected ones. The second is the unpredictability of future resale prices (DeLong, Shleifer, Summers, *et al.*, 1990). If future mispricing from a fundamental value is more extreme than when the arbitrage trade is done and the arbitrageur has to liquidate before the price approaches a fundamental value, he would suffer a loss though he may be right in the long run. This risk of a further change of noise traders' opinion away from fundamentals is called 'noise trader risk.' It must be borne by any arbitrageur with a short time horizon. These two risks limit the size of the arbitrageur's initial position, and prevent arbitrage to drive prices all the way to fundamental values.

There are several reasons that we can expect arbitrageurs to have short horizons. First, arbitrageurs may have to borrow cash or securities to implement their trades. Of course, they have to pay fees and these fees accumulate over time as the position remains open. This fact induces a strong bias towards short horizons (Shleifer and Vishny, 1990). Furthermore, the performance of fund managers is evaluated at least once or twice a year, also limiting the horizon of arbitrage.

If trading happens among noise traders with different independent models, then the effect of each noise trade should cancel each other out. In that case, noise trading as a whole would not affect asset prices. However, many trading strategies based on pseudo-signals and popular models are correlated, leading to aggregate asset demand shifts. This reflects the fact that judgement biases afflicting investors in processing information tend to be the same as overconfidence, trend extrapolation, putting too much weight on newest information, following the same market gurus or rumours and using similar technical indicators.

Due to noise trader risk, investor sentiment affects a broad range of assets in the same way. As this risk becomes systematic, it has a price in equilibrium. Consequently, assets subject to whims of investor sentiment should yield higher average returns. In other words, they must be underpriced relative to their fundamental values.

The implication for technical analysis is that if it helps predict changes in investor sentiment, it can also help predict future price changes. In addition, if noisy enough traders follow the same technical indicators, though these indicators by themselves do not reflect any fundamental values, prices might still move as predicted by these indicators, as noisy traders trade according to their signals. In other words, it can be a self-fulfilling prophecy.

2.5   The positive feedback model (DeLong et al., 1990)

In a feedback model, there are noise traders who just blindly follow a positive feedback strategy by buying when prices rise and selling when prices fall. This can result from extrapolative expectations about prices, stop loss orders, margin calls and portfolio insurance. As a result, an asset price fluctuates more wildly. It is normally presumed that rational speculation would dampen such fluctuations. Unfortunately, this is not necessarily the case. If noise traders follow positive feedback strategies, it may pay to jump on the bandwagon and purchase or sell ahead of noise demand. Such trading by rational speculators might even trigger more positive feedback trading, leading to higher volatility.

This model generates a positive correlation of stock returns at short horizons, as positive feedback traders respond to past price increases by buying more, and negative correlations of stock returns at long horizons, as prices eventually return to fundamentals. The model also predicts the market overreactions to news because such news triggers subsequent feedback trading.

The technical analysis can add value by predicting trends generated from a positive correlation of stock returns. It also helps to detect changes in trends when prices start to return to fundamentals.

2.6   Herding model (Froot et al., 1992)

In their herding model, Froot *et al.* (1992) demonstrate that the herding behaviour of short-horizon traders can lead to informational inefficiency. The reason is that short-horizon traders would make profits only when they process the same information, which is not necessarily relevant to asset values. Therefore, these short-term traders (herders) would follow the same technical indicators to make profits.

Normally, informational externalities are negative for traders or speculators. If speculators have long horizons, the returns to acquiring information fall as the number of other identically informed traders increases. Negative externalities of this sort encourage independent fundamental analysis. In sharp contrast, if speculators have short horizons, there are positive informational spillovers. As more speculators study a given piece of information, more of that information would be incorporated into the market and, therefore, the profits from learning that information early increase. In equilibrium, speculators herd on the same information.

The fact that a large number of traders use technical analysis may be enough to generate positive profits for those traders who apply technical analysis. When technical indicators are popular, it may be optimal for speculators to also apply them. Such equilibrium can persist even if the technical analysis contains no relevant fundamental information. In short, short-horizon traders would make profits when they can just coordinate their research efforts on the same set of information.

3.0   Empirical evidence

Park and Irwin (2007) provide a review of empirical studies on the issue of trading rule profitability. In their review, modern studies (papers published from 1988 to 2004) indicate that technical trading strategies were profitable in the US stock markets at least until the late 1980s. The important studies are Sullivan *et al.* (1999), Lo *et al.* (2000) and Kavajecz and Odders-White (2004). However, Brock *et al.* (1992), Bessembinder and Chan (1998), Ready (2002) and Marshall, Cahan and Cahan (2008) show that transaction costs would eliminate any trading profits. Furthermore, Bessembinder and Chan (1998) point out that the profitability of technical analysis has declined over time. As a result, technical trading strategies were no longer profitable after the 1980s. Bajgrowiczy and Scaillet

(2012) find that the early success of technical trading strategies is mainly due to the data-snooping bias. Important studies are reviewed in greater detail below.

Brock *et al.* (1992), henceforth BLL, is the first to use the bootstrap technique to test the profitability of trading based on moving averages and trading range breakout on the Dow Jones Industrial Average (DJIA). They find that buy positions across almost all trading rules consistently generate statistically significantly higher mean returns than unconditional ones. However, they do not take transaction costs into account. Later, Hudson, Dempsey and Keasey (1996) replicate the work of Brock *et al.* (1992) with the UK data. They find that all trading systems consistently generate significantly higher returns than unconditional ones. However, they find that due to transaction costs the use of trading rules would not allow investors to make excess returns. Bessembinder and Chan (1998) replicate the work of Brock *et al.* (1992) again with DJIA data. They find that the forecast ability of technical rules is at least partially due to nonsynchronous trading. They also notice that the break-even transaction costs from technical trading are not higher than estimates of actual trading costs. This means investors still could not make net excess returns.

Ito (1999) studies profitability to technical trading rules in six market indices (Japan, the United States, Canada, Indonesia, Mexico and Taiwan). The samples cover 1980–1996 for developed markets and 1988–1996 for emerging markets. The methodology follows that of Brock *et al.* (1992). They find that after transaction costs, technical trading rules outperformed the BH strategy for all indices except US indices. Interestingly, they generated higher profits for emerging markets than for developed ones. They also find that these profits could not be explained by nonsynchronous trading, but some conditional asset pricing model could explain them. Their results seem to suggest that technical profits are fair compensations for risks inherent in technical trading rules.

Lo *et al.* (2000) apply nonparametric kernel regression to a large number of US stocks from 1962 to 1996 to evaluate the effectiveness of technical analysis. They compare the unconditional empirical distribution of daily stock returns to the conditional distribution based on specific technical indicators. They reason that if technical patterns are informative, conditioning on them should alter the empirical distribution of returns. In contrast, if the information contained in such patterns has already been incorporated into returns, the conditional and unconditional distribution of returns should be close. However, they carefully note that informativeness does not guarantee a profitable trading strategy. In their results, they find that over the 31-year sample period, several technical indicators are actually 'informative'.

Sullivan *et al.* (1999) utilize White's reality check bootstrap methodology (White, 2000) to evaluate simple technical trading rules while controlling for the data-snooping bias. They expand Brock *et al.* (1992) to include more comprehensive trading rules, and apply the rules to 100 years of daily data on the DJIA. They find that the results of BLL appear to be robust to data snooping. Basically, the best performing technical trading rule is capable of generating profits when applied to the DJIA even after controlling for data-snooping effects. However, they also find that the superior performance of the best technical trading rule is not repeated in the out-of-sample experiment covering the 10-year period 1987–1996; it is not even statistically significant. They suspect that the best technical trading rule did indeed produce superior performance but that, more recently, the markets have become more efficient and hence such opportunities have disappeared.

Ready (2002) argues that the apparent success, even after transaction costs, of BLL moving average rules is a spurious result of data snooping. He points out that after the period considered by BLL, their trading rules have done quite poorly.

Bajgrowiczy and Scaillet (2012) revisit the apparent historical success of technical trading rules in BLL results. They use the false discovery rate (FDR) to address the issue of data snooping. Their results show that an investor would never have been able to select *ex-ante* the future best performing rules. In addition, even in-sample, the performance is completely offset by the introduction of low transaction costs.

Marshall, Cahan and Cahan (2010) study the profitability of over 5000 popular technical trading rules in the 49 country indices that comprise the Morgan Stanley Capital International (MSCI) Index once data-snooping bias is accounted for. They find that even profitable trading rules do not earn statistically significant profits after data-snooping bias adjustment. There is some evidence that technical trading rules perform better in emerging markets than developed markets. However, this result is not strong.

In emerging markets, there are more studies, compared to mature market cases, showing that technical analysis is profitable. Bessembinder and Chan (1995) assess whether technical analysis can help predict Asian stock market indices in the period of 1975–1991. They find that trading rules were quite successful in the emerging stock markets of Malaysia, Thailand and Taiwan. The rules had lower explanatory power in more developed markets such as Hong Kong and Japan. Overall, trading rules generated significant higher net profits. Ratner and Leal (1999) examine the potential profit of technical trading rules in 10 emerging equity markets in Latin America and Asia (Argentina, Brazil, Chile, India, Korea, Malaysia, Mexico, the Philippines, Taiwan and Thailand) from 1982 to 1995. The average difference in buy–sell returns after trading costs are compared to a BH strategy. They find that Taiwan, Thailand and Mexico emerge as markets where technical trading strategies may be profitable, though they find no strong evidence of profitability in other markets.

In a comprehensive study, Pauwels, Inghelbrecht, Heyman and Marius (2011) investigate the effectiveness of technical trading rules in 34 emerging stock market indices. The performance of the rules is evaluated by utilizing White's reality check (White, 2000) and the superior predictive ability test (Hansen, 2005) to address the data-snooping issue, along with an adjustment for transaction costs. They find strong evidence that data-snooping bias has an immense effect on performance evaluation. Their results conclude that technical trading rules are not able to outperform a naïve BH benchmark on a consistent basis. However, they find significant trading rule profits in just 4 of the 34 investigated markets (Botswana, Jamaica, Kenya and Oman).

Interestingly, more recent papers that study emerging Asian markets tend to find profitability in technical trading rules. For instance, Lento (2006), who studied the performance of nine variants of three trading rules (moving average, trading range break-outs and filter rules) in eight Asian Pacific equity markets (Australia, India, Indonesia, Korea, Japan, Hong Kong, Singapore, and Taiwan) from 1987 to 2005, finds that technical trading rules seem to be profitable in six Asian markets (India, Hong Kong, Indonesia, Korea, Singapore and Taiwan). In another study, Ming-Ming and Siok-Hwa (2006) examine the profitability of trading rules in nine Asian stock market indices (Japan, China, Thailand, Taiwan, Malaysia, Singapore, Hong Kong, Korea and Indonesia) from 1988 to 2003. Their results give strong support for trading rules in all stock markets except Japan.

Yu *et al.* (2013) study whether simple trading rules like moving average and trading range breakout rules can outperform a simple BH strategy. Their samples are Southeast Asian stock markets from 1991 to 2008. They find profitability in trading rules in the stock markets of Malaysia, Thailand, Indonesia and the Philippines, but not in the stock market of Singapore. However, they also observe that except in Thailand, trading rules cannot beat a BH strategy after transaction costs.

More recently, Tharavanij, Siraprapasiri and Rajchamaha (2015) examine the profitability of technical trading rules in the five Southeast Asian stock markets (Thailand, Malaysia, Singapore, Indonesia and the Philippines). Their results show a strong performance of technical trading rules in the emerging stock market of Thailand but not in the more mature stock market of Singapore. The technical trading rules also generate statistical significant returns in the Malaysian, Indonesian and the Philippine markets. However, after taking transaction costs into account, most technical trading rules do not generate net returns. Their paper also finds three new insights. Firstly, technical indicators do not help much in terms of market timing. Basically, traders cannot expect to buy at a relative low price and sell at a relative high price by just using technical trading rules. Secondly, technical trading rules can be beneficial to individual investors as they help them to counter the behavioural bias called 'disposition effects', which is the tendency to sell winning stocks too soon and hold on to losing stocks too long. Thirdly, even profitable strategies could not reliably predict subsequent market directions. They make money from having a higher average profit from profitable trades than an average loss from unprofitable ones.

4.0   Review of trading rules investigated in academic studies

The trading rules come from five rule families: filter rules, moving average rules, support and resistance rules, channel breakout rules and on-balance volume rules. For each type, various parameterizations would be considered. Detailed below is a summary of methods as explained in Sullivan *et al.* (1999).

4.1   *Filter rules*

The simplest filter rules involve buying (short selling) after price increases (decreases) by *x* percent. A long (short) position is closed when price decreases (increases) y percent from the previous high (low). The alternative variation involves holding a position for a pre-specified number of periods, c, regardless of other signals generated during this time.

4.2   Moving average rules

Moving average rules are mechanical trading rules that attempt to capture trends. They generate a buy (sell) signal when the price moves above (below) the longer moving average.

There are two types of filters that can be applied. The first filter requires the shorter moving average to exceed the longer moving average by a fixed amount, b. The second requires a buy or sell signal to remain valid for a pre-specified number of periods, d, before the signal is acted upon. The position can be held for a pre-specified number of periods, c.

4.3   Support and resistance rules

These rules aim to profit from the principle that trends typically start when price breaks out of a fixed trading band. Support and resistance rules involve buying (short selling) when the closing price rises above (falls below) the maximum (minimum) price over the previous n periods. The most recent closing price that is greater (less) than the e previous closing price can also be set as the extreme price level that triggers a buy or a sell. Positions can be held for a pre-specified number of periods, c. There can also be a fixed percentage band filter, b, and a time delay filter, d.

4.4   Channel breakout rules

The channel breakout rules involve buying (selling) when the closing price moves above (below) the channel. A channel is said to occur when the high over the previous n periods is within x percent of the low over the previous n periods. Positions are held for a fixed number of periods, c. There can also be a fixed band, b, being applied to the channel as a filter.

4.5   On-balance volume (OBV) rules

The OBV indicator involves adding (subtracting) to (from) the indicator the entire amount of daily volume when the closing price increases (decreases). A moving average of n periods is applied to the OBV indicator. The moving average trading rules can then be applied.

5.0   Review of testing methodologies

5.1   T-*test and round-trip break-even cost*

This part is based on my previous work in Tharavanij *et al.* (2015). To calculate the *t*-stat and the break-even cost, we do the following steps. First, we calculate

continuous-compounding daily returns from closing prices of the stock indices
$[r_t = \ln(P_t/P_{t-1})]$. The technical indicators would then provide buy or sell signals.
When the buy (sell) signal is under test, the chosen daily returns would be all daily
returns after the buy (sell) signal was generated up to the next sell (buy) signal.
Let us define Φ to be the union of all disjoint intervals generated by the buy (sell)
signals and let n be the number of daily returns in the set Φ. Then, the average
return of the tested strategy is calculated by the following equation.

$$\bar{r} = \frac{\sum_{i \in \Phi} r_i}{n}, \text{ where } \bar{r} \sim N(\mu, \frac{\sigma^2}{n}).$$

Let μ_{buy} and μ_{sell} be the population means of daily returns generated by buy and
sell signals, respectively. Also, let σ_{buy} and σ_{sell} be the standard deviations of daily
returns generated by buy and sell signals, respectively. We would expect that an
average return is positive for a buy signal and negative for a sell signal. So, we test
the following one-tailed hypotheses: $H_0: \mu_{buy} = 0$ vs, $H_1: \mu_{buy} > 0$ and $H_0: \mu_{sell} = 0$
vs, $H_1: \mu_{sell} < 0$ using the following test statistic.

$$Z_{buy} = \frac{\bar{r}_{buy}}{(S_{buy}/\sqrt{n_{buy}})}, S_{buy} = \sqrt{\frac{\sum_{i \in \Phi_{buy}} (r_i - \bar{r}_{buy})^2}{(n_{buy} - 1)}}$$

$$Z_{sell} = \frac{\bar{r}_{sell}}{(S_{sell}/\sqrt{n_{sell}})}, S_{sell} = \sqrt{\frac{\sum_{i \in \Phi_{sell}} (r_i - \bar{r}_{sell})^2}{(n_{sell} - 1)}}$$

n_{buy} = number of days the long (buy) position is held
n_{sell} = number of days the short (sell) position is held.

To test the joint effect of buy and sell signals, the hypothesis $H_0: \mu_{buy} - \mu_{sell} = 0$ vs.
$H_1: \mu_{buy} - \mu_{sell} > 0$ is also tested using the following statistic.

$$Z_{buy-sell} = \frac{(\bar{r}_{buy} - \bar{r}_{sell})}{[S.(\frac{1}{\sqrt{n_{buy}}} + \frac{1}{\sqrt{n_{sell}}})]}, S = \sqrt{\frac{\sum_{i \in \Phi_{buy \, or \, sell}} (r_i - \bar{r}_{buy \, or \, sell})^2}{(n_{buy} + n_{sell} - 1)}}.$$

We assume that the standard deviations of daily returns are the same for those
generated by buying signals and by selling signals. Therefore, we use the pooled
estimator S, the standard error of daily returns estimated from the entire sample,
to estimate both σ_{buy} and σ_{sell}.

For one-tailed test, the significant level (α) is set at 5 percent and 1 percent and
hence, the critical Z values are 1.64 and 2.33, respectively.

So far, we have not considered transaction costs yet. To investigate the profitability of each trading rule after transaction cost, we compute break-even

transaction costs to be compared with actual transaction costs. According to Bessembinder and Chan (1998), the additional return (π) generated by technical trading rules relative to a BH strategy is given as follows.

$$\Pi = \sum_{i=1}^{n_{buy}} r_i - \sum_{j=1}^{n_{sell}} r_j$$

n_{buy} = number of days the long (buy) position is held
n_{sell} = number of days the short (sell) position is held
r_i = return of the long (buy) position on day i
r_j = return of the short (sell) position on day j.

If we divide the additional return (π) by the numbers of buy and sell signals, this will give us the average additional return per signal or, in other words, the round-trip break-even cost (C) (Bessembinder and Chan, 1998).

$$C = \frac{\Pi}{(S_{buy} + S_{sell})}$$

S_{buy} = number of buy signals generated
S_{sell} = number of sell signals generated.

To be profitable, the break-even cost (C) or the average additional return per signal must be greater than a round-trip transaction cost.

5.2 Bootstrap methodology

Brock *et al.* (1992) point out three shortcomings of the traditional *t*-test and suggest that bootstrap methodology can help. First, the traditional *t*-test cannot be used to compute a comprehensive test across all rules. The reason is that such a test needs to take into account the dependencies between results for different rules. The bootstrap methodology allows a joint test of significance for a set of trading rules. This is done by utilizing bootstrap distributions for these tests. Second, the *t*-test methodology assumes normal, stationary and time independent distributions of stock returns. However, there are several well-known deviations from this assumed distribution, such as leptokurtosis (fat tail), autocorrelation, conditional heteroscedasticity and changing conditional means. A third benefit of this methodology is that it provides the standard deviations of returns during the buy and sell periods. This gives an indication of the riskiness of various trading strategies. The key limitation of this method, however, is that though it shows whether a given rule generates returns that differ from those associated with a given null model of returns, it does not takes the issue of 'data-snooping bias' into account.

The brief description of the bootstrap methodology is provided here. Basically, the returns conditional on buy (sell) signals using the raw data are compared to conditional returns from simulated comparison series. The return conditional expectations will be estimated using the sample means. These values will then be compared with empirical distributions from the simulated null models for stock returns. Basically, in this procedure each model is fit to the original data to obtain estimated parameters and residuals. The estimated residuals are then standardized by estimated standard deviations for the error process. The estimated standardized residuals are then redrawn with replacement to form a simulated residuals series which is then used with the estimated parameters to form a new representative price series for the given null model.

Each of the simulations is based on many replications of the null model. This provides a good approximation of the return distribution under the null model. The null hypothesis is rejected at the α-percent level if returns obtained from the actual price series are greater than the α-percent cut-off of the simulated returns under the null model. Representative price series are then simulated from widely used processes for stock prices such as a random walk with a drift, autoregressive process (AR), generalized autoregressive conditional heteroscedasticity in-mean model (GARCH-M), or exponential GARCH (EGARCH). Moreover, the bootstrap technique allows researchers to choose any function to aggregate results across various trading rules. Brock *et al.* (1992) use a simple average over the testing rules to compute averages over all the rules for both returns and standard deviations.

6.0   Data-snooping biases and correction for data snooping

Since a researcher can examine many trading rules for a given data set, there is a high probability that one such rule will yield superior performance for that data set by chance, even if it does not work out of sample. Multiple technical trading rules are often explored, but only the best one is reported. Statistical inference about the best rule ignores the existence of other trading rules already investigated. Since the best trading rule is only known ex post, the fact that the best trading rule outperforms a benchmark based on a usual statistical test does not necessarily imply that the rule is significantly profitable. This is called the 'data-snooping problem.'

According to White (2000), there is always the danger that good performance results might be obtained from a model by an extensive specification search. He argues that even when no forecasting relations exist, extensive data manipulation often reveals one or more forecasting models that look good, but that are, in fact, useless. To circumvent data-snooping bias, there are many proposed method as explained in brief below.

First, the most commonly used technique is that of Sullivan *et al.* (1999). This method is based on the White (2000)'s reality check (RC) approach. Subsequent researchers have attempted to improve this methodology. Hansen (2005) shows that the RC approach can be affected by the inclusion of irrelevant rules and develops a superior predictive ability (SPA) test that overcomes this issue. However, as noted by Hsu, Hsu and Kuan (2010), both the RC and SPA tests do not identify all significant rules. Second, Romano and Wolf (2005) develop a RC-based stepwise test that identifies all significant rules, but as Hsu *et al.* (2010) state, this still suffers from the irrelevant rule inclusion issue. Third, Hsu *et al.* (2010) develop a SPA-based stepwise test. This test overcomes both issues of identifying all significant rules and irrelevant rule inclusion. Fourth, Bajgrowiczy and Scaillet (2012) recently develop an FDR test which assumes that investor bases their decisions on a portfolio of strategies rather than a single strategy. Fifth, Harvey and Liu (2014), and Harvey and Liu (2015) propose a method to calculate adjusted Sharpe ratios in the multiple testing context such as back testing various trading rules. The underlying idea is to lower the *p*-value required for the statistic to be significant when there are multiple rules tested. The limitation of this method is that it assumes no correlation among test statistics. In another paper, Harvey and Liu (2013) extend the adjusted Sharpe ratio method to explicitly take the correlation among test statistics into account. Sixth, Bailey, Borwein, Prado and Zhu (2015) develop a concept called 'the probability of back test overfitting (PBO)' to measure the degree of back test overfitting. Basically, the PBO indicates the probability that a superior strategy fitted within the sample would underperform in the out-of-sample period.

References

Bailey, D. H., Borwein, J. M., Prado, M. L. D., and Zhu, Q. J. (Forthcoming). The probability of backtest overfitting. *Journal of Computational Finance*.

Bajgrowiczy, P., and Scaillet, O. (2012). Technical trading revisited: False discoveries, persistence tests, and transaction costs. *Journal of Financial Economics*, *106*(3), 473–491.

Bessembinder, H., and Chan, K. (1995). The profitability of technical trading rules in the Asian stock markets. *Pacific-Basin Finance Journal*, *3*(2–3), 257–284.

Bessembinder, H., and Chan, K. (1998). Market efficiency and the returns to technical analysis. *Financial Management*, *27*(2), 5–17.

Black, F. (1986). Noise. *Journal of Finance*, *41*(3), 529–543.

Blume, L., Easley, D., and O'Hara, M. (1994). Market statistics and technical analysis: The role of volume. *Journal of Finance*, *49*(1), 153–181.

Brock, W., Lakonishok, J., and LeBaron, B. (1992). Simple technical trading rules and the stochastic properties of stock returns. *Journal of Finance*, *47*(5), 1731–1764.

Brown, D. P., and Jennings, R. H. (1989). On technical analysis. *Review of Financial Studies*, *2*(4), 527–551.

DeLong, J. B., Shleifer, A., and Summers, L. H. (1990). Positive feedback investment strategies and destabilizing rational speculation. *Journal of Finance*, *45*(2), 379–395.

DeLong, J. B., Shleifer, A., Summers, L. H., and Waldmann, R. J. (1990). Noise trader risk in financial markets. *Journal of Political Economy*, *98*(4), 703–738.

Fama, E. F. (1970). Efficient capital markets: A review of theory and empirical work. *Journal of Finance*, *25*(2), 383–417.

Friedman, M. (1953). The case for flexible exchange rates. In: M. Friedman (Ed.), *Essays in Positive Economics*. Chicago: University of Chicago Press.

Froot, K. A., Scharftstein, D. S., and Stein, J. C. (1992). Herd on the street: Informational inefficiencies in a market with short-term speculation. *Journal of Finance*, *47*(4), 1461–1484.

Grossman, S. J., and Stiglitz, J. E. (1980). On the impossibility of informationally efficient markets. *American Economic Review, 70*(3), 393–408.

Hansen, P. R. (2005). A test for superior predictive ability. *Journal of Business & Economic Statistics, 23*(4), 365–380.

Harvey, C. R., and Liu, Y. (2013). Multiple testing in economics. Available at: http://dx.doi.org/10.2139/ssrn.2358214

Harvey, C. R., and Liu, Y. (2014). Evaluating trading strategies. *Journal of Portfolio Management, 40*(5), 108–118.

Harvey, C. R., and Liu, Y. (2015). Backtesting. *Journal of Portfolio Management, 42*(1), 13–28.

Hsu, P.-H., Hsu, Y.-C., and Kuan, C.-M. (2010). Testing the predictive ability of technical analysis using a new stepwise test without data snooping bias. *Journal of Empirical Finance, 17*(3), 471–484.

Hudson, R., Dempsey, M., and Keasey, K. (1996). A note on the weak form efficiency of capital markets: The application of simple technical trading rules to UK stock prices – 1935 to 1994. *Journal of Banking & Finance, 20*(6), 1121–1132.

Ito, A. (1999). Profits on technical trading rules and time-varying expected returns: Evidence from Pacific-Basin equity markets. *Pacific-Basin Finance Journal, 7*(3–4), 283–330.

Jensen, M. C. (1978). Some anomalous evidence regarding market efficiency. *Journal of Financial Economics, 6*(2–3), 95–101.

Kavajecz, K. A., and Odders-White, E. R. (2004). Technical analysis and liquidity provision. *Review of Financial Studies, 17*(4), 1043–1071.

Lento, C. (2006). Tests of technical trading rules in the Asian-Pacific equity markets: A bootstrap approach. *Academy of Financial and Accounting Studies Journal, 11*(2), 1–19.

Lo, A. W., Mamaysky, H., and Wang, J. (2000). Foundations of technical analysis: Computational algorithms, statistical inference, and empirical implementation. *Journal of Finance, 55*(4), 1705–1765.

Marshall, B. R., Cahan, R. H., and Cahan, J. M. (2008). Can commodity futures be profitably traded with quantitative market timing strategies? *Journal of Banking & Finance, 32*(9), 1810–1819.

Marshall, B. R., Cahan, R. H., and Cahan, J. M. (2010). Technical analysis around the world. Available at: http://dx.doi.org/10.2139/ssrn.1181367

Ming-Ming, L., and Siok-Hwa, L. (2006). The profitability of the simple moving averages and trading range breakout in the Asian stock markets. *Journal of Asian Economics, 17*(1), 144–170.

Park, C.-H., and Irwin, S. H. (2007). What do we know about the profitability of technical analysis? *Journal of Economic Surveys, 21*(4), 786–826.

Pauwels, S., Inghelbrecht, K., Heyman, D., and Marius, P. (2011). Technical trading rules in emerging stock markets. *International Journal of Social, Behavioral, Educational, Economic, Business and Industrial Engineering, 5*(11), 1731–1754.

Ratner, M., and Leal, R. P. C. (1999). Tests of technical trading strategies in the emerging equity markets of Latin America and Asia. *Journal of Banking & Finance, 23*(12), 1887–1905.

Ready, M. J. (2002). Profits from technical trading rules. *Financial Management, 31*(3), 43–61.

Romano, J. P., and Wolf, M. (2005). Stepwise multiple testing as formalized data snooping. *Econometrica, 73*(4), 1237–1282.

Shleifer, A., and Summers, L. H. (1990). The noise trader approach to finance. *Journal of Economic Perspectives*, 4(2), 19–33.

Shleifer, A., and Vishny, R. W. (1990). Equilibrium short horizons of investors and firms. *American Economic Review*, 80(2), 148–153.

Sullivan, R., Timmermann, A. G., and White, H. L. (1999). Data-snooping, technical trading rule performance, and the bootstrap. *Journal of Finance*, 54(5), 1647–1691.

Tharavanij, P., Siraprapasiri, V., and Rajchamaha, K. (2015). Performance of technical trading rules: Evidence from Southeast Asian stock markets. *SpringerPlus*, 4(552), 1–40.

White, H. (2000). A reality check for data snooping. *Econometrica*, 68(5), 1097–1126.

Yu, H., Nartea, G. V., Gan, C., and Yao, L. J. (2013). Predictive ability and profitability of simple technical trading rules: Recent evidence from Southeast Asian stock markets. *International Review of Economics and Finance*, 25(C), 356–371.

11 Testing for semi-strong efficiency under stressed market conditions

A comparative focus on Asia, Europe and the United States

Massimiliano Serati and Arianna Ziliotto

'Wall Street falls in volatile trading after Fed minutes'
(Reuters, 19 August 2015)

'World markets plunge as China stocks crash'
(CNN Money, 24 August 2015)

'China stocks fall sharpest since 2007, global markets react'
(CCTV, 24 August 2015)

'Investors welcomed the prospect of ultra low interest rates until next year. FTSE100 closed up nearly 1 percent'
(*The Guardian*, 2 October 2015)

'Markets react to the Fed's October interest rate decision: December is in play'
(*WSJ*, 28 October 2015)

1.0 Introductory overview

Worldwide financial markets have never been a soft competitive arena for traders and market practitioners. Sharp price fluctuations, wide volatility swings and dramatic liquidity crunches can always materialize as a consequence of unexpected corporate events and macroeconomic news, geopolitical turmoil and social upheavals.

In such a context, the recent Chinese market crash, the (related) US Federal Open Market Committee (FOMC) decisions on interest rates and the dramatic political unrest affecting the Middle East have all contributed to make the environment even tougher. Under this complex international contingency, it is quite reasonable to wonder whether worldwide financial markets are still able to react to 'ordinary' market-moving factors, or if, conversely, such an unexpected widespread instability has dampened the traditional 'mechanics' at work.

This study tries to address the foregoing question focusing on international equity markets' reaction to a few selected macroeconomic indicators, regularly released on a worldwide scale. Stated in alternative terms, this is a comparative study on semi-strong market efficiency under stressed market conditions, purposely conceived to investigate if (and how) stock markets in Asia, Europe and United States are affected (even in times of financial unrest) by scheduled macroeconomic releases published by some leading German, Japanese and American statistical agencies. Based on the testing framework presented by Serati and Ziliotto (2015), we will try to understand if, under the suitable volatility conditions and modelling some informational leakages from big institutional players, worldwide equity markets react significantly to macroeconomic impulses (even under stressed market conditions), thus leaving the door open (at least to some extent) to semi-strong inefficiency.

Such a wide geographical focus serves a twofold goal. First of all, this should enhance the soundness of our findings both in terms of reliability and replicability, provided that the adopted testing framework is neither country- nor economic cycle-dependent, but does conversely apply to no matter which country and/or macroeconomic contingency. Secondly, the inclusion of several heterogeneous economic systems will definitely allow us to investigate whether market reactions to macroeconomic impulses (if any) are also dependent on the complexity of the underlying financial environment and are thus different for emerging economies with relatively less developed/liquid markets. The empirical relevance of this work, however, strays beyond the strict boundaries of macroeconomics and finance, to embrace the field of market legislation: indeed, stating that worldwide markets tend to react to macroeconomic impulses and arguing that profit opportunities are likely to emerge under the suitable volatility conditions (when allowing for informational spillovers from big institutional players) basically amounts to saying that market abuse and price manipulation can materialize relatively easily on international financial markets, despite the huge legislative effort to enhance fair competition on a global scale.

The remainder of this chapter is organized as follows: Section 2 will focus on the major research contributions to the widely-debated topic of semi-strong efficiency; Section 3 will concentrate on dataset construction; Section 4, instead, will be entirely devoted to model estimation and emerging empirical findings. Section 5 will finally lay the foundations for further research and investigation.

2.0 Literature review

2.1 Theoretical foundations and emerging empirical evidence: a trade-off

Since the very beginning of the '60s, the international research community has paid increasing attention to market reactions to publicly available information, shedding progressive light on the practical implications of semi-strong market efficiency: 50 years later, this controversial topic still offers 'much food for thought' not only in strict econometric/quantitative terms, but also with respect to international market supervision and market abuse legislation.

The very first empirical evidence on semi-strong efficiency was rather supportive of the null hypothesis of market prices incorporating all the publicly available information. Fama, Fisher, Jensen and Roll (1969), for instance, focused on split announcements and found out that prices are able to adjust correctly (and almost instantaneously) to the information implicit in a split, thus automatically incorporating the informational component of the news. Ball and Brown (1968) reached very similar conclusions focusing on annual earnings announcements, thus corroborating the view that market prices were efficient processors of publicly available data.

All through the '70s and the '80s, the research focus gradually expanded to include not only corporate events, but also publicly-scheduled macroeconomic announcements: despite that, the emerging empirical evidence (though more robust) remained largely unaffected. Waud (1970), for instance, examined the effects of FOMC announcements and came to the conclusion that financial markets generally anticipated the news, given that price adjustments for the first trading day after a rate change never exceeded 5 percent. Castanias (1979), instead, mainly focused on price distribution tails and found out that macroeconomic releases tended to result into 'abnormally' large price fluctuations, brought about by prices rapidly incorporating the unexpected news.

Despite their valuable contribution to academic research, however, the foregoing studies soon let emerge a few major weaknesses that put their findings into serious question: the low data frequency, the relatively narrow geographical focus and the limited set of public indicators taken into account all contributed to make the foregoing empirical findings waver both in theory and in practice. Market efficiency was first explicitly challenged by Grossman and Stiglitz (1980) that basically argued that 'only in the extreme and unrealistic case where all information and trading costs are zero, one would expect prices to fully reflect all the available data' (Pesaran, 2005). Even on the empirical side, the evidence soon turned out to be equally challenging, as researchers and practitioners started to observe a few ever-growing 'market anomalies' (Mishkin, Bordes, Hautcoeur and Lacoue-Labarthe, 2007), that were at least controversial to justify under efficiency: the small companies and the January effects, excessive short-run volatility and mean reversion soon pushed academic researchers to look for alternative working and testing frameworks. Lo and MacKinlay (1988), for instance, showed that random walk models (one of the presumed building blocks for efficiency (Fama, 1970)) perform poorly when trying to describe market price patterns, thus paving the way to all those studies supporting the claim that stock returns can be predicted by means of several macroeconomic variables. With this respect, for instance, Pearce and Roley (1985) showed that monetary dynamics tend to affect significantly stock prices. By the same talking, Clare, Thomas and Wickens (1994) found out that the Gilt-equity yield ratio was a useful predictor of equity returns in the United Kingdom. Similarly, Black and Fraser (1995), gathered sufficiently robust evidence that the 'expected values of real economic variables are important determinants of the current values of financial variables such as discount rates and financial spreads.' Even more recent studies are largely supportive of semi-strong inefficiency: Wallenius, Fedorova and Collan (2013), for instance, examined the effects of some major EU scheduled macroeconomic announcements on CIVETS

(Colombia, Indonesia, Vietnam, Egypt, Turkey and South Africa) stock markets and found out that macroeconomic releases significantly affect both stock market volatility and stock returns. In line with the foregoing empirical evidence, Kurov, Sancetta, Strasser and Wolfe (2015) showed that major market players are likely to know the final outcome of monthly US macroeconomic announcements in advance compared to the official release time: the aforementioned news spillover clearly brings about some form of 'informed trading,' starting around 30 minutes before the release and accounting for more than 60 percent of the total market reaction to macroeconomic impulses.

Clearly enough, though relevant, stocks have not been the only asset class taken into account: FX and bonds have also been paid increasing attention. Bollerslev, Cai and Song (2000), for instance, focused on US Treasury bond futures and came to the conclusion that 'regularly scheduled macroeconomic announcements [are] an important source of volatility at the intraday level.' Kim, McKenzie and Faff (2004), instead, focused on bonds, stocks and FX and found out that market reactions to macroeconomic announcements vary depending both on the instruments type under study and on the releases taken into account (e.g. balance of trade news are helpful to predict FX market movements, bond prices tend to react significantly to news referring to the internal economy, whereas consumer and producer price information seem to be a significant driver of equity prices). Their study, indeed, provided a valuable contribution to the worldwide research community on the importance of macroeconomic variables selection. Three points, in particular, deserve special attention:

- Particular care should be paid when selecting the country/ies the public releases refer to. With this respect, since the late '80s, the vast majority of the available studies have focused on the United States as well as on the United Kingdom (see, *inter alia*, Godhart and Smith (1985), Jain (1988), Nussi and Sahlström (2001), Poitras (2004), and Bartolini, Goldberg and Sacarny (2008)), before gradually adopting a wider geographical focus. Panetta (2001), for example, concentrated on Italian releases, while Kim (2003) focused on the impact of US and Japanese announcements on the stock markets of Australia, Hong Kong and Singapore. Japan releases were also taken into special account by Hashimoto and Ito (2008), that investigated their impact on the USD/JPY exchange rate. Belgacem (2008), instead, dealt both with US and French macroeconomic indicators. More recent works also include emerging economies, thus overcoming (at least in part) the potential biases arising from country-specific distortions (Haryadi, Hallahan and Tanha (2014), for instance, concentrated both on Indonesian and US announcements).
- Once the relevant countries have been identified, it is paramount to pick out those releases with a potentially higher market impact. With this respect, no clear-cut methodology has been identified so far: some researchers have relied on 'official rakings,' like those provided by Bloomberg and the Bureau of Labour Statistics (Nikkinen, Omran, Sahlström and Aïjö (2006)); others

have opted for practical 'rules of thumb,' so that a given macroeconomic announcement is deemed to be significant insofar as it is commonly taken into account by market practitioners (Hardouvelis (1987), Li and Hu (1998), and Belgacem (2008)). A limited number of researchers have also developed some more 'theoretical' selection approaches, based on the fact that the price of any security i can be written as the sum of its expected discounted cash flows. In practice, assuming that

$$P_i = \frac{CF}{k} \tag{11.1}$$

any release is to be retained as relevant, as long as it can affect either CF or k (Chen, Roll and Ross (1986)).

• Given any macroeconomic release (independently of the indicator it refers to), what really matters for semi-strong efficiency testing is exclusively the speed with which prices incorporate the unexpected informational component (the so-called surprise) it conveys. Indeed, it is quite reasonable to assume that market prices incorporate by definition expected news, so that post-release adjustments (if any) are likely to materialize only if the said announcement provides at least some unforeseeable information. Despite its clarity, however, the practical implications of the foregoing reasoning are far from clear-cut and a formal definition of 'surprise' is still substantially missing: some researchers simply considered the difference between the actually released data and the (median) market forecast (Baum, Kurov and Wolfe (2015)); other opted for standardization (to obtain comparable units) and thus defined market surprise as

$$\frac{A - E}{\sigma} \tag{11.2}$$

with A = actual announcement, E = market expectations and σ = standard deviation of the macroeconomic variable under study (Kurov *et al.* (2015)). Kim (2003), instead, simply focused on a dummy variable approach, such that the 'news dummy takes the value of 1 if there was a news content in the announcement (i.e. actual figure announced different from market expectations) and zero otherwise.'

In the light of the foregoing discussion, it is rather clear that, in spite of the significant improvements achieved all through the last five decades, studies on market efficiency often lack a completely reliable foundation, thus potentially undermining their robustness, while leaving the door wide-open to further discussion.

2.2   *An innovative and realistic testing framework*

This work tries to fill in the existing theoretical gap through an innovative framework (Serati and Ziliotto (2015)) to test for semi-strong market efficiency under stressed market conditions, based on a minimized set of initial assumptions, with no need for unrealistic market characterizations and price equilibrium models. The adopted testing framework is based on a three-step procedure, with a special focus on:

- The **unexpected informational component** (previously referred to as 'surprise') embedded in a given macroeconomic announcement (Step 1) and defined as the difference between actual and median survey data. In the light of the discussion above, testing for efficiency is exclusively carried out when there is some unexpected information to be processed, provided that, by definition, markets have no reason to react to something that was known even before the official release time (as it is the case when actual data = market expectations).

- **Market volatility** (Step 2), computed for all the equity markets under examination, based on historical averages. The point is, anytime market volatility is found out to be 'historically high', signal extraction (i.e. correct unexpected information interpretation) soon gets to be a very hard task, as investors behave increasingly schizophrenically: if, however, markets were completely efficient, then excessive volatility outcomes would be automatically ruled out. By definition, indeed, efficiency is incompatible with high-volatility scenarios: after all, how could market prices include all the available information, if no signal extraction is materially possible? Or, stated the other way round, why should markets behave schizophrenically if prices incorporated all the information they need? In the light of the above reasoning, efficiency is only to be tested whenever volatility (on a given release day) is found out to be low, compared to historical averages.

- **Informational leakages** from big institutional players (Step 3) (also defined as 'price maker investors'). The point is, both market observation and academic research (see, *inter alia*, Baum *et al.* (2015), and Kurov *et al.* (2015)) suggest that big institutional players are very likely to have privileged access to confidential information (i.e. they know what the actual release will be well before the official macroeconomic announcement is made); now, if the knowledge of such information is somehow exploited to affect market prices starting from n minutes before the release, then 'spotting' and 'mimic' price makers' behaviours should result in successful (profitable) trading strategies: these 'abnormal' profits, in turn, if statistically significant and sufficiently long-lasting, would be enough to reject, *per se*, the hypothesis of efficiency. Notice, however, that even if no spillovers actually materialize, efficiency is still to be tested (provided that market surprise and volatility conditions are met, of course), as the absence of information leakages does not automatically imply efficiency in and of itself. For instance, pervasive ethical codes and powerful security measures may encourage certain statistical agencies to keep information as reserved as possible, until the macroeconomic datum is officially released. Or again, big institutional players (though pre-emptively informed about the release outcome) have opposite trading interests (e.g. because of triggered stop loss levels, investment policy constraints . . .) or simply consider the announce-ment of secondary importance for their investment strategy and thus decide to 'stay apart.' Stated in alternative terms, it might well happen that the lack of spillovers is not indicative of market prices incorporating all the available information, but simply reflects a negligible release market impact on the side of the big players. In this case, efficiency (if any) depends on how quickly the unexpected informational component is incorporated into market returns: if this process is 'reasonably' fast, indeed, it would be impossible for investors to profit from such misalignments, once the trading costs have been brought within the picture and the efficiency hypothesis would thus be preserved.

Adopting the aforementioned framework has a few desirable features worth stressing:

- The selected testing framework does not depend on any pre-emptive market equilibrium model and does not require any unrealistic market characteriza-tion (e.g. prices following pure random walks, no transaction costs -conversely included in our study by considering bid/ask series- . . .)
- Efficiency is tested exclusively when this makes some economic sense.
- This procedure sheds light on the importance of volatility and informational leakages within the scope of efficiency testing: profit opportunities certainly play a major role, but only under specific circumstances and are thus not sufficient to get universally reliable conclusions *per se.*

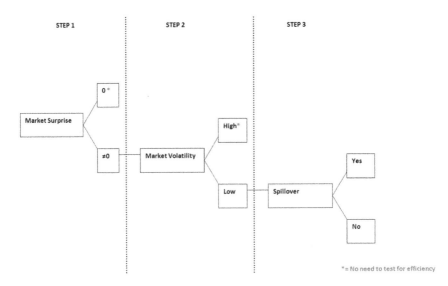

Figure 11.1 The adopted Three-step testing framework

3.0 A closer insight into the DB

Given the testing framework presented above and consistently with the general research scope of this work, the process of data retrieval and database organization has been grounded into a preliminary distinction between macroeconomic variables on one side and financial time series (prices and volatility) on the other, as discussed in the following sections.

3.1 Macroeconomic dataset: ADP, housing starts, IFO, ISM manufacturing, JPN housing starts, JPN industrial production, JPN Tankan business conditions, NFPR, university of Michigan consumer confidence, ZEW

Macroeconomic releases have been selected based on everyday market practice. In particular, all the announcements taken into account have a very high Bloomberg impact factor (at least 4 out of 5 (max)) and are actually retained as meaningful by most market players on a global scale. Clearly enough, this approach may well run the risk of being 'theoretically informal,' but it is certainly less prone to misspecifications errors. Apart from technicalities (dealt with in the corresponding Appendix 11.A), the selected macroeconomic series have three major points worth stressing. First, for all the releases taken into account, any (algebraically) positive change occurred to the corresponding market surprise indicator is deemed to be a favourable piece of news for the market as a whole, while the reverse is true in case of a negative fluctuation. Secondly, all the announcements under investigation are released on a monthly basis (except for Tankan business conditions, which is computed quarterly), so as to avoid the typical stronger volatility of higher frequency data. Third, the adopted geographical focus is wide enough to minimize the risk of country-specific distortions, while still allowing for a relatively heterogeneous insight into worldwide macroeconomic dynamics (indeed, the selected indicators actually refer to Europe, Japan and the United States, respectively).

3.2 Financial dataset: CAC40, DAX, EUROSTOXX50, FTSEMIB, HANG SENG, KOSPI, MSCI MALAYSIA, NIKKEI225, S&P500, VIX

Min-by-min bid–ask price series have been gathered for 10 futures broadly representative of France, Germany, Hong Kong, Italy, Japan, Malaysia, South Korea and US equity markets, with the ultimate aim of adopting a sufficiently wide geographical focus to eliminate country-specific distortions (if any).The main rationale for selecting futures (if compared to their underlying individual constituents) is that the former allow for a joint focus on a wide basket of securities, while benefiting from very high liquidity levels. Furthermore, ultra-high-frequency data (min-by-min) give the opportunity to concentrate even on very short-term market reactions to macroeconomic news: this is paramount, provided that low frequency observations (daily, weekly . . .) automatically rule out the possibility of assessing short-term market reactions, thus potentially biasing the final results towards zero.

In order to adopt a robust and realistic framework for analysis, also transaction costs have been accounted for by considering bid–ask series. Refer also to the corresponding Appendix 11.B to get a clearer overview of the main trading features of the selected futures.

3.3 Database architecture

As discussed, the two datasets presented above have different frequencies: monthly for macroeconomic series (except for Tankan business conditions) and min-by-min for financial variables. This discrepancy can potentially bring about several undesired consequences, not only in terms of result comparability, but also with respect to econometric estimation (matrices conformability, multicollinearity. . .). In order to preserve consistency in the final outcomes, the overall database has thus undergone a few major adjustments:

- Even though daily min-by-min market prices span from market open to market close for all the selected futures (refer also to Appendix 11.B for technical details), dealing with hundreds of observations per trading day is very likely to lead to some form of unmanageable multicollinearity: as a consequence, only a few specific time windows have been selected to monitor short-term market dynamics both before and after a given macroeconomic release, while minimizing the potential distortionary effects embedded in high-frequency data. More specifically, given any macroeconomic release among those selected (refer once again to the corresponding Appendix 11.A), the time windows that have been taken into account, in addition to market open and market close, are those displayed in Table 11.1: 'Minutes before and after a given release.' Despite being atheoretical and based on pure market observation, this choice certainly has a twofold benefit in terms of short-term monitoring and simultaneous multicollinearity reduction.
- The macroeconomic dataset (monthly/quarterly frequency) has also been adjusted accordingly to reflect the very same time spans selected for financial price series (see the previous point), so that any macroeconomic indicator is assumed to be equal to survey expectations from market open on its release day up to one minute before the official announcement, after that, it will be intuitively set equal to its actual value. This figure, in turn, will be kept unchanged until the following release day, one month/quarter later, when the new survey expectations will be brought into the picture, as explained above.

Table 11.1 Minutes before and after a given release

Minutes before release	Minutes after release
−1	+1
−2	+2
−3	+3
−4	+4
−5	+5
−10	+10
−15	+15
−25	+25
−30	+30
−35	+35
−60	+60

- Market volatility will be computed in a twofold way, both as standard deviation of bid and ask prices (formal approach) and as max-min price variation ('everyday' market approach). In practice, for all the selected time spans identified above (see Table 11.1), standard deviations and Δ(max-min) are computed, based on bid–ask market prices running from market open to the time span under examination. After that, in order to establish whether market volatility is high or low, average historical values are computed for each release day based on a predetermined number of lags (n). More specifically, considering a generic release day (yyyymmdd, hh:mm) and a given macroeconomic announcement, average volatility is computed including the n previous volatility levels referring to the very same time span. Once average volatilities have been determined accordingly, release day volatility is deemed to be high if both the daily standard deviation and max-min variation are higher than their corresponding mean values.
- Market reactions to macroeconomic impulses are assessed based on the futures under examination. Indeed, because of nonoverlapping trading windows and time zone differences, some markets are closed when a given macroeconomic release is announced: as a consequence, European and Hong Kong equity markets' responses are assessed considering exclusively EU and US indicators, Korean market's reactions are evaluated taking only Japanese announcements into account, whereas all the releases (EU, Japan and US) will be jointly taken into consideration when focusing on NIKKEI225, S&P500 and VIX, provided that the foregoing futures trade at least 23 hours per day.

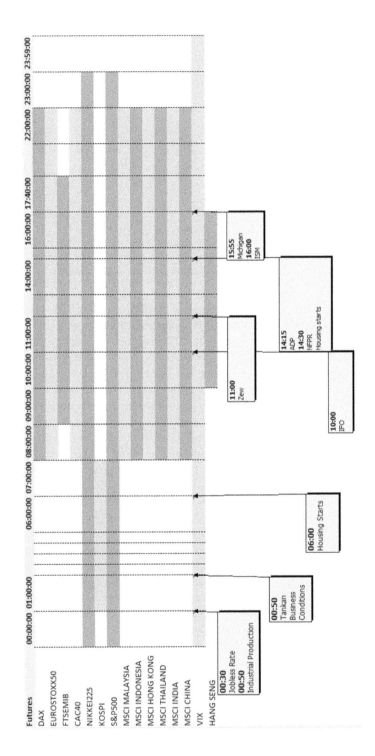

Figure 11.2 Trading windows and release scheduled times

4.0 Model estimation and emerging empirical evidence

Efficiency will be assessed considering market reactions to macroeconomic news over time under stressed market conditions: in very informal terms, the null of efficiency will be rejected only if market responses are found out to be 'strong (i.e. statistically significant) and persistent enough' to prevent market prices from instantaneously readjusting to the news embedded in unexpected information, once the macroeconomic datum has been publicly released to the worldwide investors' community. In practice, both the intensity and the time evolution path of market reactions will be investigated through impulse response functions (IRFs), as unexpected macroeconomic information can well be conceived as a sudden shock affecting security prices in a (potentially) statistically significant way. Clearly enough, in case of significance, the null of efficiency is very likely to be rejected, as this would probably open the door to persistent reactions that are not quickly reabsorbed and would thus be incompatible with market prices instantaneously incorporating all publicly available data. More specifically, in order to achieve the stated research goal, for each of the 10 futures under investigation, 2 VAR (vector autoregression) models have been estimated as detailed here below: once this first step has been completed, IRFs can then be obtained based on a suitable decomposition of the variance/covariance matrices resulting from VAR estimation. Notice finally that, independently of the various model specifications, all the estimated VARs include the three major variable types presented so far (macroeconomic indicators, volatility and market prices).

- **Macroeconomic indicators**: the single macroeconomic series previously dealt with (Section 3.1) have not been considered individually, provided that this work aims at evaluating market reactions to macroeconomic announcements in general, without making any specific reference to a precise macroeconomic release/impulse. As a consequence, Principal Component Analysis (PCA) has been carried out on the standardized selected series (refer to the corresponding Appendix 11.A), to get a single but informationally significant macroeconomic indicator, able to reduce database complexity (i.e. dimensions), while simultaneously minimizing informational losses. Clearly enough, depending on the futures under examination, the starting set of macroeconomic variables for PCA varies correspondingly, so that, for instance, for all European and Hong Kong futures this will include only EU and US macroeconomic variables; Japanese variables only will be retained for KOSPI, whereas the whole macroeconomic dataset will be considered for PCA when processing S&P500, NIKKEI225 and VIX. The resulting 'global' macroeconomic indicators will then be retained to perform VAR estimation.
- **Volatility levels**: for the sake of parsimony, only standard deviation of ask price series has been included (Section 3.3), to minimize the impact on the available degrees of freedom. Actually, the four volatility series presented

above (standard deviation of bid prices, standard deviation of ask prices, max-min deviation of bid prices and max-min deviation of ask prices) display correlations often above 0.9: taken jointly, they would simply erode the observations available for estimation, while providing no additional informational content.

- **Price series**: to keep internal consistency with volatility level indicators, price dynamics are approximated relying exclusively on ask series. Once again, this choice meets the parsimony principle outlined above (ρ(bid; ask)> 0:9), while still offering a more realistic and veritable picture of market prices and trading book dynamics compared to mid or last values. Clearly enough, both bid and ask series have been jointly taken into account when assessing profitability dynamics.

The three series presented above have then been multiplied by two dummy variables accounting for volatility and spillover dynamics, in line with the testing tree described before (step back to Chart 1). More specifically, the former (denoted global dummy [GD]) considers both steps (volatility and leakages) and equals 1 only if market volatility at release time = 'low' and spillovers = 'yes,' while the latter (denoted 'volatility dummy' [VD]) includes volatility alone, to test for efficiency even under no information leakages. In practice, the two resulting VAR models are those displayed here below (global VAR (4.1) and volatility VAR (11.4.2), respectively)

$$X_t = A_0 + A_L X_{t-n} + u_t \qquad (11.4.1)$$

with

$$X_t = \begin{pmatrix} \sigma \cdot GD \\ MacroPCA \cdot GD \\ PricesBid \cdot GD \end{pmatrix}$$

Whereas Volatility VAR:

$$X_t = A_0 + A_L X_{t-n} + z_t \qquad (11.4.2)$$

with

$$X_t = \begin{pmatrix} \sigma \cdot VD \\ MacroPCA \cdot VD \\ PricesBid \cdot VD \end{pmatrix}.$$

In both cases, the residual covariance matrices resulting from VAR estimation have been decomposed using Cholesky's factorization, in order to orthogonalize impulses for IRF determination (for a more detailed insight into Cholesky's decomposition and variables ordering, refer to Serati and Ziliotto (2015)): this has allowed to get a clearer insight into the time evolution path of market price responses to a (unitary standard deviation) shock occurred to the macroeconomic indicator.

The available empirical evidence is by far and large in line with Serati and Ziliotto (2015): indeed, the null hypothesis of efficiency is rejected for all the other futures under examination. From a purely qualitative standpoint, market reactions to macroeconomic shocks have found out to be statistically significant and persistent over the estimation horizon: indeed, this is perfectly consistent with prices gradually incorporating the unexpected information and progressively readjusting to their new equilibrium values. Prices tend to react immediately to the unexpected information, though with varying intensity, before gradually smoothing the initial peak as time goes by. The re-adjustment process, however, is generally not instantaneous and market participants consequently have all the time they need to open a 'mimetic' (observing what price makers do) position based on the just released macroeconomic announcement, before closing it to cash in a profit after a relatively short span of time. Stated in alternative terms, this amounts to saying that, though short-lived, market reactions are strong and persistent enough to reject the null of efficiency over the short term; deviations from equilibrium are then progressively reabsorbed with time and efficiency would thus be restored in the medium run.

More specifically, the available empirical evidence has shed light on a few additional points worth consideration:

- As stated above, market reactions to macroeconomic impulses are quite comparable on a worldwide scale: indeed, even in times of financial instability, significant deviations from efficiency and remarkable profit opportunities emerge whenever volatility is suitably low and information spillovers from big institutional players are relatively easy to spot (refer to Figure 11.2 as

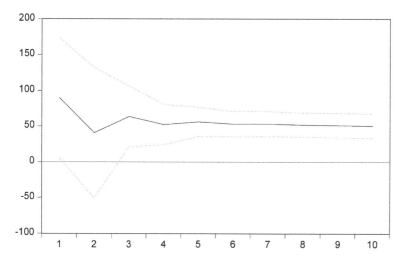

Figure 11.3 DAX IRF to macroeconomic impulses – global VAR

an example). In practice, under the foregoing scenario, whenever financial markets are 'hit' by some sort of unexpected news (like in the case of macroeconomic releases), the most rational thing to do for price takers is to adopt herd behaviours (Orléans (2007)), interpreting the available information in the light of what the big players do. This is very likely to lead to significant profit opportunities within a relatively short span of time (30–35 minutes, on average), as market prices gradually try to incorporate the new information at their disposal. On the whole, this relatively homogeneous finding is fully consistent with the increasingly more globalized competitive arena market practitioners have to deal with. Furthermore, this also amounts to saying that semi-strong inefficiency tends to hold for worldwide equity markets, independently of economic contingency (recession/growth – uncertainty/prosperity. . .), country-specific factors (developed/emerging economies. . .) and market-related features (liquidity, severity of anti-market abuse legislation as well as of the related enforcement mechanisms. . .).

- Significant market reactions clearly go hand in hand with profit opportunities, notice, however, that the latter are not to be conceived as a preliminary and sufficient condition to test for efficiency, like a sort of 'toggle tester'; based on the approach adopted so far, profit opportunities simply represent the logical consequence of a twofold interaction: whenever volatility is low and informational leakages are rather easily identifiable, mimicking the behaviours of big institutional investors (market makers) in the light of the recent release is very likely to be successful over time.

- Deviations from efficiency are still observable even under no information leakages (despite being remarkably weaker if compared to the volatility/ spillover scenario – except for DAX and HANG SENG futures): in such a context, news interpretation gets much harder for small price taking investors, that cannot benefit from the informational advantage stemming from herding and mimetic techniques. This practically means that inefficiencies are actually significant, but certainly do not leave much room for dramatic profit opportunities. German and Hong Kong equity markets conversely need further investigation, even though such exceptions are relatively easy to materialize under stressed market conditions and probably find their roots into market-specific (internal) factors.

- Equity market reactions to macroeconomic impulses tend to carry a positive sign, which is perfectly in line with the fact that market prices are very likely to increase under favourable macroeconomic scenarios (the reverse, of course, is true in case of unexpectedly bad macroeconomic news). Clearly enough, the foregoing reasoning does not apply to VIX futures, provided that market volatility and worldwide macroeconomic 'prosperity' generally exhibit negative correlations (hence the minus sign in IRFs). Stated in alternative terms, positive macroeconomic impulses bring about widespread 'optimism' within the financial community and this is deemed to reduce both average volatility levels and the uncertainty related to future economic outlooks. Once again, the reverse applies under unfavourable macroeconomic conditions. This said, however, the available empirical evidence sheds light on a couple of exceptions both referring to Asian equity markets and certainly worth additional investigation. More precisely, both for KOSPI and MSCI MALAYSIA, IRFs exhibit persistently negative signs, thus implying that favourable macroeconomic announcements tend to go hand in hand with negative market price fluctuations (adjustments). The underlying rationale of this 'unusual' behaviour is probably intimately intertwined with the two macroeconomic datasets considered for PCA and VAR estimation. In particular, as explained above, because of time zone-related issues, the macroeconomic database for KOSPI includes exclusively Japanese indicators, whereas the set of macroeconomic variables considered for MSCI MALAYSIA is based on the European Union and the United States alone. Now, as far as South Korea is concerned, the negative responses to favourable Japanese data may find their roots in the fact that, while having been close trading partners for years, South Korea has progressively turned into a fierce competitor for Japanese goods in international markets, especially for high-tech and automotive industries. With specific reference to Malaysia, instead, the rationale at the basis of the negative trend in IRFs lies in the fact that MSCI MALAYSIA is probably much more affected by the Japan macroeconomic outlook than all the other 'European' futures negotiated on Eurex Exchange: the latter, however, is closed when Japanese data are released, thus bringing about significant informational losses that have in all likelihood affected futures reactions to EU and US macroeconomic impulses. Clearly enough, this may also be the reason why MSCI MALAYSIA's reactions to macroeconomic impulses are the weakest of the whole financial dataset, as shown in Table 11.2.

Table 11.2 Market reactions (indicative absolute values) in monetary terms

	Global VAR		Volatility VAR	
	Max (EUR)	*Min (EUR)*	*Max (EUR)*	*Min (EUR)*
CAC	190	160	110	100
DAX	1650	1250	2100	1375
EUROSTOXX	200	160	140	120
FTSEMIB	375	345	280	270
HANG SENG	738	488	898	553
KOSPI	1170	780	780	390
MSCI MALAYSIA	30	27	18	9
NIKKEI 225	492	409	456	322
S&P	1612	460	690	230
VIX	368	184	92	27

Table 11.3 Adopted Exchange Rates (nr. of units of a given currency per euro as of 18 December 2015)

HKD/EUR	8.40565
KRW/EUR	1281.45
USD/EUR	1.0855

- If we exclude MSCI MALAYSIA, EUROSTOXX50 exhibits relatively weak market reactions compared to the other equity futures, probably because of its pan-European scope: indeed, such a wide geographical focus necessarily brings about some netting in international market responses, especially whenever the included financial markets do not react homogeneously to the same informational shock. DAX and KOSPI conversely exhibit strong and significant market responses, probably as a consequence of their degree of 'market openness.' More precisely, both for DAX and KOSPI, the selected macroeconomic datasets include, for most part (if not even exclusively), foreign indicators: American releases for Germany and Japanese for KOSPI, so that the aforementioned significant responses may simply be indicative of a closer economic partnership among the involved countries. In principle, the same applies to S&P (whose corresponding macroeconomic database actually includes all the selected release countries – Germany, Japan and the United States), even though such significant reactions may also be brought about by the relatively higher liquidity levels (Kurov *et al.* (2015)) typical of the American equity market. Stated in alternative terms, this amounts to saying that the intensity of equity market reactions to macroeconomic impulses seems to depend, to a great extent, on the degree of financial and economic integration within the international community: in practice, the more 'globalized' a financial system is, the more it will be sensitive to macroeconomic shocks on a worldwide scale.
- The emerging empirical evidence sheds light on the fact that, despite the huge efforts carried out at the international scale, market abuse and price manipulation are still very likely to materialize even under stressed market conditions both in developed and in emerging financial markets. Stated in simpler terms, undue informational asymmetries (clearly brought about by pre-emptive news leakages) persistently allow institutional price markers to realize significant and risk-free profits, thus seriously undermining the efficacy of all legislative efforts to preserve fair and transparent competition.

5.0 Concluding remarks

All over the last few months, both the macroeconomic outlook and the geopolitical environment have contributed to most of the instability market practitioners have had to face on a daily basis. Despite this unrest, however, the traditional macroeconomic drivers of price fluctuations do not seem to have been seriously undermined. On the contrary, based on the adopted testing framework, the emerging empirical evidence has shown that, even in times of financial instability, worldwide equity markets still react significantly and persistently (all over the subsequent 30 minutes) to macroeconomic impulses in the form of regularly released announcements. This finding clearly undermines the conditions at the very basis of semi-strong efficiency and actually opens the door to further debate with specific reference to the efficacy of both anti-market abuse legislation and release procedures adopted by the various statistical agencies (e.g. website announcements versus lock-up rooms . . .).

Furthermore, the analysis carried out so far has allowed us to cast a new light on the efficiency debate: the available empirical evidence, indeed, seems to support the claim that market inefficiencies are very likely to emerge independently of the international macroeconomic contingency as well as of all country-specific factors (emerging/developed economies. . .). This is certainly paramount to strengthen the robustness of the presented testing framework, while leaving the door wide-open to additional investigation, provided that, for instance, the proposed methodology could be extended to other instrument categories (bonds, forex. . .) and to new macroeconomic releases.

These are only a few potential developments for further discussion to lift the curtain on the efficiency debate in a realistic, market-oriented, but still rigorous way, with strong implications not only from a purely academic and technical standpoint (e.g. trading. . .), but also from a regulatory perspective.

Appendix 11.A
Macroeconomic dataset

Table 11.A.1 Selected macroeconomic indicators

ADP employment change	Description	Measure of nonfarm private employment
	Release hour	14:15 (CET)
	Unit of measurement	Thousands
	Statistical agency	ADP
Housing starts	Description	Private and residential real estate activity
	Release hour	14:30 (CET)
	Unit of measurement	Thousands
	Statistical agency	US Census Bureau
IFO	Description	Business climate (Germany and EU)
	Release hour	10:00 (CET)
	Unit of measurement	Index
	Statistical agency	IFO Institute
ISM manufacturing	Description	Manufacturing index
	Release hour	16:00 (CET)
	Unit of measurement	Index
	Statistical agency	Institute of Supply Management (ISM)
JPN housing starts	Description	New houses started during reference period
	Release hour	06:00 (CET)
	Unit of measurement	%
	Statistical agency	Ministry of Land, Infrastructure, Transport
JPN industrial production	Description	Output (volume) of industrial establishments
	Release hour	00:50 (CET)
	Unit of measurement	%
	Statistical agency	Ministry of Economy Trade and Industry
JPN Tankan business conditions	Description	Business condition forecast – large enterprises
	Release hour	00:50 (CET)
	Unit of measurement	%
	Statistical agency	Bank of Japan
NFPR	Description	Payroll jobs added/lost in nonfarm sectors
	Release hour	14:30 (CET)
	Unit of measurement	Thousands
	Statistical agency	US Bureau of Labour Statistics

University of Michigan consumer confidence index	Description	Consumer sentiment
	Release hour	15:55 (CET)
	Unit of measurement	Index
	Statistical agency	University of Michigan
ZEW	Description	Economic sentiment (Germany and EU)
	Release hour	11:00 (CET)
	Unit of measurement	Index
	Statistical agency	ZEW

Caveat: Selected Releases Time Schedule.

Release hours may be subject to variations all through the year, mainly because Europe, Japan and the United States do not switch contemporaneously from daylight saving time (DST) to Greenwich mean time (GMT) and *vice versa*.

Appendix 11.B
Financial dataset

Table 11.B.1 Selected financial indicators

CAC40	Exchange	Euronext Derivatives Paris
	Underlying	CAC Index
	Min tick	0.5
	Index pt value	10 €
	Trading hours	08:00 (CET) – 22:00 (CET)
	Available maturities	March, June, September, December
DAX	Exchange	Eurex Exchange
	Underlying	DAX Index
	Min tick	0.5
	Index pt value	25 €
	Trading hours	07:50 (CET) – 22:00 (CET)
	Available maturities	March, June, September, December
EUROSTOXX	Exchange	Eurex Exchange
	Underlying	EUROSTOXX Index
	Min tick	1
	Index pt value	10 €
	Trading hours	07:50 (CET) – 22:00 (CET)
	Available maturities	March, June, September, December
FTSEMIB	Exchange	Borsa Italiana
	Underlying	FTSEMIB Index
	Min tick	5
	Index pt value	5 €
	Trading hours	09:00 (CET) – 17:40 (CET)
	Available maturities	March, June, September, December
HANG SENG	Exchange	Hong Kong Futures Exchange
	Underlying	Hang Seng Index
	Min tick	1
	Index pt value	50 HKD
	Trading hours	02:15 (CET) – 16:45 (CET)
	Available maturities	March, June, September, December
KOSPI	Exchange	Korea Exchange
	Underlying	KOSPI 200 Index
	Min tick	0.05
	Index pt value	500,000 KRW
	Trading hours	01:00 (CET) – 07:00 (CET)
	Available maturities	March, June, September, December

MSCI	Exchange	Eurex Exchange
MALAYSIA	Underlying	MSCI Malaysia Index
	Min tick	0.1
	Index pt value	100 $
	Trading hours	07:50 (CET) – 22:00 (CET)
	Available maturities	March, June, September, December
NIKKEI225	Exchange	CME
	Underlying	USD-denominated NIKKEI 225 Index
	Min tick	5
	Index pt value	5 $
	Trading hours	00:00 (CET) – 23:00 (CET)
	Available maturities	March, June, September, December
S&P500	Exchange	CME
	Underlying	S&P500 Index
	Min Tick	0.1
	Index Pt Value	250 $
	Trading Hours	00:00 (CET) – 23:00 (CET)
	Available maturities	March, June, September, December
VIX	Exchange	CBOE
	Underlying	VIX Index
	Min Tick	0.05
	Index Pt Value	1000 $
	Trading Hours	00:00 (CET) – 23:58 (CET)
	Available maturities	March, June, September, December

Remark: All the information displayed in the tables included in Appendixes 11.A and 11.B has been retrieved from Bloomberg L.P. trading and information providing platform.

References

Ball, R., and Brown, P. (1968). An empirical evaluation of accounting income numbers. *Journal of Accounting Research*, 6(2), 159–178.

Bartolini, L., Goldberg, L., and Sacarny, A. (2008). How economics moves markets. *Current Issues in Economics and Finance*, 14(6), 1–7, Federal Reserve Bank of New York.

Baum, C. F., Kurov, A., and Wolfe, M. H. (2015). What do Chinese macro announcements tell us about the world economy? *Journal of International Money and Finance*, 59, 100–122.

Belgacem, A. (2008). Fundamentals, macroeconomic announcements and asset prices. *University of Paris Ouest-Nanterre La Défense and CNRS*. http://economix.fr/pdf/dt/2009/WP_EcoX_2009-16.pdf.

Black, A., and Fraser, P. (1995). U.K. stock returns: Predictability and business conditions. *The Manchester School of Economic & Social Studies*, 63, 85–102.

Bollerslev, T., Cai, J., and Song, F. M. (2000). Intraday periodicity, long memory volatility and macroeconomic announcement effect in the US Treasury bond market. *Journal of Empirical Finance*, 7, 37–55.

Castanias, R. P. (1979). Macroinformation and the variability of stock market prices. *The Journal of Finance*, 34(2), 439–450.

Chen, N. F., Roll, R., and Ross, S. A. (1986). Economic forces and the stock market. *Journal of Business*, 59(3), 383–403.

Clare, A. D., Thomas, S. H., and Wickens, M. R. (1994). Is the Gilt-equity yield ratio useful for predicting UK stock returns? *Economic Journal*, 104(423), 303–315.

Fama, E. F. (1970). Efficient capital markets: A review of theory and empirical work. *The Journal of Finance*, 25(2), 383–417.

Fama, E. F., Fisher, L., Jensen, M., and Roll, R. (1969). The adjustment of stock prices to new information. *International Economic Review*, X, 1–21.

Godhart, C. A. E., and Smith, R. G. (1985). The impact of news on financial markets on the UK. *Journal of Money, Credit and Banking*, 17(4), 507–511.

Grossman, S., and Stiglitz, J. (1980). On the impossibility of informational efficient markets. *American Economic Review*, 70, 393–408.

Hardouvelis, G. A. (1987). Macroeconomic information and stock prices. *Journal of Economics and Business*, 39(2), 131–140.

Haryadi, H., Hallahan, T. A., and Tanha, H. (2014). Macroeconomic announcements and volatility of equity returns: High-frequency evidence from Indonesia. *2015 Financial Markets & Corporate Governance Conference*.

Hashimoto, Y., and Ito, T. (2008). Effects of Japanese macroeconomic announcements on the Dollar/Yen exchange rate: High-resolution picture. *Journal of the Japanese and the International Economies*, 24(3), 334–354.

Jain, P. C. (1988). Response of hourly stock prices and trading volume to economic news. *The Journal of Business*, 61(2), 219–231.

Kim, S. J. (2003). The spillover effects of US and Japanese public information news in advanced Asia-Pacific Stock markets. *Pacific Basin Journal*, 11(5), 611–630.

Kim, S. J., McKenzie, M. D., and Faff, R. W. (2004). Macroeconomic news announcements and the role of expectations: Evidence for US bonds, stocks and foreign exchange market. *Journal of Multinational Financial Management*, 14(4), 217–232.

Kurov, A., Sancetta, A., Strasser, G., and Wolfe, M. A. (2015). Price drift before US macroeconomic news: Private information about public announcements? Paris Finance Meeting EUROFIDAI – AFFI.

Li, L., and Hu, Z. F. (1988). Responses of the stock market to macroeconomic announcements across economic states. International Monetary Fund-Working Papers No. WP/98/79.

Lo, A. W., and MacKinlay, C. (1988). Stock market prices do not follow random walks: Evidence from a simple specification test. *Review of Financial Studies*, 1(1), 41–66.

Mishkin, F., Bordes, C., Hautcoeur, P. C., and Lacoue-Labarthe, D. (2007). *Monnaie, banque et marches financiers*. 8th edition. Paris: Pearson Education.

Nikkinen, J., Omran, M., Sahlström, P., and Aïÿö, J. (2006). Global stock market reactions to scheduled US macroeconomic news announcements. *Global Finance Journal*, 17(1), 92–104.

Nussi, J., and Sahlström, P. (2001). Impact of scheduled US macroeconomic news on stock market uncertainty: A multinational perspective. *Multinational Finance Journal*, 5(2), 129–148.

Orléans, A. (2007). Efficience informationnelle versus finance comportementaliste: éléments pour un débat, *Axes de la recherche en sciences économiques*, CEPREMAP, Presses de la Rue d'ULM, 1–13.

Panetta, F. (2001). The stability of the relation between the stock market and macro-economic forces. *Temi di Discussione del Servizio Studi di Borsa Italiana*, No. 393.

Pearce, D. K., and Roley, V. V. (1985). Stock prices and economic news. *The Journal of Business*, 58(1), 49–67.

Pesaran, M. H. (2005). Market efficiency today. IEPR Working Paper 05.41, Institute of Economic Policy Research-University of Southern California.

Poitras, M. (2004). The impact of macroeconomic announcements on stock prices: In search of state dependence. *Southern Economic Journal*, *70*(3), 549–565.

Serati, M., and Ziliotto, A. (2015). The semi-strong efficiency debate: In search of a new testing framework. *Research in International Business and Finance*, *34*(C), 412–438.

Wallenius, L., Fedorova, E., and Collan, M. (2013). Surprise effect of European macroeconomic announcements on CIVETS stock markets. Conference Proceedings of 14th International Conference on Finance and banking, 513–523.

Waud, R. N. (1970). Public interpretation of discount rate changes: Evidence on the "announcement effect". *Econometrica*, *38*(2), 231–250.

12 Technical efficiency and stock performance of listed commercial banks in ASEAN-5

Sok-Gee Chan

1.0 Introduction

In emerging markets, the banking institution is the main source of financing for businesses due to its underdeveloped capital market for fund raising. This has made banks the main channel for monetary policy transmission, to affect the overall economic outcome in the country especially during financial crisis. Hence, the collapse of bank institution leads to destruction in the emerging country's economic performance when it creates detrimental effects on the payment system which paralyze the overall financial system. This includes the impediment to use the banking institutions as an effective tool for monetary policy. This had been documented in various empirical evidences not only from developed markets (Kroszner, Laeven and Klingebiel, 2007; Reinhart and Rogoff, 2009) but also in the emerging markets (Goldstein and Turner, 1996; Lindgren, Garcia and Saal, 1996; Williams and Nguyen, 2005). In addition, the 1997 Asian financial crisis and 2008 global financial crisis proved that the countries' economic performance was severely affected due to the fragility of bank industry. This further resulted in currency devaluation that leads to crowding the foreign direct investors out from the country and made the domestic firms perform their worst. Thus, stable and sound banking institutions had proven their footing in the domestic market as the main key driver for economic stability.

Steps have been taken over the last decades to strengthen the banking institutions with the objectives to create a more resilient and sound financial system especially in the developing region in ASEAN 5 in facing the wave of liberalization and globalization. Among others is the banking consolidations and recapitalization which had taken placed in Malaysia, Thailand and Indonesia after the 1997 Asian financial crisis. Apart of bad debt management, Lindgren *et al.* (1996) highlighted that ASEAN governments raise the protection bar for banks where they adopted the international standards supervision and enforcement policy. Furthermore to enhance the bank resilience, BASEL III emphasize the vital role of risk monitoring for banks. The BASEL III has a twofold objective i) to improve the global capital and liquidity through providing stronger and more prudent banking system and ii) enhance the capability of banks to absorb uncertain crisis, which indirectly reduce the spillover effect to the market.

In order to ensure the long-run survivability of the banking institutions in ASEAN-5, especially the locally-owned commercial banks, the performance of the bank is undeniable when it comes to bank efficiency level. Unlike the literature of finance that look mainly on bank performance in terms of profitability, efficiency provides a comprehensive picture of the banks allocation of resources. Bank efficiency is defined as the ability of the banking institution to manipulate the use of inputs to achieve a given level of financial outputs such as loans and investments. In this case, an efficient bank is believed to be able to withstand financial market turmoil and hence contribute to more efficient allocation of resources in the economy and the stability of the financial system (Shamsuddin and Xiang, 2012) as they are able to fully utilize their resources to the best usage. Besides, an efficient bank may also result in greater shareholder returns which are reflected in better stock performance and hence contribute to higher profitability and financial performance. This suggests the importance of bank efficiency for better financial performance in longer term which leads to higher investors confident, which translated into higher stock returns. In this context, efficiency becomes one of the main factors that may result in downward pressure for bank performance level which may affect the stock value of the listed banks.

Besides, according to Fama (1970) on efficient market hypothesis, the stock prices reflect all publicly available information in an efficient market. In this context, the efficiency scores estimated using published accounting numbers should also reflect the performance in the stock prices since it is publicly know information. Therefore, this study focuses on the causal relationship between the banks' stock return and technical efficiency of the listed commercial banks in ASEAN-5 from year 1990 to 2014. The study of causal relationship is useful to determine the long-run relationship between the efficiency of the bank with stock return. This is believed to shed the lights for investors and academician to understand the long-term relationship for better policy implication. The performance of the listed commercial banks is rather crucial because listed banks not only need to answer to the regulators, depositors but also to the shareholders which look mainly on shareholders' maximization. This is a contrast to the traditional operation of the banks where the main objective is on liquidity and risk management. In order to strive for balance between shareholders' maximization, liquidity and risk management, the analysis of the causal relationship between stock return and bank efficiency is rather crucial. This enables the banks to kill two birds with one stone if both are cointegrated in the long run.

This analysis is especially important upon the upcoming ASEAN Economic Community (AEC) integration for greater financial liberalization and capital market integration. AEC demands for proper planning and policy implementation so that all the member countries can benefit from such integration. This is because greater financial openness could lead to greater risk in some ASEAN countries if there is no proper planning (Almekinders, Fukuda, Mourmouras and Zhou, 2015). As the financial system in the ASEAN countries remains highly dependent on banking sector, such integration may impose greater discipline in the banking performance for a sound and resilient financial system. Thus, the relationship between bank efficiency and its stock returns served as the most basic criteria for the success of AEC. Long-run relationship is important since the monetary policy transmission within ASEAN countries largely depends on the bank channel and the disturbances in the banking institutions not only affect the individual bank but also paralyzed the whole economic situation in the region due to enactment of AEC.

In addition, the ASEAN Banking Integration Framework (ABIF) as suggested as one of the major steps forward to further liberalize the regional financial-services industry also demands for greater stability in the banking industry. Hence, the efficiency level of the banks is definitely a vital component for the success of ABIF. We select the nonparametric approach (DEA) to estimate the efficiency level of the commercial banks in ASEAN-5 which allows for decomposition of the efficiency level into managerial efficiency measures by pure technical efficiency and scale efficiency. The panel cointegration technique will be employed to study the long- run relationship between bank efficiency level and stock return using panel vector error correction model (VECM).

We will further discuss the situation of the ASEAN banking industry in Section 2.0. This is followed by the methodology employed to determine the long-run relationship between bank efficiency and stock return in Section 3.0. Section 4.0 discusses the analysis of the results obtain. Section 5.0 concludes.

2.0   The banking in ASEAN

The 1997 Asian financial crisis (AFC) remains as the most popular discussion when it comes to the banking industry among the ASEAN countries. The crisis originated from Thailand with currency devaluation that created a contagion effect to the rest of the ASEAN economies. This had led to the bailout of the commercial banks in the region and consequently the most severe economic crisis that had been documented in the Asian region as compared to the 2008 global financial crisis. The 1997 AFC awakened the regulators in the region with the collapse of major banking and financial institutions and further resulted in bank runs. Various methods had been utilized by the regulators in the region to overcome the crisis which includes obtaining financing from International Monetary Fund (IMF), closure of problems banks, banking consolidation with force mergers, re-regulation and recapitalization in major ASEAN countries such as Indonesia, Malaysia, Thailand and the Philippines.

In Indonesia, as directed by the IMF, the government and central bank took some major interventions in the banking industry which resulted in the closure of small banks, take-over and recapitalization of the state-owned and regional banks. Among the major interventions are the closures of 16 small banks in November 1997 and the recapitalization of 6 state-owned banks and 12 regional banks between 1999 and 2000. To further strengthen the banking industry after the 1997 AFC, the Indonesian government further launched the 2004 master plan to reduce the number of banks from 130 to minimum of 60 banks in the country. This is meant to strengthen the banking industry by creating economies of scale for long-term survivability of the banks to face with the wave of liberalization and globalization. Besides, steps such as raising the capital requirements, reducing ownership concentration (limit of shareholding from more than 25 percent of shares) and reducing deposit guarantee were also introduced with the objective to improve the market discipline.

Similarly, in Malaysia the banking consolidation and recapitalization also took place for the survivability of the banking industry from the collapse due to the effects of AFC. The central bank of Malaysia, Bank Negara Malaysia initiated the merger of the banking industry in Malaysia with the objective to create a more effective and efficient banking system by merging the locally-owned banking institutions into 10 major banking groups. As of 31 December 2000, it is witnessed that 50 out of 54 locally-owned banking institutions in Malaysia were consolidated into 10 banking groups following the merger program. This exercise had effectively rationalized and consolidated 94 percent of the total assets of the domestic banking industry in Malaysia as a step to save the banking industry due to the negative effects of the AFC. Continuous improvements of the domestic banking industry in Malaysia were seen with the implementation of Malaysia Deposit Insurance System in 2011, the revision of the Corporate Governance Code of Conduct since 2000 and also the adoption of Basel III requirements after the GFC. These steps are meant to further strengthen the banking institutions towards a more consolidated and efficient banking system towards the implementation of AEC as well as to ensure that the banking channel is not affected by future banking crisis which will paralyze the monetary and economic situation in Malaysia as the banking industry is the main channel of monetary policy transmission in Malaysia.

The banking industry in Thailand with no exception has to undergo a major banking consolidation and recapitalization because the banking institutions were also greatly affected by the AFC. Mergers among the Thai commercial banks and also with the foreign banks were encouraged to avoid bank bailout. Unlike other countries in ASEAN, the recapitalization of the banking institutions in Thailand was focused on the injection of foreign shareholdings into the Thai commercial banks. This includes the relaxation on the regulation of foreign shareholdings limit that permits the foreign investors to hold more than 49 percent of the share of the commercial banks in Thailand. Such strategies are meant to strengthen the commercial banks with the injection of foreign investors' shareholdings with more advanced risk management techniques into the banking industry in Thailand.

Various steps had been taken to further strengthen the banking industry in ASEAN after the AFC episode. This includes relaxing the regulation of foreign shareholdings of the commercial banks in the region. The foreign shareholdings in Indonesia were increased to 99 percent in 1999 whereas in Malaysia the foreign shareholdings increased from 30 percent to 47 percent in 2007. On the other hand, 100 percent foreign shareholdings were permitted in Thailand and the Philippines after the AFC. This move is meant to increase the risk management of the commercial banks and also towards the better disclosure and transparency to improve the efficiency of the commercial banks in this region. Besides, this step is taken in order for the locally-owned commercial banks in the region to benefit from positive spillover from the foreign counterparts such as better technology and superiority of management to further improve the banking situation in the region.

In addition, various strategies had been implemented to increase the risk management of the commercial banks in the region. For example, the Bankgko Sentral ng Pilipinas (central bank of the Philippines) required the banks to develop and implement an internal credit risk rating system in compliance with Basel II in 2004 and at the same year the central banks in Indonesia implemented master plan 2004 to reduce the number of banks in Indonesia as well raising capital requirements to further strengthen the position of the commercial banks to withhold the future economic shock.

Nevertheless, the financial system in ASEAN countries still needs to be further strengthened as it still dominated by the banking system as a whole as we can see from Table 12.1. High dependence on banking institutions could serve as a vulnerable situation for the ASEAN countries if there is no proper risk management. This had put forward the question of the survivability of the banking institutions in the process of liberalization and globalization especially when the banking industries are fully integrated under the concept of ABIF. Despite being the world financial hubs, Table 12.1 shows that the Singapore banking industry is highly concentrated with the concentration of 90.49 percent before the AFC and still remain as high as 89.80 percent between year 2009 and 2011.

The highly concentrated banking industry in ASEAN may serve as a threat for future economic development. Based on the concentration fragility hypothesis, more concentrated markets may result in fragility of the banking industry because they may take excessive risks to earn higher returns in the market (Uhde and Heimeshoff, 2009). This may result in higher information asymmetry in the banking industry which will distort the efficiency of the banking industry in terms of resource allocation (Hellman, Murdock and Stiglitz, 2000). Such views are supported by Ariss (2010) where more a concentrated market leads to higher market power due to rent seeking behaviour which will increase the moral hazard and risk-taking activities and consequently distort the banking stability. Furthermore, higher market concentration which increases the market power of the commercial banks may lead to managerial inefficiency that increase the operational and credit risk as suggested by the economic theories (Boyd and de Nicolo, 2005; Mirzaei, Moore and Liu, 2013). Therefore, the efficiency analysis of the banking industry in ASEAN is crucial to determine the current stage of banking efficiency in allocation of resources for better future planning.

In addition, banking institutions in the big ASEAN countries such as Singapore, Malaysia and Thailand still dominate the financial system which can be seen from Table 12.1 from the deposit money bank assets to GDP, private credit by deposit money banks to GDP and bank deposits to GDP. This could be an alarming issue if the banking system in the region is affected where it will distort the allocation of resources of the economies as the economies are highly dependent

Table 12.1 Banking indicator in ASEAN-5

Banking indicator	Country	1990–1997	1998–2000	2001–2005	2006–2008	2009–2011
Deposit money bank assets to GDP (%)	Indonesia	49.519	49.044	39.177	31.671	29.905
	Malaysia	110.556	149.173	122.910	103.834	120.091
	Philippines	36.766	51.838	45.545	37.184	43.778
	Singapore	95.758	121.744	125.887	107.544	126.799
	Thailand	117.132	153.574	114.199	103.884	108.996
Private credit by deposit money banks to GDP (%)	Indonesia	46.335	34.703	19.708	22.879	24.372
	Malaysia	100.702	140.272	114.515	97.146	106.347
	Philippines	28.090	39.963	29.118	23.698	28.741
	Singapore	83.374	102.982	101.722	85.992	99.657
	Thailand	109.180	141.912	98.225	92.209	96.666
Bank deposits to GDP (%)	Indonesia	37.628	48.247	40.188	33.624	31.948
	Malaysia	85.550	111.812	114.248	105.216	120.811
	Philippines	34.999	47.925	46.181	45.431	51.606
	Singapore	75.543	101.273	101.530	102.384	121.525
	Thailand	72.589	103.263	102.927	93.546	97.240
Bank concentration (%)	Indonesia	N/A	57.629	53.738	44.687	44.593
	Malaysia	N/A	38.588	55.911	71.575	63.076
	Philippines	N/A	85.080	78.108	45.687	47.561
	Singapore	N/A	90.491	98.380	88.069	89.800
	Thailand	N/A	49.678	47.529	44.794	45.598
Bank z-score	Indonesia	N/A	–0.744	2.110	2.471	2.813
	Malaysia	N/A	28.294	28.004	27.430	30.672
	Philippines	N/A	33.314	33.243	22.197	22.839
	Singapore	N/A	24.703	20.922	26.344	27.790
	Thailand	N/A	1.289	4.309	5.198	6.257

Sources: World Bank, Financial Development and Structure Database, updated November 2013; World Bank, Global Financial Development Databased, updated November 2013

on the banking industry. Hence, bank efficiency and performance are crucial for long-term survivability not only limited to the banking industry but also to the economy as a whole.

In terms of overall sovereignty of the banking industry, the bank z-score still remain low for countries such as Indonesia and Thailand as shown in Table 12.1. The z-score for Malaysia, Singapore and Philippines improved since AFC and this may be due to the prudential management and rapid banking consolidations which took place after the 1997 AFC.

ABIF is a myth to be realized for the ASEAN countries. Nevertheless, such implementation could lead to higher risk towards the financial system in the region if careful phases and sequencing of implementation are not planned accordingly. This is especially true given the current situation of the banking industry in ASEAN which is characterized with concentrated market structure, high dependency on banking institutional funding and low sovereignty as suggested by the z-score. Policy makers of the ASEAN countries had taken a cautious approach to move forward for greater financial and capital account liberalization and this definitely required strengthening the financial systems.

It is believed that the implementation of ABIF with greater financial integration facilitates the development of a deeper and more liquid market that will lower the cost of capital, enhance the resource allocation, and a better avenue for risk diversification (Almekinders *et al.*, 2015). The emphasis of ABIF is on 'inclusiveness, transparency and reciprocity' in order to enhance the overall banking industry in the region (Frost, 2015). This is aim to strengthen the disclosure and the bank efficiency in the region to face the wave of liberalization and globalization process. The success of the implementation of ABIF is believed to result in higher economic growth, employment and financial development with the benefits of a better financial system through the improvement of banking industries' performance in the region. In addition, ABIF is also believed to result in a highly competitive banking industry within ASEAN which will further force the banking institutions to increase their efficiency level in order to compete and remain in the market. Therefore, to realize the dream for a fully integrated financial system one could not ignore the fundamental question of the efficiency level of the current banking institutions rather than focus on the profitability of the banking institutions.

3.0 Methodology

This study seeks to evaluate the bank efficiency level in ASEAN-5 countries (Indonesia, Malaysia, the Philippines, Singapore and Thailand) from 1990 to 2014. The 25 years of data from the selected listed commercial banks in the region helps us in evaluating the long-term survivability and the relationship with the banking stock returns. The bank efficiency is defined as the ability of the bank to minimize the usage of inputs to achieve a given level of financial output or *vice versa*.

As suggested by Beccalli, Casu and Girardone (2006) bank efficiency is a good tool to reflect the stock performance of the banks since it's incorporated all publicly available information. The efficiency analysis utilized the information published in both the income statement and balance sheet of the banks which are crucial in the analysis of bank performance. The efficiency analysis is said to be superior as compared to the financial ratios analysis because it compares the organization of banks outputs and inputs to identify the 'best practice' banks using the frontier technique (Mercan, Arnold, Reha and Ahmet, 2003). This means efficiency not only focuses on the financial profitability of the banking institutions but also on how the bank maximizes its financial outputs by efficient allocation of resources. Instead of only focusing on a single ratio or information from the financial reports, it utilizes various financial information published such as personnel costs, fixed assets, total deposits, loans and investments to come out with the efficiency scores to determine the efficiency level of the banking industry. The superiority of the bank efficiency analysis as compared to financial ratios is also supported by Gu and Yue (2011) as well as Vardar (2013).

The analysis of the bank efficiency level is done either by using parametric method or nonparametric method. The parametric method of bank efficiency analysis such as stochastic frontier analysis (SFA) is based on econometric estimations which require priory assumptions of the production function. On the other hand, the nonparametric method is based on linear programming technique. One of the well-known nonparametric methods for measuring bank efficiency level is known as data envelopment analysis (DEA).

DEA was first developed by Charnes, Cooper and Rhodes (1978) based on constant return to scale (CRS). This is a nonparametric mathematical linear programming approach that requires no priori assumption of the production functional forms. It is widely recognized in the second stage of analysis in any econometric modelling because the DEA score does not suffer from independent and identically distributed (iid) problem. DEA compares the bank performance in the sample in formulating the best practice frontier. The best practice banks are located on the efficient frontier with a score of 1 whereas the inefficient banks are located under the frontier with a score of less than 1. In CRS, the estimation of efficiency score is based on the assumption where the bank proportionately increases both inputs and outputs in their production process. This serves as the main caveat in the efficiency estimation because in reality the World Bank did have some market power in controlling the market prices especially in concentrated markets such as the banking industry developing countries.

Banker, Chanes and Cooper (1984) further relax the assumption of CRS by introducing the variable returns to scale (VRS) concept into the DEA estimation to overcome the major caveat of the CRS for better estimation of efficiency score to reflect the true practices of the banking industry. VRS assumption allows the bank's production technology to exhibit increasing, constant and decreasing return to scale rather than only a proportionate increase in both inputs and outputs as compared to the CRS assumption. VRS are more relevant as compared to CRS assumption in the world application that is characterized by imperfect competition (Kablan, 2010). Therefore, we follow the VRS assumption in estimating the efficiency scores of the listed commercial banks in ASEAN-5 which fall into the category of imperfect competition based on the concentration ratio presented in Table 12.1. The VRS specification for the DEA approach is shown as follows:

$$\min_{\theta,\lambda} \theta,$$
$$s.t. - y_i + \Upsilon\lambda \geq 0,$$
$$\theta x_i - X\lambda \geq 0, \qquad\qquad (12.1)$$
$$\text{I}1'\lambda = 1$$
$$\lambda \geq 0,$$

where $I1$ is an $I \times 1$ vector of ones, y_i is the output i of the bank, x_i is the input I of the bank, θ is the scalar representing the value of efficiency score of the banks which range between 0 and 1 and λ represents the vector of $N \times 1$ constants.

The intermediation approach proposed by Sealey and Lindley (1977) is employed for the definition of inputs and outputs for the DEA estimation. This approach views banking institutions as firms that perform the intermediary roles in mobilizing the surpluses and deficits of funds between savers and borrowers. In this case, the outputs used in this approach are loans and investments and inputs are defined as resources to produce financial products. Therefore, the inputs used consist of deposits, physical capital measures by fixed assets and labour measures by personnel cost. All the inputs and outputs in this analysis are compiled from Bankscope database and measures in USD millions. The input-orientation is used for the estimation of bank efficiency scores with the assumption of banks seeking to minimize the use of inputs in order to achieve a given level of financial outputs.

3.1   *Panel cointegration tests*

The analysis of the long-run causality relationship between bank efficiency level and stock performance is done based on panel VECM in the second stage of analysis. Prior to the analysis of panel VECM, the panel cointegration test will be employed to test for the cointegration relationship between the two variables after testing for the stationarity of the variables in this dataset, namely the stock returns and efficiency scores of the banks. This is done to identify the long-run relationship between the two variables that suffer from stationarity properties. This is important to identify whether the two variables are integrated in the long run to avoid spurious regression modelling. Two types of panel cointegration tests are employed in this study, namely Pedroni cointegration test introduced by Pedroni (1999) and Kao cointegration test introduced by Kao (1999) which is Engle-Granger (1987) two-step residual based test.

Pedroni (1999) derives seven panel cointegration test statistics to test for the cointegration properties which are based on within-dimension and between-dimension among the series employed. For the within-dimension statistics the null hypothesis of no cointegration for the panel cointegration test is

$$H_o : \gamma_i = 1 \text{ for all } i$$
$$H_o : \gamma_i = \gamma < 1 \text{ for all } i.$$

The between-dimension statistics the null hypothesis of no cointegration for the panel cointegration test is

$$H_o : \gamma_i = 1 \text{ for all } i$$
$$H_o : \gamma_i = \gamma < 1 \text{ for all } i.$$

To compute the desired statistics, in his paper Pedroni (1999) provided the following steps;

The estimation of panel cointegration tests based on Pedroni (1999, 2004) is based on computation of the residuals of the hypothesized cointegrating regression stated in Equation (2).

$$y_{i,t} = \alpha_i + \delta_i t + \beta_{1i} x_{1i,t} + \beta_{2i} x_{2i,t} + \ldots + \beta_{Mi} x_{Mi,t} + e_{1i} \quad t = 1, \ldots T;$$
$$I = 1, \ldots N, \tag{12.2}$$

where T is the number of observation over time, N is the number of the individual members in the panel, and M refers to the number of regression variables. The series x and y are assumed to be integrated of order one. The slope coefficients $\beta_1 i, \beta_{2i}, \ldots, _{Mi}$ and specific intercept α_i vary across individual members of the panel. In this case, the residual for the first-differenced regression of the original series for each member is estimated based on Equation (3).

$$\Delta y_{i,t} = \beta_{1i} \Delta x_{1i,t} + \beta_{2i} \Delta x_{2i,t} + \ldots + \beta_{Mi} \Delta x_{Mi,t} + \eta_{i,t}, \tag{12.3}$$

where $\hat{L}_{11,i}^2$ as the long-run variance of $\hat{\eta}_{i,t}^2$ is calculated using any kernel estimator such as the Newey-West (1987) estimator. Pedroni shows that the standardized statistic is asymptotically normally distributed

$$\frac{\aleph_{N,T} - \mu\sqrt{N}}{\sqrt{v}} \xrightarrow{d} N(0,1), \tag{12.4}$$

where $\aleph_{N,T}$ is the standardized form of the test statistics with respect to N and T. Here μ and v are Monte Carlo generated adjustment terms.

Additionally, the Johansen Fisher cointegration test will be employed to test the existence of the number of cointegrating vectors in the system.

3.2   Panel vector error correction model

After identifying the cointegration properties between the stock returns and efficiency level of the commercial banks in ASEAN-5, the long-run causal relationship is determined using panel VECM shown in Equation (5).

$$\Delta Y_{it} = \alpha_{1i} + \beta_{1i} e_{it-1} + \sum_k \lambda_{11ik} \Delta Y_{i,t-k} + \sum_k \lambda_{12ik} \Delta eff_{i,t-k} + u_{1it}$$
$$\Delta eff_{it} = \alpha_{1i} + \beta_{2i} e_{it-1} + \sum_k \lambda_{21ik} \Delta Y_{i,t-k} + \sum_k \lambda_{22ik} \Delta eff_{i,t-k} + u_{2it}, \tag{12.59}$$

where:

Δeff_{it} = change in efficiency scores of bank ith in year t measure by $\dfrac{eff_{it} - eff_{it-1}}{eff_{it-1}}$

ΔY_{it} = change in average daily closing stock price of bank ith in year t

β_{1i} = long-term effect of innovations in efficiency on stock returns

β_{2i} = long-term effect of innovations in stock returns on efficiency

e_{it-1} = error correction terms that indicates the long-run adjustment process between stock returns and efficiency level

u_{it} = error terms of bank ith in year t

The advantage of panel VECM analysis as compared to normal regression analysis is it enables the determination of the adjustment towards equilibrium of the variables in the system. e_{it-1} is expected to be negative and significant if a long-run relationship exists between stock returns and bank efficiency level. In this case, it indicates that the two variables are integrated in the long run and tend to move towards equilibrium. If this is true, then the focus of the banking authority and bank management will be to enhance the bank efficiency and stock return in order to maximize the shareholders' wealth and banking performance.

4.0   Results and discussion

4.1   Return and technical efficiency

The average return and technical efficiency of the listed commercial banks in ASEAN-5 countries estimated using the DEA method is presented in Table 12.2.

Table 12.2 shows that the cumulative return on the banking stock is less than 0.05 percent even though it is from developed countries such as Singapore. In some countries such as Indonesia and Thailand, the listed banks experienced negative return throughout the 1990s especially in the AFC where the return of the stock is on average –0.106 percent for Indonesia and –0.064 percent for Thailand. The return of the Thai's listed banks was greatly affected during the

Table 12.2 Average stock return and technical efficiency (VRS assumption)

Performance	Country	1990– 1997	1998– 2000	2001– 2005	2006– 2008	2009– 2014
Stock return	Indonesia	–0.009	–0.106	0.064	–0.024	0.077
	Malaysia	–0.003	0.088	0.028	0.003	0.052
	The Philippines	0.050	0.009	–0.005	–0.039	0.063
	Singapore	0.026	0.080	0.003	–0.040	0.049
	Thailand	–0.022	–0.064	0.027	–0.097	0.074
Efficiency	Indonesia	93.122	79.951	76.701	72.200	66.613
	Malaysia	62.559	79.408	86.361	88.591	86.311
	The Philippines	62.506	57.968	60.863	71.961	68.659
	Singapore	83.195	72.690	90.325	92.056	92.202
	Thailand	67.925	77.982	84.148	85.721	73.866

Notes: Stock return is calculated based the formula $(1 + r_{month,2})\ldots(1 + r_{month,1}) - 1$ whereas the technical efficiency are estimated using the VRS assumption using DEA methods. The stock return and efficiency are expressed in percentage.

global financial crisis as compared to other banks in ASEAN with the lowest average return of –0.097 percent. This may be due to higher foreign shareholdings in the Thai's commercial banks as a result of relaxation of foreign shareholdings after the AFC as compared to the commercial banks in the same region. The significant amount of foreign shareholdings affect the performance of the Thai's commercial banks because the banking industries in developed countries such as Europe and the United States were greatly affected by the GFC in 2008.

In terms of efficiency, Table 12.2 shows that on average the banking industry is performing poorly in the early 1990s where listed commercial banks in Malaysia, Philippines and Thailand reported a lower efficiency score of less than 70 percent. This means that the banking industries in these countries were able to further improve their efficiency level with further reduction in the inputs used in production by at least 30 percent. During the AFC, as expected, the efficiency level of the banking industry in this region dropped. This includes developed countries such as Singapore. The banking industry in Philippines is greatly affected as compared to the other countries in the region with an average efficiency score of 57.968 percent. Continuous improvement in the efficiency level is seen after the AFC. This may be due to the banking consolidation and recapitalization that had been taken place in the countries in this region.

Nevertheless, Table 12.2 shows that again the efficiency level of the listed commercial banks in this region drop in the recent years (2009–2014) except for Singapore. If this continues to happen then this may serve as an alarming issue for the AEC with the implementation of ABIF because the banks are not prepared to be fully integrated and may have problems to sustain in the long-term due to inefficiency in the allocation of resources. If the stock performance and bank efficiency are integrated in the long run, a reduction in efficiency may also lead to lower return of the banking stocks and hence the needs to determine the long-run relationship are crucial.

4.2 Long-run relationship between stock return and bank technical efficiency

The results of the panel unit root tests based on Levin, Lin and Chu, Breitung, Im, Persaran and Shin and Hadri are presented in Table 12.3. The results of the unit root tests confirmed that the hypothesis of unit root properties exist in level but not at first difference. Therefore, this clearly indicates that the data are at I(1). In this case, it is crucial for us to proceed to the cointegration test to identify the existence of a long-run relationship between banking stock return and efficiency level. The results of panel cointegration tests based on Pedroni's heterogeneous panel test and Johansen's test are reported in Table 12.4 and 12.5 respectively.

The Pedroni's heterogeneous panel cointegration test presented in Table 12.4 shows that the banking stock return and efficiency scores are cointegrated. This is confirmed with the Johansen Fisher cointegration test in Table 12.5 where at least two cointegrating vectors are found between banking stock return and efficiency level of the listed commercial banks in ASEAN.

Table 12.3 Results for panel unit root tests

	Levin, Lin and Chut		Breitung t-stat		Im, Pesaran and Shin W-Stat		Hadri Z-stat	
Variable	Intercept	Trend and intercept	Intercept	Trend and intercept	Intercept	Trend and intercept	Intercept	Trend and intercept
Level								
Efficiency	−0.767	0.702	–	−0.816	0.661	1.226	11.263***	10.234***
LnPrice	−0.184	−0.209	–	0.000	−0.643	−1.234	20.359***	15.450***
First difference								
Variable	Intercept	Trend and Intercept	Intercept	Trend and Intercept	Intercept	Trend and Intercept	Intercept	Trend and Intercept
Efficiency	−10.172***	−2.773***	–	−5.489***	−23.623***	−14.188***	0.107	0.713
LnPrice	−34.758***	−36.569	–	−13.327***	−26.824***	−10.988***	1.166	2.156

Note: LnPrice is the stock price of listed banks in ASEAN 5; efficiency is the efficiency scores obtained from DEA estimation based on VRS assumption.

*, **, *** indicates significance level at 10%, 5% and 1% level, respectively.

Table 12.4 Pedroni's Panel Cointegration Results

Test statistics	Coefficient
Panel v-Statistic	−1.626
Panel rho-Statistic	−1.140
Panel PP-Statistic	−3.556***
Panel ADF-Statistic	−3.536***
Group rho-Statistic	1.329
Group PP-Statistic	−5.729***
Group ADF-Statistic	−6.309***

Note: *, **, *** indicates significance level at 10%, 5% and 1% level, respectively.

Table 12.5 Johansen Fisher panel cointegration results

Hypothesized	Fisher stat.*	Fisher stat.*
No. of CE(s)	(from trace test)	(from max-Eigen test)
None	357.400***	313.200***
At most 1	245.800***	245.800***

Notes: *, **, *** indicates significance level at 10%, 5% and 1% level, respectively.

To seek the long-run causality between banking stock return and efficiency level of the listed commercial banks in ASEAN, the analysis of VECM is performed and the estimated results are presented in Table 12.6.

The causality results from panel VECM are reported in Table 12.6. The optimal lag structure of 2-year lags is chosen based on AIC. The significance of the causality results are determined by the Wald-F-test.

From the panel VECM estimation results in Table 12.6, there is a bi-directional long-run relationship between the change in efficiency and return (change in average daily closing price) of the banking stock of the listed commercial banks in ASEAN 5 at a 1 percent significance level. This means that there is long-run causality running from efficiency to the return and also from return to the efficiency. The significant and negative e_{it-1} tell us that the speed of adjustment towards long-run equilibrium exists between the two variables. This supports the hypothesis of efficient market as suggested by Fama (1970) where stock prices incorporate all publicly available information which reflect in the efficiency level of the banks. This is supported by Beccalli *et al.* (2006) that suggest that technical efficiency measures consist of public information.

Results of short-run relationship between banking stock returns and efficiency level is presented in Table 12.7. The results suggest that there is a short-run causality running from stock return to efficiency level of the banks but not from the

Table 12.6 VECM results

Variable	ΔEfficiency	ΔStock price
e_{it}-1	-0.153***	-1.084***
	(0.024)	(0.055)
ΔEfficiency (-1)	-0.280***	-0.014
	(0.033)	(0.041)
ΔEfficiency (-2)	-0.197***	-0.105***
	(0.031)	(0.025)
ΔStock Price (-1)	-0.045***	-0.001
	(0.009)	(0.000)
ΔStock Price (-2)	-0.017*	0.000
	(0.009)	(0.000)
Constant	0.001	0.000
	(0.005)	(0.000)
Model Fit:		
R-squared	0.212	0.591
Adjusted R-squared	0.207	0.589
Sum Square Residuals	17.183	0.003
Log likelihood	532.068	4531.438
Akaike AIC	-1.136	-9.774

Notes: *, **, *** indicates significance level at 10%, 5% and 1% level, respectively.

Table 12.7 Wald *F*-test statistics from panel VECM estimation

Null hypothesis	Short-run causality test	Strong exogeneity test
ΔStock Price→ΔEfficiency	28.291***	421.916***
ΔEfficiency→ΔStock Price	2.036	385.607***

Notes: →means variable x does not Granger cause variable y.

*, **, *** indicates significance level at 10%, 5% and 1% level, respectively.

efficiency to change in stock price at 1 percent significance level. This implies that efficiency is a long-term measure of banking performance which needs to be carefully considered by the banking authority to ensure the sustainability of the banking industry in longer term. On the other hand, the short-run causality from stock return to bank efficiency may due to that stocks are frequently traded and hence the performance is highly reflective in the short-run. This explains the efficient market hypothesis, where stock price fully reflects all publicly available information if the market is efficient.

5.0   Conclusion and policy implications

It is widely recognized that the bank performance in the emerging markets are crucial because the banking industry served as the main channel for monetary policy transmission process. Stable and sound banking institutions had proven their footing in the domestic market as the main key driver for economic stability not only to withstand future economic shocks but also increasingly become an interest to the policy makers in ASEAN 5 as a result of AEC and the future implementation of ABIF. Therefore, we studied the long-run causality between the return of banking stocks and the efficiency level which we believed to serve as an insight to the policy makers to gain some insight on the direction of the banking industries in ASEAN-5 in preparing for fully integrated banking industries after the implementation of ABIF. We used data from 1990 to 2014 and utilized the panel VECM methods in order to achieve our objective.

The results suggest a long-run bi-directional causality between the efficiency level and stock return of the banks. This supports the efficient market hypothesis by Fama (1970) where in an efficient market the stock price adjusts for all publicly available information. Besides, the speeds of adjustment between the two variables are also significant. The results also conclude that the efficiency level of the banking industry did affect the stock returns in the long run but not the short run. This means that efficiency level is a long-run indicator for long-term survivability of the banks. This further reinforced the studies done by Fiordelisi (2007), Pasiouras, Liadaki and Zopounidis (2008), Gu and Yue (2011), and Shamsuddin and Xiang (2012). This study also confirmed on the influence of stock price on efficiency level of the commercial banks by and Chu and Lim (1998), and Majid and Sufian (2006) in the ASEAN region. This indicates that in order to improve the performance of the banking industry in ASEAN-5, policy makers should focus on increasing both efficiency level as well as the stock returns.

Acknowledgement

This study is part of the research supported by UMRG research grant (RP001C-13SBS), University of Malaya.

References

Almekinders, G., Fukuda, S., Mourmouras, A., and Zhou, J. (2015). ASEAN financial integration. IMF Working Paper No. WP/15/34, 1–43.
Ariss, R. T. (2010). On the implications of market power in banking: Evidence from developing countries. *Journal of Banking and Finance*, 34(4), 765–775.
Banker, R. D., Chanes, A., and Cooper, W. (1984). Some model for estimating technical and scale inefficiencies in data envelopment analysis. *Management Science*, 30(9), 1078–1092.
Beccalli, E., Casu, B., and Girardone, C. (2006). Efficiency and stock performance in European banking. *Journal of Business Finance & Accounting*, 33(1–2), 245–262.
Boyd., J. H., and de Nicoló, G. (2005). The theory of bank risk taking and competition revisited. *Journal of Finance*, 60(3), 1329–1343.

Charnes, A., Cooper, W. W., and Rhodes, E. (1978). Measuring the efficiency of decision making units. *European Journal of Operational Research, 2*(6), 429–444.

Chu, S. F., and Lim, G. F. (1998). Share performance and profit efficiency of banks in an oligopolistic market: Evidence from Singapore. *Journal of Multinational Financial Management, 8*(2), 155–168.

Engle, R., and Granger, C. (1987). Co-integration and error correction: Representation, estimation, and testing. *Econometrica, 55*(2), 251–276.

Fama, E. F. (1970). Efficient capital markets: A review of theory and empirical work. *Journal of Finance, 25*(2), 383–417.

Fiordelisi, F. (2007). Shareholder value efficiency in European banking. *Journal of Banking & Finance, 31*(7), 2151–2171.

Frost, E. (2015). Recent banking sector developments in the ASEAN region. *International Banker*. Available at: http://internationalbanker.com/banking/recent-banking-sector-developments-in-the-asean-region/. Retrieved on 12 December 2015.

Goldstein, M., and Turner, P. (1996). Banking crisis in emerging economies: Origins and policy options the role of banks. BIS Economic Papers No. 46, Bank of International Settlements.

Gu, H., and Yue, J. (2011). The relationship between bank efficiency and stock returns: Evidence from Chinese listed banks. *World Journal of Social Sciences, 1*(4), 95–106.

Hellman, T. F., Murdock, K. C., and Stiglitz, J. E. (2000). Liberalization, moral hazard in banking, and prudential regulation: Are capital requirements enough? *The American Economic Review, 90*(1), 147–165.

Kablan, S. (2010). Banking efficiency and financial development in Sub-Saharan Africa. IMF Working Paper No. WP/10/136.

Kao, C. (1999). International R&D spillovers: An application of estimation and inference in panel cointegration. *Oxford Bulletin of Economics and Statistics, 61*(S1), 691–709.

Kroszner, R. S., Laeven, L., and Klingebiel, D. (2007). Banking crises, financial dependence, and growth. *Journal of Financial Economics, 84*(1), 187–228.

Lindgren, C., Garcia, G., and Saal, M. (1996). Banking soundness and macroeconomic policy. *International Monetary Fund*, Washington, DC.

Majid, M., and Sufian, F. (2006). Consolidation and competition in an emerging market: An empirical test for Malaysian banking industry. *Economic Change and Restructuring, 39*(1), 105–124.

Mercan, M., Arnold, R., Reha, Y., and Ahmet, B. E. (2003). The effect of scale and mode of ownership on the financial performance of the Turkish banking sector: Results of a DEA-based analysis. *Socio-Economic Planning Sciences, 37*(3), 185–202.

Mirzaei, A., Moore, T., and Liu, G. (2013). Does market structure matter on banks' profitability and stability? Emerging vs. advanced economies. *Journal of Banking and Finance, 37*(8), 2920–2937.

Pasiouras, F., Liadaki, A., and Zopounidis, C. (2008). Bank efficiency and share performance: Evidence from Greece. *Applied Financial Economics, 18*(4), 1121–1130.

Pedroni, P. (1999). Critical values for cointegration tests in heterogeneous panels with multiple regressors. *Oxford Bulletin of Economics and Statistics*, Special Issue, 9, 653–670.

Pedroni, P. (2004). Panel cointegration: Asymptotic and finite sample properties of pooled time series tests with an application to the PPP hypothesis. *Econometric Theory, 20*(3), 597–625.

Reinhart, C. M., and Rogoff, K. (2009). *This Time is Different: Eight Centuries of Financial Folly.* Princeton, NJ: Princeton University Press.

Sealey, C. W., and Lindley, J. T. (1977). Inputs, outputs, and a theory of production and cost at depositor financial institutions. *Journal of Finance, 32*(4), 1251–1266.

Shamsuddin, A., and Xiang, D. (2012). Does bank efficiency matter? Market value relevance of bank efficiency in Australia. *Applied Economics, 44*(27), 3563–3572.

Uhde, A., and Heimeshoff, U. (2009). Consolidation in banking and financial stability in Europe: Empirical evidence. *Journal of Banking and Finance, 33*(7), 1299–1311.

Vardar, G. (2013). Efficiency and stock performance of banks in transition countries: Is there a relationship? *International Journal of Economics and Financial Issues, 3*(2), 355–369.

Williams, J., and Nguyen, N. (2005). Financial liberalisation, crisis, and restructuring: A comparative study of bank performance and bank governance in South East Asia. *Journal of Banking and Finance, 29*(8), 2119–2154.

13 Asymmetric effect of political elections on stock returns and volatility in Malaysia

Hooi Hooi Lean and Geok Peng Yeap

1.0 Introduction

Volatility is a fundamental issue in financial markets which has important implications for risk management. An increase in stock market volatility leads to a large increase or decrease in stock prices and shows higher stock market risk (Campbell and Hentschel, 1992). It is commonly known that stock volatility changes over time (Schwert, 1989) and tends to be persistent. Moreover, the changes of stock volatility are usually associated with the asymmetric effect. The asymmetric effect on volatility refers to the fact that stock prices react differently to negative and positive shocks of the same magnitude (Engle and Ng, 1993). In particular, a leverage effect occurs when negative shocks imply higher future volatility than do positive shocks of the same magnitude.

Schwert (1989) explains that the changes of stock volatility are due to the impact of macroeconomic factors such as interest rate, inflation rate, money supply and industrial production. Besides economic factors, political factors are important sources that affect stock volatility. Political events like government partisanship, political elections, election victory by left-wing or right-wing parties, changes in the coalition of government, the release of political news etc. will affect the financial performance of a country as well as the country's economic growth. There are numerous studies in the field of economics and political sciences that investigate the link of political events and the performance of financial markets (Siokis and Kapopoulos, 2003; Knight, 2006; Leblang and Bernhard, 2006; Mukherjee and Leblang, 2007; Mattozzi, 2008; Bechtel and Fuss, 2010; Sturm, 2013).

Among the many political events, a general election (GE) is well recognized to create uncertainty due to investors' expectation of possible policy changes resulting from the change of the government administration (Kim and Mei, 2001). Some stock markets have evidenced greater fluctuation when there are political GEs (Bialkowski, Gottschalk and Wisniewski, 2008; Floros, 2008). In the pre-election periods, uncertainty about future government policies would cause dramatic stock price changes. Besides that, according to Bialkowski *et al.* (2008), post-election shocks such as a victory with a narrow margin, a lack of compulsory voting laws, a change in the political orientation of the executive or the failure to form the government with a majority of seats in Parliament are significant contributors to stock market volatility. As such, higher uncertainty about the election outcome leads to changes in investors' sentiment during the pre- and post-election periods and increases the volatility of the stock market.

In this chapter, we focus on the asymmetric effect of stock volatility during periods of elections. There are some reasons to expect that a strong asymmetric effect might be present during GEs. Siokis and Kapopoulos (2003, 2007) explain that political elections are accompanied by information asymmetry between voters and policy makers due to the political business cycle[1] and the rational expectations[2] of voters. They describe that asymmetric information is shown when a rational voter judges the observed economic outcomes to make a decision in selecting the government, while politicians have better knowledge on their own level of competence. Moreover, the stock market tends to follow the political business cycle because the government might try to manipulate economic policy in an effort to gain popularity and be re-elected in the following cycle. Information asymmetry between the voters and the government occurs because there is limited information about the government and policies available during the election polls (Pantzalis, Stangeland and Turtle, 2000).

The objective of this study is to examine the asymmetric effect of six Malaysian GEs held during 1989–2014 on the performance of Bursa Malaysia. The contributions of our study are, first, we apply two asymmetric GARCH models to investigate the asymmetric effect of GEs on the stock market in Malaysia. Unlike previous studies (Floros, 2008; Lean, 2010) that only examine the impact of an election on stock returns, our study attempts to study stock volatility. Second, we enhance the knowledge in this field by investigating the case of Malaysia. Most of the studies on election effects are carried out in developed countries and there is relatively less study in Malaysia, except Ali, Nassir, Hassan and Abidin (2010), and Lean (2010). Third, we add two control variables, the Asian financial crisis (AFC) and the global effect, which are not accounted for in the previous studies in Malaysia. These two variables have been shown to significantly affect the Malaysian stock market (see Sheng and Tu, 2000). This study may be of interest to policy makers and investors who aim to hedge risk associated with political uncertainty.

The remainder of the chapter is organized as follows. The next section presents an overview of Malaysian GEs followed by a literature review about the impact of political events on stock markets. The subsequent section discusses the data and methodology, while the next section reports the empirical results. The last section concludes the study.

2.0   Overview of Malaysia's general elections

Similar to other democratic countries, the GE in Malaysia is held every five years, and it must be conducted within three months of the dissolution of the Parliament. The election is held at both the federal and the state levels (Ahmad, 2000). The party that wins the majority of seats in Parliament will form the federal government, and the party that has the majority of members in the state assembly will become the state government. This section discusses a brief summary of the GE in Malaysia during the sample period from 1989 to 2014. It covers six GEs (the 8th–13th GEs) under the governance of three prime ministers. During the 8th–10th GEs, the ruling coalition Barisan Nasional (BN) was led by the fourth prime minister of Malaysia, Mahathir Mohamad. For the 11th and 12th GEs, BN was under the leadership of the fifth prime minister, Abdullah Ahmad Badawi. Mohammad Najib Abdul Razak as the sixth prime minister led the 13th GE.

The 8th GE was the first time that the ruling coalition BN was challenged by a multi-ethnic coalition. There was a suggestion to transform a dominant party system into a two-coalition system. The BN coalition led by Mahathir Mohamad faced keen competition from the opposition party led by the former deputy prime minister, Razaleigh Hamzah. Besides that, the Parti Bersatu Sabah (PBS) took a surprising step by withdrawing from BN about one week before the election date (Khong, 1991) and had considerably contributed to election shocks during the 8th GE. Although the opposition was expected to win enough seats in Parliament and play a more effective role in the Parliament, the election results turned out to be unexpected. The ruling coalition remained in power with more than a two-thirds majority.

On 25 April 1995, Malaysia went to the 9th GE. BN won with a fruitful result by gaining 84 percent of the parliamentary seats and winning 65 percent of the popular votes. It was the greatest victory recorded by BN in the election history in Malaysia. Strong economic growth and political stability during the 1990s were the main contributors to the victory of BN. Since the early 1990s, new Chinese villages had undergone massive infrastructure development, and there were plenty of employment opportunities in the country. Khoo (2000) found that, overall, the Malaysian population was in a euphoric mood, which brought the desired results of BN. The BN victory showed that they gained majority supports from Malays and non-Malays and from urban as well as rural constituencies, with the exception of Kelantan (Chin, 1996). It signalled voters' confidence in the governance of BN.

The 10th GE was held in 1999 when the BN government was once again confronted by opposition spearheaded by the former deputy prime minister, Anwar Ibrahim. The most significant political event that happened before the election was the issue of Anwar Ibrahim, who was sacked on 2 September 1998 amid being accused of a sex scandal and corrupt practices. Ahmad (2000) described the 10th GE as the 'fight of the decade' with intermittent street demonstrations about Anwar Ibrahim's issue to protest against BN's government. However, the electoral outcome was that the ruling BN coalition once again won the election with a two-third majority but with fewer majority seats.

The 11th GE, held on 21 March 2004, saw the ruling coalition BN rebound from a previous setback during the 10th GE. The election result was a surprise to many Malaysians when BN won 90 percent of the total seats in the Parliament and 63.8 percent in terms of popular votes. It was the first election led by the newly appointed prime minister, Abdullah Ahmad Badawi, who promised reforms and development for the country. BN government regained the control of the Terengganu state from the opposition party.

However, the second election held under Abdullah Ahmad Badawi was not marked with a significant victory for BN. The 12th GE created election shocks when BN lost its two-thirds majority in the Parliament and five states to the opposition parties. It was the worst results for BN since independence, winning only 63 percent of the parliamentary seats and 51 percent of the popular vote. The political outcome of the 12th GE was described as a 'political tsunami' and resulted in the step down of Abdullah Ahmad Badawi as the fifth prime minister of Malaysia one year later. Besides economic factors such as high oil prices, inflation and the global economic slowdown, the failure of BN in the 12th GE was partly due to dissatisfaction with Abdullah's administration and the electoral system in the country (Moten, 2009).

The 13th GE created election uncertainty, with the greatest tension felt in the electoral history of Malaysia. Before the election date, there was a strong desire and expectation of change from the ruling coalition of BN, which had been in office for the past 56 years. The BN government was expected to lose its power in the 13th GE due to the strength of the opposition coalition (Khoo, 2013). Although BN retained its power and formed the government with 60 percent of the parliamentary seats and 47.4 percent of the popular vote, this election outcome induced surprise to the investors. These election shocks reflected political uncertainty, which could affect investors' confidence and the stock market volatility in Malaysia. Table 13.1 summarizes the percentage of votes and seats won by BN and the opposition for the six GEs.

As a conclusion, the six GEs held during 1990–2013 were accompanied by a certain level of political uncertainty. Although BN had successfully been re-elected and remained as the ruling government in all GEs, the percentages of seats and votes were significantly diminished after the 11th GE. There have been increasing concerns about the change of government in the recent two GEs. As considered by Pantzalis *et al.* (2000), the expectation of incumbent loss causes greater

Table 13.1 Results of Malaysian general elections, 1990–2013

	Total seats	No. of seats won		% Seats		% Votes	
		BN	Opposition	BN	Opposition	BN	Opposition
8th GE	180	127	53	71	29	53.4	46.6
9th GE	192	162	30	84	16	65.2	34.8
10th GE	193	148	45	77	23	56.5	43.5
11th GE	219	198	21	90	10	63.8	36.2
12th GE	222	140	82	63	37	51.4	48.6
13th GE	222	133	89	60	40	47.4	50.8

Source: Suruhanjaya Pilihan Raya, Election Report, various years.

uncertainty than when an incumbent is expected to win and re-elected. GEs in Malaysia lead to greater importance on market uncertainty.

3.0   Literature review

The studies in the United States focus on presidential elections and the performance of stock markets. The relationship between stock prices and presidential elections is called the 'theory of the presidential election cycle'; Americans elect a president every four years (Wong and McAleer, 2009). Allvine and O'Neill (1980), Gartner and Wellershoff (1995) and Wong and McAleer (2009) find that the US stock markets generally follow the four-year presidential election cycle. They see evidence that the US stock returns are significantly lower in years 1 and 2 of a presidential election cycle than in years 3 and 4. For instance, Gartner and Wellershoff (1995) demonstrate that stock prices fall in the first half and rise in the second half of a presidential cycle, while Wong and McAleer (2009) notice that stock prices decreased significantly in the second year and then increased significantly in the third year of the presidential term.

Some other authors also investigate the impact of the US presidential election results, i.e. whether a Democrat or Republican won the election, on stock price performance. Studies in the United States claim that the stock market tends to perform better under Democratic than Republican administration. For instance, Santa-Clara and Valkonov (2003) find significantly higher excess returns in the US stock market under Democratic administrations. However, at the industry level, Stangl and Jacobsen (2007) do not find significant differences in US industries' stock returns between Democratic and Republican presidencies. Similarly, Oehler, Walker and Wendt (2013) do not find significant differences on eight industries' stock abnormal returns when they specifically examined the influence of the 1980–2008 US presidential elections. They find that a transferring of the presidency from a Democrat to a Republican or *vice versa* causes stronger effects on stock returns than does re-election of the same party.

Besides the US stock markets, Foerster and Schmitz (1997) also find that the international stock markets, particularly the those in the developed Western countries, are affected by the US presidential elections. These markets are consistent with the 4-year presidential election cycle, where the lowest returns are found in the second year of the presidential term. Additionally, a delay in the announcement of the US presidential election results has been found to negatively affect the stock markets (Nippani and Medlin, 2002; Nippani and Arize, 2005). As the US presidential election is an important international factor, some authors have expanded the study to examine the effect of the US presidential election cycle on the domestic stock markets. Hung (2013) examines the impact of US presidential elections on the Taiwanese stock market. The results illustrate the lowest return in year 2, while the highest return is in year 3, which is consistent with many studies.

Other than the US presidential election, we also found studies of British GEs. Manning (1989) specifically looked at British Telecom to examine the effect of political uncertainty on the stock market during the 1987 GE in Britain. The test is stable throughout the pre-election period, which shows that British Telecom responds strongly to opinion polls. Moreover, Gemmill (1992) and Gwilym and Buckle (1994) examined the efficiency of UK stock prices during the 1987 and 1992 GEs, respectively. Both studies show that there is a close relationship between the information from opinion polls and the FTSE100 share index.

In other developed markets, Dopke and Pierdzioch (2006) find no evidence of a political cycle and election effect on the Germany stock market. However, they report that stock movements significantly affect the government's popularity in Germany. Floros (2008) finds no significant effect of the Greek parliamentary elections and European elections on the course of the Athens Stock Exchange. In New Zealand, Abidin *et al.* (2010) also find no evidence of an election effect on New Zealand stock returns in 1986–2009. However, in Egypt, Nezerwe (2013) evidences a positive impact of elections on the Egyptian Exchange in the investigation of two presidential elections.

Moreover, there are studies that test whether there exist positive or negative abnormal returns around the election dates. Pantzalis *et al.* (2000) investigated the abnormal returns of stock markets around political election dates for 33 developed and developing countries. They find positive abnormal returns during the two-week period prior to the election week, and the effect is stronger for countries with high levels of uncertainty. Chuang and Wang (2010) investigate how abnormal stock returns in the United States, United Kingdom, Japan and France react to the electoral information. They demonstrate a contradictory result with Pantzalis *et al.* (2000), where negative abnormal returns are found before and after the date of GE.

Leblang and Mukherjee (2005) examine both the US and British equity markets between 1930–2000 to find the impact of elections, partisanship and election uncertainty on the stock returns and volatility. They argue that the expectation of a lower stock return increases uncertainty about the possibility of market revival in the future and leads to higher stock volatility and *vice versa*. They find that higher uncertainty about the electoral outcome leads to higher stock volatility in the election year. On the other hand, Bialkowski *et al.* (2008) do not find excessive cumulative abnormal returns based on 27 Organisation for Economic Co-operation and Development countries data by using symmetric and asymmetric event windows. However, they observe that a strong abnormal volatility rises on the election day and that this abnormal volatility continues for about 15 trading days.

Koksal and Caliskan (2012) study the political business cycles and partisan effect on Turkey's stock market. They find evidence that the conditional volatility of returns increases prior to the GEs, and they explain that this cyclical behaviour is due to election uncertainties. Partisan effects are also found to influence the conditional volatility of the Istanbul Stock Exchange. In Greece, Siokis and Kapopoulos (2007) examine the impact of the election and partisan structure on the conditional returns and volatility of the stock market index based on an asymmetric GARCH model. They find that the stock market index is asymmetrically affected by past innovations and that the conditional variance of the stock market index is affected by different political regimes, like political parties in power and electoral uncertainties.

A number of studies have investigated the link of political events and stock markets in Asian markets, such as those of Hong Kong and Taiwan. Chan and Wei (1996) study the release of political news, i.e. news about the confrontation or cooperation between the Sino–British government, and find that it affects stock volatility in Hong Kong. They find that political news increases stock volatility in Hong Kong and the release of good political news positively correlates with the returns of the Hang Seng Index. Kim and Mei (2001) further confirm that Hong Kong's stock returns and volatility are closely associated with political news and that the impact of news is asymmetric with negative announcements, resulting in larger volatility responses. Another study in Hong Kong performed by Fong and Koh (2002) confirms that a high-volatility regime is associated with negative shocks, while a low-volatility regime is associated with positive shocks and the presence of a leverage effect in the high-volatility regime. However, the Hong Kong stock market has not been found to become consistently more volatile when the Sino–British political negotiations began in 1982.

For the case of Taiwan, Chen, Bin and Chen (2005) consider the impact of various political events on Taiwanese firms' stock performance. They find that political elections, economic policies and cross-strait relationship developments are associated with abnormal performance in Taiwan's stock market. Wang and Lin (2008) observe that a congressional effect[3] has a significantly negative effect on stock returns but not on stock volatility. The congressional effect is found on stock volatility after the first transfer of presidential power to an opposition party. Wang and Lin (2009) support the idea that congressional negatively affects stock returns but it does not significantly affect stock volatility. On the other hand, democratization[4] has significant negative effects on stock returns and significant positive effects on stock volatility.

In South Korea, Chiu, Chen and Tang (2005) investigate the impact of political elections on stock markets in terms of stock trading volume. They focus on the Korea Stock Price Index (KOSPI) 200 futures and options during the presidential and parliamentary elections in South Korea. They find that the parliamentary elections cause a distinct decrease in trading options contracts as compared to the presidential elections. The parliamentary election is also found to have more stable derivatives' trading volatility.

Turning to Malaysia, Lean (2010) investigates the link between political GEs and stock market performance over the period of 1994–2009. The result shows that the political GEs significantly affect Malaysia's stock performance, where the stock returns react positively before the election dates and negatively after the election dates. On the other hand, by examining the arrival of dramatic events such as the economic crisis and extraordinary political events on Bursa Malaysia, Ali *et al.* (2010) find evidence of underreaction behaviour during GEs. They explain that stock does not show overreaction behaviour during GEs because investors are well informed of the events with no surprise in the outcome of the GEs. Nevertheless, both studies merely focus on stock returns but ignore the possible impact of political elections on stock volatility. They also fail to show an asymmetric effect in the stock market during the time of GEs.

In summary, studies of the United States have shown that a presidential election cycle exists in the US stock returns. Moreover, the empirical results indicate that stock returns tend to be higher on average during Democratic than during Republican presidencies. Most studies on other countries provide confidence results that stock markets respond to elections. The studies in Asian markets have proved that there is a link between political events and stock volatility. Based on the above literature review, only a few studies (such as Siokis and Kapopoulos, 2007) have explored the asymmetric effect of political elections on stock volatility, and none of the studies in Malaysia has attempted this issue. Therefore, the present study would like to fill in the research gap and examine how stock returns and volatility react to the asymmetric effect of political elections in Malaysia.

4.0   Data and methodology

4.1   Data

We use Kuala Lumpur Composite Index (KLCI) daily closing prices to proxy for Malaysia stocks price. The sample period covers from 2 October 1989 to 30 May 2014, with a total of 6435 observations. All data were downloaded from Yahoo Finance and transformed into logarithm terms. The analysis covers six GEs, which were held on 21 October 1990 (8th GE), 25 April 1995 (9th GE), 29 November 1999 (10th GE), 21 March 2004 (11th GE), 8 March 2008 (12th GE) and 5 May 2013 (13th GE).

Figures 13.1 and 13.2 depict the time series plot for KLCI and the percentage change of KLCI, respectively, with the term of elections. KLCI drops significantly

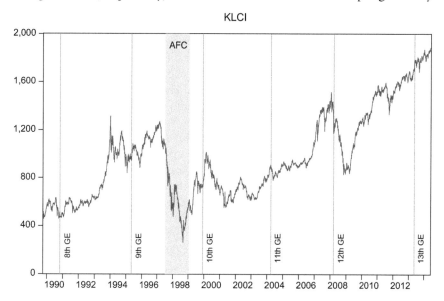

Figure 13.1 Time series plot of KLCI

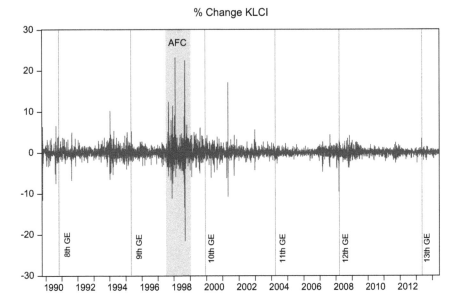

Figure 13.2 Time series plot of KLCI returns

during the AFC and results in the greatest fluctuation during the period. It is noted that the KLCI displays a high degree of volatility during the elections except for the 11th GE. A significant drop in KLCI with high fluctuation is also observed after the 12th GE and global financial crisis. During the 12th and 13th GEs, KLCI shows an unusual high spike before the election date.

We compute the daily stock returns as the first difference of the daily logarithms of KLCI. Table 13.2 shows the summary statistics of daily stock returns. KLCI has a positive average return over the sample period. The standard deviation, skewness and kurtosis are all positive. Jarque-Bera is highly significant, which shows that the return series is nonnormally distributed.

We show the price changes of KLCI before and after the election dates in Table 13.3. Overall, prior to a GE, price changes were rather mixed, with positive and negative returns before and after the election dates. The GEs do not seem to show a consistent effect on stock prices for the 8th, 9th and 10th GEs under the leadership of Mahathir Mohamad. During the 11th GE, price changes were positive before the election and negative after the election date. This was the first GE led by Abdullah Ahmad Badawi, with the largest victory won. The positive price changes before the election date could be due to market confidence in the new prime minister. The negative price changes after the 11th GE might be due to the Avian flu and SARS disease (Lean, 2010). For the 12th and 13th GEs, price changes are generally negative before and after the election dates as a result of political instability and uncertainty in the country.

Table 13.2 Summary statistics for daily changes of KLCI

Mean	2.07×10^{-4}
Std. dev.	0.0134
Skewness	0.4060
Kurtosis	52.7524
Jarque-Bera	663,764***

Note: *** indicates significant at 1% level.

Table 13.3 Malaysian general elections and KLCI changes (%)

	8th GE (21 Oct 1990)	9th GE (25 Apr 1995)	10th GE (29 Nov 1999)	11th GE (21 Mar 2004)	12th GE (8 Mar 2008)	13th GE (5 May 2013)
– 6 months	–10.98	–12.26	0.39	20.29	0.44	2.43
– 3 months	–27.19	11.31	–2.80	15.41	–9.47	3.69
– 1 month	–6.19	2.31	0.41	3.33	–8.83	0.36
– 2 weeks	0.62	1.94	2.25	2.64	–5.59	–0.68
– 1 week	–0.15	1.11	0.70	1.58	–2.61	–0.97
+ 1 week	4.94	–3.18	–2.65	–1.04	–8.15	–4.48
+ 2 weeks	0.65	–2.46	3.01	–1.91	–8.64	–4.30
+ 1 month	–0.23	6.42	7.59	–4.57	–5.60	–4.59
+ 3 month	0.73	7.34	27.52	–9.13	–5.17	–5.19
+ 6 month	21.67	–1.99	19.58	–4.44	–18.64	–6.19

Note: –/+ refers to time period before/after the election date.

4.2 *Methodology*

From the descriptive statistics and trend, we note that there could be different effects of GEs on the stock market. Thus, we aim to examine the impact of elections by modelling both the stock returns and return volatility. GARCH models are the best suited for time-varying of stock volatility in this study. We use asymmetric GARCH models, i.e. threshold GARCH (TGARCH) (Glosten, Jagannathan and Runkle, 1993) and exponential GARCH (EGARCH; Nelson, 1991). The TGARCH and EGARCH models can accommodate asymmetric volatility and allow us to examine the leverage effect where the impact of positive and negative shocks on stock volatility can be investigated. We consider the following five cases as our event windows.

Case 1: one week (five trading days) before and after the election date
Case 2: two weeks (10 trading days) before and after the election date

Case 3: one month before and after the election date
Case 4: three months before and after the election date
Case 5: six months before and after the election date

The conditional mean equation of the TGARCH and EGARCH models is expressed as

$$R_t = \alpha_0 + \alpha_1 D_1 + \alpha_2 D_2 + \alpha_3 D_{AFC} + \alpha_4 R_{MSCI} + \varepsilon_t \qquad (13.1)$$
$$\varepsilon_t \sim N(0, \sigma_t^2),$$

where R_t is the return of KLCI on day t; D_1 and D_2 are dummy variables in which D_1 takes a value of 1 for the pre-election period, while D_2 takes a value of 1 for the post-election period. For case 1, D_1 is set to 1 for all trading days one week prior to the election dates and 0 otherwise; while D_2 is set to 1 for all trading days one week after the election dates and 0 otherwise. The same steps are applied to other cases. Following Siokis and Kapopoulos (2007), we add the dummy variable for AFC and world stock returns as control variables in the GARCH models. We add D_{AFC} to control for structural change as a result of AFC. D_{AFC} takes a value pf 1 from 1 July 1997 to 31 December 1998 and 0 otherwise. We also add R_{MSCI}, which represents the returns of MSCI to control for global effect on KLCI returns.

The conditional variance equation for TGARCH (1,1) is specified as follows:

$$\sigma_t^2 = \omega_0 + \beta \varepsilon_{t-1}^2 + \gamma \varepsilon_{t-1}^2 I + \theta \sigma_{t-1}^2 + (\rho_1 D_1 + \rho_2 D_2 + \rho_3 D_{AFC} + \rho_4 R_{MSCI}), \quad (13.2)$$

where the parameters β and θ capture the ARCH and GARCH effects, respectively. The parameter γ captures the asymmetric effect where $I = 1$ if $\varepsilon_t < 0$ (negative shocks) and $I = 0$ if $\varepsilon_t > 0$ (positive shocks). In this model, good news has an impact of β on volatility, while bad news has an impact of $\beta + \gamma$ on stock volatility (McMillan *et al.*, 2000). Hence, a statistically significant γ suggests an asymmetric effect. A positive γ is consistent with the leverage effect, i.e. the arrival of negative shocks yields a greater effect on conditional volatility than do positive shocks. When γ appears to be negative, then the positive shocks are followed by greater volatility than the negative shocks (McMillan *et al.*, 2000). The parameters ρ_1 and ρ_2 show the impact of pre-election and post-election, respectively, on the conditional volatility of KLCI return. The impact of control variables, i.e. the AFC and global effect, are shown by the parameters ρ_3 and ρ_4, respectively.

The EGARCH model is also used to account for the asymmetric impact of good news and bad news on returns and volatility. The specification for the conditional variance of EGARCH (1,1) is

$$\log(\sigma_t^2) = \omega_0 + \beta \left| \frac{\varepsilon_{t-1}}{\sigma_{t-1}} \right| + \gamma \left(\frac{\varepsilon_{t-1}}{\sigma_{t-1}} \right) + \theta \log(\sigma_{t-1}^2) + (\rho_1 D_1 + \rho_2 D_2 + \rho_3 D_{AFC} + \rho_4 R_{MSCI}), \quad (13.3)$$

where the asymmetric effect of positive and negative shocks is captured by γ. If γ is significantly different from 0, then the positive and negative values of ε_t will have a different impact on the logarithm of conditional volatility. If γ is positive, then a positive shock has a larger impact on the conditional volatility than a negative shock. If γ is negative, then a positive shock reduces the conditional volatility, while a negative shock increases conditional volatility and it shows the presence of the leverage effect (Brooks, 2008). Parameter θ in the model captures volatility persistency.

5.0   Empirical results

We first examine the presence of a unit root in the level of KLCI by using augmented Dickey-Fuller (ADF) and Phillips-Perron (PP) unit root tests. The tests show consistent results,[5] which fail to reject the null hypothesis of unit root in the series, and thus the KLCI series is nonstationary at level. We further analyze the first difference of KLCI and find that ADF and PP tests reject the null hypothesis of unit root at the 1 percent level of significance, which indicates that the first difference series is stationary. The unit root analysis indicates that KLCI is integrated of order one, $I(1)$.

Table 13.4 reports the estimation results of the conditional mean and conditional variance equations of both the TGARCH and EGARCH models based on the five cases event windows, as mentioned earlier. Under the mean equation, the dummy coefficients of pre-election are positive for both TGARCH and EGARCH models. The dummy coefficients of post-election for EGARCH model are positive, but the coefficients are negative for the TGARCH model except for the one-week case. However, we lack strong statistical evidence to show that the GE has an impact on the average stock market returns in Malaysia. This insignificant result is consistent with Siokis and Kapopoulos (2007), Floros (2008) and Lean (2010). We also find that Malaysian stock market returns are negatively affected by the AFC. Moreover, Bursa Malaysia is strongly affected by the global markets environment.

Under the variance equation, there is a presence of an asymmetric effect on the Malaysian stock market. The significant γ for all cases (both TGARCH and EGARCH) strongly supports the asymmetric effect. There is also a leverage effect in both the TGARCH (with positive γ) and EGARCH (with negative γ) models. These findings imply that negative shocks from election have a larger effect on the stock volatility than its positive shocks. The sum of the ARCH and GARCH terms being close to 1 ($\beta + \theta < 1$) suggests the persistency of volatility clustering in the model.

For the TGARCH model, the pre-election dummy coefficients for all cases are positive and highly significant, inferring that stock volatility is higher in the pre-election periods. However, the post-election dummy coefficients are not significant except in the one-week case with a marginal significance at the 10 percent level.

For the EGARCH model, the pre-election dummy coefficients are also positive and significant for all cases. The post-election dummy coefficients are negative and significant for one-week, two-week and one-month cases. The asymmetric effect

Table 13.4 Estimation results

Coef.	TGARCH					EGARCH				
	1 week	2 weeks	1 month	3 months	6 months	1 week	2 weeks	1 month	3 months	6 months
Mean equation										
a1	8.20×10^{-4}	8.37×10^{-4}	1.18×10^{-4}	5.24×10^{-4}	1.95×10^{-4}	6.06×10^{-4}	7.71×10^{-4}	5.81×10^{-4}	4.08×10^{-4}	-1.12×10^{-4}
a2	6.04×10^{-5}	-0.0012	-4.88×10^{-5}	-2.34×10^{-5}	-1.55×10^{-4}	8.15×10^{-4}	4.08×10^{-4}	1.80×10^{-4}	3.44×10^{-4}	9.91×10^{-6}
a3	$-0.0026*$	$-0.0026*$	$-0.0026*$	$-0.0026*$	$-0.0026*$	$-0.0035***$	$-0.0035***$	$-0.0035***$	$-0.0036***$	$-0.0036***$
a4	$0.1467***$	$0.1469***$	$0.1472***$	$0.1473***$	$0.1477***$	$0.1565***$	$0.1565***$	$0.1567***$	$0.1551***$	$0.1566***$
Variance equation										
β	$0.0655***$	$0.0657***$	$0.0644***$	$0.0637***$	$0.0638***$	$0.1580***$	$0.1587***$	$0.1591***$	$0.1605***$	$0.1584***$
γ	$0.0385***$	$0.0405***$	$0.0409***$	$0.0432***$	$0.0426***$	$-0.0283***$	$-0.0289***$	$-0.0294***$	$-0.0310***$	$-0.0303***$
θ	$0.9084***$	$0.9073***$	$0.9087***$	$0.9084***$	$0.9090***$	$0.9893***$	$0.9889***$	$0.9888***$	$0.9882***$	$0.9886***$
ρ1	$4.18 \times 10^{-5}***$	$1.08 \times 10^{-5}***$	$5.84 \times 10^{-6}***$	$1.98 \times 10^{-6}***$	$1.219 \times 10^{-6}***$	$0.4001***$	$0.1394***$	$0.0609***$	$0.0215***$	$0.0158***$
ρ2	$-1.47 \times 10^{-5}*$	2.24×10^{-6}	-9.46×10^{-8}	1.19×10^{-7}	1.38×10^{-7}	$-0.2672***$	$-0.0629***$	$-0.0264***$	-0.0045	-9.37×10^{-4}
ρ3	$1.43 \times 10^{-5}***$	$1.44 \times 10^{-5}***$	$1.41 \times 10^{-5}***$	$1.41 \times 10^{-5}***$	$1.39 \times 10^{-5}***$	$0.0382***$	$0.0392***$	$0.0394***$	$0.0414***$	$0.0411***$
ρ4	$-2.80 \times 10^{-4}***$	$-2.81 \times 10^{-4}***$	$-2.80 \times 10^{-4}***$	$-2.65 \times 10^{-4}***$	$-2.75 \times 10^{-4}***$	$-4.1969***$	$-4.2396***$	$-4.1879***$	$-4.1071***$	$-4.2002***$

Notes: Mean equation for TGARCH and EGARCH: $R_t = \alpha_0 + \alpha_1 D_1 + \alpha_2 D_2 + \alpha_3 D_{AFC} + \alpha_4 R_{MSCI} + \varepsilon_t$. This model is added with AR(1) to account for the problem of serial correlation and heteroscedasticity.

Variance equation for TGARCH: $\sigma_t^2 = \omega_0 + \beta \varepsilon_{t-1}^2 + \gamma \varepsilon_{t-1}^2 I + \theta \sigma_{t-1}^2 + (\rho_1 D_1 + \rho_2 D_2 + \rho_3 D_{AFC} + \rho_4 R_{MSCI})$.

Variance equation for EGARCH: $\log(\sigma_t^2) = \omega_0 + \beta \left| \dfrac{\varepsilon_{t-1}}{\sigma_{t-1}} \right| + \gamma \left(\dfrac{\varepsilon_{t-1}}{\sigma_{t-1}} \right) + \theta \log(\sigma_{t-1}^2) + (\rho_1 D_1 + \rho_2 D_2 + \rho_3 D_{AFC} + \rho_4 R_{MSCI})$.

***, ** and * indicate significant at 1%, 5% and 10% respectively.

of election is clearly shown by the EGARCH model. The Malaysian stock market encounters higher volatility in the pre-election periods, whereas the stock volatility is lower in the post-election periods. Moreover, the EGARCH model captures the post-election effect on conditional volatility up to one month whereas the TGARCH model only captures the post-election effect for one week. The positive AFC dummy indicates that the stock volatility is higher during AFC. The negative sign of the MSCI return indicates that the volatility of the Malaysian stock market is lower with an increase in MSCI return.

The results of conditional variance equations confirm that there is an asymmetric effect of political elections on the volatility of stock market in Malaysia. The stock volatility is higher in the pre-election periods. This is consistent with Koksal and Caliskan (2012), who find that the volatility of the Turkey Stock Exchange increases a month before the GE due to uncertainties associated with the election. But, the stock volatility decreases after the election. As explained by Lean (2010), investors expect market stabilization after the election, especially if the election outcome is what they desired. The GEs in Malaysia have not resulted in unexpected outcomes when the BN won in all GEs. Thus, with no surprise in the outcome, the investors are less nervous and the market is restored to stability after the election.

By using a longer event window of up to six months, we find that stock volatility reacts positively six months before the election dates. This finding supports Oehler *et al.* (2013), who observe higher uncertainty in the stock market and a negative stock returns prior to an election. It is also found that the election effect decreases as time goes on. Stock market uncertainty from elections is reduced one month after the election. This phenomenon is explained by Pantzalis *et al.* (2000), who say that, as the election outcome becomes known, a large amount of uncertainty could have been resolved. While the election outcomes from the six GEs do not appear to surprise the market, the impact of the election on stock volatility decreases and slowly disappears. We also find strong evidence that the stock market is affected asymmetrically before and after the elections. During the GEs, good news will show a smaller volatility than bad news. This evidence supports Pantzalis *et al.* (2000) and Siokis and Kapopoulos (2007), who explain that there is information asymmetry between voters and the government.

6.0 Conclusions

This study investigates the impact of a major political event, i.e. the GE in Malaysia, by focusing on stock market performance. Specifically, we examine the asymmetric effect of pre-election and post-election periods on stock returns and volatility. We use both the TGARCH and EGARCH models to examine the asymmetric effect. Our results show that there is a significant asymmetric effect of election on the stock market in Malaysia. We find a significant election effect in stock volatility but not in the stock returns. The stock market volatility is indeed higher during pre-election periods but lower in the post-election periods. The post-election effect only persists for one month and it slowly disappears after one month.

Our findings have some important implications for investors. First, as the increased uncertainty in the pre-election period increases the volatility of Malaysian stock market returns, investors who wish to hedge the political risk should avoid entering the market prior to the election dates. They could enter the market one month after the polling date when the election effect on stock volatility is gradually decreased. Second, investors should use caution before an election period because the increased volatility during an election is not compensated with a significant high return. Investors are not able to make excess returns by exploiting the election effect. Third, we uncover supportive evidence that stock volatility is affected asymmetrically, which should alert investors that bad news before the country's GE will create greater volatility than good news.

Notes

1 The Political Business Cycle (PBC) model was first introduced by Nordhaus (1975).
2 See for example Cukierman and Meltzer (1986), and Rogoff and Sibert (1988).
3 Congressional effect refers to the stocks market reaction to the congressional session. and Lamb, Ma, Pace and Kennedy (1997) find that average daily return during congressional session is significantly different from those during congressional recess. Wang and Lin (2008, 2009) study Taiwan Congress corresponds with the Legislative Yuan being in session.
4 Democratization effect refers to the stock market reaction to political transition to become democratic. Wang and Lin (2009) explain that Taiwanese democracy was fully reformed when the legislative assemblies were democratically elected. They study democratic effect in Taiwanese stock market corresponds to the first transition of power from ruling party (Kuomintang) to an opposition party (Democratic Progressive Party) in year 2000.
5 The results are available upon request.

References

Abidin, S., Old, C., and Martin, T. (2010). Effect of New Zealand general elections on stock market returns. *International Review of Business Research Papers*, 6(6), 1–12.
Ahmad, Z. H. (2000). The 1999 general elections: A preliminary overview. In: N. Cunha, L. H. Freeman, L. Guan, and T. M. Sebastian. *Trends in Malaysia: Election Assessment*. Singapore: Institute of Southeast Asian Studies, 1–11.
Ali, N., Nassir, A. M., Hassan, T., and Abidin, S. Z. (2010). Short run stock overreaction: Evidence from Bursa Malaysia. *International Journal of Economics and Management*, 4(2), 319–333.
Allvine, F. C., and O'Neill, D. E. (1980). Stock market returns and the presidential election cycle: Implications for market efficiency. *Financial Analysts Journal*, 36(5), 49–56.
Bechtel, M. M., and Fuss, R. (2010). Capitalizing on partisan politics? The political economy of sector-specific redistribution in Germany. *Journal of Money, Credit and Banking*, 42(2–3), 203–235.
Bialkowski, J., Gottschalk, K., and Wisniewski, T. P. (2008). Stock market volatility around national elections. *Journal of Banking and Finance*, 32(9), 1941–1953.
Brooks, C. (2008). *Introductory Econometrics for Finance*. Cambridge, UK: Cambridge University Press.

Campbell, J. Y., and Hentschel, L. (1992). No news is good news: An asymmetric model of changing volatility in stock returns. *Journal of financial Economics, 31*(3), 281–318.

Chan, Y. C., and Wei, K. C. (1996). Political risk and stock price volatility: The case of Hong Kong. *Pacific-Basin Finance Journal, 4*, 259–275.

Chen, D. H., Bin, F. S., and Chen, C. D. (2005). The impacts of political events on foreign institutional investors and stock returns: Emerging market evidence from Taiwan. *International Journal of Business, 10*(2), 165–188.

Chin, J. (1996). The 1995 Malaysian general election: Mahathir's last triumph? *Asian Survey, 36*(4), 393–409.

Chiu, C. L., Chen, C. D., and Tang, W. W. (2005). Political elections and foreign investor trading in South Korea's financial markets. *Applied Economics Letters, 12*(11), 673–677.

Chuang, C. C., and Wang, Y. H. (2010). Electoral information in developed stock market: Testing conditional heteroscedasticity in the market model. *Applied Economics, 42*(9), 1125–1131.

Cukierman, A., and Meltzer, A. H. (1986). A theory of ambiguity, credibility, and inflation under discretion and asymmetric information. *Econometrica, 54*(5), 1099–1128.

Döpke, J., and Pierdzioch, C. (2006). Politics and the stock market: Evidence from Germany. *European Journal of Political Economy, 22*(4), 925–943.

Engle, R. F., and Ng, V. K. (1993). Measuring and testing the impact of news on volatility. *Journal of Finance, 48*(5), 1749–1778.

Floros, C. (2008). The influence of the political elections on the course of the Athens stock exchange. *Managerial Finance, 34*(7), 479–488.

Foerster, S., and Schmitz, J. J. (1997). The transmission of U.S. election cycles to international stock returns. *Journal of International Business Studies, 28*(1), 1–27.

Fong, W. M., and Koh, S. K. (2002). The political economy of volatility dynamics in the Hong Kong stock market. *Asia-Pacific Financial Markets, 9*, 259–282.

Gartner, M., and Wellershoff, K. W. (1995). Is there an election cycle in American stock returns? *International Review of Economics and Finance, 44*(4), 387–410.

Gemmill, G. (1992). Political risk and market efficiency: Tests based in British stock and options markets in the 1987 election. *Journal of Banking and Finance, 16*(1), 211–231.

Glosten, L., Jagannathan, R., and Runkle, D. E. (1993). On the relation between the expected value and the volatility of the nominal excess return on stocks. *Journal of Finance, 48*(5), 1779–1801.

Gwilym, O. A., and Buckle, M. (1994). The efficiency of stock and options markets: Tests based on 1992 UK election opinion polls. *Applied Financial Economics, 4*(5), 345–354.

Hung, L. C. (2013). U.S. Presidential Elections and the Taiwanese stock market. *Issues & Studies, 49*(1), 71–97.

Khong, K. H. (1991). *Malaysia's General Election, 1990: Continuity, Change and Ethnic Politics.* Singapore: Institute of Southeast Asian Studies.

Khoo, B. T. (2013). *13th General Election in Malaysia: Issues, Outcomes and Implications.* Available at: http://www.ide.go.jp/Japanese/Publish/Download/Kidou/pdf/2013_malaysia_03.pdf. Retrieved November 18, 2013, from Institute of Developing Economies Japan External Trade Organization.

Khoo, K. K. (2000). Malaysian election 1990–1999: A historical perspective. In: N. Cunha, L. H. Freeman, L. Guan, and T. M. Sebastian. *Trends in Malaysia: Election Assessment.* Singapore: Institute of Southeast Asian Studies, 15–22.

Kim, H. Y., and Mei, J. P. (2001). What makes the stock market jump? An analysis of political risk on Hong Kong stock returns. *Journal of International Money and Finance, 20*(7), 1003–1016.

Knight, B. (2006). Are policy platforms capitalized into equity prices? Evidence from the Bush/Gore 2000 Presidential Election. *Journal of Public Economics, 90*(4–5), 751–773.

Köksal, B., and Çalışkan, A. (2012). Political business cycles and partisan politics: Evidence from a developing economy. *Economics & Politics, 24*(2), 182–199.

Lamb, R. P., Ma, K. C., Pace, R. D., and Kennedy, W. F. (1997). The congressional calendar and stock market performance. *Financial Services Review, 6*(1), 19–25.

Lean, H. H. (2010). Political general election ad stock performance: The Malaysian evidence. In: Ismail, M. T., and Mustafa, A. (Eds.), *Research in Mathematics and Economics*. Penang: Universiti Sains Malaysia, 111–120.

Leblang, D., and Bernhard, W. (2006). Parliamentary politics and foreign exchange markets: The world according to GARCH. *International Studies Quarterly, 50*, 69–92.

Leblang, D., and Mukherjee, B. (2005). Government partisanship, elections and the stock market: Examining American and British stock returns, 2930–2000. *American Journal of Political Science, 49*(4), 780–802.

Manning, D. N. (1989). The effect of political uncertainty on the stock market: The case of British Telecom. *Applied Economics, 21*(7), 881–890.

Mattozzi, A. (2008). Can we insure against political uncertainty? Evidence from the U.S. stock market. *Public Choice, 137*, 43–55.

McMillan, D., Speight, A., and Apgwilym, O. (2000). Forecasting UK stock market volatility. *Applied Financial Economics, 10*(4), 435–448.

Moten, A. R. (2009). 2004 and 2008 general elections in Malaysia: Towards a multicultural, bi-party political system? *Asian Journal of Political Science, 17*(2), 173–194.

Mukherjee, B., and Leblang, D. (2007). Partisan politics, interest rates and the stock market: Evidence from American and British returns in the twentieth century. *Economics and Politics, 19*(2), 135–167.

Nelson, D. B. (1991). Conditional heteroskedasticity in asset returns: A new approach. *Econometrica, 59*(2), 347–370.

Nezerwe, Y. (2013). Presidential Elections and stock returns in Egypt. *Review of Business and Finance Studies, 4*(2), 63–68.

Nippani, S., and Arize, A. C. (2005). U.S. Presidential Election impact on Canadian and Mexican stock market. *Journal of Economics and Finance, 29*(2), 271–279.

Nippani, S., and Medlin, W. B. (2002). The 2000 Presidential Election and the stock market. *Journal of Economics and Finance, 26*(2), 162–169.

Nordhaus, W. (1975). The political business cycle. *Review of Economic Studies, 42*(2), 169–190.

Oehler, A., Walker, T. J., and Wendt, S. (2013). Effects of election results on stock price performance: Evidence from 1980 to 2008. *Managerial Finance, 39*(8), 714–736.

Pantzalis, C., Stangeland, D. A., and Turtle, H. J. (2000). Political elections and the resolution of uncertainty: The international evidence. *Journal of Banking & Finance, 24*, 1575–1604.

Rogoff, K., and Sibert, A. (1988). Elections and macroeconomic policy cycles. *Review of Economic Studies, 55*(1), 1–16.

Santa-Clara, P., and Valkanov, R. (2003). The Presidential puzzle: Political cycles and the stock market. *Journal of Finance, 58*(5), 1841–1872.

Schwert, G. (1989). Why does market volatility change over time? *Journal of Finance*, *44*(55), 1115–1153.

Sheng, H. C., and Tu, A. H. (2000). A study of cointegration and variance decomposition among national equity indices before and during the period of the Asian financial crisis. *Journal of Multinational Financial Management*, *10*(3), 345–365.

Siokis, F., and Kapopoulos, P. (2003). Electoral management, political risk and exchange rate dynamics: The Greek experience. *Applied Financial Economics*, *13*(4), 279–285.

Siokis, F., and Kapopoulos, P. (2007). Parties, elections and stock market volatility: Evidence from a small open economy. *Economics and Politics*, *19*(1), 123–134.

Stangl, J. S., and Jacobsen, B. (2007). Political cycle in US industry returns. *Journal of International Finance and Economics*, *5*(1). Available at: http://ssrn.com/abstract=1106023.

Sturm, R. R., (2013). Economic policy and the presidential election cycle in stock returns. *Journal of Economics and Finance*, *37*(2), 200–215.

Timmermann, A., and Granger, C. W. J. (2004). Efficient market hypothesis and forecasting. *International Journal of Forecasting*, 20, 15–27.

Wang, Y. H., and Lin, C. T. (2008). Empirical analysis of political uncertainty on TAIEX stock market. *Applied Economics Letters*, *15*(7), 545–550.

Wang, Y. H., and Lin, C. T. (2009). The political uncertainty and stock market behavior in emerging democracy: The case of Taiwan. *Quality and Quantity*, *43*(2), 237–248.

Wilson, E. J., and Marashdeh, H. A. (2007). Are co-integrated stock prices consistent with the efficient market hypothesis? *The Economic Record*, *83*(1), 87–93.

Wong, W. K., and McAleer, M. (2009). Mapping the Presidential Election cycle in US stock markets. *Mathematics and Computers in Simulation*, *79*, 3267–3277.

Index

For Product Safety Concerns and Information please contact our EU
representative GPSR@taylorandfrancis.com
Taylor & Francis Verlag GmbH, Kaufingerstraße 24, 80331 München, Germany

www.ingramcontent.com/pod-product-compliance
Ingram Content Group UK Ltd.
Pitfield, Milton Keynes, MK11 3LW, UK
UKHW021008180425
457613UK00019B/855